ENGLAND'S LOST EDEN

ENGLAND'S LOST EDEN

Adventures in a Victorian Utopia

PHILIP HOARE

FOURTH ESTATE · *London* and *New York*

First published in Great Britain in 2005 by
Fourth Estate
A Division of HarperCollins*Publishers*
77–85 Fulham Palace Road
London W6 8JB
www.4thestate.com

1 3 5 7 9 10 8 6 4 2

A catalogue record for this book
is available from the British Library

ISBN 0-00-715910-2

Typeset in PostScript Linotype Sabon with Janson display by
Rowland Phototypesetting Ltd, Bury St Edmunds, Suffolk
Printed in Great Britain by
Clays Ltd, St Ives plc

For Mark

CONTENTS

PART III *Arrows of Desire*

PART IV *The Countenance Divine*

PART V *A New Jerusalem*

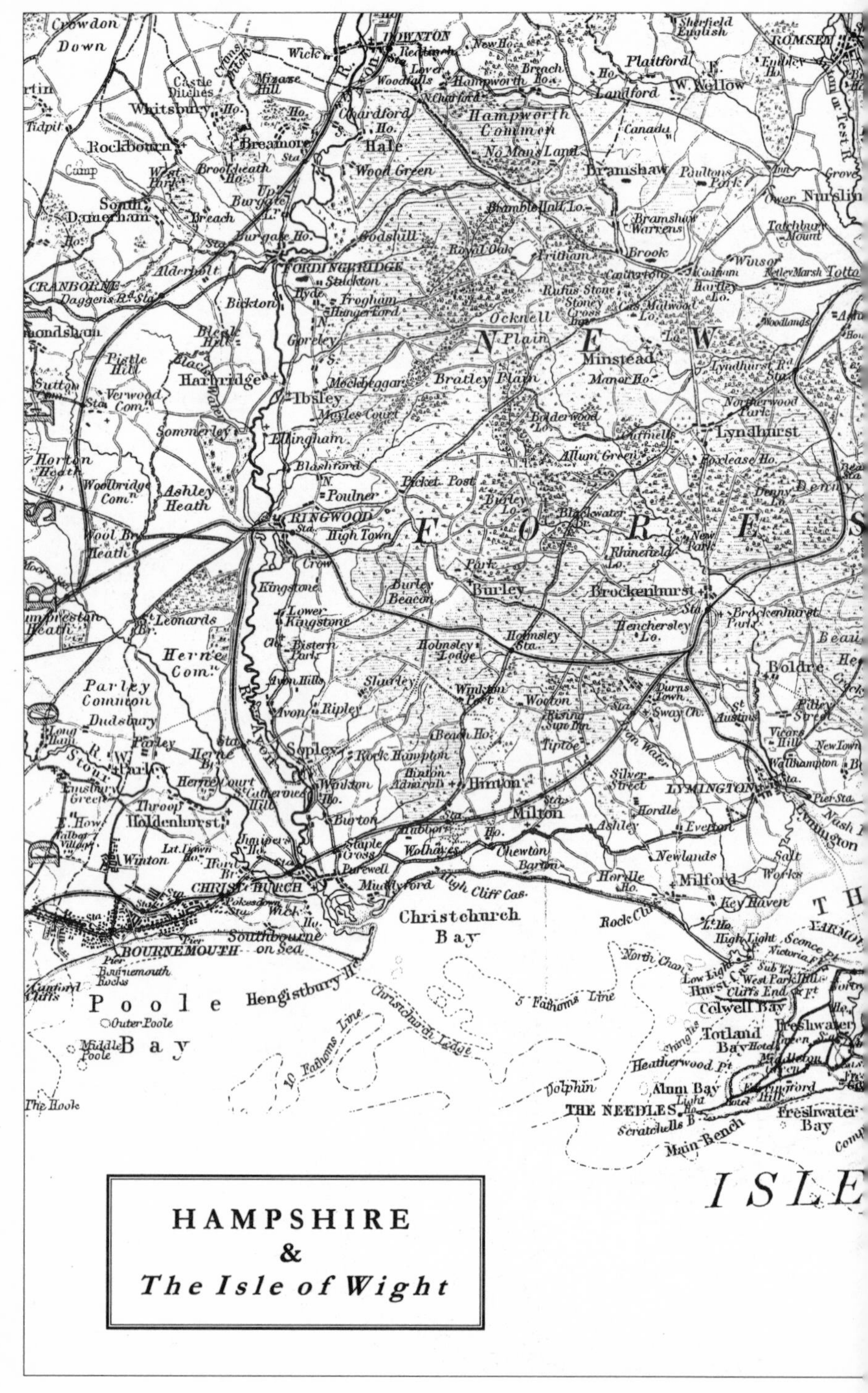
HAMPSHIRE
&
The Isle of Wight
Crowdon Down
DOWNTON
Whitsbury
Rockbourn
Breamore
Hale
Wood Green
Hampworth Common
No Mans Land
Landford
W. Wellow
Plaitford
ROMSEY
Bramshaw
Canada
Nursling
South Damerham
FORDINGBRIDGE
Godshill
Royal Oak
Fritham
Brook
Cadnam
CRANBORNE
Bickton
Frogham
Ocknell Plain
Minstead
Lyndhurst Rd. Sta.
Harbridge
Ibsley
Bratley Plain
Lyndhurst
Ellingham
Blashford
Poulner
Picket Post
Ashley Heath
RINGWOOD
High Town
N E W
F O R E S
Burley Beacon
Burley
Brockenhurst
Rhinefield Lo.
Leonards
Herne Com.
Holmsley Sta.
Boldre
Parley Common
Dudsbury
Sopley
Ripley
Hinton
Milton
Sway
LYMINGTON
Holdenhurst
Winton
CHRISTCHURCH
Mudeford
High Cliff Cas.
Chewton
Everton
Milford
Hordle
Key Haven
BOURNEMOUTH
Southbourne on Sea
Christchurch Bay
Poole Bay
Hengistbury Hd.
5 Fathoms Line
10 Fathoms Line
Christchurch Ledge
Colwell Bay
Totland Bay
Freshwater
Alum Bay
THE NEEDLES
Freshwater Bay
Main Bench
Heatherwood Pt.
Dolphin
The Hook
ISLE

Bambridge
Marwell Lo.
Belmore Ho.
Exton
East Meon
Upham
Crowdhill
Corhampton
Meon Stoke
Combe
Bishop-stoke
Eastleigh
Fair Oak
Ashton
Droxford
Chidden
Lake
Durley
BISHOPS WALTHAM
Middlington
Soberton
Hambledon
West End
Bitterne
Sidwell
Curdridge Ho.
Botley
Barn Green
Wickham
West Lo.
Bursledon
Swanwick
FOREST OF
Southwick
Netley Abbey
Sarisbury
Lunatic Asylum
Roche Court
Hamble
SOUTHAMPTON WATER
Titchfield
FAREHAM
Wymering
Cosham
Drayton
Widley
Beaulieu Heath
Cadland Park
Fawley
Hollam Hill
Crofton
Porchester
Portsmouth Harbr.
PORTSEA
Stubbington
Rowner
Calshot Cas.
Langley
Exbury
Lee on the Solent
Landport
Milton
PORTSMOUTH
Southsea
Alverstoke
GOSPORT
Stanswood Bay
Stone Pt.
Bramble
Lee Pt.
Stokes Bay
Gilkicker Pt.
S P I T H E A D
S O L E N T
Egypt Pt.
West Cowes
E. Cowes
Norris Cas.
Osborne B.
Barton Pt.
Wootton Pt.
Fishbourne
Gurnet B.
Thorney Bay
Whippingham
Northwood
Binstead
RYDE
Wootton
Newtown
St. Helens
Shalfleet
NEWPORT
Carisbrook
Road
Bembridge
Foreland
Calbourne
Arreton
Brading
Yaverland
White Cliff Bay
Culver Cliff
Gatcombe
Newchurch
Brighstone
Shorwell
Sandown
Sandown Bay
WIGHT
Mottiston
Godshill
Kingston
Shanklin
Shanklin Chine
Brighstone Bay
Luccomb Chine
Chine Head
Atherfield Rocks
Chale Bay
Chale
Whitwell
Wroxhall
DUNNOSE
Bonchurch
Niton
St. Lawrence
VENTNOR
Blackgang Chine
Rocken End
Steep Hill

Prologue

Early in May 1100 – the exact date is uncertain – the king's bastard nephew was hunting deer in the New Forest when he was killed by an arrow loosed by one of his own party. Thirty years before, his uncle, the king's brother, had been gored to death by a stag in the same forest. Both deaths were seen as a judgement on the Norman invaders who had imposed their rule on the land, sweeping aside entire villages to create a vast hunting ground, a kind of royal Eden. An elderly victim of that enclosure cursed the reigning family, predicting their demise within its woods; and so when, later that fateful year, a stray arrow claimed the life of the king himself, it was seen as a death foretold, an ironic end for a man whose father had claimed to love deer more than his own flesh and blood.

William Rufus, forty-year-old son of the Conqueror, was named after his florid complexion rather than his hair, which was flaxen like that of his Viking ancestors. Rufus had ruled England for thirteen years: a fair-minded king to many, but to others, especially the Church, his rival in temporal power, a godless man of pagan leanings. Some called him a warlock; others accused Rufus of the more worldly vice of sodomy. In that last year, the Devil appeared to men 'in the woods and secret places, whispering to them as they passed'. One bishop exiled by the king saw him in a vision, condemned to the fires of Hell.

In his final hours, these stories began to accelerate around Rufus, as though the forest itself were closing in upon him. As day broke on the morning of 2 August 1100, a monk appeared before the hunting party, relating a dream in which the king had swaggered into a church and seized the crucifix from its altar, tearing its arms and legs 'like a beast . . . with his bare teeth'. The cross had hurled its assailant to the ground, and 'great tongues of flame, reminiscent of the stream of blood, spurted from his mouth and reached towards the sky'. Later that day, the Earl of Cranborne went out hunting and met a black goat with the body of a naked, wounded man on its back. The animal said it was the Devil, crying, 'I bear to judgement your King, or rather your tyrant, William Rufus. For I am a malevolent spirit and the avenger of his wickedness which raged against the Church of Christ and so I have procured his death.'

Disconcerted by these portents, Rufus delayed his sport until the evening. Riding with the king's hunting party was his brother Henry, Walter Tirel of Poix, and other powerful men, jangling arrogantly through a forest they regarded as their private domain. The deer were to be driven towards them and, accordingly, a stag entered the clearing in which the king waited, the long shadows of the summer's evening cast before him. It was as if the entire affair were choreographed and lit to give it theatricality; shielding his eyes from the rays of the setting sun, Rufus loosed his arrow. As he watched the animal stagger, another appeared, distracting the king's attention, and 'at this instant Walter . . . unknowingly, and without power to prevent it, Oh gracious God! pierced his breast with a fatal arrow. On receiving the wound, the king uttered not a word; but breaking off the shaft of the weapon where it projected from his body, fell upon the wound, by which he accelerated his death.'

The horror of the scene – played out in slow-motion, as it were – was counterpointed by its setting: the silent beauty of the glade, the swift arrow seeking its pre-ordained target, the venal king falling to the forest floor. It was a death given transcendence by its victim's sovereignty, and by the reaction of the royal body to the arrow's penetration, *by which he accelerated his death*. And in the multiple perspective of historical record, the act acquired other meanings, as though filmed by another camera. It was claimed that the arrow was aimed away from the king, but was deflected by an oak tree, while others discerned conspiracy at work among those with rival claims to the throne. Over the next millennium, myth and legend gathered round this royal assassination. Some saw Rufus as 'the Divine Victim, giver of fertility to his kingdom', killed on the morrow of the pagan feast of Lammas in order to propitiate the gods. The notion of ritual sacrifice linked William Rufus's murder with that of Thomas à Becket; with witchcraft, Cathar heresy and Uranianism – 'the persistence of "unnatural love" as a mark of the heresy'. To others, however, the king's demise was just 'a stupid and an accidental death'.

The oaks still stand that witnessed these deeds, although their hearts have been eaten away by fungus as old as the wood itself, leaving hollow crowns, shadows of their living selves. In the eighteenth century, a stone was erected where Rufus fell, although even this site, near Minstead, was disputed, as if elusive myth rejected hard fact. Here, it was said, a ghostly hart would appear at times of national crises and, like King Arthur sleeping in Avalon, Rufus would wake and fight for his country. The spectral animal was sighted during the Crimean War, again in 1914, and on the eve of the deaths of George IV and Edward VII. It has yet to be seen again.

Leaving Southampton, westwards, monstrous cranes straddle the estuary's upper reaches, where mudflats meet the industrial port on land reclaimed from the sea. The dock wharves are strewn with tank-like containers and row after row of brand new cars awaiting export, shiny from the production line. Electric pylons stalk across this confluence of water and land, while herons pick their way gracefully through the mud and ponies perch on the grassy bank of the dual carriageway, their bodies improbably tilted at right angles to the busy road. In high summer, dare-devil lads balance on the old stone bridge beneath the flyover, yanking off their shirts and jumping into the water, the brief arch of their leap caught in freeze-frame by the cars speeding overhead.

I once flew over this interzone in a balloon, rising noiselessly from the city's common at dawn, borne up by a raw flame roaring under the neon nylon tent which billowed between us and infinity. Our wickerwork cradle creaked as we were lifted into the sky and over the park, its green carpet falling away as we sailed silently into the air, bumping with the unseen thermals. We drifted over the Civic Centre and its needle tower, built to emulate an Italian campanile, and over the port in whose great dry docks ocean liners were once prised out of their element like stranded cetaceans while workers examined their barnacled hulls. Southampton Water opened out ahead, and in the distance, on an horizon below rather than level with the eye, the Solent and its fluttering yachts held the Isle of Wight in a silvery embrace.

For a brief moment, in the hour after dawn, we were caught out of time and space, suspended above the world and the suburban plots whose tenants were just beginning to surface that Saturday morning, waking to see our airy leviathan floating noiselessly over their heads. In that moment ordinary life stopped: all that was below had been disconnected as the lines between us and the earth snapped as we had tugged away from the field and pulled up the anchor. Now we were left to nothingness, in limbo, supported by no more than a thin layer of fabric as we hung in mid-air, dangling like puppets.

Then, just as imperceptibly as we had gained this strangely unvertiginous height, the great sphere above us began to lose its tautness. The crimson licking flame diminished, and slowly, with pathetic gasps, the heat and air began to go out of our inflated world. The wind caught us, and we went with it, gliding past the military port at Marchwood and its ordered terrain, then dipping over the wetlands as the ground rushed up to meet us faster and faster until, ordered into landing positions, we crouched down in the basket, backs braced, knees drawn up to our chests like parachutists ready to return to earth. Through the willow-woven cracks, the bright light was dimmed by approaching land. Suddenly we hit the grass, ripping up clods and biting into the field before dragging to a violent halt, our bodies tossed about in the basket like so much fruit. We climbed out on uncertain legs, as though we'd experienced zero gravity and had to reaccustom ourselves to firm ground. But we really were in another world, for we had flown free of the city and into the forest itself.

Walking into the woods is like entering a rainforest. In the stillness, which isn't still at all, birds sing and boughs sigh, unseen in the translucent green canopy above, which filters a subaqueous light. The world is dampened here, muffled by brilliant green moss and held in by sinuous roots, as though the earth were bursting with its own fertility. The forest floor clings to the feet, the senses heightened by the silence; intensely aware of cracking twigs and rustling leaves and rotting vegetation dragged down into the soil by worms and beetles, adding another layer to this fecund, decaying, self-regenerating organism. You must tread carefully here, for you are walking on the living and the dead.

Once all of England looked like this; even a thousand years after its enclosure, the New Forest still feels medieval: an ancient domain which ought not to exist at all, and which, ironically, owes its preservation to an invader. It has no physical boundaries to mark its beginning or its end, and yet it encompasses a third of Hampshire. It is barely an hour and a half's drive from London, but it is a liminal region, for all its apparent accessibility. In the Dark Ages, this was one of the last parts of the country to remain pagan; in the Second World War, witches gathered here to ward off an invasion force invested with its own occult beliefs. This place of purity has ever been suffused with the alien: from the Romans and the Vikings, to whom I owe the kink in my little finger, to the gypsies who first came here from Europe five hundred years ago, and who until recently sent their children to school wearing rabbit-skins under their clothes.

Even its name is deceptive – 'forest' was the word for a hunting ground, rather than woods – and modern visitors wonder where all the trees are. For mile after mile, the eye sees nothing but great stretches of heathland flattened by the sky: the spaces where the woods once were. *Erica vulgaris* and *Ulex europaeus* – the pink-belled heather and the coconut-scented gorse – colonise these gravelly expanses with relentless efficiency. These are tough, hard-bitten plants used to the hooves of the ponies that congregate idly on the verges, their thick hides, shaggy manes and round bellies stolid and unmoving as their big black eyes reflect the cars which occasionally cull one of their number, each sweet stupid victim awaiting its turn.

Yet for all its contradictions, or perhaps because of them, the forest is a compendium of myth. It reaches back to an age before the cruel Norman laws which would amputate the fingers of poachers and mutilate their dogs' feet, to dark woods peopled by Herne the Hunter, a man in stag's guise, his antlers 'spreading like mantling in the breeze'; and to the wise wild men, strange figures part way between animal, vegetable and human who had their Victorian counterpart in Brusher Mills, the snake-catcher who allowed his reptiles to slither through his beard.

A place where the pagan worship of trees conflated with the verdant cross of Christian immortality, ever subject to the immemorial cycle of life, death and resurrection, this new-old forest stands for all threatened wildernesses. It promises a sylvan idyll, the greenwood of all our imaginings, invested with certainty and superstition, hope and fear; a place of sanctuary, mystery and magical transformation, here in the heart of England, our lost and ancient Eden.

PART ONE

Green and Pleasant Land

Midway this way of life we're bound upon, I woke to
find myself in a dark wood
Where the right road was wholly lost and gone

Dante, *The Divine Comedy*

ONE

A Voice in the Wilderness

I am the voice of one crying in the wilderness,
'Make straight the way of the Lord'

John 1:23

When I was a boy, we'd often drive into the forest. With my father at the wheel of our Wolseley and my mother at his side, the world seemed as secure and bound and polished as the big old car itself. I would lie back and look up through the rear window at the trees passing hypnotically overhead. They seemed both remote and near as I looked out for a particular row of pines which reminded me of the day I lost my toy koala bear – his rabbit fur and shiny snout the source of deep solace – on scrubby cliffs above a Dorset beach where, for all the hours of searching, he was not to be found.

Now, forty years later, the westbound train crawls through Southampton's outer suburbs, as if the city's gravity were reluctant to let it go. This is the rear view, where England turns its back on itself, as if ashamed of its own history. Here the houses look into their few square yards, denying their communality with leylandii and larch-lap; here where subtopian dreams meet suburban reality. Then, gradually, the tarmac gives way to gravel, concrete to grass, allotments to wide heaths where pole-straight silver birch stake out new territory, screening the sky with their filigree bronze branches, standing guard over rutted ground riven with stony rills like frozen waterfalls. This land is open and limitless, laid bare in a way we have forgotten; we know contours only through gear changes, as our towns and cities gather together, seeking safety in numbers for fear of nature and its unpredictable ways.

At Brockenhurst, I haul my bike onto the empty platform. The forest station still seems rural, with its two-stop line to Lymington and a waiting room decorated with photographs by Julia Margaret Cameron, given in memory of her son and intended to beautify this connexion between London and her home on the Isle of Wight. But now visitors are greeted by letters spelt out in ballast on the side of the track *Welcome to Brock*. Beyond the village, with its butcher selling venison and its stockbroker-belt guarded by expensive cars, the B-road races the railway to the coast, while on the horizon the Island hovers where clouds should be, a lowering landmass separated by the unseen sea.

The wind is against me as I cycle over the open heath, and I'm grateful for the descent into the village of Sway, its outskirts marked by a tall stone cross. Remembrance wreaths still lie on the war memorial, their scarlet paper poppies faded by the sun and spotted by rain; propped up on the railing is a discarded hubcap. Dipping into the valley beyond, the lane darkens with tall trees. I turn off into Barrows Lane, where a hand-painted sign announces *Arnewood Turkeys*, but this is no ordinary farm building. Concrete where the rest of the forest buildings are brick, its classical proportions, domed roof and pillars resemble some strange escape from the Italian countryside. Beside it, in an overgrown field, is a stubby campanile, a plastic bag flapping from its unglazed window. Seemingly unfinished – as if its creator intended to return to his handiwork – this fairytale towerlet labours under an ivy burden. But it is dwarfed by the structure in whose shadow it lies, an eminence impossible to ignore, yet so unexpected that you could pass by without raising your eyes and miss it entirely. Reaching up out of the forest is an immense grey column, rising two hundred feet into

the sky. Its very shape seems to change with the clouds – a sun-lit gnomon from one angle, a mad church steeple from another.

It is so bizarre that it seems completely detached from its surroundings. Over the road, a hard-hatted engineer perches at the top of a telegraph pole, barely aware of the tower that looms over him, just as I cannot remember it from my childhood visits to the forest. Perhaps it is a mirage, appearing only fitfully. Or perhaps it is part of some vast underground complex, some covert scientific experiment. The stillness of this unnamed country lane invites conspiracy: there is no sign of life, no one to acknowledge or explain this extraordinary structure. Omnipresent but forgotten, it refutes the curiosity of the modern world, as though gagged by its own mystery.

As I cycle on, past hedgerows which billow up like green pillows on either side, the tower's shadow seems to follow me. The houses and cottages multiply as I approach Hordle. Here the roads have names, oddly evocative – Silver Street and Sky End Lane – but it is a disparate place, this arbitrary settlement rescued from the suburbs of nearby New Milton only by the proximity of the forest, whose presence is ever obvious and yet remote. These houses stand just outside its invisible boundaries, yet they cannot but be a part of it, as if its greenness were drawing them in, ineluctably.

I cross the busy east–west road, with its traffic hurtling towards Bournemouth, and ride up Vaggs Lane. Here the land is palpably higher, blown by secondhand gusts from the sea. Behind an orchard of exhausted apple trees is a petrified pine stripped of its bark, skeletal, as if lightning-struck. I knock at the door of a nearby house. A young teenage boy in combat trousers appears, restraining a dog.

'Alright mate,' he says, his chummy tone undermined by hesitancy and poshness.

I explain my mission. He points me back in the direction from which I came.

'Are they friendly?' I ask.

The boy shrugs: it was an old people's home before the new owners took over. I retrace my tracks and pull up outside the gates. Opposite is a metal-barred entrance on which a notice has been pasted: NO DUMPING OUTSIDE THESE GATES BY ORDER OF THE DEPT OF THE ENVIRONMENT. Below it is a rusty white van, bits of old car engine, and an assortment of scrap metal and tin cans.

The gravel crunches as I walk up to the door. No-one answers the bell, but a pair of dogs growl at the side gate. The house is bigger than it appears from the road, the land around it lush pasture. I peer through the windows and try to imagine what this place was like a century and a half ago, when its inhabitants sought heaven on earth and this country lane erupted to scandal and sensation. Back down the lane I wander into the village churchyard, where gravestones stand shoulder to shoulder, many decorated with artificial flowers. Screwed to a buttress of the building, overlooking an oddly empty part of the churchyard, is a plaque of the kind made by shoe repairers in shopping malls.

Yet no trace of Mrs Girling's grave remains. It is an absence which is doubly appropriate, for her followers claimed that three days after her interment, their leader rose from the dead.

Once these fields echoed to one hundred and sixty-four men, women and children speaking in tongues and dancing in ecstatic rites, living celibate, communal lives as they awaited the millennium. Now there is nothing left to show for their utopian aspirations: no buildings, no books, no artefacts; nothing more than this small plastic sign. How could the memory of Mary Ann Girling and her Shakers have vanished so completely? Surely it is no coincidence that just a few fields away, that conspiratorial tower rises over the trees, wreathed in its own dumb mystery. But as I look around me, the bare grass of the quiet Hampshire churchyard gives nothing away.

The facts of Mary Ann's early life are equally unrevealing. She was born on 27 April 1827 in a cottage at Little Glemham, a village in rural Suffolk, between Woodbridge and Aldeburgh. It is a faintly threatening landscape of corn fields and black crows, often over-lowered by rain clouds which sweep in from the east, streaking downwards as if to suck water from the sea and unload it over the unsuspecting countryside. Mary Ann's family, the Cloutings, lived in a cottage on Tinkerbrook Lane, an undulating country road now empty of the slate-roofed cottages which once lined it, long since consumed by the expanding fields of modern farming. But it is still bounded on one side by the estate and substantial brick mansion of Glemham Hall, and on the other by the river Alde, which widens into marshland before it reaches the sea at Aldeburgh. There, on a shingle spit, stands a pillbox-like Martello tower – the northernmost link in a chain to defend against Napoleonic invasion which stretched along the shape-changing Orford Ness and down the English coast as far as Hampshire. In Mary Ann's time, the houses of the fishing village of Slaughden clustered round the tower; but like its outer defences, they were long ago lost to the grey-brown waters of the German Sea.

Both Constable and Turner painted this watery landscape, but in the early nineteenth century the lives of Suffolk's 'wild amphibious race' were also recorded by the 'poet of the poor', George Crabbe, whose verse discerned the grimness as well as the beauty of this countryside and its people. Crabbe practised as a surgeon in Aldeburgh, and was addicted to opium, but later became a curate and preached in Little Glemham's parish church, St Andrew's, its characteristic Suffolk flint-knapped square tower rising over the land and its porch painted in gothic letters, enjoining worshippers, 'This is the Gate of the Lord'. Inside, a neo-classical chapel and a white marble statue still bear testament to the master of Glemham Hall, Dudley North, Crabbe's patron. Crabbe made his name in London with the help of friends such as Edmund Burke and Charles Fox; but in 1810 he wrote *The Borough*, and its tale of 'an old fisherman of Aldborough, while Mr Crabbe was practising

there as a surgeon. He had a succession of apprentices from London, and a certain sum with each. As the boys all disappeared under circumstances of strong suspicion, the man was warned by some of the principal inhabitants, that if another followed in like manner, he should certainly be charged with murder'. The story of Peter Grimes – who, it was implied, violated his charges – would provide Benjamin Britten with his opera. Its author – whom the Cloutings may well have heard preach in St Andrew's – died in 1832, leaving his son, John, to become vicar of Little Glemham in 1840.

Like the New Forest, this corner of England has its own peculiarities. Its bleak, rattling coast stretches from Lowestoft to Felixstowe, passing the drowned churches of Dunwich and the ominous concrete bulk of Sizewell's nuclear reactor which towers over black clapboard cottages that look as though they were painted with pitch. In Mary Ann's day, the landscape was studded with windmills and church towers, a scene described by M. R. James in 'A Warning to the Curious': 'Marshes intersected by dykes to the south, recalling the early chapters of *Great Expectations*; flat fields to the north, merging into heath; heath, fire woods, and above all, gorse, inland'. James' eerie story, 'Oh, Whistle, and I'll come to you, My Lad' – with its ghastly pursuer on the beach, 'a figure in pale, fluttering draperies, ill-defined' – was set on this coastline; Dickens' collaborator, Wilkie Collins, another writer of mysteries, used Aldeburgh for his novel, *No Name*. And up the river Deben at Woodbridge, Edward FitzGerald, translator of *The Rubiyat of Omar Khayyám*, lived as an eccentric recluse, sailing his yacht in a white feather boa, eating a vegetarian diet, and mourning the death of his young friend, William Browne.

Parts of the Suffolk coast remain the least populated in southern England, yet its emptiness is as deceptive as the New Forest's heath. In 1827, the year in which Mary Ann was born, 'seven or eight gentlemen from London' descended on the burial mounds at Snape, taking 'quantities of gold rings, brooches, chains, etc' away after their excavations; a century later, in the 1930s, a Saxon treasure trove would be discovered at Sutton Hoo, on the outskirts of Woodbridge. More recently, a mysterious circle of upturned oaks, reaching down to the watery otherworld of the ancient Britons, was found on the shore. Later, medieval Christianity produced its prophets: Julian of Norwich, the mystic and anchoress who endured 'showings' in 1370; and Margery Kempe of Kings Lynn who, thirty years later, was inspired by visions to renounce the marital bed, fine clothes and meat for communion with Christ. Modern science would discern other symptoms in these phenomena, but to the faithful of the fourteenth century, they were signs of a metaphysical universe.

They may have been lowly, but the Cloutings could trace their Suffolk roots back to the age of Julian of Norwich, when Wilmo Clouting was born, in 1327. In the five hundred years since, the family had barely moved fifteen miles, from the villages of Laxfield, Stradbroke and Saxmundham, to Orford – where Mary Ann's grandfather, William, was born in 1760 – then inland to Little Glemham, where her father, also named William, was born in 1804.

Born before Victoria ascended the throne, Mary Ann came into a very different world to the one she would leave six decades later. 'It was only yesterday, but what a gulf between now and then', wrote William Makepeace Thackeray in 1860, looking back on his childhood. '*Then* was the old world. Stage-coaches . . . highwaymen, Druids, Ancient Britons . . . all these belong to the old period . . . We who lived before railways and survive out of the ancient world, are like Father Noah and his family out of the Ark.' This often flooded corner of England was a remote, self-sufficient community in which lives were lived within themselves, as the reiteration of Suffolk surnames entered in the census and carved on village tombstones – Benham and Folkard, Todd and Barham, Girling and Clouting – suggest.

The Cloutings' was certainly a crowded household. The first modern census, taken in 1841 when Mary Ann was fourteen, records that her father, William, and mother Emma (née Gibbs, and born in nearby Benhall), were then both thirty-five. Mary Ann had five younger brothers: John, aged twelve, Robert, ten, William, eight, Henry, six, and Charles, one; her only sister, Emma, was four. Later two more girls, Jane and Susan, would be born, along with another boy, Mark. They lived in a village of some sixty houses with a population of about three hundred, most of whose men were farm labourers like William Clouting, or blacksmiths, coachmen or wheelwrights. Like many such settlements, it had grown up in a haphazard fashion along the road, and its life centred around the parish church and its vicar, John Crabbe, the Red Lion Inn and its patrons, and the Norths of Glemham Hall; a semi-feudal existence which depended on a good harvest and the ability to pay the rent.

Yet even this rural backwater was moving into the modern world. In the 'Hungry Forties' of bad harvests and poverty, the

People's Charter for universal sufferage became an emblem of the stirring power of the working class. In 1845 the Chartists' champion, Feargus O'Connor, set up small-holdings in which Shelley's 'helots of luxury' could escape industrial tyranny and unemployment in a bid for self-sufficiency; at the same time, railways and new roads spread across the country and provided another network for social change. Meanwhile the Anglican church, despite a similar boom in construction, was threatened by an equivalent growth in nonconformism and a decline in belief. In March 1851, the first religious census held in Britain found that of a population of 17,927,609, fewer than half, 7,261,032, attended at Divine Service in chapels and churches; it was estimated that 5,288,294 people who could have gone to worship did not. While evangelism had touched the entire country in the 1830s, science would weaken orthodox religion. 'It is said that in tropical forests one can almost hear the vegetation growing,' wrote W. H. Mallock in 1877. 'One may almost say that with us one can hear faith decaying'.

Suffolk's own *Woodbridge Reporter* noted, on the occasion of the laying of a foundation stone for a new Wesleyan chapel, that the town hardly lacked the 'means for spiritual instruction. More than a century ago there dwelt in it Presbyterians, Anabaptists, and Sabbattarians, but whether these sects had any public accommodation for performing their religious duties . . . does not appear.' Other eclectic beliefs had sprung up in East Anglia, such as the New Lights and the Old Lights, still there in the twentieth century, their black-bonneted adherents walking miles from outlying villages to spend the entire Sabbath day worshipping in their chapels. There were secular sects, too, such as the vegetarian colony which flourished in Stratford St Mary, near Ipswich, from 1848 to 1851, where cultivation of the land was combined with cultural pursuits and an interest in shorthand writing. But family memory indicates that the Cloutings were being drawn to Primitive

Methodism, whose itinerant ministers were particularly active here; Mary Ann's own younger brother Mark, a wheelwright, would become a preacher.

His sister, however – now a striking young woman, 'impetuous, strong-willing and passionate, somewhat tall, and in figure well made' – had had little education, and was said never to have read the Bible. She spent her early adolescence in domestic service to local families, and at a house on Woodbridge Road in Ipswich; but later she learned the skills of a milliner and dressmaker, working for farmers' wives and more well-to-do inhabitants of the district. But it was in Lowestoft, England's most easterly port, that, at the age of sixteen, Mary Ann married the nineteen-year-old Mariner, George Stanton Girling, on 2 May 1843.

Girling was originally from Theberton, a village close to Dunwich. His parents were menial, and George grew up unable to write his own name; but if a photograph of his son is any indication, he was a handsome man, and like others thereabouts, he was probably a 'half and halfer', spending part of his time working on land, and part of it at sea. While her husband was away, Mary Ann continued to earn a living by dressmaking, but she seemed restless with her half-neglected married life, and 'went forth in search of fresh and more congenial scenes'. Some reports claim that she made a living selling brandy and other spirits, 'which she conveyed about surreptitiously, and of which she disposed as opportunity favoured'. Perhaps because of such less reputable interludes, there are great gaps in Mary Ann's story – not least as self-told, or relayed second- or third-hand. What happened to her in the years between her marriage to George Girling and the beginning of her mission, two decades later? Did she go to sea with her husband – perhaps even visit America, as some have suggested? Whatever course her life took until then, it was soon to alter in the most dramatic manner possible.

By now George Girling had become a fitter in an iron foundry in Ipswich, where the family name was and is well known: a 1920s edition of the *Michelin Guide to Great Britain* recommends the services of Girling & Dolan's garage, and notes that the town was renowned for its agricultural implements. The company which employed George made ploughs, while traces of local history reveal other Girlings with occupations as disparate as farm labourers, police detectives and mariners. George and Mary Ann lived close to the docks in a terraced house on Arthur Street, with other iron fitters and mariners as neighbours; their daughter Mary Jane was born there on 6 September 1853. Two years later, at nearby Fore Street – one of Ipswich's oldest thoroughfares, still partly lined with Tudor houses and then home to dressmakers, carpenters, pawnbrokers and makers of straw bonnets – Mary Ann had a son, William, on 27 December 1855.

But these bare facts hide another story. In the first ten years of her marriage, Mary Ann had lost or miscarried several other children – one account puts the figure at as many as eight. Even in an age of high infant mortality this was unusual; and for some reason Mary Ann felt she was to blame. The bitter toll of dead infants turned her against religion, and for years she avoided any place of worship as melancholy overcame her. Then one day she went to a church – evidence suggests the great docklands parish church of St Clement's, which towered over Fore Street and the river Orwell – and there heard words which comforted her soul. Convinced that her violent temper had brought judgement upon her, she joined the congregation and became a 'female missionary' – although she still yielded to her sin of rage. 'It was after one of these outbursts that the climax came.' For Mary Ann the dressmaker, the real and the imagined were about to be sewn together in a fantastic way, and in the process her body itself would be changed.

* * *

Years later Mary Ann would describe the precise moment at which the vision came to her, at the age of thirty-two (although some accounts put her age at twenty-one, others at thirty-seven). That night she lay restless in bed – perhaps in guilt for her 'unsubdued temper' – and after hours of misery, rose feeling wretched and began to pray for delivery from her sin. Suddenly the room filled with 'a flash of light, brighter than the sun', and she heard a voice say, 'Daughter! thy sins are all forgiven thee'.

As she watched, Mary Ann saw its source coalesce before her: a luminous figure which she identified as her Saviour by the nail-marks in His hands and feet. As she came face to face with this shimmering apparition in her Ipswich bedroom, 'his body became more glorious and beautifully translucent, and he looked young and of a benign countenance'. Now he spoke: if she loved him, would she give up something for him?

'What is it, Lord?' she asked.

'Leave the world's ways, and give up earthly and all carnal usages, and live for me.'

'I don't know that I can,' said Mary Ann.

'Do you not love me?' replied the Lord.

'And as he spoke, the divine love in his countenance came from his face into her, and the rapid communication of his thoughts to her was such, that her will became his, and she said, "I will do anything for thee, my Lord."'

And with that, the vision vanished.

Mary Ann had never felt such ecstasy before; it sent 'a thrill throughout her organism', filling her with love for the whole human race. Yet she kept her vision to herself, as if there was something shameful about what she had experienced alone in her bedroom. The modern world might diagnose sleep paralysis, a vivid hallucinatory state with sexual overtones, said to account for dæmonic possession from the evil spirits of the Bible to Henry Fuseli's eighteenth-century painting, *The Nightmare*, and contemporary claims of alien abduction. Or perhaps, like Fuseli's friend William Blake, she was able to produce eidetic images of what has previously been seen – in some religious tract or biblical illustration, for example – and which she saw 'in the literal sense . . . not memories, or afterimages, or daydreams, but real sensory perceptions'. Or maybe hers was an epileptic fit, during which the sufferer may sense a presence in an otherwise empty room, and afterwards assert absolute moral certainty and religiosity, as Paul's conversion on the road to Damascus has been explained. Was Mary Ann's vision a short circuit in her brain, or was this itself a gift? Whatever the truth, for an uneducated woman of a pre-Freudian age there was only one explanation for what she saw, and what came after it.

Mary Ann returned to her duties, fired with an undeclared determination; her heart must have been bursting to speak of it, but she told her fellow chapel goers only that they must observe holy lives. Five hundred years previously, Julian of Norwich had written of her own revelation:

> When I was 30 years old and a half, God sent me a sickness, in which I lay three days and three nights . . . my sight began to fail, and it was all dark about me, save in the image of the Cross, whereupon I beheld a common light . . . Suddenly my pain was taken from me, and I was as whole as ever I was. Then came . . . to my mind that I should desire the second wound of our Lord's gracious gift. In this moment I saw the red blood trickle down hot and freshly and right plenteous, as it were in the time of His Passion when the Garland of Thorns was pressed on His blessed head. And suddenly the Trinity fulfilled my heart most of joy.

Now Mary Ann received a second vision, although, just as the gospels diversify in their accounts, so her story relies on different writers and her own fluctuating pronouncements; and where one claims six years between her visions, another records just days before the Spirit appeared in the form of a fiery dove commanding her,

> *I have called thee to declare my immediate coming, and it is now the close of this dispensation; a new era is opening on the world, and thou art to be the Messenger.*

From this point, it seemed, Mary Ann's life was determined as parable, to be replayed in situations which would reflect biblical events. The heaven-borne message echoed John's baptism of Christ, when 'the Holy Spirit descended upon him in bodily form, as a dove, and a voice came from heaven, "Thou art my beloved Son; with thee I am well pleased"'. Yet still she said nothing: Mary Ann lost herself in her work, afraid that a public declaration would subject her to 'odium and opposition'. But the visions continued, more potent than ever. She was taken 'into a realm far above the earth; and she ascended out of it, and beheld a vista of ages; and then she looked at Christ, whose glory illuminated her, and she discovered that she was in a glorified ethereal body'. In this astral experience, the Lord appeared 'in the form of a man'. This was no dream: like Moses and Elijah appearing to Jesus, the vision was as real as she could say. Now the Bible was opened to her, and its written word revealed 'all its truth concerning the life of the spirit within the tabernacle of the body'.

Mary Ann's eyes had been opened, just as the scales had fallen from St Paul's eyes. And as with millenarian prophets of the past, her discovery resulted in a literal interpretation of St John's Revelations and its apocalyptic predictions for the end of time. Her visions told her that the Second Coming would happen in her lifetime, and that she was its Messenger, 'to declare an end of sin, and a judgement; and, further, that if she yielded and obeyed, *she should not see death* . . . and that as a witness to her call and work, the outpouring of the Holy Ghost should be to those who believed;

that they should speak with tongues, and do marvellous works; which would be the seal of her messengership'. It was a mirror of St Paul's mission, and in order to fulfil her duty, she must leave her home and family 'and go forth into the streets, declaring the message; and . . . all who believed must be prepared to do the same'.

The cumulative weight of these supernatural events proved too much for a woman's body already weakened by miscarriage. For six weeks Mary Ann was stricken by a paralysis which twisted her mouth, as if in punishment for her ill-tempered tongue, a God-sent witch's scold. This physical ultimatum, in her own account, also caused blindness in one eye and seized her body – perhaps the result of a minor stroke. She was faced with a choice: she could either disregard the visions and remain in this helpless state, or obey her holy orders. And so she told the Lord that He must do with her as He would. As a result of this epiphany – in its original meaning, the manifestation of a god – she immediately recovered. But later, Mary Ann would claim that the last of her visions left her with a yet more extraordinary legacy. At Christmas 1864 she received the sign for which Julian had prayed. The stigmata appeared on her hands, feet and side, erupting in imitation of Christ's crucified body. Like some sacred statue brought to life, Mary Ann's flesh itself bore testament to her Saviour's sufferings. It was as if these wounds were symptoms of her death, as though she had died and been reborn without sin.

Was she a sinful woman, this sometime purveyor of illicit liquor, turned evangelist? Records do not tell us more, nor does Mary Ann, although the guilt she felt for her dead children indicates something for which she needed to atone: a recovered memory, perhaps of abuse within the crowded childhood home. Nor was she beautiful; her face was no lure to lust, and what was interbred emerged in sharp features set awry by harsh experience. Yet she was tall and imposing, with a magnetic stare; as if, in compensation for her lack of beauty, she relied on other means to command attention. There was a sensuality in the way her hair curled in dark locks over her shoulders, although her physical stance spoke against desire and her wide, thin lips bore the memory of paralysis. Her gaunt frame rejected consumption and sexuality in favour of asceticism and spirituality; a visionary aspiration in retreat from the world and its demands. In retrospect, it seems Mary Ann may have suffered some kind of dietary disorder; certainly her body was unnaturally slender. 'The only emaciated being we saw was the prophetess herself', one witness would note, 'and her desperate enthusiasm would burn the flesh from any flame.'

Perhaps her passion fed on her body, exchanging the one for the other. In the process, her resolve was stiffened, as if that heaven-sent rictus were a physical reaction to or a prevention of sin, tensing her body against evil. And if she had been a sinful woman, then her sins were forgiven. Her manner, once inflexible and intolerant, was now gentle and generous. Seeing this, her husband gave up his initial opposition – an acquiescence he would maintain throughout all that was to come. Mary Ann explained that having experienced the 'perfect presence of Jesus', it was impossible to remain with him, 'for her spirit being once set free to enter the paradisiacal state, it was not lawful to enter the state of matrimony again'. Instead she became a bride of Christ, and returned to her chapel – only to find that the congregation refused to listen.

It is easy to imagine their reaction, faced with this woman whose duty lay at home with her children, yet who chose to lecture them on their sins. Mary Ann burned to communicate the wonder of what she had seen, and rejection merely made the fire glow brighter. Shortly after, she saw a crowd listening to a male preacher on a street corner. Someone asked her to speak, and soon, like Wesley, she had her own audience in the open air. But for Mary Ann there was something more to her commission than human history, and she was reminded of it every day by her hidden, holy scars, as if God's words were written on her skin.

We all reinvent ourselves. We conflate memory and fact, and reinterpret the pleasure and pain of the past to suit the present and form our future. Mary Ann too was convinced of her story, and felt the need to share it – a desire only heightened by the obstacles placed in its way, not least that of her sex. Yet being born a woman was not necessarily a bar to her calling: not only were there precedents for female preachers among the Methodists and the Quakers, but her experience – the loss of her children, her lowly origins – made her message more immediate. It was said that her 'thrilling, and often overpowering speeches had a vivid effect on sympathetic lady hearers, for she observed proprieties of behaviour, and there was nothing coarse or vulgar about her'. And like other female mystics, from Julian of Norwich and Margery Kempe, to Hildegard of Bingen, Teresa of Avila and Joan of Arc, she cited higher authority; like the Maid of Orleans' armour, her visions were a defence against male prejudice. Who could doubt the Word of God, even if it came from a farm labourer's daughter?

The world had always been reluctant to give women a voice; yet more so when their prophecies crossed the barrier between Christian and pagan, between witch and saint. In Yorkshire, Mother Shipton had seen the future from her Knaresborough cave and its dripping well, where I was taken as a boy to see strange objects dangling from a rock ledge, the pale brown mineral-rich water turning soft toys into modern fossils. Around the same time as Shipton made her predictions of telegrams and aeroplanes, the Holy Maid of Kent, Elizabeth Burton, was hanged for prophesying Henry VIII's death. In Mary Ann's native East Anglia, the power of magic lingered long after it had faded elsewhere. The eastern counties became home to the Family of Love, a heretical cult imported across the sea from the mirror-lowlands of Holland, which preached that heaven and hell were to be found on earth and that it was possible to recreate Eden through communal living; Ely was declared an 'island of errors and sectaries', and parts of this countryside were said to be heathen until the draining of the fens in the 1630s – as if the act of reclamation deprived the land of its ancient aquatic spirits.

Perhaps devils took hold instead. In 1645, Matthew Hopkins, Witchfinder General, instituted his campaign in Suffolk, when neighbour denounced neighbour and women were walked to keep them awake until their demonic familiars came to betray them. Those who miscarried or whose children were stillborn were accused of sacrificing their offspring. At Aldeburgh, seven women were hanged as witches, and the Borough paid Hopkins £2 for his work. Had she been born two centuries earlier, Mary Ann too might have been stripped and searched for the devil's marks – although her searchers would have found Christ's.

Two hundred years after Matthew Hopkins' reign of terror, Mary Ann left Ipswich to travel the villages around Woodbridge and Saxmundham, the land she knew so well from her childhood and where she thought her words would be heard. As she preached in the open air at Little Glemham, it must have been odd for her young children to witness the change in their mother, leaving the family home for the fields of rural Suffolk. Mary Jane, then in her teens, would assist at the services by teaching and playing the piano, although she was soon to marry; William, however, just six years old when Mary Ann's mission began, would find himself caught up in her cause.

The Primitive Methodists were well represented in these places, and Mary Ann was invited to preach at their chapel at Stratford St Andrew's. But her unorthodox ideas offended them, and many of those who had listened now refused to hear her increasingly radical ideas. So Mary Ann sermonised in market squares, a soapbox orator in shirtwaist and curls. Unconfined by marriage or maternal duties, she took her message to the disenfranchised and the dispossessed – just as the first British Christians had been lowly peasants who found a new sense of community in their faith, and just as the same common people had been identified as God's chosen ones during the religious revolutions of the seventeenth century, with its own dreams of 'utopia and infinite liberty' and a theocracy led by another East Anglian prophet, Oliver Cromwell. In her version of Christ's elegantly paradoxical beatitudes, which called for the poor to be rich and the downtrodden to be free, Mary Ann promised social justice and heaven on earth. Those who had failed to find a place in the world could find a home with her, by choosing a new family. And in questioning the morality of marriage, she offered women the right to choose God over slavery; to be freed from the shackles of sexual demands and the dangerous burden of child-bearing. Mary Ann had issued a challenge to the nineteenth-century family, even as she sundered her own: it seemed she really was set to turn the world upside down.

Girlingism, as it became known, embraced those over whom industrialisation had ridden rough-shod. It offered an alternative way of life almost revolutionary in its aims, although its communist ideas were rooted in Scripture. Consciously or not, Mary Ann appeared to be influenced by sects such as the Family of Love and the Diggers and the Ranters of the Interregnum who took the Acts of the Apostles – 'And all who believe were together and had all things in common' – as precedent for their communality. In 1649, the Diggers had staked out their allotments on St George's Hill in Surrey, and although their attempt at Eden, seeing the Second Coming as an earthly return to paradise, lasted little more than a year, the visionary William Everard, whose followers spoke with angels, went on to found other rural Digger communes. These provided patterns for what Mary Ann would attempt. And while she would admit a spiritual kinship with the early Quakers – more extreme in their early expression than in their later quietude – there was another echo to be detected, in the newly emancipated Catholic Church. In 1858, as Christ appeared in Mary Ann's Ipswich bedroom, another young peasant girl saw the Virgin Mary in a French cave, as if her solemn, beautiful statue had come to life, her robe as blue as the sky from which she had fallen in augury of her Son's return. Bernadette knelt on the ground and seemed to eat the earth: to some, a symptom of psychological disturbance; to others, an indication of the passion of her visions. In an increasingly secular century, it was no coincidence that the visitations at Lourdes and the agitations of the Girlingites registered simultaneously on the spiritual scale.

Back in Suffolk, Mary Ann's mission had a direct and intensely personal effect on another young woman. Eliza Folkard, a carpenter's daughter from Parham, sang in the Methodist choir, but one day she attended a Girlingite meeting and suddenly got up and began to dance. She then spoke for an hour, describing 'how she had been convinced of sin at the age of 17, but did not give her heart to God until after a long illness'. In a further reflection of Mary Ann's conversion, she declared that Mrs Girling was truly the herald of the Second Coming, and as she emerged from her trance she embraced her new mother. To others, however, Eliza's closeness to Mary Ann would lead to the notion that she was in fact her daughter, and perhaps an indication of sin. And where Mary Ann was dark, Eliza had blonde hair, a race memory of Viking invaders: she would become the pulchritudinous face of Girlingism, the angelic obverse to Mary Ann's darker power.

Eliza's conversion was followed by that of Henry, or Harry Osborne, described as a 'rough, uncouth and illiterate farm-labourer, of pugilistic tendencies' – a useful person when danger threatened. In fact, Harry was a thirty-one-year-old widower and shoemaker; but in this gallery of types, he became Mary Ann's right-hand man, completing the trinity that she presented to the world – and introducing new rumours about their own relationship.

Within eighteen months Girlingism had fifty adherents, for whom it was compulsory to receive 'the Spirit, or the baptism of the New Life' and to practise celibacy, without which they could not be accepted by the Saviour on His return, 'which was expected to be sudden as the lightning's flash'. Anyone joining the group had to give up all their worldly goods; from there on 'the old ties of husband, wife and lover were to be lost in a fraternal bond'; they were now all brothers and sisters, living 'a pure and holy life'. Mary Ann was known as Sister: her sororial title was levelling and egalitarian, but it also gave her a sense of pre-ordained mission. As a universal relative, she cast off her wedded status and assumed a new role, that of a secular nun or religious nurse.

This was neither an unusual self-discovery, nor a disreputable one: the most famous sister of the age, the high-born Florence Nightingale, had recently entered imperial iconography as the Lady with the Lamp, inspired by her own three visions of Christ; while the empire itself was ruled over by a matriarch queen from her seaside home on the Isle of Wight. But it was also the coming era of the New Woman, and Mary Ann would be seen as part of these powerful moves towards a new female identity: 'She stands forth, in this age of "woman's mission", fearlessly to lead and encourage a pure society based upon the inward law of her nature', claimed one new age magazine; although a more hostile account saw her as 'a curious growth of the "Women's Right" genus, from a theological point of view; and when she stretches her bony arms, in all the warmth of native eloquence, she reminds one of a pious scarecrow tossed in the winds of fanaticism and superstition and set up as a terror to evil doers in the way of religious enthusiasm.'

A woman's power was still to be feared; and like those new women, this universal sister's tenets, intended to create an alternative clan, were not entirely welcome as they sundered families and married couples and separated children from parents. When a later visitor asked Mary Ann, 'Why not procreate?', she replied that the earth was already too full. Such sentiments echoed those of Reverend Malthus, who believed mankind was doomed if it continued to reproduce without check. But they also threatened the defining unit of an age which relied on reproduction. The family yoked the workers of the industrial revolution to the demands of capitalism; Mary Ann directly opposed that economic adhesion. For such a person of such a background and of such a sex to set up such a challenge was unacceptable. Mrs Girling made a travesty of her married name, and in the process became an anti-woman.

There were other reasons to fear Girlingism: it created tensions not just between families, but between communities. In an era of insecurity and high unemployment – exemplified by the agricultural strikes which hit East Suffolk in the early 1870s as the newly formed Agricultural Labourers' Union clashed with the Farmers' Association – men lost their jobs because of Mary Ann. In the market and barrack town of Woodbridge, her teachings began to concern clergy and upset landowners, anxious at her effect on their flocks and labour force: 'Many of the males were discharged from their situations, and others suffered loss in a variety of ways'. To some it seemed they had lost their senses to religious mania, and were suitable subjects for the local lunatic asylum at Melton – an establishment of more than four hundred disturbed souls, their occupations, listed next to their initials in the 1871 census, representative of Mary Ann's constituency: farm labourers and their wives; factory girls and seamen's wives; soldiers and needlewomen; chimney sweeps and policemen's wives; brush makers and lime burners; or simply, in the case of 'V. F.', a 'loose character'.

They were the psychiatric casualties of an industrial era, the kind of minds susceptible to a woman who might have found herself similarly incarcerated. Or perhaps Mary Ann evoked an older belief, when people had laid votive offerings in the lakes and rivers, reaching down to that elemental world beneath their feet. Whatever the source of her power, it seemed there was a primal force gathering around this prophetess, one which would invoke spirits and provoke opposition. One man bet his friends that he would shoot Mary Ann on a certain night – although in the event the would-be assassin himself converted and became a Girlingite, a miracle taken by her followers as proof that their leader was protected by God. That which did not kill her made Mary Ann stronger, and in this sensational narrative – something between penny dreadful and missionary tract – she had become a symbolic, almost revolutionary figure.

A later image of Mary Ann depicts her as an androgynous angel from some Renaissance woodcut, wearing indeterminate, anachronistic dress, her head encircled by a band in simple recognition of her sacred mission. Her stare challenges the viewer and imbues the portrait with the air of an icon. This idealised Mary Ann is far from what we know of her true features; more Joan of Arc as seen in a Victorian picturebook than the face of a farm labourer's

daughter. But equally, it could be an advertisement for the latest nostrum, lacking only the caption, *Mother Girling Saves*.

Girlingite meetings took a set form. Bible verses were read and debated, followed by prayer. But then came the strange dancing and trance-like speaking in tongues which Eliza Folkard had exhibited, and which were already attracting crowds. These shaking fits earned the sect the nickname Convulsionists, although they preferred to call themselves Children of God, from St John's gospel, '. . . to all those who received him, who believed in his name, he gave power to become children of God; who were born, not of blood nor of the will of flesh nor of the will of man, but of God'. Like the Corinthians in the wake of St Paul's mission, they would 'jabber and quake' when in the spirit, led by Mary Ann herself, leaping from foot to foot while waving her arms as if beckoning while she exhorted the Lord's name. To some these antics resembled the dance of a savage; others watching the 'springy, elastic movements and considerable waving of her arms . . . could hardly resist the comic aspect of the scene'.

Soon enough these rites attracted the attention of the press, and on 20 April 1871 a headline appeared in the *Woodbridge Reporter & Aldeburgh Times*:

MOBBING A FEMALE PREACHER.

The accompanying story may have been the first occasion on which Mary Ann's name appeared in print; it was certainly not the last.

Reporting on a case heard at the Framlingham Petty Sessions by F. S. Corrance, the local Member of Parliament, and two clergymen – the Reverends G. F. Pooley and G. H. Porter – the newspaper gave details of five young men, William Goldsmith, James George, Samuel Crane, James Nichols and John Barham, who were charged by a farmer with 'riotous behaviour in his dwelling, which is registered as a place for religious worship'.

At first it seemed a matter of mere youthful high spirits. The farmer, forty-eight-year-old Leonard Benham of Stratford St Andrew, worked 138 acres – belonging to the Earl of Guildford – where he employed three men and a boy, as well as two household servants (one of them being twenty-year-old William Folkard, a kinsman of Eliza's). But Benham was also a member of the Children of God, and had resolved to support Mary Ann 'at any cost'. He would pledge his entire family – his wife Martha, forty; his daughters Ellen, twenty, Emma, thirteen, and Mary Ann, then four years old; together with his sons Arthur, then aged sixteen, William, fifteen, and George, just five – to the cause.

That Sunday afternoon, a meeting had been held in Benham's house which was attended by the five defendants – not by invitation. As the Girlingites prayed, one of the young men, John Barham, began to talk and laugh. When asked to be quiet, he replied by singing and hallooing, with his friends joining in.

'I went to the door and stood near them,' Leonard Benham told the court. 'They said, "Take your sins off your own back, we won't believe you, you're a liar." I told them mine was a registered house. They told me not to daubt them up with untempered mortar' – an obscure metaphor which would pursue the Girlingites, along with mobs hurling slack, or slaked lime.

The hooligans then began pulling off his wallpaper, and declared that 'they would be d— if they wouldn't kiss Mrs Girling before they left'. Failing in this, they tried to kiss another member of the congregation, Robert Spall. 'Not being able to do that, they said they would kiss Mrs Spall, but did not attempt to do it.'

That night the gang came back to finish what they'd started. 'What a pity it is you young men come here and make a disturbance,' Benham told them. 'The law is very stringent about this, and you'll hear something from me about it.' But Nichols strode into the room and began shouting and stamping, while Goldsmith mockingly held up a stick to which he'd attached a red handkerchief, saying, 'This is a flag of distress.' He then began to declaim a text of his own, and sat down to light his pipe. Crane, also smoking, cried, 'Pinpatches and sprats at three pence a quarter.' The scene turned violent as the gang began to break up the furniture, with Barham sitting on the window-sill shouting, 'My wife has run away with a man that has three children, and when she comes back I'll be d— if I have her again.'

The mob had tailored their insults to the Girlingites, and their actions had the air of a concerted assault rather than the casual vandalism of bored young men with nothing better to do on a Sunday night in a small country village. The explanation became clear when Benham told the court that such meetings were held every three weeks at his house.

'We have two or three places where we worship under the head of Mrs Girling. Singing hymns is part of the services, which were usually well attended. I have never seen anyone on the floor fainting. Mrs Girling has a husband and two children at Ipswich. The rooms will hold one hundred people.'

Mr Jewesson, acting for the defence, asked, 'You're one of the disciples, ain't you?', his biblical overtones somewhat undermined by his grammar.

'Yes, and thank God for it,' replied Benham, who proceeded to give intriguing details of the sect and the power of their leader. 'There is silence generally when Mrs Girling reads the word of God . . . It is customary for any person to pray who likes. I never saw two or three praying at once – one stopped till another had finished. Mrs Girling was the only one that read and expounded.' He admitted, modestly, 'I am not sufficiently high to read and expound the Word of God; I wish I was.'

It wasn't clear whether he was referring to his stature or his spiritual status. Mary Ann had first come to his house eighteen months ago – 'Eliza Folkard sometimes expounded, but not publicly' – and although he had never seen anyone faint at any of these services, 'I have seen them fall under the power of God.' As an elder of the Children of God, Benham sought to counter some of the more extraordinary rumours already gathering around them. He told the court that their services differed little from those of other dissenting chapels:

'It is just the same with the exception that other people give out a text while Mrs Girling only expounds the word of God.'

Yet there was the sense of something other at work, not least in the shape of Mary Ann herself and the transcendence to which she aspired.

'By our people I mean the people who follow Mrs Girling. We subscribe money amongst ourselves. We only provide Mrs Girling with clothes and boots. We pay nothing for the rooms; I give mine gratis.'

'You speak of falling down,' remarked Mr Corrance, 'when does that occur?'

'Very often, sir,' replied Benham. 'We see people fall down by the power of God.'

'What do you mean by that?' asked Corrance.

'They go into a trance, sir, and can see all things that are going on around them. We allow them to remain till they come to themselves.' Benham insisted that they never disturbed anyone: 'We have never recognised these roughs as part of our congregation . . . They are the Devil's congregation, and ours are the children of God.'

This testimony was supported by key figures in the movement: Alfred Folkard, Eliza's father; Cornelius Chase, a twenty-seven-year-old coachmaker, and Isaac Batho, postmaster and shoemaker, both of Benhall; and Sally Spall, wife of Robert, a machinist from Hascheston, with whom Mary Ann had been staying during her missionary work. Sally Spall bore witness to the 'kiss of charity' which had prompted the gang's sarcastic amorousness.

'It is usual to kiss each other indiscriminately?' Mr Jewesson asked Mrs Spall.

'Yes, sir,' she replied.

'Both males and females?' inquired Mr Corrance.

'Both, sir.'

'Men, women and children, I suppose?' prompted Jewesson.

'Yes, sir.'

This sounded decidedly immoral, so Mr Hill stepped in, acting on behalf of the Girlingites: 'I suppose it was only a brotherly and sisterly expression of affection?'

'That's all,' said Mrs Spall.

'You don't rush into just anyone's arms – it is only the members of the congregation?'

'It's a salutation, I suppose,' remarked the Reverend Pooley.

'Just so, sir,' said Mr Hill.

Mary Ann was as much on trial here as any of her potential assailants. 'The members of this sect were led by a woman,' Jewesson was reported as saying, 'of whom, without imputing anything wrong to her, he might say that it was to be regretted she should leave her husband and children, and put herself forward in the way she did, creating as she must necessarily do so, a disturbance wherever she went.' Thus Mary Ann was portrayed as a troublemaker, a woman who, by her very sex, sought to disturb the status quo. Jewesson went on to claim that his clients had gone to the service as potential converts, 'and the confusion which took place was not caused by them or anyone connected with them'. It was a lame excuse. Hill said his client was willing to drop the charges if his expenses – and the fine – were paid there and then; and in an extraordinary intervention which to some seemed to compromise the impartiality of the Bench, Mr Corrance himself advanced the required sum for the defendants.

* * *

A legal resolution had been reached, but the wider question of the Girlingites and their freedom to worship remained. The *Woodbridge Reporter* may have been a local paper, but it reported on national issues: 'the Rights of Women'; 'Spirit Rapping Extraordinary in Woodbridge' (which turned out to be a skit advertising alcohol); Primitive Methodism; the vaccination debate; and emigration, 'a subject uppermost in men's minds now'. Disturbing events across the Channel – the 'Literary, Scientific, and Artistic Communists' in the Paris Commune – sat alongside reports of riots in Dublin and an apocalyptic editorial on cholera, 'the most destructive of human diseases', whose invasion no '"streak of silver sea"' could prevent. Amid such signs and wonders – as if plague and famine might yet sweep the land, just as the sea could break its defences – the appearance of a local prophetess was of more than a little interest; especially when her crusade provoked a riot at the Mechanics' Institute in Woodbridge.

Mechanics' institutes were established in the 1820s as educational centres for artisans. Often used for lectures on sectarian beliefs and spiritualism, they provided the working man with 'an opportunity to ride the wave of the new pseudo-sciences'. On 2 May 1871, the *Reporter* noted that 'some printed handbills circulated in the town announced that Mrs Girling would preach the Gospel in the Lecture Hall, on Tuesday evening, at half-past seven'. Such advance publicity ensured that the hall was packed, with a crowd of one hundred clamouring for admission, and 'a great number who went were not prompted with the desire of hearing the Gospel preached . . .' Mr Joseph Cullingford attempted to address the crowd, 'but was frequently interrupted. Mrs Girling stood on the centre of the platform, and by her side was . . . a Miss Folkard from Parham.' While many were still trying to get in – some by forcing the door – others were trying to get out, overcome by the heat and noise inside. It was the first indication of a mass reaction to the Girlingite gospel: a frightening spectacle to some;

to others, rather farcical. Mr Cullingford tried to leave the hall, but as he did so the door was suddenly locked, leaving his coat tails trapped and the unfortunate man 'subject to the rude remarks of the roughs for some time' while he banged on the door unheard, such was the furore within.

Meanwhile, Mary Ann had begun to speak. She told the audience that she lived at 58 Victoria Street, London Road, Ipswich, at which point a voice piped up, 'Where is your husband?', to roars of laughter. Mary Ann replied that she had his permission to speak the Word of God. Indeed, on the night of that year's census, Mrs Girling was not at home with her husband, her seventeen-year-old daughter Mary Jane, now a dressmaker, and her son William, just fifteen but, like his father, already employed in the iron works. Instead she was roaming Suffolk – not preaching, but practising, as she declared. She was about to read from the Book of Revelations when a loud noise was heard outside and the door burst open, releasing Mr Cullingford's coat. 'Outsiders rushed in, insiders rushed out, jostling with each other, and a little fresh air was obtained by this indecorous breach. With some difficulty the door was shut and locked, but the interruption continued.' Mary Ann said she'd been in worse places in Ipswich, but had never experienced such a disturbance. This merely made matters worse.

'Where's Osborne?' went up another shout.

'Are you going to mesmerise us?'

'Sit down!'

'Go home!'

'Look out, Osborne! no harm sleeping with a saint.'

The hall-keeper tried to eject some of the troublemakers, but his efforts only resulted in an increase in the riot, 'and the noise and disturbance that ensued were indescribable. A stone was thrown through one of the back windows and nearly hit a person on the head.'

At this point it was decided that it would be better to call off the entire service. The gas was turned out, and in the darkness Mary Ann made her escape through a rear exit, running across the fields towards Bredfield. In the meantime the police finally arrived, in the shape of Superintendent Fitzgerald and three or four officers. They cleared out the remaining roughs, who then went to the nearby Sun Inn where they thought the Girlingites had sought refuge, and where they 'saluted Mr Banyard with a handful of slush, which they threw into his face, and the doors were kept shut two hours'. Mr Phillips, the local magistrate, was sent for, and the *Reporter* concluded that 'Such a disgraceful riot has not occurred in Woodbridge for a very long time. We are informed that proceedings will be taken against some of the parties concerned in it.'

It seemed Suffolk had joined battle with Mary Ann's blasphemy; but what appeared to be a popular uprising was more likely organised by disgruntled squires determined to rid the county of such unsettling influences. While Phillips blamed Mrs Girling for the uproar and called for police intervention, Superintendent Fitzgerald said that as he understood the meeting 'was for religious controversy, he did not think he had any right to interfere nor to send any of his men so long as personal violence was not resorted to, nor any injury to property done'. Girlingism was to become the focus for contemporary concerns about religious freedom, pursued with a ferocity which was a legacy of the English Revolution. In the *Reporter*, 'A Lover of Fair Play' bemoaned 'a lot of blackguards being *encouraged* to injure our property and howl down free discussion', and thought it 'very unseemly, to say the least [that] a Magistrate could . . . advance the money to pay the fine of one of those worthies to prevent him from going to prison. I can only hope he is in the habit of showing the same sympathy when a poor wretch is about to be sent to gaol for killing a partridge or a hare . . . Mrs Girling and her friends will *not* be silenced by mud and riot and brawling'; rational debate was the only way to 'expose her folly and delusions'. And while a 'Lover of Civil and Religious Liberty' asked, 'Will you tell me which is the worst of the two – heathenism in Madagascar, or heathenism in (so-called) Christian England?', another 'Layman' declared that Mary Ann had been 'misrepresented and ought to be heard'.

As she was. On 1 June at Dallinghoo, Mary Ann preached at Mr Cooper's cottage: the congregation numbered twenty, five of whom were police constables, and two females fainted during the service. Landowners complained that the police 'would have been better employed in their own parishes looking to the public-houses . . . rather than being in a labourer's cottage with this fanatic, who, with her disciples, declares she can never die, and, therefore, requires not mortal protection'. The *Reporter* meanwhile 'deplored that such opinions as Mrs Girling enunciates should "delude" even a Suffolk labourer; but orthodoxy is not the test of citizenship, and her success in these parts shows that they must be included amongst the dark regions of the earth'. The imperial sway represented justice, whether in the remoteness of Madagascar, or in East Anglia.

Just when the readers thought they'd heard the last of the Children of God, came the headline:

MRS. GIRLING AGAIN!

William Brooks, a labourer, and William Leggatt, a cobbler, both from Charsfield, were charged with having assaulted John Cooper of Dallinghoo, a gardener. Around 9.30 pm on a summer evening, in the meadow next to his cottage, Cooper confronted some men throwing stones and rotten eggs at his door, and then proceeded to throw them at him.

Leggatt, standing behind a tree, hit the gardener over the head with a stick, and when Cooper said, 'I know who you are', Brooks struck out with a bigger stick, shouting, 'You old b—, I'll split your head.' 'My head was tender several days from the blow,' said Cooper. He said he couldn't understand why the gang were there, but his testimony showed precisely the reason: Mary Ann had been conducting services at his cottage for the past two months.

His evidence was a further insight into the sect's practices:

'We only sing, pray, and read the Bible,' Cooper told the court. 'It lasts one and a half hours, we sometimes stay as late as eleven, we have been as late as three or four o'clock in the morning at other places. I call myself a child of God; I belong to Christ. Mrs Girling has no particular name for the sect. We greet each other with a kiss. Mrs Girling kisses them all; she did on that occasion. My wife was present; she was kissed. I kissed Mrs Girling, and the men as well; that is our general salutation – kissing each other.'

This was decidedly unEnglish behaviour – men kissing men and persons to whom they were unrelated. Cross-questioned, Cooper painted an even stranger picture.

'We never had any seized with hysteria or fits, or carried out at mine. Some persons do see visions and are overcome by the Word of God, but that is not hysterics. I never saw any person in hysterics. When they are taken up we let them remain the Lord's time; we set them up; we use no hartsthorn . . .; we give them no brandy and water; we never tried what effect a pail of cold water would have by throwing it on them.'

Hartsthorn was a solution of ammonia, used as smelling salts, and originally made from the shavings of antlers. Cooper's description evoked pagan rites and folk magic, as well as scenes of possession unseen in Suffolk for two centuries, and the magistrates decided it was time to put a stop to this nonsense: 'If these services were met with silent public contempt and disgust they would drop, but while they were opposed in the manner they have been, the leaders of them would endeavour to claim sympathy as being the subjects of religious persecution.' Leggatt and Brooks were each fined 1s and 12s 8d costs.

But a curious sidelight is revealed by the census: Leggatt was the nineteen-year-old stepson of a David Spall. Not only was he related to the Spalls, who had converted to Girlingism, but in the same village, Charsfield, his forty-six-year-old uncle, also a shoemaker, was a minister at the Baptist chapel. Meanwhile, Henry Osborne would marry Eliza Barham, his second wife, whose kinsman had harried Leonard Benham. This was a close-knit, internecine society whose families had been divided by faith, and it is not hard to see, in this light, why the reaction was so extreme in rural Suffolk: Girlingism pitted brother against brother, sister against sister, and Mary Ann had exhausted the temper of the county. She would claim that a new vision prompted her departure, but the threat of violence was a forceful factor, while an invitation from an elder of the Bible Christians, who had asked her to preach in London, provided a good excuse to leave. Or perhaps, as the sea ate away at the Suffolk coast, she too was in retreat from its depredations, seeking a new life and a new communion in the ever-growing metropolis. Whatever her reasons, that summer of 1871 – which would prove to be a heady season for Victorian utopians – Mary Ann, her flaxen-haired chorister Eliza and her pugilistic cobbler Harry, left Suffolk to take on the capital itself.

TWO

Turning the World Upside-Down

These men who have turned the world upside down have come here also . . .

Acts of the Apostles, 17:6

Each day in London, I walk over a path of broken gravestones, slippery with moss and imprinted with the sooty shadows of long-decayed leaves. Most of the inscriptions have been eroded over the years, but one word remains –

Memory

– and every time I walk over it, the letters are slowly reduced by an infinite degree.

Bunhill Fields is a residual city square of lawn and plane trees, enclosed by tall buildings, as though part of the forest had been left behind as a museum of extinct specimens. But the reason for the survival of this ancient site is evident from its original, uncorrupted name: Bone Hill. Since 1315, layer upon layer of London's dead have been laid here, a compost of 123,000 bodies. During the pestilence of 1665, Bunhill was registered as a plague pit; instead it became a burial place for religious dissenters, who chose this unconsecrated ground beyond the city walls. Its tight-packed headstones, obelisks and urns mark the resting place of John Bunyan, Daniel Defoe and Isaac Watts. William Blake is also interred here, although his bones do not lie under his memorial, but in an unmarked part of the cemetery nine feet down in a common grave, as if even now, the mystic who saw angels in the trees of Peckham Rye and who lived in the poverty of Jesus remains as elusive as his visions.

This is a shadowy place, even at noon. Over one grave grows an oddly suburban privet hedge, trimmed in the shape of a table-top tomb; some stones assume the shape of coffins themselves, while others mimic Egyptian temples. They bear laconic elegies – *Affection Weeps – Heaven Rejoices* – or more morbid epitaphs:

<table>
<tr><td>Here lyes Dame Mary Page</td><td>on</td><td>In 67 months she was tapd 66 times</td></tr>
<tr><td>Relict of Sir Gregory Page Bart</td><td>one side</td><td>Had taken away 240 gallons of water</td></tr>
<tr><td>She departed this life March 4 1728</td><td>and on</td><td>Without ever reping at her case</td></tr>
<tr><td>In the 50th Year of her age</td><td>the other</td><td>Or fearing the operation.</td></tr>
</table>

the unfortunate Dame being a victim of dropsy. But perhaps the most famous presence here is buried on the other side of the City Road, where Wesley lies next to his house and chapel. From there pilgrim tourists spill out into the narrow alley that runs through Bunhill, mingling with the office workers taking a shortcut through the necropolis, all of them unaware that these fields once witnessed sensational events.

On 15 September 1784, the first hot-air balloon to ascend from English soil rose from the Artillery Ground abutting Bunhill Fields. It was piloted by Vincent Lunardi and watched by the Prince of Wales and 150,000 others. Monsieur Lunardi ate chicken and drank wine as he surveyed the scene from his gondola, the first to broach the space above London and look down on its warrens of streets and churches. It was an experience for which history had not prepared him, seeing a city

> so reduced on the great scale before me, that I can find no simile to convey an idea of it. I could distinguish Saint Paul's and other churches, from the houses. I saw streets as lines, all animated with beings, whom I knew to be men and women, but which I should otherwise have had a difficulty in describing. It

> was an enormous bee-hive, but the industry of it was suspended. All the moving mass seemed to have no object but myself, and the transition from the suspicion, and perhaps contempt of the preceding hour, to the affectionate transport, admiration and glory of the present moment, was not without its effect on my mind.

Lunardi's view was that of the eye of God; in his ascent, he seemed to have broken some natural law and assumed the divine, looking down on this vast still life, its numinosity directed by himself. This was eighteenth-century science fiction, a triumph of technology over nature; confirmation of an age in which Man took central stage and perhaps even superseded the Creator Himself. It was also a public spectacle: Lunardi's vehicle was exhibited in the Pantheon, Oxford Street's hall of brash attraction, and drew great crowds, some sporting the latest fashion in balloon hats; even Blake was inspired by Lunardi to write his verse 'An Island in the Moon'. The new invention caught the imagination of the young Shelley, too, who saw it as a means of discovery, both physical and philosophical –

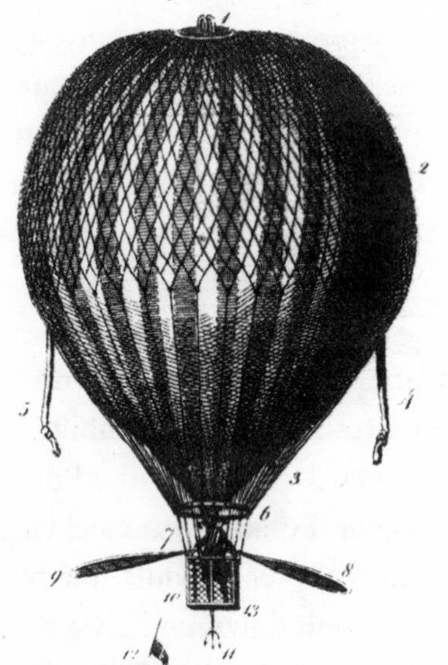

The ENGLISH BALLOON and Appendages
in which Mr LUNARDI ascended into
the Atmosphere, from the Artillery Ground,
Sep. 15 1784.

> The balloon has not yet received the perfection of which it is surely capable . . . Why are we still so ignorant of the interior of Africa? – why do we not despatch intrepid aeronauts to

> cross it in every direction, and to survey the whole peninsula in a few weeks? The shadow of the first balloon, which a vertical sun would project precisely underneath it, as it glided silently over that hitherto unhappy country, would virtually emancipate every slave, and would annihilate slavery for ever.

– but his optimism was counterpointed by Horace Walpole, who hoped that

> . . . these new mechanical meteors will prove only playthings for the learned and idle, and not be converted into new engines of destruction to the human race, as is so often the case of refinements or discoveries in science. *The wicked wit of man always studies to apply the result of talents to enslaving, destroying, or cheating his fellow creatures.* Could we reach the moon, we should think of reducing it to a province of some European kingdom.

Walpole's vision presaged Zeppelin raids and firestorms; Shelley's, a socialist utopia. Later, stranded in Devon yet keen to pursue his radical campaigns, the poet made miniature silk balloons and sent them over the moors laden with his *Declaration of Rights*, little airborne devices of sedition suspended by spirit flames, invested with their own subversive futurity, 'Twinkling amid the dark blue depths of Heaven'.

Two generations later, in 1850, the architect, artist and aerialist Philip Brannon displayed the remarkable properties of the hot-air balloon above Southampton. He produced an image of the town from 'a framed point about 400 feet above Hill Farm', the same site from which my own flight would begin. Brannon's painting, made from a photograph, was part chart, part panorama; in other images he would envisage a utopian Southampton laid out in imperial avenues, while his guide to the town described an urban Eden in which antediluvian monsters had become a kind of sideshow:

> The Whale and Grampus have been captured in Southampton Water, and on such rare occasions there have been of course the usual arrangements for sight-seers. Small shoals of Porpoises often visit the estuary; and the visitor from inland counties may be pleasingly surprised, as he walks the Quays and Platform, to see at a short distance from the shore many of these singular fish rolling and springing on the surface of the water, then disappearing, and rising again at another point to renew their awkward gambols.

But back in the London graveyard over which Lunardi had floated, events born of yet more fantastical dreams had taken place.

The dissenters buried in Bunhill Fields were heirs of the Interregnum, when it seemed 'that the world might be *permanently* turned upside down'. Among them was one Jane Leade, a widow and prophetess whose followers, the Philadelphians – named after the future city cited in Revelations – expected the millennium. In communion with the spirit world, Mrs Leade issued tracts such as *The Sign of the Times, Forerunning the Kingdom of Christ and Evidencing what is to come*, but she died, still waiting, in 1704, by which time new prophets had arrived in London with their own eschatological gospel. Just as Bunhill lived in the memory of the years of the Beast, of famine, plague and fire, so forty years later, the French Prophets seemed to augur a new apocalypse.

The Camisards were Protestant insurgents from southern France who took their name from the black shirts they wore in their nocturnal raids. They were heirs of the Cathars and their Gnostic heresies – rejecting organised religion, seeing men and women as equal before God, believing in mystical knowledge attained through divine revelation – and since the 1680s they had conducted a guerilla war directed by visions. Attended by a strange 'aerial psalmody' when hymns were heard in the heavens, 'many fell down as if dead . . . affected with sobs, sighs, groans, and tears'.

Eyewitnesses said that they looked like 'persons moved by a power outside or above themselves'. To others they resembled victims of St Anthony's Fire, a nervous disorder caused by ergot, a fungus on wheat, which in medieval times had its own relationship to the apocalyptic Dance of Death.

One Camisard experienced nine months of 'sobs and mental agitation' before falling 'into an ecstacy, and God opened my mouth. For those three days and nights I was continually under the influence of the spirit, and neither ate, drank, nor slept'. Some claimed the ability to exorcise and heal, 'passing unharmed through the fire, and practising clairvoyance'. At their secret rites, held at night to avoid detection, young recruits 'learned to perform the strangest contortions, and generally wrought themselves in a sort of trance'. They were then breathed upon to receive four degrees of divine afflatus: *L'Avertissement, Le Souffle, La prophétie* and *Le dons*, a refinement of the holy fire of Pentecost – although others ascribed these ecstatic states to the excessive fasting practised by the Camisards.

In their battles they were led by a former shepherd, Jean Cavalier, guided by God and punished by the Beast. Apprehended Camisards were tortured by being broken on the wheel, their limbs smashed until they could be made to fit its circumference, just as the orthodox world demanded that they should conform their beliefs. Fleeing from persecution, some were exiled to New Orleans (where, in a later civil war, black troops would call themselves Camisards, as rebels within a rebellion), while in 1704 another group, led by Cavalier, escaped to London. They settled in Spitalfields where 'they ranted profusely, and made converts of many English people, chiefly of the devouter sex . . . Miracles, too, were performed in abundance.' Their 'mystical phalanx' was promulgated in tracts such as *An Account of a Dream at Harwich, In a Letter to a Member of Parliament about the Camisars*, a portent-filled reverie to rival Revelations and haunted by two figures: a horseman in golden armour, and a monstrous female, 'her Eyes glaring like Lightning':

> Out of her Nostrils came a sulphurous Smoke, and out of her Mouth Flames of Fire. Her Hair was frizled, and adorn'd with Spoils of ruin'd people; her Neck bare, with Chains about it of Dice, mix'd with Pieces of Gold; which rattling, made a horrid Noise, for her Motions were all fierce and violent, her garment was all stain'd with Tears and Blood: There hung about her several Pieces of Parchment, with Bits of Wax at the end, with Figures engraved on them. She cast her Eyes often with Rage and Fury at that bright appearance I have describ'd [the golden horseman] over whom having no force, she toss'd her Head with Disdain, and glared about on her Votarys, till we saw several possess with her . . .

This nightmare, experienced on the Suffolk coast close to Mary Ann's own birthplace, seemed to engulf all England; another pamphlet, *Clavis Prophetica*, feared that these French Prophets had imported anarchy, and would cover 'the whole Face of our Heaven with Darkness'.

At Christmas 1707, an English Camisard convert, Dr Thomas Emes, died on the eve of the millennium he had predicted. He was buried in Bunhill Fields, but it was foretold that God 'wou'd attest this Publication of our Lord's Approach as Bridegroom, and Return as a King, by raising Dr *Emes* from the Grave on the 25th of next Month, above 5 Months after his Interment . . .' Accordingly, on 25 May 1708, a crowd estimated at between twenty and sixty thousand gathered in Bunhill Fields to await the doctor's resurrection. Their disappointment was blamed on 'the fact of some unfaithful person looking on'; denied their miracle, the mob managed to do great damage both to Emes's resting place and other graves as they rioted through the cemetery. Yet the French Prophets' fire still burned fiercely: four hundred converts spread out through the country, bearing their pentecostal message like Shelley's miniature balloons, and holding nocturnal meetings at which crowds gathered to see prophetesses sigh and quake. By the 1740s, their influence had reached the north of England, where it was claimed to have inspired James and Jane Wardley of Bolton-le-Moors, with that 'further degree of light and power' which would define their own and yet stranger sect.

They called themselves the United Society of Believers, to differentiate from the Quakers' Society of Friends, founded by George Fox on his Mount of Vision, Pendle Hill. But just as the latter were so called because they quaked at the word of the Lord, so the Wardleys earned the nickname of Shaking Quakers, or Shakers, a term of abuse which they turned and took upon themselves. The same soubriquet had been given to the Ranters in 1648: it was as if Shakerism was a delayed reaction to those revolutionary sects – the Familists, the Grindletons, the Seekers, the Diggers, the Ranters and the Levellers – who were themselves influenced by foreign heresies.

The early Quakers had interrupted church sermons to castigate the preachers, and had stripped naked as a protest. In the 1650s, John Gilpin wanted to cut a hole in his throat to let out the spirit's tongue. Local lads were encouraged to throw stones at itinerant Quakers, and in their stronghold at Bristol, Wakefield's James Nayler re-enacted Christ's entry into Jerusalem, with his long hair, riding on a donkey with women strewing palms before him – a blasphemy for which he had his tongue bored and his forehead branded. But with the Restoration, Quakerism lost its messianic fervour and settled into silent meditation. The Shakers, however, rejoiced in noise. It was as though they registered a seismic pre-echo of the impending industrial revolution. One Shaker described how 'a strange power begins to come on, and takes place in the body . . . which sets the person agaping and stretching; and soon sets him a twitching, as though his nerves were all in convulsion. I can compare it to nothing nearer in its feelings, than the operation of an electerising machine.' These tremors were symptoms of a new revolution to which the operators of Manchester's mechanised cotton looms would be shackled, in thrall to the processes of mass production while their children scurried perilously beneath eternally shuttling frames. Shakerism would offer an alternative to such slavery.

'. . . Amend your lives,' demanded Mother Jane Wardley. 'Repent. For the kingdom of God is at hand. The new heaven and new earth prophesied of old is about to come . . .' Her female ministry had its precedent in the French prophetesses, such as the fifteen-year-old Isabeau Vincent, who conducted services while sleeping and maintained, 'It is not I that speak, but it is the spirit within me'; or the elderly Dorothy Harling, the 'Permanent Spring' who whipped her followers and urinated on their limbs. Here in the northern forests of Pendle and Knaresborough a dangerous memory lingered; that of a holocaust in which as many as eleven million, mostly women, had died throughout Europe. The same suspicion would taint all female prophets, whose daughters would inherit what their mothers had endured. It was not until 1736 that the laws against witchcraft were repealed – the year in which Ann Lee was born in Manchester.

Even her street had the name of a witch's familiar: Toad Lane, an alley in a pre-industrial city still surrounded by wilderness, a devil darkness which Saddleworth Moor does little to dispel today. Like Mary Ann, Ann Lee was the daughter of a labourer – her father was a blacksmith – and she too was subject to divine inspiration, 'especially concerning the lusts of the flesh'. Ann would admonish her mother against sex and, as her father attempted to whip her, 'threw herself into her mother's arms, and clung around her to escape his strokes', a scene in which we might detect the traces of other abuse. And like Mary Ann, we have little record of how Ann Lee looked, only a strange phrenological portrait, an imaginary impression.

After working at a cotton loom and as a velvet-cutter, Ann became a cook in the Manchester Infirmary, while her father joined the Wardleys' congregation. In September 1758, aged twenty-two, she too became a Shaker and was soon disrupting services in Manchester's cathedral, questioning the priest's words. Four years later, she was persuaded to marry John Standerin, another blacksmith. The lateness of their union owed much to Ann's mistrust of marriage – legacy of seventeenth-century radicalism which saw marital union as another form of slavery. For Ann it was a protest vindicated by a terrible sequence: the death of her four children in infancy. And as with Mary Ann, these losses became the catalyst for her own rebirth.

ANN LEE.

After the painful and dangerous forceps delivery of her youngest daughter, Ann lay for hours in a kind of coma, as if by giving life her own had been suspended. When she recovered, her fear of her husband's concupiscence had grown. At night she paced the floor in her stockinged feet so as not to awaken him, moving through a nightmare – one which seemed to evoke her own memory of abuse. 'When I felt my eyes closing with sleep, I used to pull them open with my fingers, and say within myself, I had better open my eyes here, than open them in hell.' Where witches had been walked to make them summon their familiars, Ann forestalled her hellish visions by remaining conscious. She starved her body so that her soul 'might hunger for nothing but God'; tears 'cleaved off' her cheeks, blood 'gushed from under her nails', and when she lay down at night, the bed shook so that her husband was glad to leave it. Denying herself every gratification, her 'earthly tabernacle' was so reduced that she had to rely on others to feed her.

'My flesh consumed upon my bones, bloody sweat pressed through the pores of my skin, and I became as helpless as an infant.' As she fasted, 'a kind of down came upon my skin' – a symptom of malnutrition, elsewhere responsible for the animal appearance of feral children. In her personal wilderness, Ann 'labored, in strong cries and groans to God, day and night, till my flesh wasted away, and I became like a skeleton'. It seemed she was about to make of her marriage bed a sepulchre. Reduced to a living *memento mori*, Ann was now granted an 'astonishing vision of the Fall, in which Christ appeared to her in all his glory'. She was shown a 'full and clear view of the mystery of iniquity . . . *and of the very act of transgression committed by the first man and woman in the garden of Eden*'. The impact of this sacred, sexual vision was to set Ann on a new and extraordinary course, one which would take her across the world. But others saw it differently, and in 1770 Ann was admitted to the asylum of the same hospital in which she worked.

Thus confined, as if with child, Ann faced her final confrontation. There, in the Lunatick Ward of the Manchester Infirmary, God revealed that she was the woman whose appearance was foretold in Revelations, 'clothed with the sun, and the moon under her feet, and upon her head a crown of twelve stars', crying out 'in her pangs of birth, in anguish for delivery'. At this Ann 'felt unspeakable joy in God, and my flesh came upon me, like the flesh of an infant'. Released from the infirmary and out of madness, she was born again, just as two centuries later psychotics would be reborn through insulin coma or electrical therapies which themselves resembled the Shakers' trembling rituals. In this rite of her own body, she had become a different being: the Bride of the Lamb, or simply Ann the Word; and as she emerged from her confinement, like a butterfly from its chrysalis, she asserted her power over her mentors, the Wardleys.

It was a religious coup in which Ann installed her own followers, among them her brother William, a former cavalry officer, a tall, powerfully-built young man who would act as Ann's protector and yet who would also acknowledge her as his mother. As the new figurehead of the Shakers, Ann pursued their principles, taken from the Pentecostal or Primitive church: communal property, celibacy, pacifism, self government and power over disease. As with her familial conflicts, these claims enraged the mob, threatened by the promise that they might be saved if they too rejected sex. One of Ann's own brothers took a broomstick to his sister: 'He then beat me over my face and nose, with his staff, till one end of it was much splintered. But I sensibly felt and saw bright rays of the glory of God, pass between my face and his staff, which shielded off the blows, so that he had to stop and call for drink.' Having refreshed himself, he resumed his assault, and yet a spiritual *souffle* infused Ann: 'While he continued striking, I felt my breath, like healing balsam, streaming from my mouth and nose, which healed me, so that I felt no harm from his stroke, but he was out of breath, like one which had been running a race.' His breath was merely human; Ann's, divine.

Like the Camisards, the Shakers moved by night to safe houses, chanting as they went, their leader miraculously preserved as though enveloped in some sacred bubble; when being stoned by the mob, Ann was 'surrounded by the presence of God to such an effect that she felt joy and comfort while her unprotected enemies were utterly confused and distressed'. On another occasion, after 'wilfully and contemptuously' haranguing a Manchester congregation, Ann was interrogated by the church authorities who, she claimed, threatened to brand her cheeks and bore her blasphemous tongue with a hot iron – an attack which echoed the punishment meted out to James Nayler and portended Mary Ann's paralysed lips, as if the word of God were as much an affliction as a blessing. And like Mary Ann, Ann Lee too had her would-be assassin: one

Elizabeth Bishop, who declared she wished to shoot Ann with a silver bullet – only to fall under her influence and become a Shaker herself. It was as if Mary Ann's trials had all been run before her, incarnate in Ann Lee.

One Sunday morning the local constabulary broke in upon the Shakers' worship and dragged Ann downstairs by her ankles, an act of humiliation in which her skirts rode up about her waist. In Manchester's House of Correction, she was confined in a cell so small that she was unable to straighten herself. 'She had nothing to eat or drink, except some wine and milk mixed, put into the bowl of a tobacco-pipe, and conveyed to her by inserting the stem through the key-hole once every 24 hours. This was done by James Whittaker, when a boy, whom Mother Ann brought up.' It was a modern version of the medieval torture of 'little ease', in which, as Linder Sterling observes, the victim became an involuntary anchoress. Or perhaps this was a political imprisonment, an augury of hunger-striking suffragettes who used consumption and its denial as an offensive weapon, only to be punished by force-feeding with mechanical contraptions and rubber tubes.

Freed once more, Ann declared, 'It is not I that speak, it is Christ who dwells in me. I converse with Christ.' She was the Elder Sister to Jesus's Elder Brother: mortal beings to be followed, not worshipped; yet in her 'the *Christ*, NOT *Jesus* . . . should make a *Second Appearance*'. The Shakers would reject physical resurrection as 'utterly repugnant to both science, reason, and Scripture'. With their foundation, the Day of Judgement had occurred; they were now living 'in the Resurrection Order, surrounded by, and in communion with, the spirits of the dead' – a communion in which they looked to the new world for salvation.

Over the wild Atlantic, America seemed to reflect its absence of history in its very vastness, as if the unending forests, prairies and lakes were waiting for its story to be written by the clouds scudding across its gigantic skies. This *terra nullis* evoked Eden before the Fall; a place in which to be reborn, as the Puritans believed, out of a state of fallen grace and back into perfection. Unseen and sublime over the horizon, this brave new world was itself a religious experiment, implicit with redemption. Even the passage there was a test of faith, just as *The Tempest* was inspired by a shipload of Irish rebels, gypsies, dissenters and criminals who had set off for Virginia, 'Earth's only Paradise', only to founder on Bermuda, Prospero's Island.

Since their foundation by the Puritans, the colonies had been home to many such refugees. The Quaker William Penn had established Pennsylvania – a place of sylvan woods named after his father – with its biblical capital, Philadelphia. Mennonite and Amish communities would follow, as would a young Rosicrucian, Kelpius, who exchanged 'millennial convictions' with Mrs Leade in London, before taking his followers on a voyage during which the storm was calmed as Christ had done on Galilee. Led to their 'new forest-homes beyond the mighty sea', they set up their wooden tabernacle near Germantown in Pennsylvania, there to await the Second Coming, living communally and identifying with the woman clothed with the sun from whom they took their name, *Das Weib in der Wüste* (*The Woman in the Wilderness*). For seven years they scanned the skies with telescopes for signs, but were rewarded only with 'a white, obscure, moving body in the air . . . which, as it approached, assumed the form and mien of an angel' before receding 'into the shadows of the forest . . .'

Back in Manchester, the woods also beckoned to Ann Lee. One night the Shakers were resting at the roadside when James Whittaker saw 'a large tree, and every leaf thereof shone with such brightness as made it appear like a burning torch'. Like the burning bush from which Moses was commanded to lead his people out of slavery, this 'Tree of Life' was a sign of their new order; and so, in the words of their chroniclers, the Shakers 'fled to the wilderness of

America, from the face of the "fiery flying serpent"' – the church and state which they saw as the Image of the Beast. During their voyage – financed by a wealthy supporter, John Hocknell – the captain threatened to throw his human cargo overboard when they persisted in their strange rites, but a tempest blew up, and as waves sprang a plank in the hull, Ann saw two bright angels standing by the mast. At this another wave pounded the plank back into place.

On their arrival in New York, the Shakers strode up Pearl Street and stopped outside the house of Mrs Cunningham, whose name Ann seemed to know. 'I am commissioned of the Almighty God to preach the everlasting Gospel to America, and an Angel commanded me to come to this house, and to make a home for me and my people,' she declared, whereupon they were immediately taken inside. There they stayed until the spring of 1776 when they established a new Albion at Niskeyuna, on land bought by Hocknell in upstate New York, a place reached through 'the immense pines and hemlock trees' of 'that dreary forest, which blackens so large a portion of North America'. Around them raged the battle for the new nation, a revolution which, their visions had assured them, would 'terminate successfully, and that a Civil Government would be founded, protecting all people in their liberty of conscience, person, and press'. Indeed, they had come to save Americans 'all sunk in their pollutions'.

It was a mission rooted in the virgin forest. Ann Lee was the woman living unknown in the woods of the Apocalypse, asking the trees to pray for her followers, who ran wild, hooting like owls. Witnesses claimed to have seen them dancing naked, in the belief that 'they were angels, and invisible, and could go out among men and not be seen'. There was a precedent for such behaviour: the Ranters had preached unclothed, and the Quakers went 'naked for a sign'. These were symbolic states, just as Blake and his wife would sit naked in their Lambeth garden, reciting from *Paradise Lost* and greeting a visitor, 'Come in! it's only Adam and Eve, you know!'

The Blakes' back garden represented the perfection of paradise, 'to the scandal of wondering neighbours'. Neighbours of the Shakers' Eden were also suspicious – not least of the sect's claims to commune with the dead: 'Sometimes while eating at the table, they say their dead parents and brethren come on the table and set on a pyre and they see them.' The Shakers had inherited the early Quakers' belief in 'a certain efflux or effluvium of animal volatile spirits . . . that flow from their bodies by the command of their will into the bodies of . . . new proselytes', while Ann saw God's power 'visible on the faces of the believers and even on their clothing . . . It looked perfectly white and run in veins'. At other times a 'strange milky substance . . . seemed to run over the skin and clothes of converts'. Such phenomena recalled the breath that had protected Ann like balsalm and foreshadowed spiritualistic ectoplasm – the mysterious cloudy matter which possessed its own methods of bodily extrusion as it was brought forth from mediums' mouths and even their vaginas.

In fact, in the New World their rituals had become even more extreme. The Shakers struck grotesque shapes – 'shaking their heads, in a violent manner, turning their heads half round, so that their face looks over each shoulder, their eyes being shut' – as if God was fighting the Devil for control of their bodies. To some, such contortions were indistinguishable from the possessed victims of witchcraft. As the ritual rose to fever-pitch, worshippers would be 'groaning most dismally; some trembling extremely; others acting as though all their nerves were convulsed; others swinging their arms, with all vigour, as though they were turning a wheel, etc. Then all break off, and have a spell of smoaking, and some times great fits of laughter . . . this they call the worship of God'.

Sometimes the dancing grew so intense that the entire company would jump up and down, making the house tremble 'as if there were an earthquake'. Nor were these convulsions confined to indoors. They could happen while travelling by foot or horseback, digging in the fields, or cutting trees; their subjects would not interrupt their chores, but carried on working as their heads turned from left to right, 'with eyes closed or raised towards the sky, with an expression which proclaims ecstasy, anguish, and pain'. Such scenes must have been truly disturbing for passersby, and perhaps even for the Shakers themselves. Yet they had been licensed to act in this way by the freedom of America, as though their removal to a new world had liberated them from England's little ease and allowed their ranks to swell. The American colonies had already witnessed George Whitefield's Great Awakening and the revival known as the New Light Stir. Now, with the Dark Day of 10 May 1780, when candles had to be lit at noon – in fact, the clouds were the carbonised remains of the forest itself, burnt in clearings and suspended in the air like great trails of incense – hundreds came over to Shakerism, drawn by this apocalyptic sign.

It seemed the Shakers were summoning spirits, or were possessed by them, sometimes to be purged by Mother Ann. After all, was not Christ an exorcist? But in New England, these were dangerous ideas in the lee of Salem, the harbour town due east of Niskeyuna. Only eighty years previously, in 1692, several girls of the town had begun to display strange symptoms. 'Their motions in their fits are preternatural, both as to the manner, which is so strange as a well person could not screw their body into,' wrote Reverend Lawson, while Reverend Hale noted: 'Their arms, necks, and backs were turned this way and that, and returned back again, so as it was impossible for them to do of themselves, and beyond the power of any epileptic fits, or natural disease to effect.' Others spoke in voices which were not their own; some felt bitten or pinched, and even had actual marks on their skin. Later explanations for these phenomena would include multiple personality, an extreme form of 'hysterical fugue', or even ergotism, St Antony's Fire, in which the victim contorts their body in pain, shaking and suffering delusions. But such pathology was not available to those who witnessed the Shakers' strange convulsions; and as Matthew Hopkins' campaign would haunt Mary Ann Girling, so Salem's memory cast these forest rites as a kind of Goyaesque coven.

For the Shakers, who saw time in heaven-directed dispensations which extended beyond human measure, it was the beginning of a new age. To seal the success of their 'federated communal order', an echo of the new states of America, they set off to tour New England. Travelling by night, they sang to keep their spirits up in the pitch-black darkness of the forest, and carried their faith as far north as Maine and the plantation by Sabbathday Lake. Yet in these shadowy sorties they were accused of unAmerican activities, of harbouring weapons and 'being *unfriendly to the patriotic cause*, from the fact of their bearing a testimony against *war in general*'. Their pacifism was in itself an offence, and Mother Ann was abducted by vigilantes with blackened faces like the 'Red Indian' protesters of the Boston Tea Party, and her dress torn off to reveal 'a British emissary in a woman's habit', while her followers were accused of being Indian-lovers. And just as Salem's witches were suspected of contracts with the devil – to 'over Come the Kingdome of Christ and set up [his own] Kingdome' – so the Shakers seemed to pose a new threat to the virgin territory. They had become the enemy within. Enraged by their enacted, allegorical war between Michael and the dragon, colonists besieged the Shakers in their houses or route-marched them out of town. Still they bore their sufferings selflessly, like Christian and Faithful in Bunyan's *Pilgrim's Progress*, jumping on each others' backs to save one another from the whippings, and thanking God 'that He had found them worthy of persecution'.

These years of opposition took their toll on Ann Lee, and on 8 September 1784 she succumbed to what may have been leukaemia, visible as bruise-like marks on her body: pathological stigmata. Ann had never believed in her own immortality, although her followers expected her ministry to last a thousand years. Under her appointed successor, her surrogate son James Whittaker, the sect financed the building of a ship, the *Union*, 'to bear the testimony to foreign lands'. With its Shaker crew and cargo of horses, flour and other supplies, this latterday *Mayflower* must have made an extraordinary sight as it sailed out of Boston Harbour, bound for Haiti and Havanna. We know nothing of its journey, nor is there any record of Cubans converting to the cause, no secret Caribbean colony of Shakers conducting their rites in the tropical wilderness, observed only by parakeets and snakes.

In the Old World, rationality had triumphed. England had rejected Ann Lee's visions and sent her troublesome sectarians to one colony, just as it would transport its criminal outcasts to another. Faced with its own republicanism and radicalism, a new English revolution was averted by John Wesley and his peculiar people, who subsumed rebellion in religion and what Charles Kingsley called 'the opium of the masses'. Yet faith remained an outlet for lives in thrall to industrialism, and open-air Methodist gatherings were prey to 'swooning, groaning, crying out, weeping and falling into paroxysms'.

Although Wesley opposed such extreme reaction, it had grown rather than subsided among people alienated by enclosure and the age of the machine; and in an era paradoxically attuned to madness and hysteria by its own rational aspirations, metaphysical questions gathered currency as the century moved towards its end. Anton Mesmer, discoverer of animal magnetism, believed that the universe was filled with a mystical fluid which permeated everything and was the conduit of the influence of the stars – an alchemical connexion between the Shakers' effluvium and the modern notion that our bodies are made of stardust. Like Isaac Newton searching for the Philosopher's Stone even as he wrote his *Principia*, or the earlier scientist Sir Kenelm Digby, who had developed his curative 'powder of sympathy' and who joined others such as Francis Bacon in the belief in sympathetic magic –

that bleeding could be stopped at a distance by applying a handkerchief soaked in the injured party's blood to the weapon which had caused the wound – Mesmer moved between philosophy and the preternatural. Mozart was said to have written *Così Fan Tutte* under his influence, although in 1784 the French Academy decided that 'imagination with magnetism produces convulsions and that magnetism without imagination produces nothing'. Yet mesmerism, in its scientific reincarnation as hypnotism, would become a treatment for the neuroses which afflicted the industrial world and which filled its asylums with the mad. Was religious mania, then, a neurosis? The behaviour of Richard Brothers made a good case study.

In March 1795, Richard Brothers was arrested on the orders of the Privy Council and confined to an asylum. His crime – his madness – was to have predicted that the Thames would run with human blood in advance of the Second Coming. As his popularity grew, Brothers issued prophetic tracts whose comprehensive titles – *the Downfall of the Pope; a Revolution in Spain, Portugal, and Germany; the Death of Certain Great Personages in this and other Countries. Also a dreadful Famine, Pestilence and Earthquake* – evoke the apocalyptic scenes painted by John Martin, with their angel hosts on one side, and on the other, hordes thrown into hell like those Shakers who felt themselves teetering on the precipice of the inferno. In Brothers' imagined future, France would be infected with 'contaminated blood', Catholicism and Islam would be destroyed, and a universal brotherhood take their place. Such predictions were a heady narcotic for those excluded by the changing centre of economic gravity. But Brothers was arrested and confined to Bedlam, and only released in 1806, still insisting that he had seen the Devil 'walk leisurely into London' – by which time he had been superseded by an even greater cult.

The *fin de siècle* had produced new prophetesses, women such as Elspeth Buchan, a contemporary of Ann Lee who claimed that

God's power 'wrought such a wonderful change' that she was able to live without food for many weeks. She too employed holy breath, decried marriage as 'the bondage of the law', and bid her Buchanites sleep on heather bundles in a barn. She would stand in a circle of young men and touch each with her palm, at which they would swoon away and lie about her like some human crop circle, springing upright when touched again. She also set a date for the Second Coming in July 1786, when her followers, their heads shaved save for tufts by which angels could pluck them up, waited on a wooden platform built on a nearby hill – only instead of the Lord a wind arrived and sent them crashing to the ground.

But none gathered greater crowds than Joanna Southcott. Born in Gittisham, Devon, in 1750, Southcott was a farmer's daughter, and a zealous Methodist. At the age of forty, a change came over her: modern doctors might have discerned the menopause, but Joanna said she had been called by God and, like Elspeth Buchan, she assumed the starry mantle of the Woman Clothed with the Sun. By 1801, when she published her booklet, *The Strange Effects of Faith*, her Christian Israelites were particularly numerous in the North and South-West. From London, Joanna issued ominous warnings – 'O England! O England! England! the axe is laid to the tree, and it must and will be cut down; ye know not the days of your visitation' – while in Hampshire, William Cobbett despaired, 'It is in vain that we boast of our *enlightened state*, while a sect like this is increasing daily.'

One day, sweeping out a house after a sale, Southcott 'was permitted by the Lord to find, *as if by accident*', a commonplace seal. In

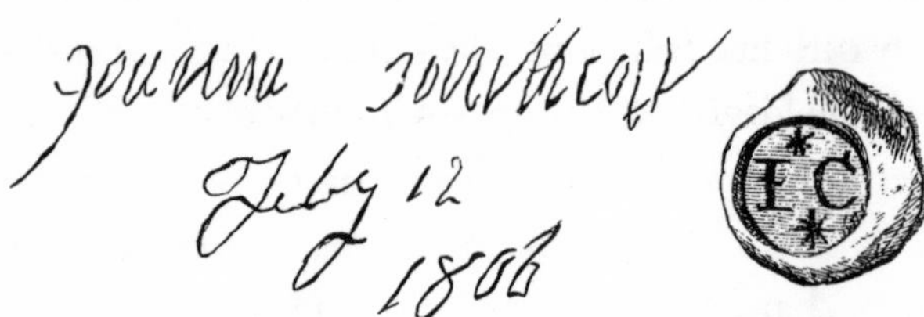

her hands it became the English Seal of Revelation, and her SEALED PEOPLE rapidly approached the mystical number predicted in the book of the Apocalypse: 'Then I heard the count of those who were sealed, a hundred and forty-four thousand of them'. This was followed by a yet more extraordinary announcement: that the sixty-three-year-old Southcott was pregnant with the messiah who would rule the nations with a rod of iron. This was not a new phenomenon – in the Interregnum, Ranter women had professed to be with Christ's child – but now all England awaited Shiloh's birth. Expectation grew, as did Joanna's belly, but fatally she cast doubt on her state, and when no child appeared, she fell ill and died on 27 December 1814. Her followers waited three days for her resurrection, keeping her body warm with hot water bottles (and thus accelerating its putrefaction). On the fourth day they permitted a postmortem, which revealed that her phantom pregnancy (as if to bear the Holy Spirit) was due to dropsy, the same watery disease which had flooded the unfortunate corpus of Bunhill's Mary Page.

Southcott left behind twenty-five boxes filled with her visions, one sealed and to be opened only in time of national crisis. Attempts were made to have it opened during the Crimean War and the First World War – the same points at which a ghostly hart appeared at the Rufus Stone. The Panacea Society – formed in Bedford by the suffragette Mary Bulthrop, who believed herself to be the reincarnation of Shiloh – campaigned for its opening, but when it was finally unlocked in 1927, the box was found to contain some insignificant papers and a lottery ticket. The Panaceans, however, contend that this was not the authentic box, and that even now, Joanna's secrets lie in a rural repository awaiting ultimate revelation, while her followers prepare for Christ's arrival at 18 Albany Street, Bedford, the original site, they claim, of the Garden of Eden.

* * *

In New England, Shakerism had settled down to become an institution, with a written constitution and divided 'orders' as if in mimesis of the new republic. The Shakers lived like monks and nuns, their daily routines of worship and work strictly regulated, even as to how they should eat: noiselessly and without conversation. The outside world was kept at bay: surgeons were summoned only in the case of broken bones or serious wounds; otherwise, trust was put in God's healing. Industry became an expression of their faith; as Ann Lee had declared: 'Put your hands to work and give your hearts to God'. Their clothes were symbols of their unity and their otherness – and, perhaps, of suppressed individuality, a uniqueness in itself homogenous. With long gowns, aprons and caps for the women, and coats, capes, breeches and stocks for the men, they resembled a cross between Puritans and workers in a Lancashire factory. Such subfusc costumes reflected their connexion with nature, in felt and wool and linen and cotton, woven and dyed with the levelling unchemical colours of drab, nutgall, butternut or pursley blue to blend with the land – just as the paint used by the Sabbathday Lake family for their meeting house was composed of crushed blueberry skins, sage leaves, and indigo. The Shakers saw God in the natural kingdom, in the animals they kept, in the food they ate: many were vegetarians or even vegans.

Their villages aspired to a similar purity. Built of plain white clapboard, they were unadorned places in which to live out lives of innocence. They now rehearsed their steps before dancing, and on Sundays, carriages would arrive at Sabbathday Lake from the spa hotels of Poland Springs, as though the Shakers were another attraction laid on for their amusement. In a complicated world, Shakerism presented an uncluttered appeal. Free from possessions and responsible to no government but God, they were 'the children of one family, enjoying equal rights and privileges in things spiritual and temporal, because . . . love is the only bond of their union'.

Bonded by love: it was that simple.

The Shakers seemed to reinvent the way the world could work, and they inspired the Welsh-born reformer Robert Owen in his plans for a new society, founded on a series of co-operatives – although Britain remained sceptical about his plans: 'Can Mr Owen reverse the decrees of Fate, and so regulate the *accidents* to which human beings are liable, as to remove from them all temptation to sin, and exempt them from all chance of mistery?' Nonetheless, this wealthy visionary arrived in America in the wake of Ann Lee, with an equally presumptuous ambition. 'I am come to this country,' he declared in 1825, 'to introduce an entire new system of society; to change it from an ignorant, selfish system to an enlightened social system . . . and remove all causes for contest between individuals.' And as he explained to President John Adams, who himself opposed slavery, he would achieve his aim by *building* utopia, for that was the only way Man might change, if his circumstances dignified his ambitions.

Owen's vision was a new Jerusalem, about to rise in the New World – in Indiana. He proposed a great hollow square, one thousand feet long, which would contain all his community needed: a school and a university, a library, chapel, ballrooms. Kitchens, dining rooms and laundries would occupy other blocks, while the upper storeys would house the inhabitants like some gigantic hotel. This 'new empire of peace and goodwill' foresaw the city of the future; but just as that would for many become a dystopia, Owen and his architect, Stedman Whitwell, also had to accept a different reality. Having taken over a former Rappite community, hundreds flocked to Owen's New Harmony, drawn by its utopian dream or its founder's substantial fortune. But the colony did not live up to its name: it lacked the religious principles, the discipline and the cohesion of celibacy, as practised by the Shakers, and there were disputes over the system which should be adopted to run the place. Yet it sowed radical seeds, not least in the work carried on by Owen's son, Robert Dale Owen, who would join Fanny Wright (one of the first to arrive at New Harmony and founder of Nashoba, a community to educate liberated slaves) in proposing free education and women's rights, ideas which would influence the Democratic party, while among other Owenites championing these same radical ideas was an Englishman, Frederick Evans. In a reverse arc to Owen's inspiration, Evans would convert to Shakerism in 1831 and become its most able proponent. He was also the man who would oversee their venture into another world.

THE WHIRLING GIFT

In 1837, Shakerism was suddenly disrupted by a violent eruption. That August at Niskeyuna, a class of adolescent girls 'began to shake and whirl'. In the summer evening, 'the senses of three of the children appeared withdrawn from the scenes of time . . . They began to sing, talk about angels, and describe a journey they were making, under spiritual guidance, to heavenly places.' It was the start of 'Mother Ann's Work', a revival directed from beyond the grave by Ann Lee herself.

The Shakers had ever believed that they were surrounded by the spirits of the dead. Mother Ann had written to one Shaker, 'I see the dead around you, whose visages are ghostly and very awful.

Their faces almost touch thine. If you did but see what I see, you would be surprised . . .' Now the sect had witnessed the birth of spiritualism, and it was a violent genesis. The music created by these human instruments was an eerie composition which superseded time and space, connecting all things in the Shakers' eternal dance. It threw its subjects to the floor, 'where they lay as dead, or struggling in distress until someone near lifted them up, when they would begin to speak with great clearness and composure', although the words came in 'native speech' or 'mongrel English'. These events may have recalled those at Salem, but to some, the extremity of the reactions in these, adolescents was more clearly than ever an erotic sublimation. As the phenomenon spread, the instruments were possessed by figures from the past; by dead Shakers or a panoply of Sounding Angels, Angels of Love, of Consuming Fire, and the Holy Witnessing Angel of God bearing scrolls of 'heavenly thoughts' from the Apostles and Old Testament prophets, from Alexander, Napoleon and George Washington, or from their 'Heavenly Parents', Jesus Christ and Ann Lee herself.

'Mother Ann's Work' was breathtaking in the detail with which it imagined another plane. Where Enlightenment scholars had debated whether one would drink claret in heaven, Shaker feasts of invisible food were consumed and drinkers made giddy by invisible wine in what were in effect mass seances. There were extravagant manifests of fantastic objects echoing those of Revelations and the eschatological banquet of the Lamb, a festival to mark the final unfolding of time: 'diamonds of charity', 'chrysolites, emeralds, sapphires, and other precious stones; golden censors, bowls, and chains; gold boxes filled with various treasures; cakes of love and "sweet-scented manna on shining plates" . . . plates of wisdom, baskets of simplicity, balls of promise, belts of wisdom, bands of brightness and robes of meekness; heavenly doves; leaves from the tree of life . . .'

It was as if the after-life was providing the Shakers with the luxuries denied them on earth, all listed in dream-like, Byzantine indices worthy of Huysmans' *À Rebours*. Like later mediums, instruments employed Indian spirit guides, with brethren as braves and sisters as squaws, whooping and yelling in strange antics, 'such as would require a Dickens to describe', while predictions of the invention of the telegraph and coming revolution in Europe seemed, like Mother Shipton, to map out the future, opening doors to the unknown. Although the Shakers were reluctant to make public the phenomena they were experiencing, the instruments announced that 'similar manifestations would soon break forth in the world'. Accordingly, in 1847 at Hydesville, a small town in New York State, two sisters, Margaret and Kate Fox, aged twelve and ten, heard 'a brisk tattoo' of raps on their bedroom wall and saw their furniture move of its own accord.

As newspapers began to report these strange events, Mrs Fox sent the girls to their married sister, Leah, in Rochester, five miles away. But the phenomena followed them, delivering messages for which Leah charged visitors a dollar a head. The Rochester Rappings ushered in commercial spiritualism. Moving to New York, the Fox sisters set up operation in P. T. Barnum's Hotel, where they were visited by Manhattan society and such figures as the singer Jenny Lind, so impressed that she left 'with her eyes full of tears'. Despite an investigation which concluded that the noises were made by snapping certain tendons, and Margaret Fox's confession – subsequently retracted – that 'the whole business is humbug from beginning to end', an air of mystery lay over the affair. It was as if the sisters had fulfilled a need for belief in a rational age. Among those who paid their dollar admission were the members of a Shaker committee, who 'at once recognised the presence of the spirits, and believed it to be the prelude to extensive manifestations of different kinds'. However, as spiritualism began to grip the country, other Shakers professed to be uncertain about its manifestations, declaring that 'this form of communion with the spirit world is not for Believers in our faith'.

In those years America seemed open to a hundred Edens, from Thoreau's Walden in Massachusetts to Keil's Aurora in Oregon; from Josiah Warren's Equity in Ohio to Étienne Cabet's Icaria in California. In 1840, Emerson told Thomas Carlyle: 'We are all a little wild here with numberless projects of social reform. Not a reading man but has a draft of a new community in his waistcoat pocket...' However, Boston Transcendentalists distrusted spiritualism (a 'Rat-revelation', said Emerson); and Nathaniel Hawthorne, visiting the Shaker village of Hancock with his friend Herman Melville, then in the midst of writing *Moby-Dick*, professed to be disgusted by its 'utter and systematic lack of privacy', the 'miserable pretence of cleanliness and neatness' and the fact that two men shared a narrow bed. Yet ten years before, Hawthorne had been a shareholder in Brook Farm's brief commune of intellectuals on 160 acres of farmland, where he laboured all day in the fields – only to find himself too tired to write at night.

Even shorter-lived was Fruitlands, a commune inspired by the Shakers and founded by Amos Bronson Alcott, the great Transcendentalist, after a visit (funded by Emerson) to the 'Concordium', an English commune at Ham Common which was run by his friend, Charles Lane. Back in New England, Alcott and Lane, nine other adults, and the Alcotts' four daughters – among them the ten-year-old Louisa May – set up camp on ninety acres in Harvard, where many adopted new identities for the venture. One man, Samuel Bower, declared that clothes stifled his spirit and became a nudist, while another lived only on apples. Apart from Mrs Alcott, there was only one other woman, Ann Page, although she was expelled for eating fish. The community was strictly vegan, taking nothing whatsoever from animals – no dairy products, eggs, honey, wax, or wool. No manure was used to fertilise the land, nor animals to work it. There was no lamp oil, since it came from whales and so the commune was dark at night; cotton was forbidden as it was produced by slavery. Yet such admirable, contemporary-sounding sanctions caused problems – not least what their adherents could wear (for those unwilling to adopt Samuel Bower's sky-clad solution) in an era before man-made fibres. 'Since cotton, silk, and wool were forbidden as the product of slave-labor, worm-slaughter, and sheep-robbery', as Louisa May Alcott wrote in *Transcendental Wild Oats*, her fictional account of the commune, 'a new dress was invented. Tunics and trousers of brown linen were the only wear ... Some persecution lent a charm to the costume, and the long-haired, linen-clad reformers quite enjoyed the mild martyrdom they endured when they left home.'

Fruitlands was a utopian may-fly, lasting only one summer. Its failure lay in its membership of people already unable to cope with life, men such as Samuel Hecker, who 'had nervous fits, heard imaginary voices, and suffered from an unidentified sexual disorder for which others advised marriage but which convinced him always to remain celibate'. Hecker tried to purify himself by eating only unleavened bread, fruit and water, and aspired to the ultimate diet of wanting 'to do away with the digestive system entirely'. He later became a Roman Catholic priest.

By now Brook Farm and its tenants had fallen under a powerful new spell: that of François Marie Charles Fourier, a man whose influence spread across the world, even though he had never left France between his birth in 1772 and his death, kneeling by his bedside in a lowly boarding house, in 1837. Yet Fourier devised a world of mutually interdependent communities built up through layer over layer of human endeavour, and inhabiting gigantic three-storey dwellings spread over three square miles. In order to succeed where Owen had failed, these colonies would contain a high proportion of farmers and mechanics to capitalists, artists and scientists; the least pleasant work would receive the highest pay, and leisure hours be devoted to the uplifting pursuit of pleasure. This hedonistic army paraded – in Fourier's mind – in ascending phalanxes of one thousand six hundred and twenty individuals ready to take over the world when their number reached 2,985,984. By that time, Fourier predicted, the sea would have turned to lemonade, the stars and planets ('sentient beings like ourselves') continued to reproduce, and men would have grown tails with eyes in them. The dangerous beasts of the wilderness would be replaced by 'anti-lions' and 'anti-sharks', and the Arctic would dispense perfumed dew.

Not since Thomas More's Island of Utopia had paradise been so specifically charted. And such were these promises, so precise and so wonderful, that in an industrial century longing for its own lost Eden, Fourierism was taken up with a wild popularity. Brook Farm itself became a phalanx, but in the process lost its intellectual sheen: the transcendentalists stopped coming, and the farm burnt down. Meanwhile, part of New York State was declared a Burnt Over Region through which revivalism had raged, leaving behind the stubble of faith. From this eschatological geography – from the Great Awakening to the New Light Stir and now this incindered zone – a gothic New England was created, evoked in Hawthorne's *Shaker Bridal*, *The Blithedale Romance* and *The House of the Seven Gables*. The latter was set in his hometown of Salem, with its 'Daguerreotypist' as a latter-day witch, a photographer-radical suspected of practising animal magnetism and who had 'the strangest companions imaginable; – men with long beards, and dressed in linen blouses, and other such new-fangled and ill-fitting garments; – . . . who acknowledged no law and ate no solid food, but lived on the scent of other people's cookery, and turned up their noses at the fare'; while in *Moby-Dick*, Melville depicted the young 'archangel Gabriel' as a maniacal figure in a 'cabalistically-cut coat of a faded walnut tinge' who was 'nurtured among the crazy society of Neskyuna Shakers', and who declared the White Whale itself to be 'the Shaker God incarnate'.

One New England sect truly prospered, however: John Humphrey Noyes' Perfectionists or 'Bible Communists'. In 1834 Noyes had announced that Christ had absolved him of sin, and that the Second Coming had actually occurred thirty years after the Saviour's crucifixion. The Perfectionists were now living in a state of regenerated innocence – 'In a holy community, there is no more reason why sexual intercourse should be restrained by law, than why eating and drinking should be' – and where the Shakers sublimated desire in the dance, Noyes liberated women via *coitus reservatus*. He even envisaged a kind of early eugenicism by preaching against 'random procreation'. Members lived in a centrally-heated Mansion House at Oneida in New York State, with a visitor's parlour and a library which contained the latest works by Huxley and Darwin. Next door there was a school, photographic and chemistry laboratories, and a printing press producing the weekly *Circular*, with mock 'classifieds' advertising 'Shares of Second-Coming Stock'. Entertainment was provided by an orchestra, with a stereopticon for the children. Inhabitants rose when they liked, their workload lightened by hired labour. From its graceful lawns, Oneida presented a civilised image, with men in suits and women in liberated short skirts and bloomers; only the notion of radical sexual practices lent an edge to such genteel scenes.

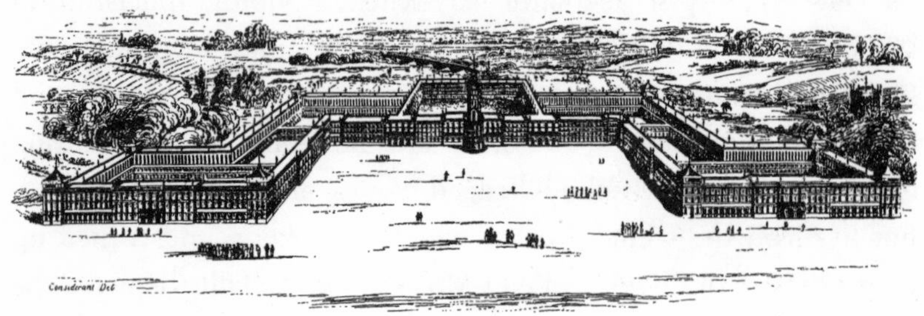

DESIGN FOR A FOURIERIST PHALANSTERY

THREE

Human Nature

> . . . Considering the poverty of Pekin, the beggary in Constantinople, the infanticide in Paris, the political corruption in New York, and the fifty thousand thieves, one hundred thousand prostitutes, and one hundred and sixty-five thousand paupers of London, is it strange that noble souls in all lands yearn for social reconstruction? . . . Are not present political and social systems falling to pieces? What mean their panics, strikes, internationales, trades' unions, and co-operative fraternities? Does not Whittier, writing of recurrent cycles, say 'The new is old, the old is new?'
>
> 'J. M. Peebles on Robert Owen', *Human Nature*, June 1874

At the end of the twentieth century, I visited a monastery on the Isle of Wight. Quarr Abbey, close to Victoria's retreat at Osborne, was constructed in 1911 to a modern design by one of its own brothers, Dom Paul Bellot, employing Belgian bricks and three hundred builders. Reached by a tree-lined avenue and surrounded by walled orchards, it lies on the shores of an island remaindered in time; a perpetually sunlit place where at any moment I might see a 1960s car, laden with my own family, en route for our holiday in a converted railway carriage around which the bats flew at night while the incandescent, moth-wing gas mantles glowed inside.

At Quarr, the monks rise in the dark to sing their divine office, and work until it is time to eat their high-ceilinged refectory at bare wooden tables, facing across a space from which the outside world is proscribed. As they serve themselves soup and pale cider from their orchards, an ancient silence seems to reside in the building itself. Their black habits seem to be from some remote past, too, but underneath they wear trainers on their feet.

For our rational age, faith is problematic. We find fervour suspicious; but perhaps you need faith to see. From Plato's Atlantis to Thomas More's *u-topos* and Fourier's phalanxes, Utopia was ever a human ideal: its hope is one of the appeals of religion, for that is where paradise lies. But paradises are lost, too, and by its very perfection, Utopia's history is a virtual one, to be created out of a metaphorical wilderness. Crowded nineteenth-century England, its primal forests felled long ago, was constricted and controlled; conversely, the vast reaches of America allowed for adventure. But it too was being privatised and industrialised, and the attraction of such sects began to pall in inverse proportion to the inexorable pull of capital. The new republic's economic expansion reined in its religious experiments by the simple expedient of the equally expanding price of land. Utopia was priced out of the market, and among those to suffer in the exchange were the Shakers, their decline an ironic result of the progress which they had embraced as inventors of the washing machine and the clothes pin. At their peak in 1840 there were six thousand Shakers in America; by the end of the century that number would be reduced to just one thousand. The United Society of Believers had been superseded by the United States of America, and as the secular replaced the sacred, a new revival was required: one which would withstand the test of an industrial age, yet which could draw on the passion of Mother Ann's Work. And if anyone could save Shakerism from decay, it was Frederick Evans.

Born in Worcester, England, in 1810, Evans, the former Owenite, would become the intellectual face of Shakerism, drawing radical strength from the virtues of his plain-clad sisters and brothers: 'To the mind of the simple, unsophisticated Shaker, it seems marvellously inconsistent ... that more than one half the citizens should be disfranchised because they happen to be females ... while still millions of other fellow-citizens are treated as property, because they chance to possess a darker-coloured skin than their cruel brethren.' That these objections remain is a testament to the Shakers' moral code. From their village of Mount Lebanon, Evans would correspond with Tolstoy on the subject of non-resistance, while his other protests have the ring of modernity, as the elder spoke out against animal cruelty, class education and religious persecution. He also sought to apply Shaker principles to the government itself, suggesting that leadership be confined to 'intellectual celibates', male or female, 'who would be married only to the state'.

In search of new recruits, Evans planned to reimport these ideas to the mother country. England had been alerted to Shakerism by such writers and reformers as Robert Owen, Charles Lane and Harriet Martineau, but it was the new power of spiritualism that truly prepared the way for Evans' mission. Writing to Owen in 1856, Evans reminded his mentor that 'Spiritualism originated among the Shakers of America ... In truth, all the members, in a greater or less degree, were mediums', for whom 'physical manifestations, visions, revelations, prophecies and gifts of various kinds ... were as common as is gold in California'. Indeed, Evans had discovered his own mediumship at the height of Mother Ann's Work, and would invite the medium William Eddy to Mount Lebanon to conduct seances using special cabinets built by the Shakers, in which Eddy was locked while thirty-one spirits manifested themselves in 'ancient costume'. But among those ancestral voices, one would become all-important: 'That noble, wonderful man Thomas Paine laid the foundations of the New Earth, as Ann Lee laid the foundations of the New Heavens.'

Thomas Paine, an ex-corset maker from Norfolk, had come to America in the same year as Ann Lee. As the author of *Common*

Sense and *The Rights of Man*, he had inspired revolution on both sides of the Atlantic. He died in a back room in Greenwich Village, New York in 1809, and ten years later, William Cobbett, exiled from his farm in Botley near Southampton to Long Island, would bring Paine's remains back to Britain as a symbolic act. But now Paine's spirit was claimed for a new revolution. In 1850, three years after its infamous Rappings, Rochester's Reverend Charles Hammond, who styled himself as a medium, claimed to have received an account of Paine's posthumous conversion from sceptic to believer. Three years later, David Richmond, a Shaker convert, member of the Concordium, and witness to the Rappings, came home to Yorkshire, ostensibly as a missionary for the Shakers; but also as a proponent of spiritualism. He established a spiritualist sect in Keighley over which Paine's spirit presided; the advance guard of a movement in which both Robert Owen and Fredrick Evans would claim Paine as a kind of patron saint.

Such esoteric faith was a response to uncertain times. Since 1848, European revolution and the publication of the *Communist Manifesto* had served to destabilise old regimes while offering hope to the oppressed. The British Empire was threatened by mutinies in India and Africa and, later, a possible French invasion, in response to which the Prime Minister, Lord Palmerston, ordered a series of fortresses to be built on the south coast and even on the sea bed of the Solent. Island Britain felt embattled, and new prophets rose to pronounce on this troubled age.

In 1857, John Brown, a soldier-turned-visionary preaching in Nottingham, presaged an apocalyptic conflict in which the Russians would invade Europe, leaving only Britain and America to hold out on the battlefields of Armageddon. He proposed a spiritual defence – among the locations in which his Community of the Great Organisation took root was the Isle of Wight – while he divided the map of England with compasses, each circled area to be entrusted to one of his twelve pseudo-apostles in a campaign directed by the Angel Gabriel through Brown's crystal ball. At the same time, Owen's own predictions were becoming increasingly bizarre: at his last Birthday Congress, held in May 1857, he foretold that by the end of the century, 'the English and Irish channels [would] be crossed on dry land, the seas and oceans . . . navigated on islands instead of ships'. He had already proposed that Jesus Christ was 'an inspired medium from his birth', and that famous figures such as Shelley and Jefferson, whom he had known in life, came back in spirit form to guide him. Now Owen declared that spiritualism was either 'one of the greatest deceptions ever practised on human credulity', or 'the most important event that [had] yet occurred in the history of the human race'.

Fourteen years later, as Evans prepared his own mission, utopia remained a topic of the day. In 1871 no fewer than three English texts proposed visions of utopia or apocalypse, from the social Darwinian science fiction of Lord Lytton's *The Coming Race*, to George Chesney's *The Battle of Dorking*, a John Brown vision of a war to end all wars; and Samuel Butler's *Erewhon*, a Swiftian satire on the impossibility of utopia, the 'nowhere' of the book's anagrammatic title. It was as if that summer had been ordained as a new season of utopian intent. Evans' transatlantic adventure was a mirror image of Ann Lee's American venture a century before: he intended to exorcise the old country of its 'spirits of devils', and as spiritualism had been exported from America, so he was determined that Shakerism should follow in its wake. Indeed, his campaign was made possible by two highly influential spiritualists. Reverend James Martin Peebles was a professor at the Eclectic Medical College, Cincinnati; an anti-vaccinationist and honourary Shaker, were it not for Peebles, Evans 'would have come to an unploughed field unfit to receive the seed'. His other sponsor was one of the most important British practitioners. James Burns had come south from Scotland to work as a gardener, but was inspired by American tracts to found his Progressive Library and Spiritual

Institution in Holborn. A longtime vegetarian and teetotaller, he also began spiritualist Sunday schools to which believers could send their children for corrective education, and in 1865 proposed a People's University at which would be taught 'Cosmology, Spiritualism, Immortality etc.' – a notion which had its echo a century later in the Anti-University of London, founded in Hoxton in 1969 with a syllabus featuring R. D. Laing on anti-psychiatry, Yoko Ono on 'The Connexion', and Francis Huxley on dragons.

Burns was satirised in a contemporary novel, *Maud Blount, Medium*, as Mr Blathersby of the Spiritual Lyceum, 'a kind of Universal Provider for Spiritualists from the cradle to the grave, catching them at the former extremity of life in the hope of making Infant Phenomenons of them, and retaining their hold upon them until the last, on the chance of converting them into Rapping Spirits when *in articulo mortis*. It was a kind of school, clubhouse, and chapel rolled into one, and all comprised in the not very spacious accommodation of a first-floor over a barber's shop, in a back street of the W. C. district.' Here, 'where the spiritualistic force of the metropolis was concentrated', Burns edited *Human Nature*, a veritable compendium of new beliefs, as its first edition announced on 1 April 1867:

James Burns

HUMAN NATURE

A Monthly Record of Zoistic Science and Intelligence, embodying

PHYSIOLOGY, PHRENOLOGY, PSYCHOLOGY, SPIRITUALISM,

PHILOSOPHY, THE LAWS OF HEALTH, AND SOCIOLOGY

An Educational and Family Magazine

Human Nature – which took its cue from the *New Age* journal published by the Ham Common Concordium – was a kind of esoteric *à la carte* from which readers could pick and choose. The 'Psychological Department' had features on 'What is Mesmerism', while the 'Physiology and Hygiene' section included a pertinent essay calling for 'REFORM IN WOMEN'S DRESS', noting that at a recent inquest, 'Dr Lankester remarked that there were 300 women burnt to death annually in England and Wales . . . this being the case, it might well be said that there was room for a reform in women's dress, not only in the mode, but in the material'. Victorian crinolines were indeed a fatal fashion: in January 1875 there were two such immolations in Southampton alone: Elizabeth Cleall, seventy-eight, was discovered 'with the upper portion of her body enveloped in flames . . . dreadfully burnt about the arms and head', telling witnesses 'to take the lamp out of her hand', while Harriet Mills, a fifteen-year-old servant, was found in the wash-house, 'exclaiming repeatedly, "Oh! Oh!" . . . her clothes being all in flames. She was told to lie down so that a rug could be put over her, but was too frightened to do as she was instructed . . .' Other victims of this incendiary epidemic included Oscar Wilde's half-sisters, who perished in 1871 when one's dress caught fire and the other attempted to put out the flames.

A sense of social justice underpinned *Human Nature*. One article on 'Life in the Factories' attacked Victorian philanthropy; noting that a Bradford factory had recently given a 'substantial knife and fork tea' for their workers, its author complained that 'No slave is so helpless as the factory operative. He is doomed to privations, of which the savage negro cannot complain, viz., want of fresh air and sunshine. Till the radical defects of this iniquitous system are altered, we feel that gluttonous suppers and "mutual admiration meetings" are only opiates to induce the victims to submit to further injury, and thus postpone the day of readministration and retribution.' It was no coincidence that Bradford was a stronghold of spiritualism, or that in 1851 the philanthropic Titus Salt was moved to build his industrial utopia, Saltaire, on the outskirts of the town, where my own father was born in 1915.

In publishing such critiques, Burns allied spiritualism to a radical agenda, and addressed other means of social control. In 'The Vaccination Humbug', he examined the harmful effects of compulsory immunisation – medicine as violation – and quoted Richard Gibbs of the Anti-Compulsory Vaccination League: 'I believe we have hundreds of cases here, from being poisoned with vaccination, I deem incurable . . . We strongly advise parents to go to prison, rather than submit to have their helpless offspring inoculated with scrofula, syphilis, and mania . . .' Diet was another issue, and although *Human Nature* did not go as far as Fruitlands, it exhorted the readers to abandon 'alcoholic liquors and hot stimulants, such as tea, coffee &c . . . and substitute the juicy fruits which will at once remove a heavy tax from the pocket of the individual, and promote health, happiness, and long-life'.

In this era of mass production, questions of consumption and abstinence defined the new age. Burns published a report on *The Cases of the Welsh Fasting Girl & Her Father. On the Possibility of* LONG CONTINUED ABSTINENCE FROM FOOD, a bizarre account of Sarah Jacobs, the daughter of a Carmarthenshire farmer, who had gone without food for two years. Burns had visited the girl at her parents' farm, where he found her lying in a bed covered with books and pamphlets. 'In length she measures about 4 feet 8 inches. She has not the power of moving her body [and] has fits several times a day,' he noted. In 1869 the case was investigated by a committee which appointed four nurses from Guy's Hospital, under whose scrutiny the girl died. 'Her death was a triumph for science, which took no account of the influence of these four death-watchers upon a frail hysterical girl living on the very precipes of this life, whom a puff of air or of feeling threw into convulsions.' Her parents were found guilty of manslaughter and sentenced to long terms of imprisonment; the judge decided that their daughter must have been fed in the previous two years, 'and that when she was watched she of course died'. It seemed a drastic manner in which to prove the fact. Citing instances of living toads found in rocks, Burns proposed a number of reasons as to how Sarah had been able to survive, including the possibility of absorbing nutrition through the skin and from organic particles in the air.

Human Nature's -isms would not be out of place in a modern Sunday supplement. Subscribers could turn to fiction by Eliza W. Farnham (*The Ideal Attained*), pick up hints on the conservation of fuel, and read essays on 'Walt Whitman; or, the Religion of Art' and extracts from Thomas Lake Harris's poetry, 'Music from the Spirit Shore'. They might wonder WHY WE SHOULD NOT BE POISONED BECAUSE WE ARE SICK, and under the heading PSYCHOLOGICAL PHENOMENA, discover titbits on 'Mysterious Photographs on Window Panes' in Milan, Ohio, or an account of a nine-year-old negro girl from Kentucky able to memorise entire pages from books. But *Human Nature*'s most important function was to assemble news of spiritualist progress in places as far apart as Liverpool, Paris and America, from where J. H. Powell reported on Vineland, a 'modern miracle of some 10,000 human beings, who are solving the question of colonisation with spirit. Six years ago, it was a houseless tract of 50 square miles, mostly covered with timber; now, a considerable part of it is a blooming township. Here are congregated men and women of intellect', among them Robert Dale Owen, himself a committed spiritualist. Meanwhile, the English medium J. J. Morse attended a psychic festival of 15,000 spiritualists at Lake Pleasant, complete with displays of animals, 'alive and stuffed', and a tent for 'mesmeric entertainments'.

But if there was a particular 'science' to which *Human Nature* was drawn, it was spirit photography. The capture of psychic manifestations in photographic emulsion was an exciting development; and in the excitement, it seems, rational observers suspended their critical faculties. *Human Nature* incorporated actual examples – all the more unreal for being stuck onto stiff, pale cream pages and outlined in thin red frames like photographs in a Victorian album. Yet their glossy physical presence still speaks of implicit faith: someone fixed them there; someone believed in them.

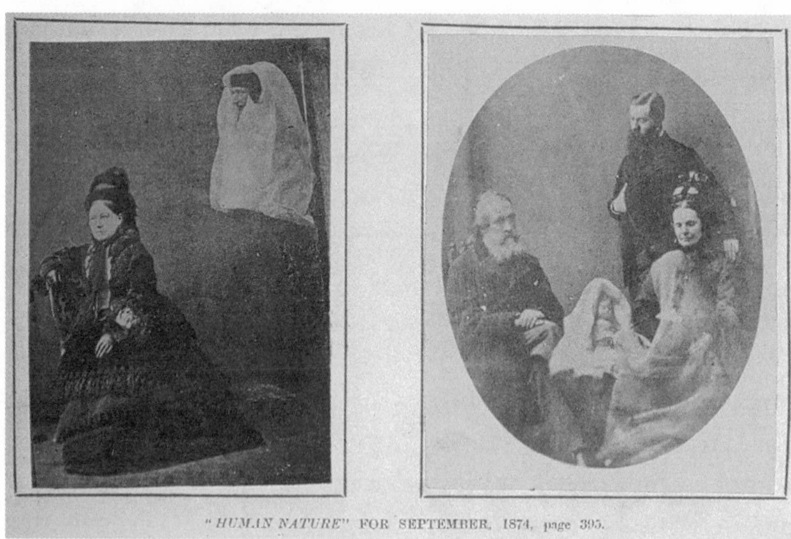
"HUMAN NATURE" FOR SEPTEMBER, 1874, page 395.

Particularly favoured was the work of Mr Hudson, of 2 Kensington Park Road, London, the first of the English spirit photographers. One of a pair of his pictures in the September 1874 edition displayed 'the baby sister of Dr Speer . . . and the shadowy form in the right front is the mother of the infant . . .' The author of the accompanying article, 'MA (Oxon)', was William Stainton Moses, an Oxford graduate, Anglican minister and himself an accomplished medium. 'I have written before how this child-spirit has persistently manifested at our circle almost from its formation . . . She passed from this sphere of life more than fifty years ago at Tours, being then only seven months old. Her joyous little message, "*Je suis heureuse, très heureuse*", was the first indication we had of her presence . . .' Yet to our eyes this cloth-swaddled figure is quite obviously a china doll and looks more like baby Jesus in a school Nativity than the shade of a dead infant.

Photography was still a young and plastic art, and to those untutored in its sly deceptions, the camera could not lie. Spirit photographs seemed to demonstrate the survival of the soul, and a happy survival at that. It was as if the camera were able to peer into another dimension. The immortalising power of photography had been taken one step further, and in such pictures, *Human Nature* revealed the extent of the desire to believe, a thirst for hard proof satisfied by cotton-wool fantasies. Encoded with an occult unconsciousness, these images prefigured the surrealist constructions of the next century, the uncanny imagined in silver nitrate. Yet their moral instability – their essential *untruthfulness* – turns such putative glimpses of eternity into mere psychic pornography; glossy, titillating images carefully concealed within the pages of the periodical. One print by W. H. Mumler of Boston, a jewellery engraver and pioneer of American spirit photography, shows Mrs Abraham Lincoln (whose husband was a believer, as was Wild Bill Hickok) with the assassinated president looking over her: '. . . The evidence for the genuineness of Mr Mumler's photographs, and for the integrity of Mr Mumler himself, is as strong as can well be conceived.' But in 1871 Mrs Lincoln was declared insane and Mr Mumler was later prosecuted for witchcraft in New York.

In its acceptance of such pictures, *Human Nature* was betrayed by its own innocence. Opening the pages of the journal now, I look at these images with a childish sense of revelation and disappointment: in an ironic reversal of their intended function, they resonate with charlatanism and fakery, undermining my own will to believe, as much as if I had been shown videotape of Christ's crucifixion and seen Kensington gore rather than blood oozing from His wounds. This was faith as theatre, 'by way of a singular intermediary . . . by way of Death', a sensational sequence of manipulated images: from nineteenth-century *tableaux vivants* to Eadweard Muybridge's calibrated human graphs and Julia Margaret Cameron's angelic children, bedecked with wings and suspended in amniotic fluid, innocent emblems of infant mortality at the beginning of life. With the aid of muslin, montage and double exposure, the spirit photographers created equally convincing, equally fantastical visions of life after death. The final irony is that spiritualism invested its faith in such evidence, for the passing of time would ensure that these images undermined the movement more comprehensively than any amount of improbable table-tapping or levitating chairs.

The powerfully eclectic editorial stance of *Human Nature* was to provide a natural platform, and excellent publicity, for Frederick Evans, while James Burns was keen to promote Shakerism for his own ends. This earthly alliance suited their spiritual ambitions – a vivid example of the cross-pollination of utopian belief between England and America. Evans and Burns were as much prophets of their age as their more colourful antecedents – and they had the added benefit of new media. Cheap publishing, burgeoning literacy and photographic reproduction allowed spiritualism to be widely disseminated via the self-promoting identities of its practitioners, feeding on a trend which was even more evident: the American genius for self-invention, and an attendant sense of glamour. Thus the meeting of Evans – the intellectual embodiment of American Shakerism – and Burns – the motivating force of British Spiritualism – was an enormously potent encounter. Yet behind these men lay two female spirits; and just as the progenitor of their meeting was Ann Lee, so Mary Ann Girling would be its progeny.

That summer of 1871, as Mary Ann was making preparations for her mission to London, Evans and Peebles left New York on the new White Star liner, S.S. *Atlantic*. 'The whole ship is under the influence of Shakerism to some extent,' Evans told his fellow elders. Turning the voyage into an extension of his mission, he used an onboard accident – when a cannon exploded during the Independence Day celebrations and blew off a seaman's arms – as an endorsement of Shaker pacifism, and persuaded the captain to have the fireworks thrown overboard: 'Thus we preached non-resistance and non-powder-explosions, at the same time, *on the 4th of July*.' A week later, Evans arrived in London and set up his office at the Progressive Library and Spiritual Institution at 15 Southampton Row. In the 'dark little shop', Evans was 'crowded with letters, papers, books, visitors, inquiries, and deputations of various kinds', while Burns took the opportunity to make a phrenological examination of his guest, as 'we have seen only one Shaker'. It was as if the sect were an exotic tribe from some remote corner of the Empire: Burns advertised copies of Evans' photograph and 'stereoscopic views of groups of Shakers and their houses and gardens, all of which afford valuable data to the student of human nature'.

Elder Frederick Evans

Evans' arrival also stirred up considerable interest among men such as the Honourable Auberon Herbert, Liberal Member of Parliament for Nottingham, with whom Evans and Peebles breakfasted at 11 o'clock (an hour which shocked Evans, who broke his fast around dawn). Their interview was 'most interesting and profitable', wrote Peebles. 'Elder Frederick expounded to him the principles of Shakerism. He was deeply interested – pricked in the heart; and, upon some points at least, convicted.' That afternoon, Herbert took both men into the House of Commons, where Evans 'preached the Gospel of Progress and Reform'. 'Many in this English speaking nation are almost ready for the harvest,' declared Peebles. 'They feel that something must be done . . . many are inquiring the way to Zion, and asking, What shall I do to be saved . . . England is ripening up rapidly for the forming of Shaker Societies.' And Evans was determined to reap the benefit. Invited by Herbert to 'splendid rooms' to address a 'fashionable gathering' ('some of the women not dressed as they ought to be, for *modest women*'), he was subjected to cross examination by lawyers, doctors and secretaries for nearly three hours.

But this mission was not to be limited to the professional classes. Evans' lectures at Cleveland Hall proved so popular that they soon required a larger venue, as *The Times* announced on 3 August:

> *An Opportunity*
>
> Elder Frederick W. Evans, of Mount Lebanon, State of New York, USA, will discourse on the principles of his order next Sunday, at the St George's Hall, Langham Place, Regent St. Mr Hepworth Dixon, author of *New America*, will take the chair, supported by Mr Auberon Herbert, MP, and other Members of Parliament.

William Hepworth Dixon had recently published his first-hand account of American sects; as a guest of Evans and Eldress

Antoinette Dolittle at Mount Lebanon, he had been struck by the 'singular beauty and perfect success' of the Shaker way of life, and his book was evidently *The Times'* source of information. 'The order of Shakers has been in existence for nearly 100 years . . . They are celibates, hold property in common like Primitive Christians, are free-thinking Spiritualists, and firm believers in present Divine inspiration. They neither manufacture nor use intoxicating drink, and they entertain peace principles. They have solved those vexed problems, war, intemperance, poverty, the social evil [prostitution], and crime, with all its concommittants of police-courts, gaols, and such like.'

SHAKER LADY.

The paper also reported positively on Evans' lecture itself:

> The proceedings were commenced with a hymn, 'The Day is Breaking', and a short prayer, after which Mr Hepworth Dixon introduced 'Elder Frederick' to the meeting with a few words expressive of the pleasure which he had felt some years ago in visiting Mount Ephraim [sic], and seeing with his own eyes the well-ordered community of the Shakers, and the peace, contentment, plenty, and morality which reigned among them, where they had 'made the desert smile'.

Such a life must have seemed attractive to many readers caught up in their quotidian duties. Cheered regularly throughout his speech, Evans warned 'that both England as a country and London as a great city had need to reform their social code and habits of life', and 'that other empires and cities as large and as powerful . . . had perished by the sword . . .' Privately, he discerned a 'desperate, drugged determination . . . to do or die' in that 'great Babel of a city of 3½ millions of human bodies, supposed to have souls in them', and where he felt like a 'pilgrim and a stranger'. 'The poor breed like rabbits; and, when the boys are old enough, the Government *takes* them as soldiers. But labor is so cheap, they are willing to be shot at, if they can get food to eat . . . This city, and all great cities, rest upon volcanoes liable to eruption at [a] time when least to be looked for or expected.' Such observations were redolent of the *Communist Manifesto*. 'This Government is wise, with all its wickedness. It watches sharply the signs of popular uprising, and yields to the demands of the great *middle class*, so as to propitiate them . . .' While he noted that five thousand a day were dying in the siege of Paris, Evans claimed that 'Communism is the greatest good that thousands can see in the future; and the fact that the Shakers make it a practical thing, a success, is a constant source of congratulation, and of hope . . . I am quite sure that our Gospel will be preached and received in England before long.' He even envisioned his own North Family at Mount Lebanon coming to London to save its citizens, 'I am quite sure souls would gather to them as fast as they could be taken care of.'

Shakerism had caught a public imagination already alert to utopian notions. *Human Nature* reported that 'from one end of the country to the other the principles of Shakerism were being eagerly discussed'. Evans addressed four thousand at two open-air meetings in Bradford, 'convened by the Spiritualists and largely attended by them'; other meetings followed in Bishop Auckland, Birmingham, and Manchester, the birthplace of Ann Lee, erstwhile home to Friedrich Engels, and host to such events as a 'Spiritualists' Vegetarian Banquet'. Yet Evans was warned by a friend that 'I should do better not to be identified with Spiritualists too much . . . the Shakers are in good order and famous with the public; while the Spiritualists are in unease [sic] condition than ever before'. 'They are holding dark circles,' Evans noted. 'Peebles was at a house this afternoon and the spirits threw things about, and did damage – He took no part. We ignore them.' Evans worried that spiritualists such as Emma Hardinge – one of the most famous American mediums working in England, herself sponsored by Burns, and who had sent Evans tickets for her appearance at the Albert Hall – were doing 'harm rather than good'. And yet the link was undeniable. 'What have Spiritualists to do with Shakerism?' Burns asked the readers of *Human Nature*, and answered his own question, declaring that the Shakers were 'an illustration of the ultimate influence of Spiritualism in its highest form upon the mind of man . . .'

The *Shaker and Shakeress* – edited by Evans – also acknowledged these claims. With reports on 'women's rights (including the right to live a virgin life)'; sleeping on the right side (so that the stomach was in the correct position for digestion); and a debate on the notion, 'Will Shakerism depopulate the world?' the periodical bore comparison with *Human Nature*. It also featured miscellanea from other newspapers, such as one article on Mother Shipton, who 'would have taken high rank as a medium in our day' and whose last couplet was especially ominous: 'The world to an end shall come/In eighteen hundred and eighty-one'. But *The Shaker* too was concerned with spiritualism as an instrument of its aim 'to inaugurate Shaker Communism on British soil . . .' Recruiting advertisements appeared in Shaker tracts published by Burns: 'Single persons, who are free, may come at their own option, bearing in mind the important fact that SHAKERISM is "RELIGIOUS COMMUNISM".' Yet for all Evans' sterling efforts and Burns' positive public relations, few answered the call. When he sailed home from Liverpool on 24 August, the elder took with him just four recruits – and of that 'party of proselytes', two would return to England to join the Girlingites. It was ironic that, while the Shakers had tried to stir up their land of origin through the ministry of an intellectual, adoptive American, it was an uneducated English woman who would capitalise on the new public awareness of Shakerism. For Evans, the summer of 1871 had proved an anti-climax; for Mary Ann, it marked the beginning of her most successful phase.

From the start, the rather disparate party which accompanied Evans home across the Atlantic were not entirely convinced of what they were doing. James Haase was a twenty-six-year-old businessman whose wife Martha had died earlier that year at the age of thirty-one – perhaps a factor in his willingness to leave England. In his diary, Evans noted Haase's address – 12 Cross Street, Islington – and that he was 'a young man who is the first that I have opened the testimony unto . . . James has just lost his wife'. It is possible that the grieving Haase was a visitor to Burns' shop and a subscriber to spiritualism; certainly the bachelor Evans found him an attractive young man: 'it is as easy to talk with him, as to breathe the air; I have hope that he will "be obedient to the Heavenly Mission".' Evans told Eldress Antoinette that 'if things suit him' at Mount Lebanon, Haase would return to England to settle up his business: 'His report . . . will be looked for with an amount of interest you can hardly realise.'

Evans had hoped for good, solid, practical recruits, with their own financial backing. 'There is a family by the name of Stephens who are going to send a boy, sixteen, and a girl, 11. They are real business people, and engaged in co-operation. That is all I know of, except a young man about 17, who wants to come, but has not the means.' Robert Stephens, father of eleven-year-old Annie Stephens and her sixteen-year-old stepbrother Edwin Clarke, was a socialist weaver from Manchester who had run a co-operative store in London 'for political reasons'; while their parents sorted out the sale of their business, it was agreed that Annie and Edwin would go on ahead. Reverend Alsop and his two daughters, ten and fourteen, said they would come too, and Evans also worked on a Mr Atkins, 'a great scientific man'; although a 'bore', Evans thought he might 'get something useful out of him'. Another application – 'if I wd pay their passage' – came from a family in Edinburgh. But in the event, the party was complemented by its oldest, wealthiest and most eccentric member. Fifty-three-year-old Julia Wood, born at Codsall, Staffordshire, was the third of eight children whose father had made his money from distilleries – a somewhat uneasy source which, given the temperance of the new age, may have made for family disagreements. As a young girl, Julia had exhibited a fervent spirituality, to the extent that her own family had had her confined to the Staffordshire Asylum on grounds of religious mania. Like Haase, she lived in Islington – in one of the grander Georgian terraces of Duncan Street – but was a less certain recruit: next to her address, Evans noted merely 'thinks of going'.

Thus this ill-matched group of would-be Shakers arrived at Mount Lebanon, where they were greeted warmly as the vanguard of a new contingent: there was even a hymn written for them, 'A Welcome For the Company from England'. One hundred and fifty miles up the Hudson River from New York and just across the state border from Massachusetts, Mount Lebanon's setting seemed paradisiacal. 'Hills, mountains, and valleys, trees, gardens, farmhouses and farms spread around and above you in ever-varying beauty,' wrote Henry Vincent, another Englishman who accepted an invitation from Evans, and who declared, 'The dream of Utopia is here realized . . . they work hard; they enjoy the fruits of their industry; they live simply and frugally. For ten years they have ceased to eat swine, or drink alcoholic drinks . . . Within the past forty years, the Owenite experiments in England and America have failed; but *Shakerism is a living and triumphant fact.*'

Such transcendentalism eluded David Brown, another young man drawn to America by Evans' mission. A northerner of communist inclinations, Brown had heard the elder lecture at the Temperance Hall in Manchester. He listened patiently, but thought Evans took liberties with the facts: 'He stated that while every other community in America had been a failure, the Shakers alone had been a success. But this was a wrong statement. There are the German Rappites in Pennsylvania who have acquired immense wealth. There are also the Free Lovers at Oneida Creek, and others who have been very prosperous, and are established on a better basis in many respects than the Shakers. If Elder F. W. Evans had stated that there had been a falling off among the Shakers, and that he had come over to England to replenish their number, he would have come nearer the truth, but he knew better than that.'

At Mount Lebanon, Brown found his hopes fractured by reality, just as later visitors to communist states would be disabused of their utopian expectations. Brown thought the sect overdisciplined and its religious principles claustrophobic; he was also suspicious of Evans' eagerness for publicity. 'Whenever any person visits Mount Lebanon who is of high standing in literature, the elders are most anxious for such to write on Shakerism . . . Elder F. W. Evans wanted me to write to Mr Burns, editor of the *Medium and Daybreak*, England, but I refused, saying that I wished to give it a fair trial, and then I would write.' Brown's account, published in *Human Nature* in 1876, voiced the opinion that the Shakers must wholeheartedly embrace spiritualism or perish, and was hardly likely to gather converts with its statement, 'Shakerism is most unquestionably slavery modified'. It was a conclusion with which Burns would come to agree.

David Brown's unhappy experience may have reflected that of Julia Wood and James Haase. Of the four English visitors to Mount Lebanon, only one – Annie Stephens – found Shakerism compelling enough to become a permanent member. The others all returned to England – James Haase and Julia Wood as soon as 23 September, barely a month later. Still considering his position, Haase wrote to Evans from Islington on 8 November, complaining that his 'trials have been very severe and persecutions great from family relations. But I feel the more opposition I meet with, the firmer and more steadfast I become . . .' James was evidently a passionate young man: 'Life to me is earnest, life to me is real. I know that I am going to live for ever and am conscious that every thought and every action is moulding my character for eternity . . . I will follow the truth – at any cost.'

That pursuit for immortality would lead him to Mary Ann. Haase told Evans that 'the interest manifested by the English Spiritualists to know what my experiences have been has been very interesting. The brief account I gave to the *Medium* brought forth many enquiries from several parts of the Country which I responded to. A brother from Manchester intends visiting me at Christmas and intends returning with me in the Spring.' But Haase also noted that his neighbour, Miss Wood, 'has called upon me once or twice since her return and I have visited her as often. She has grown very dissatisfied having been told by the "*spirits*" that she is not to go. She considers herself a lady and much more advanced than her Shaker Sisters – more refined – which I very much doubt. I felt inclined to say to her on one or two occasions whilst making frivolous objections "get thee behind me Satan'. She dwells considerably on her fortune, giving up her fortune and being placed at the wash tub.' Evans had good reason to doubt Julia's seriousness, but as she paid her own fare to America (the others had been subsidised by the Shakers), he had not dissuaded her, perhaps seeing in her a potential source of funds for future missions. Indeed, Evans would return to England twelve years later, but by that time the country had heard of a new and different kind of Shaker altogether.

PART TWO

O Clouds Unfold!

The great majority of interpretations of Apocalypse assume that the End is pretty near. Consequently the historical allegory is always having to be revised; time discredits it. And this is important. Apocalypse can be disconfirmed without being discredited. This is part of its extraordinary resilience.

Frank Kermode, *The Sense of an Ending*

FOUR

The Walworth Jumpers

> Blessed are you when men revile you and persecute you and utter all kinds of evil against you falsely on my account. Rejoice and be glad, for your reward is great in heaven, for so men persecuted the prophets who were before you.
>
> Matthew 4:11

The train from Ipswich, a steam-spewing monster, slouched into the maw of Liverpool Street where the brick arches of the terminus, newly-built over the site of the original Bethlehem Hospital, seemed to suck the visitor into the nerve-jangling immensity of the city, exciting the spirit as much as the third-class carriages had shaken the flesh. Detraining into the hot, fetid hubbub of the subterranean concourse, Mary Ann dusted down the smuts from her gown and prepared to resume her mission, not in the heart of some dark continent, but in the backstreets of London, where factory chimneys rivalled church spires for the skyline above and the fate of the souls in the lowly terraces below.

The world had changed dramatically since the decade of Mary Ann's birth, not least in the way one could move around it. It was one of the ironies of the modern world that many of those responsible for building the new railways were themselves Quakers; forbidden from swearing oaths which would admit them to professional positions, they excelled at other trades. It was a Quaker, George Bradshaw, who published his *Railway Time Table* in 1839, not for profit, but to assist his fellow man. The expanding network had standardised time itself, unifying the country and metering modern history, yet Bradshaw's publication still bore Quaker designations – 'First Month' instead of January, and so on – while one visitor to the Friends' meeting house at King's Cross found their tracts shelved on the walls like 'the time tables . . . in the stations of the Metropolitan Railway'. So too would Mary Ann's mission be conducted by railway – under the tracks themselves.

The myth of Mary Ann's arrival in London, like the other stories that surround her, remains almost wilfully obscure. The Bible Christians said to have invited her were originally Primitive Methodists from East Cornwall, and therefore rural imports like the Girlingites. They too had female ministers, such as Mary Toms, a faith-healer who left Tintagel for the Isle of Wight in the 1820s and was seen 'standing on a borrowed chair one Sunday morning at East Cowes, lashed by the wind and rain'. She also claimed to have been followed down a dark lane by a 'dimly visible creature . . . thought by some to have been a heavenly visitant sent to protect her, but by herself to have been a diabolical creature sent to scare her'. But 'Bible Christian' was a term applied to a number of sects (not least the Girlingites themselves), and on closer inspection it seems more likely that Mary Ann's invitation came from the Peculiar People, a sect founded by a fellow Suffolk preacher and erstwhile Wesleyan, William Bridges.

Born in Woodbridge in 1802, Bridges had left Suffolk soon after his marriage in 1824, but his family still lived there and had probably come into contact with Girlingism, which seemed to share common ground with the Peculiar People. The 'Plumstead Peculiars', as they were later known, took their name from God's commandment to Moses to lead His 'peculiar people'. They believed in faith-healing, the anointing of oil and the power of prayer, and they opposed vaccination; in 1872 George Harry of Plumstead would be sent to Newgate Prison 'for refusing to provide medical assistance or remedies of any kind' for his daughter

Cecilia who was dying of smallpox, while his wife was summonsed by a coroner's court for the manslaughter of their second child who had also died. In the 1830s, Bridges had set up a chapel in Gravel Lane, Kennington, but one of his followers, a cobbler named John Sirgood, extended the Peculiar Gospel to rural Sussex, assembling a congregation of two hundred in the village of Loxwood – only to attract the same antipathy which the Girlingites had suffered in Suffolk. Sirgood complained that his faithful were 'derided, reproached, insulted . . . thrown down into the mud . . . and women and children filled with terror'. One particularly terrifying night, assailants armed with bludgeons, their faces painted and 'disguised in the most grotesque manner . . . beat about the house to the breaking up of the windows and the crockery, threatening the life of the Preacher'. And just as Mary Ann had left Suffolk, so by 1860, Sirgood had returned to south London.

Despite their obscure history, it is clear that these part rural, part city evangelists paved the way for Mary Ann. Through their south London mission she would gain access to a new following, and in the process she would divide Bridges' Southwark citadel. At first the Peculiar People allowed Mary Ann to preach in their chapel on Sunday evenings, where she maintained she was only the 'Messenger' of the Second Coming. But when she began to claim her own divinity, it proved too much for the Peculiars. Like the Methodists, they asked Mary Ann to 'withdraw from their communion', which she did, taking many of their followers with her. As in Suffolk, she began preaching in private houses, where 'spiritual manifestations' took place. Emboldened by their move to the imperial capital as the Shakers had been by their American migration, the Girlingites' fainting fits were now fully-fledged ecstasies; quivering, quaking rites. And like the Camisards before them, news of these strange phenomena attracted crowds wanting to see this woman from Suffolk, who was publicly declaring that she would not die.

It was an exhortative season for the esoteric gospel. That

summer, as Elder Evans hired ever larger halls to enable his words to be heard, Mary Ann acquired a new place of worship – an altogether more unconventional venue for one of the most extraordinary eruptions of religious zeal London had ever seen. In the sinful city which Cobbett had called the Great Wen, she would meet with opposition all the more violent for its metropolitan cynicism. Yet hadn't Christ instructed his apostles to leave their fishing nets and families and follow in His footsteps? Her rural sectaries shamed the city-dwellers with their faith. Entire clans had given up their worldly goods and birthrights to be born again; and while their peers made similar migrations in pursuit of employment and wages, the Girlingites rejected work for anyone but God, and saw money as personally worthless. They placed their faith in Mary Ann. And just as her predecessor Joanna Southcott had drawn supporters to her House of God in the Elephant and Castle, so Mary Ann's mission would operate from a railway arch off the Walworth Road.

The Southcottians had proved to be pervasive in south London, where their loud orisons still brought irate neighbours out into the street. Other preachers inspired the people of Southwark, too: the evangelist Charles Spurgeon drew thousands to his Metropolitan Tabernacle at the Elephant and Castle, a theatrical auditorium with a grandiose façade of Corinthian pillars still visible from today's pink-painted roundabout. With 'triumphant' acoustics and curving stairs ending in a deep pool where believers were baptised, the chapel was host to visitors such as John Ruskin, a resident of nearby Denmark Hall who contributed £100 to the Tabernacle fund, and whose taste for Spurgeon's sermons would emerge in his own apocalyptic essays, *Unto this Last*.

In fact, the entire city seemed sensitised to new beliefs. In the teeming streets of Southwark and Bermondsey, in meeting houses in King's Cross, in Hoxton's dark squares and along Belgravia's rich terraces, all manner of practitioners gathered believers to their causes. The salons of the wealthy might host after-dinner entertainment by a mesmerist or medium, while hastily-built chapels or squatted semi-industrial spaces became cells for lower-class dissent. The sheer range of creeds available to mid-Victorian Londoners was a reflection of the extent of the imperial project; in a commodified world, the choice of faiths mirrored an age of mass production. From its centre to its suburbs, the world's biggest city encompassed Peculiar People and phrenologists, Quakers and Swedenborgians, homeopaths and hypnotists. For this cosmopolitan parish, the catchment area was the Empire itself, an ever-shifting congregation swelled by the Thames' wide reach and supplied by the speedy railway. Here a home could be found for any belief, no matter how odd. And here was a ready-made market for Mary Ann's offer of immortality.

In that summer of 1871, a third and equally eccentric figure embarked on his own metropolitan mission. The Reverend Charles Maurice Davies was compiling a series of reports for the *Daily Telegraph* – 'strictly descriptive . . . expressing no opinion pro or con' – on the remarkable spectrum of alternative beliefs, later to be collected in a volume entitled *Unorthodox London, Or, Phases of Religious Life in the Metropolis*. As a Fellow of Durham University, this sinecured cleric struck an authorial stance between a sceptic relaying the latest craze for the amusement of his *Telegraph* readers, and an intellectual with an interest in the strange sects sprouting up almost weekly. Like one of M. R. James's learned professors, Davies' religious-academic background gave a sense of authority to his narrative as he explored the city's penumbral streets, reporting from the shadows thrown by the imperial glare. His 'unorthodox London' was a spiritual precursor of the colour-coded chart to be created by the radical statistician Charles Booth (on which my own street in Hoxton is coloured black and described as 'the leading criminal quarter of London and indeed of all England'). As Booth presented his socio-economic topography of the city, so Davies surveyed its dark heart of faith: 'On the plane of working from the circumference to the centre, I set off on a recent Sunday morning, resolved to make my first study at the widest possible radius, the very *Ultima Thule* of religious London.'

Turning the pages of his book in the British Library, with their indented type punctuated by the odd squashed fly preserved as if in amber, the clergyman's gothic peregrinations come to life. He travelled by the newly-installed Underground, tunnelling into esoteric arenas like some clerical mole: from the Theists of the South Place Chapel 'close to the Moorgate Street Station of the Metropolitan Railway', to 'Colonel Wentworth Higginson on Buddha' (author of *Army Life in a Black Regiment*, Higginson had commanded one of the Black Camisard regiments in the American Civil War), taking in the Tabernacle Ranters of Newington, with their 'loud and long-continued' hallelujahs, along the way. It was as if these nodes of unconvention were intimately connected by rail – the neural network by which their dissension spread – and on these public transport expeditions into urban anthropology, Davies' own character and opinion emerged slyly, as though in an aside to a passenger.

Ordained in 1852, Davies had served the Church in Somerset and London, but had since concentrated on writing as a career, contributing to the *Western Morning News* and the National Press Agency, as well as producing religious novels such as *Philip Paternoster: A Tractarian Love Story*. His true interest lay in spiritualism, however, as his skittish *Maud Blount, Medium. A Story of Modern Spiritualism* indicates. The book follows the adventures of 'a splendid specimen of a spoiled child' who, as 'a splendid specimen of womanhood, too', discovers her psychic talents. 'The very latest novelty had been Spiritualism . . . Young ladies called it "charmingly dreadful". Scientific men scoffed at it, and clergymen said it was either conjuring or the devil', although one character – the Reverend Ball – proposes 'these modern miracles . . . to be evidential just as those we find in Scripture'. It was the same justification employed by Christian spiritualists, who equated the exorcism of demons with the work of the seance table.

'Spiritualism is emphatically a question of the hour, and has been fairly described by one of its adherents to be "either a gigantic delusion or the most important subject that can possibly be broached",' Davies declared. And like so many, he had a personal sense of its importance. In 1865 his young son died of scarlet fever, and Davies found that spiritualism gave 'hope at a time when we are mostly hopeless'. His wife developed a facility for automatic writing, receiving messages from the guardian spirit who now cared for their little boy. Davies would spend fifteen years seeking 'to prove unbroken continuity between the life in this world and the life beyond', a quest in which he was guided by influential spiritualists.

Despite this hidden agenda, the clergyman's commentary was often acidulous. He found the Irvingites of Bloomsbury singular for their spirit voices and three-hour rituals, for which they adopted every colour of robe – 'black tippets ... puce tippets ... short surplices ... coloured stoles', while in the Swedenborgians of King's Cross he detected other traces of spiritualism. The eighteenth-century Swedish scientist and mystic Emanuel Swedenborg had experienced 'a sort of middle state between sleeping and waking'; a kind of permanent Near Death Experience, not the stuff of dreams, but of a spiritual 'future life'. He believed that man and angel were consubstantial, and 'decoded' Scripture in his book, *The Apocalypse Explained.* An influence on writers and artists from Blake to Browning and Emerson, his presence still lingers in the Swedenborg Society, its panelled rooms presided over by his marble bust – just a street away from the site of Burns' institution, where Davies was drawn in search of yet stranger beliefs.

Having discovered the availability of 'shilling seances' at Burns' premises, Davies decided to attend this psychic pot-luck, where the visitor could not summon spirits at will, but had to take them as they came. As a 'slim, artistic-looking' young man in his early twenties played the piano, the gas was turned down and the seance began.

'Had I been altogether unused to the manners and customs of trance mediums, I should have thought that the poor young man was taken suddenly ill, for he turned up his eyes and wriggled about in his chair . . . in the most alarming manner.' One 'simpering voice' belonged to 'Maria Crook, late of the Crown and Can, Clerkenwell, and now of Highgate Cemetery'; another to a navvy who had worked on the south London drains; and when a third declared, 'I never break my word, sir; Thomas Paine never did whilst on earth', Davies deduced 'that we had been listening to the voice of the author of the "Age of Reason," *redivivus*'. 'It does certainly seem remarkable that such things should be going on amid the very roar of Holborn in this nineteenth century,' Davies concluded; and in that pioneering vein, he set off on another foray, this time to Hackney to visit a medium who claimed to be able to produce 'spirit-faces': 'a pretty, Jewish-like little girl' of sixteen 'managed' by her father at their home in the eastern suburb.

It was an authentically bizarre scene. 'Little Miss Blank' sat inside a 'sort of corner cupboard . . . like a pot of jam or a pound of candles' with a rope on her lap, while the rest of the party sat round, 'grown-up children waiting for the magic lantern'. As the gathering – which included the editor of a spiritualist journal, a country doctor and an elderly gentleman from Manchester – sang spiritualist hymns, the cupboard doors opened to reveal 'pretty Miss Blank tied round the neck, arms, and legs to the chair, in a very uncomfortable and apparently secure manner'. The knots were sealed and the cupboard shut again, leaving an opening at the top, like that in a seaside Punch and Judy show.

> After some delay a face rose gently to the aperture rather far back, but presently came well to the front. It was slightly pale, and the head was swathed in white drapery. The eyes were

> fixed, and altogether it looked ghostly. It remained for some time, disappeared and re-appeared; and the lamp was turned full upon it, but the eyes never lost their fixed stare, and showed no symptom of winking. After several minutes it went altogether.

The cupboard was then opened and its inmate revealed still tightly bound, the seals unbroken. The exhausted girl was taken into the garden for a walk to revive her, and repeated the process three times that evening, summoning a 'Parsee doctor' with a turban and a 'decidedly Eastern expression of countenance and dark complexion', and another face, 'still surmounted by white drapery, but a black band was over the forehead, like a nun's hood. The teeth were projecting, and the expression of the face sad. They fancied it was a spirit that was pained at not being recognized.' The spirit guide, Katie, invited Davies to touch her face and hand after asking him, 'Do you squeeze?' Assuring her he 'did not do anything so improper', Davies was permitted his 'manipulations'.

The image of this bound and closeted girl recalls Julia Margaret Cameron's 'Despair', for which she shut her adoptive daughter Cyllene in a cupboard in order to reproduce an authentic expression of terror when she was let out. There was something unsettling about this passive girl and her audience of men: a scene of contained violence and sexuality, pitched somewhere between circus sideshow and a vision of the unknown. Davies, 'sufficiently struck' to attend another seance at that address, wondered whether he had really been 'in direct contact with supernatural beings or simply taken in by one of the most satisfactory "physical mediums" it was ever my good fortune to meet'.

His suspicions were well founded. The young girl was Florence Cook, whose spirit guide, Katie King, was said to be the daughter of the seventeenth-century pirate Henry Morgan. Nine years later, in the rooms of the British National Association of Spiritualists, Sir George Sitwell, father of the famous literary trio, would squeeze

Katie's hand, and in the process prove that the 'vivacious and apparently youthful ghost' was 'a common cheat'. Even then, many refused to believe that Katie was composed of anything other than ectoplasm.

Yet astounding as Florence Cook's manifestations were, Davies' annals of the Victorian uncanny were about to produce even more extraordinary scenes as he went south of the river and into another enclosed space. This time it was to the very belly of the city's industrial catacombs, where the fraudulent met the faithful and where those who could not afford even 'shilling seances' might pursue the quest for life after death; a place where believers might yet be reborn, never to die again.

'Sect-hunting, like misery, makes a man acquainted with strange companions, and familiarises him with strange experiences,' wrote Davies, 'but of all the religious phenomena with which I had yet been brought into contact, the latest and certainly the very strangest, have been those connected with the "Jumpers" at Walworth – the Bible Christians, or Children of God . . .' Having been tipped off about these odd goings-on, Davies proceeded 'to a certain railway arch in Sutherland Street, Walworth Road, beneath which . . . I had been given to understand that the Bible Christians gathered thrice a week to listen to the preaching of an inspired woman from Suffolk'.

Walworth Road was then, as it is now, a bustling thoroughfare leading south from the Elephant and Castle and running parallel with the railway from Blackfriars. Leading off the broad strand of shops, businesses and trams were narrow residential streets clustered with terraces of newly-built villas. Those on Sutherland Street were tall, not without some pretensions, and led to the enclave of Sutherland Square, with its ornate railings and miniature oval park. Most residents would have worshipped at St Peter's, whose domed tower, designed by Sir John Soane, cast its graceful shadow over the area; an orthodox venue compared to the sensational Spurgeon Tabernacle up the road.

This was the inner city parish Mary Ann chose to colonise. Davies was told that the Girlingites had been in existence for seven years, and now numbered more than two hundred. Their place of worship was leased from the London Chatham & Dover Railway by Samuel Burrows, a Girlingite and kinsman of William Bridges. Burrows, who lived in Walworth, may have been responsible for inviting Mary Ann to London: he and unnamed 'others' had registered the arch for 'Divine service'.

It may have been down a back street, but the arch was easy to find. By 6.30 pm a mob had already gathered round the rough-tarred hoarding at the entrance, where a lone doorman was admitting the crowd one by one. 'Young Walworth in the shape of ragged shock-headed boys and draggle-tailed girls, was rigidly excluded'; the local dandy-ruffians known as the New Cut swells got in only by 'considerable manoeuvring and no little physical persuasion'. Negotiating planks laid over mud, Davies entered the arch, which smelt of the stables next door and was boarded up with an assortment of window-sashes partly smashed by 'the missiles of the Walworth Gentiles'. A few forms and planks faced a green baize table on which stood two cups and a collecting box; a sole gas pipe ran the length of the arch, 'whence descended two burners that shed a dim if not exactly a religious light . . .' It was a weird sight, this gloomy cavern, lit with flickering flames. A century later such arches would house car workshops or illicit nightclubs; now, this subterranean temple – a negative void in the no-man's-land formed by the railway's onward march – was charged with expectation. Part sacred space, part profane sanctuary beyond the jurisdiction of the common law, its barrel-vaults and restive audience echoed those of the music halls whose limelight illuminated other feats of Victorian entertainment.

By now the arch was filled with 'fustian-clad men, women in

about the proportion of two to one man, and babies in more than adequate force'. The swells – who declined to remove their hats – sat at the back, talking loudly. The crowd craned their heads, waiting for the show to begin. There was a ripple of excitement as the 'Jumpers' made their entrance, greeting each other with the kiss of charity – 'no half-and-half stage salute, but a good whacking kiss' – to the amusement of the swells, who 'proceeded at once to imitate the sound, and to remark audibly, "Ain't it nice?"'. Then, as seven o'clock struck, Mary Ann entered, her appearance all the more remarkable within this wayside grotto.

Taking the stage with the drama of an actress, she presented a potent combination for an age which demanded entertainment with its religion; the bizarre venue and its rag-tag congregation invested her with a sense of revelation. Here was a woman who claimed divine inspiration, an extraordinary assertion to make – yet more so in a railway arch in south London in 1871 – but Mary Ann drew on all the visionaries in whose footsteps she walked, a demotic parade of mystics and charlatans, believers and deceivers. She was a messiah for an industrial age, borne here to redeem the wicked city – even as the London to Dover train rattled overhead.

She was not, however, quite what Reverend Davies had expected. The figure he saw resembled less a seeress than one of those suburban mediums in whose vaguely disreputable company he had dallied. Dressed in a red merino gown and a 'somewhat jaunty black bonnet', to Davies she appeared to be a 'tall, thin, Suffolk peasant woman, of middle age, with high cheek-bones and piercing eyes' (elsewhere ascribed with a 'peculiar bright gleam' and an 'almost unnatural lustre' when excited). Davies' pathological description seemed to have some pre-knowledge of Mary Ann's past, as though her mission were written on her face. 'She had a large prominent mouth with projecting teeth, and the muscles around the jaw bore that peculiar appearance often observed in habitual speakers, being strongly developed, and giving a sort of animal appearance to the lower portion of the face' (others saw her thin lips as 'betokening an energetic and excitable temperament').

Flanked by the loyal Eliza Folkard, 'a young, good-looking girl of twenty', and Harry Osborne, 'an inane-visaged man in a broad-cloth coat and corduroys', Mary Ann asked – in a 'somewhat affected tone' – that anyone who could not stay until nine o'clock should leave at once, as the door would be closed and no exit allowed until then. This confinement was necessary 'on account of the outsiders, whose noisy clamours for admittance combine with the frequent passage of trains to mar the tranquillity of the evening'. It was religious worship determined by railway timetable and human interruption, although in her airs and graces, Mary Ann was quite equal to the heckles of the New Cut swells: 'I had heard . . . of the superior wisdom of the Londoners, but if this be London wisdom commend me to my Suffolk ignorance.' As another observer noted drily, it was a voice 'that could have been well heard in a place much larger than a railway arch'.

Apologising for the 'ill-convenience' of the venue, Mary Ann called for a prayer from Eliza, 'who lifted one hand and prayed with a fervour and a certain rough but gentle eloquence for ten minutes'; Davies was reminded of Dinah Morris, the Wesleyan preacher in George Eliot's *Adam Bede*. He was less impressed by Osborne's oration. Mary Ann herself 'prayed volubly, and used her long arms freely in gesticulation', which to Davies resembled mesmeric passes, 'but in this I was probably mistaken'.

The reverend summed up the sect's tenets for the benefit of his *Telegraph* readers. 'Now it must be premised that the distinguishing doctrine of these Children of God is the assurance that they will never die,' he noted. 'Belief not only does away with previous sin, but exempts them from bodily death. The Lord is to come speedily and gather them to Himself, without the previous process of dissolution. From the date of their conversion, in fact, they are immortal. They die at conversion, and die no more.' Where the Quakers 'were often believed to have claimed to raise from the dead when they only meant that they had effected a conversion', and where Swedenborg experienced a 'future life' between life and death, Mary Ann said that her followers had never 'given the undertaker a job yet, and didn't mean to'.

'Why did Lazarus come back?' she asked her congregation.

'Because he had got a return ticket,' someone shouted.

Riding the laughter and the noise of the trains, Mary Ann answered, 'No; he never was dead. He had died before . . .'

As she spoke, Davies noticed 'more than one lady subside into an apparently comatose condition' with 'a peculiar twitching of the limbs, and an expression of face like that which I have observed on the features of the mesmerised . . . what mesmerisers call "the superior condition"'. The women woke up at the end of the sermon 'as though nothing had happened'. It was time for a performance, and the Jumpers duly obliged.

Two young girls got up and began to dance, 'much in the same way as they might do if a grinding-organ had struck up an appropriate air'. These infant phenomena were then joined by a young man aged about eighteen: it seemed to Davies that their strangely vacant expressions were 'suggestive of animal magnetism', and he could only conclude there was more than mere abandon in their antics. It was as though they drew on some primal energy within the modern city, whose darker alleys could still encompass such mysteries as Spring-heeled Jack, a caped ghoul breathing fire in its own devilish leaping; or later, Jack the Ripper, an apocalyptic, sacrificial reaper stalking the harlot-strewn streets. In such places residual belief sought shamans to counter evil times, and Mary Ann offered an alternative to the shackles of working-class life.

On engaging a 'respectable woman' in conversation, Davies was told, 'Every member of this sect, upon conversion, undergoes *death*

– an actual process analogous to physical death, and exactly corresponding with it in external signs, only that it is not permanent.' Even for a man accustomed to mediums summoning the dead, this was a remarkable development. 'Some die very hard, in great agony,' said the woman, 'others quite peacefully. Only then would they 'jump'; and like the Shakers, 'once under the influence, it may recur at any moment'. In order to obtain the complete gift, 'probationary believers' had to embrace celibacy; this would ensure their immortality. This was no allegorical state, no erudite metaphor teased out from biblical texts by a learned parson; it was the literal truth: 'Once dead, not only will they die no more, but they suffer no pain, they feel no sorrow.'

The Children of God believed they had discovered the secret of eternal life, and in a world in which death was a daily fact, this promise was beyond prize and almost beyond imagination. Suspended in their state of grace, they awaited the millennium. Where Ann Lee had lain for hours 'with but little appearance of life' before her own rebirth, Mary Ann's Children emerged from their comas into the bright light of an assured place in heaven. Like Ann Lee, Mary Ann was living out a biblical narrative of her own. Why should she not be a prophet of modern times? After all, if Scripture was a battleground over which faiths had fought for centuries, then her exegesis looked back to the original, Primitive Church. It was as if she had only just discovered the Word of God (as indeed she had), and was now a missionary in her own country. And where the Shakers had believed they were living 'in the Resurrection Order, surrounded by, and in communion with, the spirits of the dead', here in Walworth Christ's coming was divined daily, to a timetable set by Mrs Girling, as though that railway arch were a portal through which some spiritual steam engine might take them all into another world.

* * *

When James J. Morse attended his first spiritualist meeting in Whitechapel in 1868, he found himself 'endowed with another personality . . . I shouted, rolled around the room, I swore, and . . . the more I tried not to do these things, the more perfectly were they accomplished!' After three-quarters of an hour the fit subsided, and he 'sank exhausted upon a settee'. As a connoisseur of such events, Davies equated the altered states of mesmerism and spiritualism with the Jumpers' ecstasy (in its original meaning, *exstasis*, to stand outside oneself), although when he interviewed Mary Ann, she was eager to disown such comparisons. Nevertheless, Davies was convinced that 'whatever be the origin of the so-called mesmeric condition, the same is the cause of "jumping". The magnetic "sleep-walking" may be produced without contact or passes . . . and religious excitement is certainly an adequate cause to produce such an effect.'

The vexed question of whether Mary Ann hypnotised her followers would haunt her mission – and produce new accusations of witchcraft. That night in the railway arch, one woman who had been 'grimacing and gesticulating in a slightly idiotic manner, jumped up and joined the dance. Her demeanour, however, was anything but happy; she prayed as in an unknown tongue, and called out "The devil! the devil!"' Davies was told by his confidante, 'Yes, there is something wrong. You see when they are in that state they have the gift of prophecy and clear vision. She can see the state of those around.' Perhaps, like the Shakers, the Girlingites could see the dead walking – although Davies offered the explanation that, like the onlookers who had spoiled Dr Emes's resurrection from Bunhill Fields, the New Cut swells had '"disturbed the conditions" . . . as the spiritists would say . . . When deprecating to me any use of mesmerism or chloroform, the minister said, "I wish I had been able to use the one or the other once or twice tonight".'

The reference to anaesthesia was apposite. Hypnotism and chloroform were seen to induce bodily abandonment beyond the control of consciousness; both evoked notions of surrender and perhaps violation (in 1865, Sir William Wilde, Oscar's father, had been accused of 'chloroforming' a young patient before seducing her), and spiritualists and mesmerists were accused of taking sexual advantage of their entranced subjects. Similarly, Mary Ann would stand accused of moral transgression when her followers danced themselves into unconsciousness and 'death', as if experiencing the *petite mort* of sexual ecstasy. For a world which would be shocked by the waltz, it was little wonder that such rites were regarded with suspicion and fascination. This peasant woman had imported pagan ways into the city and had thrown the formalised choreography of polite society into uninhibited abandon; these diseased fits presaged the St Vitus-like jerks of jazz dancers yet to come: one newspaper compared the Jumpers' rituals to 'a performance between a nigger break-down and the jig of the wandering Savoyards that we see in our streets'. Or perhaps their terpsichorean excesses were fuelled by narcotics imported from the Orient to the nearby docklands of the East End, where the exports were said to include the drugged and abducted young women of the white slave trade.

In Davies' conspiratorial narrative, cloaked in mystery like a clerical detective novel, anything might be possible, and the plot deepened with an invitation to a private meeting at an address given to him in confidence by his Girlingite friend. Here, he was promised, 'deaths' were more frequent – perhaps because they were conducted out of range of the swells' ridicule, and more lethal antipathies: 'Some of the men wait for our brothers and almost kill them', Davies was told. South London was a wild place, as the clergyman found for himself on leaving the rented railway arch. 'It took two policemen to get us quietly out . . . lest some honest Walworthian should mistake me for a "brother".' With that somewhat edgy exit, the reverend concluded his account, for the time being.

*   *   *

London was undergoing a transformation. Vast new buildings were rising at its centre like new geological formations, from the gothic cliffs of Kensington's Natural History Museum – built by the Quaker, Alfred Waterhouse – to Charles Barry's Italianate canyons of Portland stone along Whitehall, and the jagged stalagmites of Westminster. It was a city skyline newly framed by medieval crenellations; Gilbert Scott's St Pancras, seen romantically against a fiery sunset like some gigantic monastery out of Ruskin's *The Stones of Venice*, was in fact a modern hotel undercoursed by grinding locomotives and commuters hurrying through its tiled caverns. The entire metropolis was in a state of reinvention; one giant construction site for secular cathedrals dedicated to the imperial saints of science, technology, governance and capital. So too Mary Ann's arrival had seen an extension in her mission, as if London's burgeoning architecture encouraged her to produce yet more extraordinary effects. But hers was a spiritual phalanx populated by her Children of God, and unlike the leviathan monuments which her fellow Victorians were erecting, it did not need a grand temple to state its certainties. The Girlingites' rites were conducted underneath those constructions, in the dead space which progress had left behind – a vacuum filled by their immortal faith.

Mary Ann lodged with a family in Chelsea (possibly apostates of the Peculiar People), whose twenty-four-year-old daughter Violet was chosen, like Eliza Folkard, to receive the 'gift of the Spirit'. Having accompanied her parents to Walworth to hear Mary Ann speak, Violet fell unconscious to the floor where she remained for two hours, then suddenly she began to speak under inspiration, prophesying 'great and terrible judgements from God' on anyone who refused to accept Mrs Girling's message. Violet declared that she too would leave her family and follow Mary Ann wherever she went. Her conversion – which went one step further than the Peculiar People's gospel of salvation, and resembled the trance-like fervour of the young Shakeress instruments – was a cornerstone in the Girlingites' mission. It became a talisman for Mary Ann's followers, raising their sense of identity and encouraging new converts.

That winter at Walworth, Violet's visions had a galvanising effect. Many exhibited similar manifestations in the services, which attracted up to three hundred people – as well as the attention of the press. Crowds milling around the arch had swollen tenfold to two or three thousand, and the *South London Press* in particular followed the 'extraordinary proceedings . . . among the "Shakers" at Walworth' – reports all the more notable for their comparison of the Girlingites with the American sect. Next to an article on 'Mr Spurgeon's Return to South London' (from Rome, where 'the Papal system [was] as full of idolatry as ever Hindooism was'), the journalist 'C.E.P.' posed the question, 'What is a Shaker?' It was one which would 'naturally be asked by those who have not read Mr Hepworth Dixon's "New America"' – or perhaps by those who had attended one of Frederick Evans' lectures that summer – and it might be difficult to answer 'were it not for the fact that in South London, scarcely a hundred yards from the Walworth-road station, is the meeting-house of a Shaker community, where the inquirer may see with his own eyes . . .'

Arriving at Sutherland Street for a Sunday morning service, C.E.P. found Mary Ann seated behind her green baize table, a cup of tea at her side 'with which she occasionally refreshed herself'. The atmosphere was electric. Despite the winter weather it was hot and stuffy inside, and the correspondent watched as a group bent over a heavy-looking youth who lay in his companion's arms. Two young women had their arms around the boy's neck and were mumbling in excited, incoherent tongues. They then jumped up to dance, twirling and twisting 'as if they were bitten by the tarantula' (it was no coincidence that the poisonous spider also lent its name to a leaping mania and a feverish Italian dance). All the while another young man with slicked-back hair and a sickly smile dabbed at their faces with a handkerchief, helping an 'unhealthy-looking girl' out of her jacket when she grew too hot.

C.E.P. was particularly disgusted by 'a pale child of stunted growth' and the way she threw her head back over her shoulder 'and cast her eyes upwards, until almost nothing but the whites were visible . . . one almost felt tempted to jump up and rescue the silly fools . . .' But the dance went on. One girl began to stagger with her eyes closed and 'a wild unmeaning smile on her features', her cheeks 'streaked with white and red patches'; another respectably-dressed man in his fifties danced on one leg. The two young women had grabbed hold of the recumbent youth's head and were pulling his face towards them, kissing him violently as he submitted in a placid, cow-like manner'. The Brueghel-like scene was completed by a dark, swarthy man who performed like a dancing bear, his appearance 'as if . . . mesmerized' and his face 'more like that of a corpse'.

Evidently Mary Ann felt some explanation was necessary for this bizarre circus. She told the audience that the spirit of the Lord had a quickening effect. 'Ah', she said, 'if you could get people to do this, you might shut up all your dancing places.' Then she declared that 'Parents have a difficulty to get their children to places of worship; we have nothing of that kind; so far from it, we can't keep our children away. They like dancing, and cry to come.' To others, however, the presence of children in these rites – like that of adolescent mediums – was worrying, and would lead to questions about the Girlingites' treatment of their youngest and most vulnerable members.

One 'matron of some 35 years' attested that 'having once died the relation of a husband and wife ceases: A wife is ever after a housekeeper – nothing more'; while the preacher that night – probably Harry Osborne – declared, 'My sisters, if your desire be to your husbands, I pray you let it be so no more; for *every child born is the offspring of lust*!' The sect had inverted the relationship between adult and child; by surrendering to Mary Ann's control, they gave up responsibility for their own lives and became Children of God, leaving their offspring to be moulded in the Girlingite faith. Later, it seems, they would adopt orphans, as well as caring for children whose parents had joined but then left the sect; these young members would ensure a new generation for the celibate Family. Their role in such wild scenes was discomforting – especially when they made the front page of the *Illustrated Police News* (a consequence of the fact that the local police station stood directly behind Sutherland Street). The front page of the issue for January 1872 was a Grand Guignol display of a man eaten by rats, a lion tamer killed by his charges, and a violent poaching 'affray'. Set below these exhibits in a graphic predella, as though caught in a photographer's stark magnesium flash, were thrilling glimpses of the arch, with the figure of Mary Ann presiding over two dancers almost levitating in their ecstasy.

Such voyeuristic images made the Jumpers' chapel look more like Bedlam; and although the sect may have regarded their place of worship as an asylum in the other sense of the word, their disruptive presence was not beyond the law – whether used for or against them. In a rerun of their Suffolk trials, the Girlingites now appeared in London's courts, and at Lambeth on 8 February 1872, an Edward Ball was charged with 'indecent behaviour in a certain chapel of the religious denomination called Bible Christians'.

The magistrate, Mr Chance, heard how the 'excitement and turmoil' at the arch necessitated a constant police presence from the nearby station to maintain order. The sect had decided to prosecute Ball, having been 'so much annoyed by parties interfering with them for some time'. Samuel Burrows maintained theirs were 'manifestations', not dances, and an integral part of their worship. Then Harry Osborne testified that he travelled with 'the female speaker'. This did not sound entirely respectable.

Mr Chance: What do you mean by travelling with her?

Witness: We go about reading the word of God.

THE ILLUSTRATED POLICE NEWS

LAW-COURTS AND WEEKLY RECORD

SATURDAY, JANUARY 13, 1872. PRICE ONE PENNY.

TERRIBLE SCENE AT MANDERS MENAGERIE – THE LION TAMER KILLED –

PECULIAR PEOPLE OR DANCING IN AID OF RELIGION

THE MEETING PLACE IN SUTHERLAND ST

INSIDE THE MEETING HOUSE

Mr Chance: Do you live with her?

Witness: I live in the same house.

Now came Mary Ann's court debut. '. . . Gurling [sic] . . . said her husband allowed her to travel about, which she had done for six years. She now travelled with the witness Osborn [sic] and a young girl from the country, who were helpers in the work.'

Edward Ball was allowed to cross-examine his accuser:

Defendant: Are you not called the 'Shakers'?

Witness (sternly): Some may call us so.

Asked to explain their manifestations, Mary Ann said, 'When they take place I have no power. It is when they feel the word of God, and when it falls on them they remain in an unconscious state for a time, followed by a quickening effect which turns to a dance.' Fired by the laughter which greeted this statement, she confronted the mockers with their own mortality: 'All who dance have passed from death to life, and if you read the Bible you will understand it to be so.' This was met with a sharp intake of breath.

'Well, I am at present in the depths of darkness concerning it,' said Mr Chance. 'When are the dancers supposed to die?'

'They do not dance for dancing sake,' said Mary Ann, 'but it is the spirit of God moved them. I can tell when they pass from death to life by the symptoms. There is always some indication, such as their not being able to move. I have known some upwards of seven hours passing from the old state of Adam to the new.'

Inspector Fife of P Division told the magistrate that he had seen a crowd of some five hundred trying to gain entry to the arch. Despite the 'sad delusion' of its inhabitants, it was registered as a place of worship and had the right to be protected as such, Mr Chance conceded; but he also advised 'sensible people' to keep away from the place. As they left the court late that night, the Girlingites 'were scrutinized in a most unenviable manner'.

With Mary Ann's court appearance came the first reports of her millenarian message to the metropolis, 'to the effect that the end of all things was at hand and that she was to gather together the "hundred and forty and four thousand" who are to meet the Lord at His second coming . . .' It was a reiteration of Southcott's call to the 'sealed' of the Apocalypse. Meanwhile the *South London Press* reported on another local inhabitant with an interest in eschatology: 'Why Mr Ruskin leaves Denmark Hill: Frankenstein flying from monsters of his own creation is the character Mr John Ruskin declares he now personates.' Twenty years previously the author of *The Stones of Venice* had helped revive gothic architecture; now he protested, 'I have had indirect influence on nearly every cheap villa-builder between here and Bromley, and there is scarcely a public-house near the Crystal Palace but sells its gin-and-bitters under pseudo-Venetian capitals . . .' As an habitué of Spurgeon's Tabernacle and the Camden Chapel on Walworth Road, Ruskin must have known of the Girlingites; although with their enemies outnumbering friends in the area, they too were on the move. The residents of Sutherland Square complained that the streets were 'infested, from 6 o'clock until after 9, by a swarm of overgrown boys . . . hooting and shouting every time a member of the sect passed in or out', and by April Mary Ann had switched her operation to Salisbury Row, Lock's Fields, near the Old Kent Road, where she took a room in a private house. Her landlord soon regretted the lease. On Tuesday nights, when the sect assembled, the house was besieged by 'a crowd of women fearful lest their husbands should be converted and become "dead" to them in the flesh'. These wives 'smashed every pane of glass in the windows, tore up the palings round the house', shouting 'Down with the Shakers!' and 'No more dead-alive husbands!' It was, in its way, an augury of the prostitutes who would demonstrate outside the Old Bailey during Oscar Wilde's trial.

Mary Ann now assumed the title of Mother, as had Ann Lee, an action which symbolically coincided with the conversion of her own son, William Walter, now seventeen, to the cause. The comparison with the Shakers was also underlined by two more new recruits: James Haase and Julia Wood, newly returned from Mount Lebanon. They were important additions. Haase brought his business sense to this English eruption of religious communism – perhaps with the prospect of gathering the Children of God for Elder Evans – while Miss Wood's money would finance their establishment as a community. When told of the poverty of the followers back in Suffolk – where Mary Ann's mission had continued in her absence, a kind of holding bay of the faithful as converts awaited her confirmation – Wood acquired a home for the Girlingites at 107 Battersea Bridge Road. Here, by the banks of the river Thames, was a London Mount Lebanon, founded by 'the first twelve', the dozen Suffolk elders who sought to follow the lives of the apostles. For their neighbours, however – who included the congregation of a Wesleyan chapel and William D. Sumner, a professor of music – the arrival of this commune, preceded by reports of riots and court cases, was probably as welcome as that of a bail hostel in a modern suburb.

In April 1872, Mrs Dawe, the wife of a mechanic living at 4 Agate Street, Walworth, told Lambeth court that her husband 'had for some weeks belonged to the "Shakers". He had not entirely left her, but had ceased cohabitation, and she believed he would shortly proceed with the party to America.' The case was heard by Mr Chance, who was becoming all too familiar with south London's sects (two months later he would direct one of the Peculiar People 'to have his son vaccinated on pain of a fine of 2/6'). The magistrate told Mrs Dawe that he could hardly interfere between man and wife, despite her protests: 'What she had witnessed on Sunday week, when she went with her husband, was quite shocking, and enough to outrage any decent woman. She saw men and women embracing one another for a quarter of an hour at a time . . .' When her husband came home, he 'looked vacant, and seemed lost, and took no notice of anything. He had what the "Shakers" called "died", and had passed from death to "newness of life",' and she feared he was about to leave for America.

The recruitment of Evans' erstwhile acolytes seemed to encourage such ideas: the lure of the New World as a religious refuge held as good in the 1870s as it had in the 1770s, and perhaps – with Julia Wood's patronage – Mary Ann even considered a Girlingite exodus across the Atlantic, just as John Hocknell had financed the Shakers' move. In the event, however, theirs was only a trek up the Old Kent Road. The equally familiar figure of Inspector Fife told the court that the sect had 'received notice to leave Sunderland Street, and on Thursday would open Milton Hall, near a railway station'.

Although he would remain with Mary Ann for the next ten years at least, James Haase was ambivalent about Girlingism, as if he could not quite bring himself to embrace its more extreme tenets. That May, a labourer named John Tyseen was charged with using abusive language to Haase. In court Haase claimed that he was not a member of the group, and 'did not altogether agree with the worship of dancing'. It was a disclaimer which, with its overtones of Peter's denial of Christ, seemed to echo Mary Ann's generally equivocal relationship to the Shakers. What did she know of the American sect with which she was associated? Did she draw on their beliefs in the same way as she had parasitised the Peculiar People? Her new recruits must have discussed their experiences at Mount Lebanon with Mary Ann; it is even possible that she had attended one of Evans' lectures, although there is no trace of any encounter. The connexion, as indisputable as it is in one respect, is at the same time comprehensively denied. It is one reason why Mary Ann remains such an elusive figure.

Even now, the influence of the Shakers on Girlingism is impossible to pin down. The English sect left almost no records of its own, and those accounts which survive in the press are often wanton in their reporting, compounding the errors of others. In the search for sensation, the complicated lines of millenarian genealogy were obscured, not least through Mary Ann's own publicity-worthy assertions. For editors, it was easy to associate the two sects, especially as Mary Ann's arrival in London had coincided with the advent of Elder Evans; just as Girlingism was associated with spiritualism, for the same reasons. In the wake of Hepworth Dixon's *New America* and the comic sketches of Artemus Ward – a popular cartoonist who had also visited the Shakers – it was assumed Mary Ann was a Shaker and perhaps even American herself. The confusion was encouraged by the way in which the Girlingites were seen through the filter of popular culture, and remarks about Mary Ann's apparently American accent and dress and the transatlantic mannerisms of her followers were rooted in this media confusion.

Even to informed observers, it seemed plain that Girlingism drew on the same kind of itinerant preachers and radical sectaries who had sought refuge in the New World. Ann Lee's struggle had been one of Manichean polarities, a narrative of pioneering faith. Mary Ann's fate, as related in the press, would follow a similar trajectory. But hers was a distorted drama enacted, not in a colonial wilderness, but under the sophisticated surveillance of the imperial metropolis. Her mission was compromised by the burgeoning press and accelerating means of communication, as if the century itself sped her story to its inevitable dénouement.

Back at Shaker headquarters, word of Mary Ann's ambitions had reached the Society, which moved swiftly to deny the impostors, as *The Times* announced: 'We have received from Elder Frederick W. Evans, of Mount Lebanon . . . a communication disclaiming on the part of his community all connexion with a sect known as "the Walworth Shakers", but whose proper cognomen, according to Elder Evans, "would appear to be Jumpers or Bible Christians".' Evans may have been concerned at the effect on his own recruitment drive, but his protest underlined other paradoxes. Where the Americans had become regularised in their rituals, the Girlingites were wilder, more passionate, like the early Shakers, or the Quakers. It was as if they were re-enacting Mother Ann's Work – and gaining the kind of support which Evans had hoped for. Indeed, had Girlingism been a little more practical, its satellite communities, which would spring up in the Isle of Wight and Bristol, might have seen a national network to rival the Shaker families of America. 'Had she been supported by men of similar calibre to those who followed Ann Lee, and Joanna Southcott, there can be no doubt but that her work would have continued like the Shakers, and the Christian Israelites,' observed one contemporary.

But the times were already moving too fast. From the outset there was a sense of a lost cause to Mary Ann's mission, undermined, ironically, by her distinct lack of insight and administrative ability: 'she . . . would not permit any interference with her absolute rule of affairs, or allow any practical person to organise the Family on sound economic principles'. The chaos in the Walworth arch had been emblematic of the essential anarchy of the Children of God. They looked forward to the millennium, but not to the immediate future. Instead, Mary Ann insisted on her immortality – an ultimately fatal mechanism – and at the same time rejected identification with the Shakers: to do otherwise would be to acknowledge another messiah. It was a crucial component in the creation of Mary Ann's myth: she sought to obscure parallels and influences in order to make her own appearance that much more remarkable (while on a personal level, she may have been envious of Evans and antipathetic towards his masculine erudition). Although Mary Ann seemed at times to be a reincarnation of Ann Lee – and all the other prophetesses before her – for her once-orphaned, now reborn Children, there was only one Mother. And so it would remain, until they were made orphans once more.

* * *

It was left to Julia Wood, who had first-hand knowledge of both creeds, to make the distinctions. 'The American Shakers believe in Christ only as a prophet and a great man,' she told *The Times*, 'the followers of Girling believe in Him as God-man.' 'On the other hand,' observed the newspaper, 'dancing, celibacy, and community of goods are common to both sects', and, indulging in its own little pun, it predicted that it would not be easy 'to shake off the name'. Mary Ann's comments were rather more disingenuous: 'She believed there was a sect of the name in America, but she had never been there and she knew nothing about them . . . She and her friends were more like the Quakers, but they preferred to be called the children of God . . .'

Nonetheless, the Girlingites and the Shakers continued to be connected, often in a manner which reflected well on neither. One commentator on the Walworth Jumpers quoted from Charles Dickens' 1842 visit to Mount Lebanon which, like Brown and Hawthorne's accounts, contradicted the rosy pastoral portraits of that New England paradise. The novelist particularly disliked Shaker chairs, which 'partook so strongly of the general grimness, that one would have much rather sat on the floor than incurred the smallest obligation to them'. His greater complaint was philosophic, however. Like Hawthorne, Dickens saw Shakerism as forever living in the shadow of an apocalyptic future rather than rejoicing in the pragmatic present; and where Evans' *Autobiography of a Shaker, and Revelation of The Apocalypse* (*with an Appendix*) had the epigram, 'The spirit searcheth all things, yea, the deep things of God', Dickens declared, 'I so abhor, and from my soul detest that bad spirit . . . which would strip life of its healthful graces, rob youth of its innocent pleasures, pluck from maturity and age their pleasant ornaments, and make existence but a narrow path towards the grave . . .'

That struggle for spiritual integrity had its casualties back in Walworth, where the Girling whirlwind had left the Peculiar People and John Sirgood in disarray. Sirgood had initially been won over by Mary Ann, and that August had written, 'I do not think any of them knows what the power in the soul is but the woman that is their chief . . .' Like some vampire, Mary Ann fed on the Peculiar People, seducing them with her promise of immortality; the glamour of Girlingism put Bridges' beliefs in the shade, and 'those who believed the new docrine are of course getting the joy', observed Harriet Sirgood. She attended a meeting 'under the Arch', where Mary Ann pressed the urgency of gathering the 144,000: 'You better make haste, don't wait for others or the number will be made and the Saviour come.' Harriet watched as one member 'died' at the meeting and was still unconscious at ten o'clock. Her husband now felt that he had been 'led astray' by Mary Ann, and saw her as an equivalent of the vision of Satan as an angel of light which had once appeared to him. It was as if he feared for his own attraction to Mary Ann: 'the more I gave place to her the less I felt towards others, which caused me to see that it was a deception of the devil come closer to me than ever before'. William Bridges went so far as to claim: 'They had even brought the tar to tar the woman over; to set fire to her but was prevented.' It was a potent vision of violence: Mary Ann in flames, a tarred but not feathered witch, a blackened angel, her gown afire, too late for any *Human Nature* campaign to save this Joan of Arc of the Walworth Road.

After three weeks at Milton Hall – which appears to have been a generic name for a railway arch, this time a dark and damp void close to Waterloo station – the Girlingites were driven out by 'a volley of stones, a general melee, and a grand "skedaddle" of the saints'. After a brief stay in Finsbury, by June they were in West London where, under the management of James Haase and financed by Julia Wood, they rented Victoria Hall, in Little College Place, 'a back slum in Chelsea . . . situated about midway between the South Kensington and Sloane Square Stations on the Metropolitan District Railway', as Maurice Davies reported.

Davies duly arrived by tube to find the sect newly installed in a whitewashed and well-lit chapel, a contrast to their chimney-sweep neighbour. It seemed that in their move to Chelsea, the Girlingites were 'gravitating towards common sense': the meeting was conducted 'in a more decorous fashion', with a 'most excellent choir'. But this raised a new problem: with sensation came income, especially in a city with so many rival sideshows, and as the meeting ended without any manifestations, some of the congregation demanded their money back. Having stayed behind to engage Mary Ann in conversation – she was perfectly amenable to questions on Scriptural theory, but her answers were less satisfactory – Davies left thinking he had heard the last of the Jumpers. He could not know that of all the sects he had visited on his capital-wide trawl of the eerie, the faithful and the fraudulent, the Children of God would soon return to the pages of the newspapers, and in a manner more sensational than anyone could have predicted.

Their services may have calmed down in Chelsea, but the Girlingites still found themselves assailed by the mobs they thought they had left behind in Walworth. Paying threepence to view their antics, sightseers came expecting marvels or freaks, just as visitors to the East End's Commercial Road would gawp at John Merrick, the Elephant Man. Some were disappointed with what they found; others took exception to the 'Shakers' Tea Meeting' and its orgiastic scenes: 'The men kissed each other, the women kissed each other, then the men ran about kissing the women, and the girls then ran and kissed the men. Their kisses were not single kisses or mere salutes of love and peace: they were regular running fires of kisses and love chirps, which lasted for several minutes. Their arms were first round each other's waists, then round each other's necks: then they were looking into each other's eyes, then laying their heads on one another's shoulders, and then kissing again, as though entirely lost to all around in feelings of the most exquisite ecstasy.'

A
SHAKERS'
'SERVICE.'
BY
EYEWITNESS
SECOND EDITION—Revised.
All rights reserved.
PUBLISHED AND PRINTED BY
MONTAGUE & Co., 42, CASTLE STREET, HOLBORN.
PRICE ONE PENNY.

Audiences stood on their benches to get a better look: 'Oh crikey, look here at that girl: ain't her having it nice: I should like to be kissing her', while an offended observer said, 'You all ought to be ashamed of yourselves, you ought: it's disgraceful.' Then, as Eliza – assumed to be Mary Ann's daughter – sang a hymn, the crowd struck up a rival tune, sung to the air of 'Old Brown's Daughter' –

> There lives an ancient party
> At the end of Ipswich town,
> Who keeps a little preaching shop
> In Chelsea college town.
> She has only got one daughter,
> Such a party I never saw;
> By jingo I would like to be
> That woman's son-in-law

– with the ironic refrain, 'Mother Girling's daughter is a proper sort of girl'. The parody was itself an indication of Mary Ann's celebrity, as was a satirical *A Shaker's 'Service'* pamphlet, cashing in on the sensational Girlingites. Accordingly, the crowd at Chelsea were rewarded with yet more extraordinary manifestations, as if in reaction to that fame. 'Numbers of people were thrown into trances, from which they were not aroused, and apparently could not be aroused, at the time of leaving. In their apparently mesmeric state they related visions and prophesied most startling events. While in their unconscious state they danced and violently jumped to a height of several feet. They also spoke and sang in unknown tongues. There were several professed spiritualists present . . .'

Littered with comatose bodies and supercharged with emotion, it is little wonder that the chapel attracted spiritualists, for its jabbering tongues and ecstatic rites rivalled mediumistic trances for sensation, and seemed to tap into the same strange energies. Another newspaper witnessed an uproarious atmosphere akin to 'the gallery of the "Vic" on Boxing Night'. The noise was 'absolutely deafening; cat-calls, whistling cries for "the old woman . . . to come on", groans and shouts of mocking laughter . . . No one took the trouble to take off his hat, and stale cutties and penny smokes filled the place with sickening odours'. Mary Ann finally descended from the loft, dressed 'in the orthodox black silk dress, whose glories had long since departed, leaving a rusty brown predominant in its shades' – as if London's acid pollution had begun to eat away at the prophetess. 'A tight-fitting jacket of the same material, and a black and white bonnet of puritanical simplicity completed her attire . . . Ascending the platform she surveyed her audience for a few seconds in silence, then in accents which almost set one's teeth on edge, shouted, "Get hoff them seats, or I'll close the meeting. If you are gentlemen show yourselves sich".'

As the hubbub rose, Mary Ann folded her arms like a long-suffering school mistress and stared at the rafters until the noise subsided. Some took this to mean that she had 'seen something' ('"Cobwebs", suggested a shock-headed youth'), while a greengrocer offered, ''Ave a drop of short, missus.' 'Turning sharp round, the goddess thundered forth, "You are a disgrace to the name of Englishmen; if you were in the lowest place of worship in the land you would not behave so".' After the dancing, during which Eliza's flaxen hair flew 'as wildly as the snakes that ... supply the Furies with chignons', Mary Ann declared, 'I'm not afraid of death', to an 'Oh, Oh' from the audience. 'You are, but I am not,' she replied. 'I shall never die. I was dead once' – at which a voice interrupted, 'What a shake you must have given to have got out of yer coffin' – 'but I have been born again.' As the meeting disintegrated, Mary Ann 'abused the press' and 'maintained that she and her followers were not such fools as they looked. She repudiated the assertion that their religion was an American importation, but gave no explanation of its origin.' The session ended with the police clearing the room. Afterwards, the reporter spoke to one of the elders: '"Is your religion an American invention?" we inquired. "Certainly not." "Let us look at your hymn-book." The saint looked confused, but seeing we would take no refusal, he let us open it. It was headed "The *American* Sacred Songster".'

Accusations of transatlantic influence came suffused with a certain prejudice, a legacy of lost colonies and the threat of hostilities between the two countries – as well as resentment at American imports, or the lack of them (the civil war – which, like its English version was seen as an augury of the last days by such millenarian American journals as the *Prophetic Times* – had caused a cotton famine and much hardship in England). That most patriotic of periodicals, *John Bull*, detected in the 'showily dressed' and 'stentorian voiced' 'Sister Garling' [sic], 'a decidedly American accent, though she called herself a "poor Suffolk woman"'. To some, Mary Ann was nothing more than an outrageous and possibly traitorous imposter – like Ann Lee – and her ideas decidedly dangerous in this, the year of the Paris Commune, whose rebels were being executed in France even as the papers reported on the Walworth Jumpers. That winter the mob flung slack lime at the Girlingites and broke their chapel windows. It was the kind of casual violence which, back in the Walworth Road, had come close to being murderous, and once again the sect proved willing to take their assailants to court – and occasionally won. But it was clear they could not stay in London much longer.

With the millennium ever closer, and the need for a new home more urgent in the growing opposition of the city, Mary Ann now experienced a new vision. She was told to gather her Children together for the Second Coming, and was issued with a specific instruction: 'God had given to her New Forest Lodge at Hordle, Hampshire, for this purpose', as if from some heavenly estate agent.

Although Mary Ann professed to have no knowledge of this apocalyptic location, there were precedents for her sect's imminent removal to southern England. Not only were there the examples of Sirgood's Society of Dependants at Loxwood, the Ham Common Concordium, and Stratford St Mary's vegetarian commune, but in 1839, Robert Owen had established his Harmony Hall at East Tytherley, just north of the New Forest. By May 1843, forty-five adults and twenty-five children were living in a three-storey, red-brick communal house in the style of a Fourier phalanstery. Owen envisaged a £600,000 estate from whose towers 'would be reflected at night, by powerful apparatus, the new koniophostic light, which would brilliantly illuminate its whole square'. The commune aspired to the self-sufficiency and craftsmanship of Shaker villages, but after six years it faltered under mismanagement, parodied by Cruikshank's cartoon of foolish figures dancing to the caption, *Harmony Hall – All Owin' – No payin'*. Meanwhile, a more venal sect was established in 1850 at Spaxton, Somerset, by a former curate, Henry James Prince, who claimed to be incapable of sin and that 'those who had faith in him would never die'. Prince attracted wealthy female followers to his Agapemone or 'Abode of Love' and its 200-acre estate, through which he would drive in a carriage with four white horses and a footman, sounding the horn and crying 'All hail! All hail! The Messiah!' Prince's union with Miss Paterson, one of his 'soul wives', was 'sealed in the flesh . . . in a public act of worship on a sofa after prayers in the billiard room', and by 1860, moral opposition had caused the sect to sink under a series of lawsuits from its former members.

Perhaps with good reason, Mary Ann acknowledged none of these as influences, although others saw them as such: the *Pall Mall Gazette* would note that the Girlingites had chosen their site 'at no great distance . . . from the spot where Robert Owen made his celebrated experiment in Socialism and failed . . .' Rather, for Mary Ann the move acquired its own spiritual, biblical uniqueness: 'A London house afforded no fit place for the development of her system and the exercise of faith,' reported *The Times*. 'Land should be tilled; and, in another sense, there must be room to grow.' Like the radicals of two centuries before, the Children of God were to dig for their Eden: 'He that works for another, either for wages or to pay him rent, works unrighteously,' the Digger, Gerrard Winstanley, had declared. 'True religion and undefiled is to let every one quietly have earth to manure.'

Yet Mary Ann's choice of their new Zion remains a mystery. Was her vision so precise, sending her to the New Forest just as Shakers had been directed across the Atlantic by a burning tree? Or did Miss Wood see it advertised in a newspaper? Whatever the truth, their home had been found, and now all that was needed was the money to buy it. Here the obligingly solvent Julia played her part. In December 1872, she arranged to buy the property and thirty acres of land for £2,250, but – perhaps on advice – paid only £1,250, leaving the community with a mortgage of £1,000. The mechanics of the deal did not concern Mary Ann; she was about to lead her Family to the lee of the sheltering forest. Away from the antipathy of London and its rival attractions, she could renew her mission. She had exhausted the temper of the town, and its source of new recruits; now she would till fresh and fertile ground. The *Daily Telegraph* would recall the sect's last days in London, 'howling and jumping about in a chapel to which the public were admitted indiscriminately', although 'Brother Prince and his people at the Agapemone were really much more offensive to public feeling than these Shakers, about whose creed scarcely anybody seems to know anything'. Nonetheless, 'it was deemed a good riddance when the poor people betook themselves, with their yelling and capering orisons, to the peaceful county of Hampshire'.

FIVE

The New Forest Shakers

> Had they searched England through these peculiar people could not have pitched their camp at a more suitable place for quietness and repose. The New Forest is the sleepiest hollow we have left to us. Dartmoor and the Isle of Portland answer admirably as convict settlements; wastes like Chat Moss and Cannock Chase would be most eligible lots for men contemplating the hermit line of business . . . But to those who can enjoy existence without the iron and stone and turmoil of Babylon, the New Forest offers the most delightful advantages. In truth, spite of its ancient designation of 'New', it is not merely the oldest, but the only forest worthy of the name remaining in the land.
>
> *Daily News*, 18 December 1874

Two days into the new year of 1873, Mary Ann and her Family arrived in Hordle. The Osbornes, Henry and Isaac, came with their wives and children, as did Thomas Todd; Eliza, Violet, and three older men – among them, Isaac Batho – made up this advance party. Villagers must have been amazed and aghast to see their caravan pitch up on Vaggs Lane. The Children of God had been led to the 'gate of heaven', and their new neighbours could not know what had been visited upon them. William Henry Spackman, the vicar of Sway, only found expression at the appearance of Mary Ann in a letter to *The Times* two years later: 'Her assertions were of a most astonishing character,' he wrote, as though still coming to terms with them. 'She claimed to have direct communication with Heaven, to obtain supernatural revelations, and to be the elected head of those saints on earth who were waiting for Christ's coming, whose advent she confidently affirmed would be made in the neighbourhood of the New Forest. In religious fanatics these claims are not extraordinary, the marvel is that in the nineteenth century she could obtain converts.' But it was an age of marvels, and holy feet might yet walk upon this land.

Hordle in the early 1870s had little to distinguish it from other such places in and around the New Forest; a disparate, vague settlement, caught between the forest and the sea, barely a coherent community at all, save in those few cottages which surrounded the parish church, itself a new construction. It was as if Hordle were an approximation of a traditional English village, lacking the heart of an ancient chapel and immemorial green.

In fact, Hordle had once had such a church. For seven hundred years it had stood to the south on the sea cliff, its wind-blown graveyard home not only to parishioners, but to the often anonymous victims of shipwrecks and drownings. An 1809 entry in the burial register records, forensically, 'Woman, unknown, aged from 20 to 24 found on Hordle shore 13th Augst. – naked except her stockings, with a gold ring, and apparently a nurse, with bruises on breast and head'. Another entry, from 1834, reads: 'John Johnson, a negro from Sierra Leone, wrecked from a trading ship, the *William Hamilton*, on Hordle coast. No funeral service read the man being a heathen.' Forty years later, a Frenchman who survived a wreck recorded an encounter with a strange religious group in the village, as if he had arrived on the shores of Africa rather than southern England.

For all its proximity to civilisation, this could be a desolate place. The narrow straits between here and the Isle of Wight were as wild as any wide ocean, haunted by the forests beneath the waves through which the river Solent once flowed, and by the memory of even older, primeval seas in which monsters once swam, their fossilised remains still found in the cliffs known as the Crocodile

Bed. There were other traces, too, of worship and invasion: from grassy tumuli (it was said that the name of Hordle itself derived from the word for 'treasure', perhaps from these pagan burials), to Roman camps and battlefields where resident Saxons had fought marauding Danes.

The population of Hordle had since moved inland, seeking shelter from the unrelenting sea and winter storms, and the site of their old church became increasingly inconvenient. In 1830, its medieval walls were demolished and a new gothic pile rose on Downton Common using their stone for its foundations, but these proved to be so badly constructed that forty years later a replacement was required. Hordle's third church, All Saints, was built of red brick and Bath stone and consecrated by the Bishop of Winchester on 8 June 1872, just six months before the arrival of the Girlingites, attended by their own storms.

Beyond All Saints lay Hordle's crossroads, marked by the Bells Inn, a social centre for the parish and witness to its comings and goings. To the east, along Silver Street, lay Arnewood (chosen by Captain Marryat as the name for the house from which his children of the New Forest had fled for the woods), Brockenhurst and the railway line to Southampton and London. To the west was Milton, Christchurch (with its priory and its miraculous beam, placed there by a mysterious holy carpenter), and the 'wonderful new town' of Bournemouth, a Victorian resort 'which, some twenty summers ago, was all but a wild, barren heath, but which is now like the vast fashionable suburb of a great city, with its thousands of splendid villas . . .' To the south lay the sea, but northwards the road ran through Tiptoe and Sway and into the forest itself. Here the land opened up from the inclosures of Set Thorns onto the heath of Wilverley Plain and the Naked Man, a skeletal tree from whose branches both good and bad thieves were hanged.

The countryside around Hordle was coursed with high hedgerows and studded with oaks and beeches which seemed to have

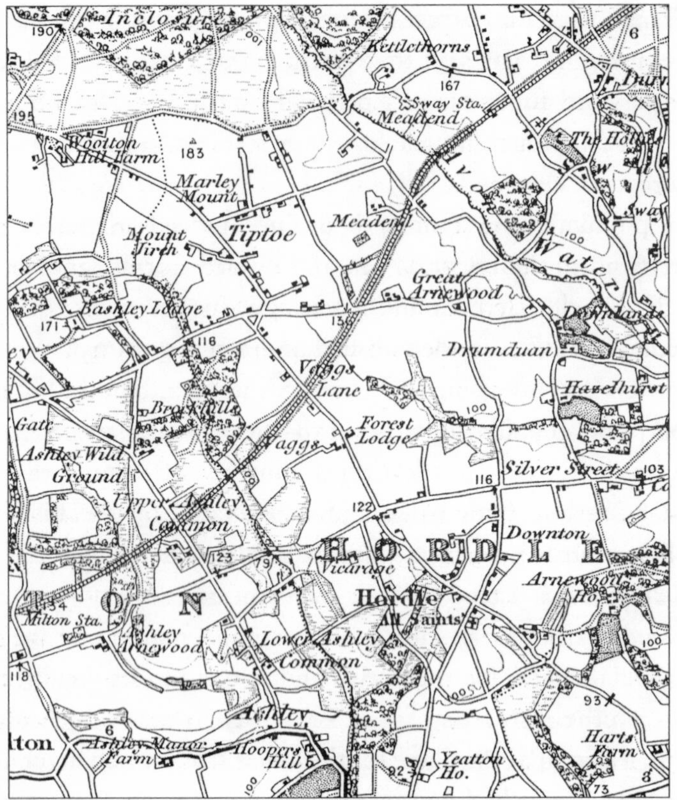

Ordnance Survey of England, 1876

escaped from the forest. There were orchards and small fields growing cereals and vegetables, while gravel pits provided other evidence of progress eating away at the wilderness, as the newly-levelled and engineered network of roads opened up the land, flattening it out for public inspection and access. The forest itself, however, remained 'an out-of-the-world haunt, full of picturesque nooks, and delicious solitudes', where ponies, said to be descended from ships wrecked during another attempted invasion – that of the Spanish Armada – ran wild, and where 'a primitive forester, or cow-boy' would be as 'amazed at your appearance' as a 'startled fox or hare'. The nearest town was Lymington, recently connected by a branch line from Brockenhurst, running 'through a bona fide bit of forest, out of which your train startles the pheasants and rabbits'. Lymington was the local centre of commerce and authority, with its own court and workhouse, the dreaded Union. Its high street of elegant Georgian houses and bow-fronted shops narrowed down to the cobbled Quay Hill, where ferries connected the mainland to the Isle of Wight. A toll bridge over the river led to the dissolved Cistercian foundation of Beaulieu, once sanctuary to Perkin Walbeck. Further down, where the river met the sea, were the eerie salterns, first worked by the Romans, now a rush-sown expanse redolent of the Alde valley where Mary Ann had grown up.

This countryside would have been familiar to those Suffolk exiles – and all the more welcome for that, after the teeming streets of London. It was a landscape which had been shaped in a sweep of enclosure 'from Christchurch Bay to Brockenstand', a process which had reduced the forest and at the same time brought its outlaws under control and into the workforce. Hordle's agriculture meant that it was not a particularly deprived area, and it rode the mid-century depressions by supplying the burgeoning resort of Bournemouth with produce. Half of the parish population – estimated at eight hundred and sixty-eight in the 1871 census – worked the land for themselves or its owners; the rest were artisans, or retired clergy or gentry occupying estates and larger houses, some of them naval and military men. Yet this quiet place still played a role in the defence of the realm. The parish included Hurst Spit, the shingle strand which reached out like an arm from the coast; barely a mile stood between its lighthouse and its newly-built counterpart at the end of the Island's chalk stack Needles.

This vulnerable entry point to England was guarded by Hurst Castle and its sixty-strong garrison, a grander version of the Martello tower which stood at Aldeburgh. This fortress had been built by Henry VIII using stone robbed out of Beaulieu; during the civil war its isolation made it a suitable jail for Charles I, and it would also house Catholics convicted under the anti-popery acts: one Franciscan imprisoned in 1700 was still there at his death, twenty-nine years later. In the decade before Mary Ann's arrival, Hurst had been massively reinforced in response to the threat from Napoleon III – and at the same time tethered to the modern world by means of 'communication by submarine telegraph with London and Osborne'.

Hurst's monumental buttresses of brick and stone were still under construction as the Girlingites arrived that bleak January day, along with the chill winds blowing inland from the Solent. Their advent was a reminder of other strangers equally worthy of suspicion: the Romany who moved around the forest, some seventy families living in tents and caravans, plying their trades but keeping their distance; and the navigators or 'navvies' working the new railway lines and living in temporary mud huts close by. Mary Ann's colony would suffer in the comparison. 'An indulgence is being granted to the Shakers,' one parishoner would protest, 'which is refused to the bands of working gypsies and other itinerant classes.' For these religious outlaws, the central conflict would also be one of ownership and otherness; and as self-displaced persons professing communist beliefs, the Girlingites would be doubly distrusted and resented.

The vicar under whose spiritual control this restive, disparate parish lay was the Reverend James Rushton, MA, also chaplain to the Hurst garrison. All Saints was valued at £90 per annum, and benefited from the patronage of the widowed Mrs Ashley Chute, and the wealthy John Peirse Kennard of Hordle Cliff, who had contributed most of the money for the new church. There the parishioners of Hordle worshipped quietly, listening to the vicar's sermons and the words of the King James Bible. Yet such orthodoxy was deceptive, for like Suffolk, Hampshire had its own tradition of dissent. There was a Primitive Methodist chapel in

Nomansland – originally a Gypsy settlement, a 'nowhere' to echo its utopian neighbours – while since the seventeenth century there had been a substantial number of Anabaptists in Hordle; in 1725, out of a parish of one hundred and fifty-seven, seventy-nine were Anabaptists, along with twenty-three papists. Although the Baptists were now an accepted faith, 'Anabaptist' had been a generic term, as pejorative as 'Shaker' for those who believed only adults could receive baptism, who refused to take oaths and even aspired to communal property; they too were seen to oppose the status quo. Forests and heaths had ever been places outside society where squatters and cottagers could live free of feudal masters; the forest's mysterious geography, its scattered settlements and large parishes encouraged such autonomy, and the after-shock of the English Revolution and its millenarian beliefs still seemed to reverberate here in Hampshire.

And yet for all these precedents – the familiar and the strange, and the familiarity of the stranger – the arrival of the Children of God caused sensation. Many would come to wonder at their abandonment of normal behaviour; but others would be attracted by New Forest Lodge and its alternative to the orthodoxy of All Saints – and would be gathered into the fold by Mary Ann. She presented a compelling contrast to the Reverend Rushton: her figure, so ramrod straight, and her eyes, so magnetic, seemed to summon the faithful. Perhaps they thought her skirts would shelter them from the coming storm.

Forest Lodge, as it was known, was a new building, constructed in the late 1860s, for a farmer, George Smith, and his family. Built in the characteristic style of the period, it had a pair of gables with bay windows, and a glazed area forming a kind of conservatory to the front of the building. Surrounded by fields and ancient hedgerows, with oaks and Victorian specimens of macrocarpa and pine lining its driveway, the house presented a quiet, unassuming aspect to passersby who glimpsed it through the trees – a place which had minded its own business until now, and might have expected to accommodate a retired businessman or army officer. Instead, it was occupied by an apocalyptic commune overseen by a female messiah.

To locals, it must have seemed as though the Lodge had turned into a kind of gothic asylum inhabited by a deranged cult. For the Girlingites, however, it was simply 'the Home'. In layout, the building formed a horseshoe shape, with two wings: the front door opened into a wide hall with a low pitched ceiling and a fireplace, and a long corridor ran to the two main reception rooms, with others facing into the courtyard behind. Upstairs were four or five bedrooms and servants' quarters. There were neatly planted gardens and at the rear, stables and a cottage which Miss Wood would occupy.

In March, Leonard Benham arrived from Suffolk, bringing his wife, six children, horses, tools and £100 in cash, a welcome addition to the commune. With thirty-one acres of pasture and fields, there was land enough to sustain the sect; although agriculture was incidental to their mission, as was evident when the new tenants turned the brick stables into a hall whose industrial plainness echoed the dissenting chapels which had sprung up across the country. The horses' stalls were replaced by benches fixed to the walls – similar to those in Shaker meeting places – leaving the floor clear for dancing. At one end was a stool on which Mary Ann stood to preach, illuminated by oil lamps. Here the faithful gathered, listening to the words which had drawn them to this place; a space which once echoed to hooves now resounded to ecstatic dance steps and hymns conducted by Isaac Batho, the community's choirmaster:

All hail, our risen Head!
We, thy children dear,
Look for thy appearing,
We, by thy spirit led,
Nothing here are fearing.
Come and gather us home, dear Lord!
Come and gather us home.
We long to be in Heaven with thee,
Our cry is, Come, Lord, Come!

All hail, thou Mighty One!
Display thy glorious power,
These last days revealing,
Man's race is nearly run;
Light from them is stealing.
Come and gather us home, dear Lord!

All hail, thou Perfect One,
Time is drawing nigh;
Things around are telling
The work is nearly done.
Our hearts with joy are swelling.
Come and gather us home, dear Lord!

All hail, thou King of Peace,
We know thou'rt at the door.
We yearn for our meeting,
Bring Thou our release.
We want to give Thee greeting
Come and gather us home, dear Lord!

Soon the Lodge and its shared bedrooms – resembling something between a cottage hospital and a convent – proved unable to accommodate the swelling numbers, especially as, like the Shakers, they were strictly segregated by sex. The loft above their chapel, reached by a ladder and a trap-door, was converted into a dormitory for fifty beds. Meanwhile, the brothers were busy erecting new buildings to accommodate their sexual division; Mary Ann would later claim that they spent £2,000 in alterations and furnishings. A 'New Hall', workshops and other outbuildings rose in the

field next to the house, made out of the earth itself, using clay dug from pits on the site and fashioned into rudimentary bricks waterproofed with bitumen. These adobes – a cross between ancient cob barns and the mud huts built by railway navvies – irritated the mortgagee, who complained that he had sold the Lodge to a spinster, not to a hundred religious zealots 'who considered themselves entitled to dig large holes for brick earth, to erect unsightly and dangerous structures . . . and to otherwise injure the house and property'. As his solicitors noted: 'Had we or our client been aware of this, or that the house would have been overcrowded by such a "peculiar people", no advance would have been made by him.'

But Mary Ann's mission was growing exponentially with the success of her ministry, and the Hampshire colony had become a settlement in its own right, aspiring to self-sufficiency, using livestock and implements bought by Julia Wood. Two-thirds of the fields had been dug for vegetables, and five acres of wheat had been planted. The Lodge also entailed forest rights which allowed the sect to graze cattle there. And yet despite other beneficial factors – the fertile soil, the ready markets of Lymington and Ringwood – the Children of God were allowed to sell neither their produce nor their labour. Like the Diggers, whose allotments had annoyed earlier landowners, their cultivation was a symbolic act, almost perversely beyond the mechanism of nineteenth-century capital. And as a contemporary would point out, '. . . Any one, other than a fanatical zealot might have seen the consequences that too soon followed . . .'

To sympathisers and enemies alike, such prohibitions seemed a fundamental madness. When one member who had run a co-operative store in his former life started a similar venture at the Home with 'the promise of fair results', Mary Ann closed it down, saying that 'buying and selling formed no part of the Kingdom of God'. Had her prophecies extended to more practical matters, she might have seen that in the success of her mission lay its downfall: all those incomers needed to be fed, and yet the sect could not create the system needed to support itself. She merely stated, 'God will amply provide for all our wants', and they believed it was true. To encourage fellow spirit, a contract was drawn up which all had to sign and obey; it was revealing statement of utopian intent:

> All persons joining this Community must give evidence of new life or belief in Christ as the way of life, according as the Gospel sayeth:–
>
> 'And the multitude of them that believed were of one heart and of one soul: neither said any of them that ought of the things which he possessed was his own; but they had all things common.
>
> 'And with great power gave the Apostles witness of the resurrection of the Lord Jesus: and great peace was upon them all.
>
> 'Neither was there any among them that lacked: for as many

as were possessors of lands or houses sold them, and brought the prices of the things that were sold.'

Acts iv., verses 32–34.

On entering the community every person must willingly give up to M. A. Girling, the accepted Stewardess, all they possess – gold, silver, goods, and all clothing except what they are wearing, without the exception of ever having them again. Articles so given up are not to be asked for again, nor will any article be allowed to be taken off the place without M. A. Girling's permission.

No parents will be allowed to inflict any punishment on their children, nor to interfere in any way with their management; and no person under the age of fourteen to be left by their parents in this community.

No marrying or undue intimacy between man and woman allowed.

No teaching or doctrine to be introduced into this community different to what has been observed and advocated by M. A. Girling, her teaching being in strict harmony with the Apostolical order and Gospels of Christ.

All disputes, either temporal or spiritual, to be submitted to M. A. Girling, and her decision to be final.

No masters. All to do what is appointed them as under God.

No wages paid.

No one allowed on the premises without leave. No one to sell anything off the place, or take anything off the premises.

No goods to be secretly brought on to the premises, or to be concealed; all to be given up for equal distribution.

Men to rise from 6.30 to 7.0 a.m.

Women to rise from 7.0 to 7.30 a.m. Breakfast at 8.0 a.m.

By order of the Twelve Founders.

These commandments were rather more prosaic than those handed down to Moses from Mount Sinai, although they too demanded absolute obedience of the modern Israelites, and critics compared them to the Shakers' 'modified slavery': 'At the expense of loss of individuality they were, in every sense, treated as children, whose wills, and even intelligence and reason, were to be in rigorous and abject (although they saw it not) obedience to the behests of their "Mother". But to others, they were the pattern for heaven on earth, reinventing the whole notion of family life for a putative new age.

They were a heterogeneous assortment, these souls who waited here in Hordle for the Second Coming. Of their ever-growing communion – one hundred and sixty-four chosen by God and gathered by Mrs Girling – forty or fifty were infants, and around the same number men, 'a few mechanics – blacksmith, carpenter, shoemaker, tailor – but more agricultural labourers'. But most were women: seventy wives, teachers, widows and servants drawn from their households in London, Suffolk or Hampshire by Mary Ann's call. The core of the community centred around the Elect: the Osborne families (headed by Henry and his brother Isaac), the Coopers and the Benhams. They encouraged conversions and enforced the rules. Each recruit gave their money to the communal fund and, like the Shakers, entered an austere regime. They ate little meat; many were vegetarians. At meals they sat separated by their sex, and at night they were likewise divided in order to minimise the temptations of the flesh: male and female met only during daily tasks or worship, and so were kept pure and apart for God. Members could leave the compound only by permission; beyond its bounds lay temptation. Yet for all its regulations, theirs was an innocent state, unencumbered by possessions, desires or vanities. Nothing from the outside world was allowed unfiltered into theirs: their welfare and their souls were given up to the Lord through His representative, Mother Mary Ann.

The Girlingites rejected the modern, as though time had stopped still on the day that Christ first appeared in their leader's Ipswich bedroom. Like others who sought to return to the values of the Primitive Church, they turned back to the past even as they looked to the future. It was as if the nineteenth century had never happened. Mary Ann reached back to an age of belief before the age of reason; an era when miracles and spirits were evidence of God and symbols of the end time. Dehumanising industry was written out of the Girlingites' world; the harnessing of steam, the remorselessness of the railway and all the other imperial creations were undone by this one woman and her prophecies. They had no need of such things: there was no point in material acquisition when there was so little time left to run.

This was a back-to-nature existence in an age when the rich and powerful were removed from the cares of the ordinary people; a world divided by the railway lines which even now were bisecting the forest. The Girlingites looked into the wilderness, just as the Cistercians before them had sought a 'horrible' or wild place at Beaulieu. New Forest Lodge might lack the grandeur of that foundation, but it also lacked the wealth which had corrupted it. Without ownership, there could be no envy, and without envy, no greed.

In return for absolute happiness, Mary Ann demanded absolute obedience. It was a simple enough equation. As the rules asserted, her decision was final: she was God's referee, and the withdrawal of her favour was the ultimate sanction. 'The "Mother" cast off several who sought parish relief at Lymington, and one night she called up a woman who had three children and told her that she must leave, and leave she did at once, she and her little ones, and sought refuge at Lymington, saying that the Lord had willed that she should leave; but not a word of complaint against the "Mother" for turning her out in the night.' Yet this was an emancipated band: led by a woman, its female members might even be exalted over men. What annoyed some – mostly men – was that Mary Ann was not at home performing the duties of her sex, but abroad, preaching as an equal, and denying men the rights of the marital bed. Whatever its other proscriptions, Victorian Britain was not a celibate state, and as it was predicated on the family unit, so it relied on a producing, consuming and expanding populace to sustain it. By proscribing against sex, capital and reproduction, Mary Ann not only questioned their morality, she subverted the tenets of the age.

Yet for all their apparent impracticality, the Girlingites' commune seemed to work – at first. The men laboured in the field or maintained the property or made shoes and boots. Harvesting carried out for others was seen as employment for the love of God – although contributions to the common fund were allowed. The women sewed and cooked and planted and, like the orphans in *The Children of the New Forest* (themselves refugees from a proscriptive regime), ventured into Lymington to buy supplies, using the common fund to pay for 'such goods as . . . cloth for garments and leather for boots and shoes, all of which were made on the premises'. They were a strange sight on the high street, these sisters in their mannish bloomers, as alien as the black-clad Amish in modern-day Pennsylvania – a colonial image enhanced by the broad-brimmed wide-awake hats worn by the Girlingite men. There was a bohemian, Rousseauesque air to these religious pioneers, and they wore their otherness as a badge as they intersected with the secular world. 'Several of the girls and young women took music lessons; they drove into Lymington and were taught the piano and singing; they always conducted themselves with propriety, and no vulgarity or anything bearing on immorality was ever observed by the Lymington people or the neighbours.' This was the idyll they were promised, as they danced on the green to 'the pleasing strains' of 'a Shaker band comprising fiddle, piano, triangles etc' playing 'The Campbells are Coming'; a gypsy bohemia here at the forest's edge.

Nor was theirs a lavish existence. 'Upon the land they grew many vegetables, but little corn, buying bread – not, I fear, all the bread they wanted, but such as they could', wrote the man from *The Times*, sent to report on Mary Ann's latest venture. 'Although none of them can be said to be educated, those to whom I spoke answered my questions intelligently and with a certain softness and refinement of manner and language by no means common to their class. In their talk with each other you could trace the same influence, showing itself in mutual deference and respect, and a quiet cheerfulness which was pleasant to see . . . The habit is cultivated, Mrs Girling said, and is soon communicated to new members.'

Glimpses of life among the Girlingites reveal snapshots of an innocent existence, 'on the lines which she believed had been lived by the Christian converts in the time of the Apostles'. Both young and old women curled their hair in ringlets, 'and threw it back over their necks like children – suggesting, no doubt, that they were children – the children of the Lord'. Inside the Lodge pet pigeons and doves flew freely, settling on the shoulders of the inhabitants who imbued these creatures of God with supernatural power, symbols of immortality and divine favour – a shamanic belief in animal spirits and the forces of nature. But these efforts towards Eden, in which one might imagine the Girlingites talking like St Francis to the deer and other fauna of the forest, did not seem entirely happy to visitors, who saw the sect's children dawdling in the yard, not playing, but moping in silence as if cowed by their elders' faith. Infant Girlingites were taught by 'two of the most capable young women' in a schoolroom which was decorated with a coloured print of the Madonna and Child and a woodcut of Napoleon III – a strange pairing of icons, not least because some (notably the Canadian eschatologist Michael Baxter, who had come to London in 1867 to publish his periodical, *Signs of Our Times*) claimed that the emperor was himself the anti-Christ.

Education was not a priority at the Lodge. Mary Ann believed 'that the smaller the acquaintance with the things that may be learned in books the better for their spiritual health, and a young

Shakeress who was found with a novel which a farmer in the neighbourhood had lent her was promptly told that such naughty reading would not open for her the gates of eternity'. Where other sects embraced progress, the Girlingites rejected it. Yet in other ways they presaged the future; and if the women's bloomers were emblems of equality associated with dress reform (as recommended by *Human Nature* to prevent fatal combustion), they also possessed an ambiguous sexuality: these pyjamas were both androgynous and drew attention to their gender. Loosened hair, too, was a symbol of moral laxity as well as innocence. And like their fellow bloomer-wearers, the Oneidans (with their own decidedly uncelibate approach to sexual relations), such signs encouraged others to believe that something wicked might be under way within that mysterious compound.

These paradoxes were amply exemplified by Mary Ann herself. In contemporary engravings she wears bloomers, but her sororial solidarity went only so far: 'however rigidly the other female members of the community renounce the pomps and vanities of dress and fashion, "Mother" Girling . . . affects great care as to her own personal adornment, even allowing her natural charms to be heightened by the glittering effects of jewellery'. Her Children might wear costumes consonant with their communal beliefs, but their matriarch maintained a sense of apartness, even glamour. She was a dressmaker, after all.

On the Lord's day, however, the utilitarian bloomers were put away and the women wore white dresses which, along with their uncovered hair, made them seem yet more ethereal as they spun about, their skirts billowing like clouds. Their lifting tresses and the oddly vacant expressions on their moon-like faces began to blur in the dance, as if, like the speeding scenery watched from a train, they moved too fast for the eye to focus upon. When one fell swooning from exhaustion, another took her place. The otherworldly yet sensual vision of these whirling virgins with their flying ringlets endowed them with fantastic appearance – and encouraged persistent rumours that Mary Ann mesmerised her followers to keep them under her control. Soon suspicion began to turn in on the sect. To nonbelievers, the Girlingite way of life and its most conspicuous expression – the weekly services to which the public were admitted in a spirit of openness and honest faith – was not just irreligious; it was evidence of a preternatural power. Surely no Christian faith could make these people spin so? As witchcraft's greatest threat was seen as the ability of its practitioners to recruit the souls of the possessed, so Mary Ann was accused of enchantment – as if, even now, the hysteria of the seventeenth century might resurface in the nineteenth.

Such beliefs had certainly not died away. Only three years before, the *Telegraph* had reported the trial of Emma Gregory, 'a woman living in a wild district in North Hants . . . called "the cunning woman of Newbury"', who claimed to be able to locate some goods stolen from two local women. 'She went through an absurd ceremony, and pretended to bring the image of the man who had stolen the things in a glass which she produced. She said she ruled the stars, and that if the nights were fine she would be able to get the lost things back tomorrow.' Having charged a shilling for this service, Gregory was found to have had seven previous convictions 'for offences of a like nature', and was sentenced to five years' penal servitude. It seemed that the authorities were of a mind to come down hard on such trickery: 'The Recorder said that such practices as those by which the prisoner had gained a livelihood for many years were a scandal to society.'

Scientific minds had an answer to the sorcery practised by Mary Ann. They reasoned that she must be exerting some sort of psychological slavery, and they looked to the spiritualist and mesmeric experiments which Maurice Davies had witnessed. As another cleric would conclude, how else could one explain her 'extraordinary influence and power . . . in this matter-of-fact age', other than by 'some secret attraction, some powerful magnetic drawing force'? It was the kind of mystery that both scandalised and fascinated Victorian observers. But for one man, these intimations of unknown forces were about to change the course of his life.

Far from the forest and its cool depths, Andrew Peterson had had enough of the Indian sun. For half his working life he had endured the heat and the dust, seen the poverty, and laboured in the shadow of Calcutta's whitened minarets and the dry hills beyond. It was time to return to England's green fields.

At the age of sixty-one, Andrew Thomas Turton Peterson could look back on a colourful life. Born in Wakefield in 1813 to a trading family of American-Dutch descent, after three years at school he had run away to sea and later worked at an Indian salt works. Back in England, he trained as a lawyer and married Charlotte Myers St Clair, daughter of a Royal Artillery colonel. In 1846, with their daughter, Anna Augusta, the family left for Calcutta, where Peterson spent twenty-two years before the Supreme Court, an occupation which earned him fees of up to £24,000 and a place in the city's expatriate society, presided over by the official hostess at Government House, Julia Margaret Cameron. Her father was a judge and her husband President of the Law Commission, and the future photographer would have known Peterson well. But now, like the Camerons, he wanted to return home, to pursue his hobbies: farming and building. 'Fearing the English climate and thinking of picking out a spot where I could feel the benefit of the Gulf Stream . . . I purchased a small house and a hundred acres of ground a few miles from the sea, almost opposite the Needles in the Isle of Wight.'

Drum Duan (named by its former owner, another retired Anglo-Indian) lay just across the Solent from Freshwater and the Camerons' Dimbola Lodge. Here, on the edge of the forest, between Hordle and Sway, Peterson acquired more land, and built a new mansion; not of Hampshire brick, but of concrete, a material he had seen used in India but which had been little employed in the West since Roman times. With another empire turning the globe pink, it was a propitious time to revive its qualities: taking gravel from forest pits, sand and shingle from the beach and cement from Portland, Peterson sought not to construct new imperial cities, but to facilitate another world entirely – that of the spirit.

'But what is concrete? the reader may ask', wrote Peterson's new friend – none other than James Burns, publisher of *Human Nature* and its weekly counterpart *Medium and Daybreak*, for whose readership he duly supplied the answer. 'The word signifies a compound or combination. A plum pudding is undoubtedly "concrete", and indeed the material of which we write bears not a little resemblance to that well-known and highly relished viand.' While Mary Ann invited journalists to her commune, Peterson summoned Burns to Arnewood Towers to witness his experiments. The editor was by turns culinary and alchemical in his enthusiastic metaphors: 'The pebbles and sand are carefully washed, so as to purge them of any earthy matter . . . In due proportions they are combined with a brown powder supplied in bags, and water is added till the whole acquires the consistency, as a wag put it, of brown sugar properly wetted and sanded by the honest grocer, before the family retire to prayers.'

Burns was as excited by this wonder stuff as was his friend, as though it bore a relationship to the cloudy ectoplasm which constituted his own psychic experiments. 'Soon it becomes harder than any building stone. The pebbles and particles of sand seem so detachable that a projecting piece might be broken off with the finger and thumb, but to do so would require some labour with a hammer and chisel. The whole structure becomes one solid stone, and it is said the longer it stands the harder it grows.' These constructions would stand for perpetuity, growing stronger rather than weaker with the years: this was indeed the material with which to build empires on earth or in the sky. Yet there were other, political reasons for Burns' interest in Peterson's project: its spiritualistic overtones (which we shall soon discover), and its philanthropy.

Arnewood Towers had been transformed 'from a small villa into a commodious country residence of somewhere near forty rooms, with the necessary outbuildings, built entirely of concrete . . . The proprietor was his own architect throughout, and the whole work was performed under his personal superintendance by the unskilled labour supplied by the district. Everything is substantial, elegant, capacious and convenient'; from 'roomy and well-ventilated' cellars to ceilings 'formed of gently undulating arches resting on iron girders', all was of a whole, 'as much so as if it had been carved out of quarry'. It also had the added benefit of being 'practically indestructible': 'The contents of a room might be consumed, but the house itself would not burn, and in the case of an accident the conflagration might be confined to the apartment in which it occurred.'

Like the later technological wonder, the unsinkable *Titanic* with its water-tight chambers, this was a design to defy disaster: a futuristic, utopian, Jules Verne architecture, aesthetically and practically pleasing at the same time. 'The drawing-room presents a succession of these graceful arches, and the effect contrasts most favourably with that of the common flat ceiling. Where the arches meet on the girder, the under surface is ornamented with elegant mouldings.' In tones reminiscent of *The Stones of Venice*, Burns evoked a new Renaissance in concrete; an uplifting edifice which might play host to angels, even as it augured the modernism of a century to come – more Le Corbusier than Charles Barry in its conflation of architectural and philosophical ambitions.

To Burns, it seemed that Peterson was building a new world, here in the heart of Hampshire: 'Concrete is seen everywhere; in the stables and other offices; the cottages of coachman, gardener, bailiff and others.' 'There is not a solid foot of stonework or brick to be seen anywhere. Ponds, aqueducts, gate-pillars, steps, garden walls, sheds, – even the table on which the gardener pots his plants – are all of concrete. All the moulding and ornamental work about the place – and taste and beauty are shown everywhere – are composed of the same material.' Soon it seemed the entire county might be housed in concrete. Yet preoccupied as he was with construction, Peterson was moving towards another dimension – one to which Mary Ann Girling had shown the way.

'At the time when I was beginning to get wearied of the life I was leading, an event happened which has entirely altered the whole tenor of my life, and which for nearly ten years has in one form or the other occupied my attention.'

> This event was the arrival of Mrs Girling and her followers, who have since attained so much notoriety under the name of the 'New Forest Shakers'. Her strange doctrines, the dancing, twisting, and contortions of her proselytes made a considerable stir . . . Many from the neighbouring villages joined her ranks, over whom she had a complete sway as if they had been mere children.

Peterson was fascinated by Mary Ann's strange power. Two of his own workers had joined the sect, 'and after that became not only utterly useless, but . . . greatly disturbed the minds of their fellow labourers'. His neighbours were experiencing similar problems, among them a gentleman 'who had had church preferment somewhere in Suffolk, near the place from whence came Mrs Girling and some of her leading proselytes'. By remarkable coincidence, Reverend Edward Mortimer Clissold, MA, had been rector at St Nicholas in the parish of Wrentham, just fifteen miles or so from Little Glemham.

Born in 1828, and therefore a coeval of Mary Ann, Clissold came from a clerical family with interests as unconventional as Maurice Davies'. One of his kinsmen was Reverend Augustus Clissold of Stoke Newington, Swedenborgian, and author of

SANCTA COENA; or, The Holy Supper, Explained on the Principles Taught by Emanuel Swedenborg and *A Review of the Principles of Apocalyptical Interpretation.* Edward Clissold – who had served at Wrentham in the 1850s and 1860s, when Mary Ann first became active in the area – had a more sceptical attitude towards psychic matters. He was also rather wealthy, and had retired to Yeatton House, a substantial white stucco villa set back from the road in park-like grounds, close to Peterson's Arnewood Towers – and to New Forest Lodge.

Clissold was to become a nemesis for the Children of God. Knowing their reputation from home, he would become a kind of sect-rescuer, to whom Suffolk families turned in the hope of retrieving loved ones. 'There has been a constant ebb and flow of deluded fanatics and ruined outcasts,' he wrote.

> Some have come here with money, furniture, and tools, and in a few weeks have had to tramp their way home sadder and wiser men. Fathers have come down seeking in vain for their daughters. I hold now in my possession a letter from a poor woman who in the most piteous manner begs me to rescue her two daughters (both under 21 years of age), who have for two years been members of this community. Another case is that of a poor man, a platelayer on the Great Eastern Railway, who has come down here twice in search of his two daughters, both under 21 years of age. He was only able to rescue one, while the younger girl (under 16 years) is still with Mrs Girling.

Although he did not admit to it in his letters on the subject to *The Times*, it was Clissold's pre-knowledge of Girlingism which had established Mary Ann's mesmeric powers as 'fact'. He told the newspaper how, shortly after the sect arrived in Hordle, his gardener came to him one morning to announce that he and his wife and children were leaving to join the commune; not only that, but Clissold's boot-boy was going too. 'You cannot wonder, Sir,' the clergyman wrote, 'that I began to feel an interest in a religious society which deprived me of two such useful members.' Clissold was convinced his staff had been mesmerised – just as a footman at the newly-built Palace House at Beaulieu had persuaded Lord Henry Scott's butler to accompany him to the Lodge, where the underling had 'caught the contagion of the dancing, and began himself to twirl around'. Having dragged the footman outside, the butler took him back to the great hall to serve at a grand dinner party that night, only for the underling to start spinning again. Such scenes compare to early Shaker history, in which the young came to scoff, only to be 'surrounded by the brethren and sisters . . . so great was the strength and power of God in the assembly, that they were unable to make any resistance; but were compelled to dance . . .' A generation earlier, Robert Southey had suggested that the mass hysteria of Primitive Methodism was a kind of mesmerism, 'a new disease'. It was a diagnosis which both Clissold and Peterson would apply to Girlingism.

Since Anton Mesmer's experiments in the eighteenth century, mesmerism had become a means by which the metaphysical might be explained. As science struggled to interpret the world, progress threw off eccentric sparks, and mesmerism had followed 'the aftershock of electricity' in a quest which equated as much with alchemy as alienism. Mesmer's mysterious, unseen and universal fluid echoed Newton's theory that space was occupied by an Aetherial Medium, and that 'every movement in the world was the immediate effect of God's power' (itself a precursor of modern chaos theory). Newton, who was depicted by Blake in a kind of undersea cave, measuring the ocean floor as though weighed down by the material world he had defined, also believed in alchemy and Rosicrucianism and had calculated the date of the Second Coming. For an era trying to reconcile the Communion of Saints with natural philosophy, the empirical search for the soul produced strange, chimeric conflations of magic and science – such as those conducted in a London suburb in the late 1830s by the mesmerist and clairvoyant John Dove during his search for 'an occult spiritual essence . . . a special tincture which could not only convert the baser metals into gold, but transmute the physical, corrupt and decaying man into the Angelic, Immortal and Christ-like Man'.

Andrew Peterson, too, had his own experience of mesmerism: 'I had seen some of it in the early days of Dr Elliotson; and some of my personal friends had operated, and others of them had been operated on.' John Elliotson had established Mesmeric Infirmaries in London and Bristol in the 1830s and had founded the *Zoist*, a journal dedicated to explaining the power behind mesmerism. A Fellow of the Royal College of Surgeons and one of the first doctors to use a stethoscope (and acupuncture), Elliotson employed mesmerism both to heal and to anaesthetise, and had many upper-class adherents. He practised in his own drawing room, using mesmerised water, gold and silver – as if irradiating inanimate matter with a part homeopathic, part alchemical charge – and his clients included 'some fifty or sixty of the highest society in London'. Among them were William Makepeace Thackeray, Wilkie Collins and Charles Dickens, who wrote, 'If my own life, or my wife's, or that of either of my children were in peril tomorrow, I would trust it to him, implicitly.' Dickens took lessons from Elliotson and practised mesmerism on his wife. Harriet Martineau was another patient and tried to convert Charlotte Brontë. 'Scarcely', said Brontë, 'yet I heard miracles of its efficacy and could hardly discredit the whole of what was told me.' Even the Queen had recourse to 'magnetism' to cure the ailing arm of her son.

Patronised by the great and the good, mesmerism spread around the world. 'Mr Lewis, a gentleman of colour', recorded successful healings with the mesmeric pass in Africa and the Caribbean, and in Calcutta in 1845 James Esdaile had persuaded city officials to give him his own hospital – although tellingly, his patients, or subjects, were Indian. 'Esdaile had persistence like Elliotson's,' wrote Frederic Myers, the psychical researcher, '. . . the long series of carefully-noted, carefully-figured operations which he performed under mesmeric anaesthesia upon Hindoos in the Calcutta Hospital made it impossible for any candid inquirer to doubt longer that the mesmeric trance was a real, a valuable discovery.' As a result of these colonial experiments, Esdaile was promoted to the highest medical post in Calcutta – a position in which he inevitably came into contact with Peterson, who noted that Esdaile had done 'wonderful things'. Peterson's interest in mesmerism reflected the curiosity of the age, and many agreed with the Queen who believed that mesmerism and spiritualism drew on the same mysterious force; but it was not until the arrival of his phenomenal neighbours, 'these New Forest Shakers' and 'their fantastic movements', that the former lawyer began a more serious investigation.

One Sunday afternoon, a group arrived in Hordle from Southampton, led by a Sergeant-Major Millin. A retired soldier turned travelling mesmerist, Millin was something of a showman himself. He called at Yeatton House, where he told Clissold that he and a Wesleyan minister had attended a Girlingite meeting 'and felt certain, from what he had seen, that the whole affair was managed by mesmerism . . . He had witnessed the peculiar dancing, stupors, visions, &c, and that he, as a professional mesmeriser, was in this habit of producing similar delusions at his lectures.' At the Lodge, Millin and Clissold watched as 'a Shaker man was spreading dung in front of the house, when he threw down his fork and began to dance', much as the American Shakers had done while tending their fields. Millin 'went and brought him to' (although Mary Ann would later identify the dancing young man as one of the outside brethren, Harry Buttles, and said that Millin 'struck him on the shoulder, but it had no more effect than though he never touched him'). Millin then taught Clissold 'how to do it, and he brought 10 or 15 to their sense. Then Mrs Girling called all the people inside and said they mustn't go to work for the wicked people any more, and from that time they had done nothing beyond working for themselves. They were under her influence. When the influence was not quite removed, a person was just as likely to carry on the experiments at any time, in the night, or in the street.'

These semi-public demonstrations convinced Clissold 'that the simple folk – my gardener, to wit, and the shoe boy, and others – who saw the pretended visions, and were under the firm impression that the Holy Spirit was operating on them, in reality were the unconscious objects of animal magnetism'. He conceded that this was an unpopular explanation, 'seeing that it at once knocks on the head all the poetry and romance, to say nothing of the religious element', but he would hold it until he was 'better informed'.

Millin would become an earthly instrument in Clissold's anti-Girlingite campaign. Peterson, however, took the investigation to another level. Having invited the sergeant to give private 'mesmeric entertainments', he was fascinated by the way in which Millin brought subjects under his influence: 'He could will them to do what he wished without a word spoken by him.' Soon Peterson was taking private lessons from Millin, 'and after a time . . . I found that I could put in abeyance both the mind and body of the patient under my influence. I could make him do what I willed; I could make him think, talk and see what I willed . . . I could make him insensible to force operating on his body, but at the same time painfully sensitive to any pain inflicted on mine.'

To Peterson this will to power seemed to go beyond human physicality. 'I could silently picture to my mind a particular tableau, and Will him to see and describe it,' Peterson reported of his experiments with an unwitting employee. 'I could Will him to eat cabbage leaves and think them plum cake, or drink water and fancy it wine. I could Will a limb to be limp or rigid as I liked.' But what use were these feats? Surely they had more meaning than 'amusing exhibitions . . . utterly useless as far as regards the masses of mankind'? As a man of radical ambitions, Peterson saw that if mesmerism could displace one will with his own, then this was proof that the soul existed separately from the body. This realisation sent him on an extraordinary and potentially dangerous journey of self-discovery – one which would change the skyline of the forest itself.

In the villages and towns around the New Forest, there was already a discernible opposition to the Girlingites. *Our Social Circle – A Manuscript Magazine devoted to the interests of Young Men*, 'published' in Ringwood as a hand-written journal and intricately lettered in black and violet ink with verse, anecdotes and delicate drawings of ships, included a clipping from the *Hampshire Independent* describing the scene in the Lodge's chapel when the village postman had fallen groaning to the floor, seemingly dead, only to be brought back to life by Mary Ann. 'With all due respect for all that is *real* and *good* in the religious life & practices of the "Shakers",' wrote the high-minded young editor, 'we do not hesitate to characterise such performances as described in this "cutting" as being most detestible & disgusting. We never indulge in feelings of bigotry, but cannot really wink at innovations in the professed worship of the true God, which are copied from the heathenish practices of idolators.'

Yet for other young people there was something exciting, romantic and magnetic about what was going on in Hordle, and they were drawn there by the heady promise of religious revolution and drug-like euphoria. The forest seemed to enable such magical, shamanic transformations. Even in the mid-nineteenth century it remained a place of residual supernatural belief, the 'very home of fancy and imagination' where the shape-shifting Puck or Robin Goodfellow played tricks on unwary mortals. One contemporary historian claimed 'no one is so superstitious' as the New Forest peasant, for whom 'fairies lived among the trees'; other spirits could abduct unwary infants should they step inside a fairy ring or pick bluebells in the woods. These tales would haunt the Girlingites, too, in their own troublesome relationship with children – even as they themselves were lost or enchanted innocents in the wilderness.

Myth seemed to gather around the Hordle colony. The Victorian psyche embraced Robin Hood as a forest outlaw, an incarnation of the Green Man or Herne the Hunter in his guise of antlers and mantling. It was an escapism enacted through Alfred Tennyson's *Idylls of the King*, Julia Margaret Cameron's fantastic tableaux and William Morris's fascination with Malory's *Morte d'Arthur*, a Pre-Raphaelite dream of a lost England. Arthurian romance permeated popular culture: Gustav Doré's etchings reimagined Merlin as a Druid mage in woods where roots and branches curled like entangling serpents, while Richard Dadd, sequestered in his asylum cell, painted nightmarish visions of fairies and goblins in some semi-subterranean forest bower. It was a potent alternative to industrial modernity. From William Rufus to rumours of still-surviving covens, the forest had ever been a site of sacrifice and magic. Now it was a locus for the century's psychic struggles, contained within its abiding remoteness – for all that it was three hours' train ride from London.

In this legendary setting, Mary Ann achieved a power beyond herself – despite, or perhaps because of her lowly rural origins. She was both witch and demagogue, weaving a spell with her wild gestures; beckoning, hectoring, cajoling, offering a new way of life entirely. It was the same strange dynamic which operates when a group falls under the influence of a leader – a collective experience which permits the domination of the will as faith tips from trust to blind obedience. In an uncertain world, it is reassuring to have someone tell you what to do and how to live; to submit like a lover to a superior power. It is a force communicated in prophetic signs and emotionally-charged wonders, more to do with instinct than intellect. Little wonder, then, that Girlingism, drawing on folk memory and disseminated by an ill-educated and possibly psychologically-damaged Suffolk housewife, exerted an awful control.

Years later, the local Baptist minister was told of a young man who had run away to be married, only to be found in a relative's house, hiding in terror under the bed 'as Mother would be after him!'

And yet there was an ambivalence to the fascination – perhaps even obsession – which men such as Clissold and Peterson felt for Mary Ann. On one hand they sought to disprove or explain her feminine powers; on the other they were beguiled by them, like John Sirgood, or the priest obsessed by the gypsy Esmeralda in Hugo's *The Hunchback of Notre Dame*. Or perhaps they saw their own potential for control, like Svengali bringing Trilby under his sway. Inevitably, that vexed question of sexuality encouraged yet more rumours. The Girlingites' effusive kisses and ecstatic dances, their emancipated dress, the families persuaded to live apart as brothers and sisters with their 'sacred mother'; all these broke the bounds of normal relationships and rendered young men and women prone to unnatural or illicit ones. Mary Ann's anti-marriage message of celibacy brought with it paradoxical notions of free love, if not incest. Their chapel doors may have been open on the Sabbath, but who knew what went on in the Lodge during the week? Overflowing dormitories and a closed compound deepened such suspicions, while those men and women who did 'escape' reported that while 'praising God in the dance', both sisters and brothers took off their clothes. It was even said 'that several children have died since their residence at New Forest Lodge, and have been buried in the grounds of their place *sans* ceremony'. Ann Lee's Shakers had faced similar accusations – with their overtones of ritual magic – a century before. Perhaps stillborn babies were interred on the site; certainly rural areas were susceptible to the 'disposal' of unwanted children: from the legend of the Babes in the Wood, to Thomas Hardy's tales of pools 'wherein nameless infants had been used to disappear', and newspaper reports of the bodies of five-day-old infants found washed up on the sea shore.

But Mary Ann declared that 'sin and shame . . . came into the world together', and denied 'any indecency in worship or elsewhere'; she insisted that great care was taken to 'divide the sexes and to make life blameless'. Fifty years later, the last Girlingites would testify to 'only one lapse from strict morality . . . during the whole time of their occupation of Forest Lodge . . . It is true that some of the children were fatherless and motherless, whose parents had joined the community then deserted it, leaving their little ones behind. But no steps were taken against them. Mrs Girling just took the children as an additional call for service to God in caring for his little ones as Jesus had taught them.' It was as if these orphans had taken the place of Mary Ann's own lost infants.

The currency of rumour was the price of Mary Ann's success. As visitors to the colony came not only to stare but to stay, local churches lost parishioners to the charismatic new cult. Reverend Spackman of Sway watched aghast as a rival congregation grew before his eyes, 'aided by the fluency of the mother and by the glowing descriptions of penny-a-liners who were invited to gain information by living among them, and by the reports circulated even by religious papers of their fervency, self-sacrifice, and devoted piety – reports with about as much truth as that of the pretended dwarf and dog fight in the Midland Counties'. With their commune now constituting more than one-fifth of the population of the seven-hundred-strong Hordle parish, the Girlingites were a substantial body with potential new colonies in Ryde and Bristol, and new believers back in Suffolk and London awaiting confirmation.

This was the heyday of Girlingism, fast becoming a movement – with all the implications that might entail. Its tenets reflected greater anxieties about social change and raised questions of order and freedom, and as such began to concern the state – from the practical problems of how to deal with a large group of people who rejected the authority of law, employment and property, to the philosophic dilemma of their insistence on their own immortality. How could one impose the regularities of normal life on a people who not only believed they would not die, but imminently expected the Second Coming of Christ? A people who, indeed, believed they had *already* died, and now lived without sin? It was this sense of opposition – the faithful Girlingites versus the venal State, religious freedom versus social control – which made the situation so implacable. In this light, Spackman's reservations as a representative of the Established Church, part of that vested estate, were understandable. It was hardly in his interest to encourage this ragged band of communists.

The vicar's concern grew as the Family and their compound swelled: a place of dancing sectarians speaking in tongues and seeing visions; a foreign presence on Hampshire soil. 'Converts – chiefly from Suffolk, or from a distance, enrolled themselves, some bringing as much as £300 with them; these were mostly old ladies,' Spackman wrote. 'Sheds were built, one large one as a place for prayer meetings, others for workshops and dwelling-houses . . . carpenters, bricklayers, mechanics, farmers, increased the number (the poor were not so welcome), and by June [1874] they counted 150.' As part of the recruitment drive, journalists were invited to the Lodge (as they had been to the Girlingites' London venues) to observe and even live with the sect – a technique employed by Frederick Evans at Mount Lebanon and perhaps suggested by James Haase. Indeed one correspondent turned Girlingite himself: having witnessed Mary Ann's power, he went home and prayed for eleven days, 'and shed thousands of tears before he was able to believe, and that happened one evening in his own home as he was reading in the Bible about the conversion of Paul and Silas's gaoler, and he cried and laughed for joy all that night'.

It seemed that the entire neighbourhood might go Girlingite. The compound was taken up with the faithful: every available space was filled. Some were reduced to sleeping in the barn, like stabled cattle or bundled Buchanites; to them, Mary Ann would cite the circumstances of their Saviour's birth. Her mission even overflowed into the outer world, with the establishment of 'outside brethren' – such as Thomas Ackland, a young carpenter from neighbouring Tiptoe – who practised in their own homes, and who would soon prove valuable allies.

Yet none of these willing hands was making any money. There was a modern precedent for this proscription: in the 1850s, John Brown, the crystal seer of Nottingham, had been told by the Angel Gabriel, 'Behold! God hath said that buying, selling, or traffic for gain in the produce of the earth is an abomination to him.' For the Girlingites, communality was itself a manumission: Mary Ann declared 'that they should be perfectly free; that they were not to work for hire'. But to others the embargo seemed perverse and the Children of God merely lazy. Reverend Spackman turned a sardonic eye upon their Canaan, and contrasted its ideals with the control effected by their Mother: 'Here liberty, however, does not seem to have been so well understood as equality and fraternity, for soon some few of the members . . . wishing to retire from a body for which they felt themselves unfitted found a difficulty in doing so, at least with any of their property.' Yet such tyranny was contradicted in parables resonant with the kind of devotion shown to Ann Lee: 'An adult male who wished to leave the Society sought the intervention of the police for the purpose of reclaiming his property from the common stock. But when his little package was made up and he went to say good-bye to "Mother", his heart sank, and he returned like a lamb to the fold.'

Some accounted for Mary Ann's autocracy as a result of previous sins; far from a holy woman, they saw her as a moral recidivist. 'Her old imperious temper showed itself . . . she thought only of the increase of her "Family", and this was coupled with the conception of Queenship; for she would tolerate no rival in her government, or to share her prerogative.' In her attempt at autonomy, Mary Ann might be accused of not really knowing what she was doing; at worst, her doctrines were a fraud and her commune built on nothing more than hot air. 'Those who had brought money, thinking themselves entitled to subsist on the labours of those who had brought none, lived a life of idleness, the disregard of those social laws the observance of which is necessary for the preservation of any community threw them into debt.' And ironically, it was money which proved to be their undoing.

In December 1873 the Family were unable to meet the half-yearly interest of £25 on their mortgage. Although they were given time to pay, in April 1874 the sum remained outstanding. A writ was issued and in May the bailiffs arrived and seized two horses and three cows. These were auctioned for £130, although one of the elders, probably Isaac Batho, said he'd been offered £70 for one horse alone. As their debt amounted to £40, this meant that they were now owed £90. The elder also pointed out that 'the execution was levied on the goods of Miss Wood as the mortgager, but the goods actually taken were those of the whole community'.

Like any other victims of financial misfortune, having fallen below the plimsoll line of solvency, the Children of God began to sink fast. In June the interest period came around; again they were unable to pay. Deprived of their stock and with sixty elderly or underage members to support, their position grew desperate. Without their cows they could no longer give milk to the children – 'of whom there are 40, mostly taken by the society out of charity' – and they had to buy in supplies, 'which . . . left them in lower water than ever'. Brethren began to leave, 'some openly and others surreptitiously'. Their diet was reduced to vegetables, mostly potatoes, and by the end of the year the adults were living without food or hot drinks for three days at a time. Yet still they would not ask the sheriff for the balance due to them from the sale of their stock, as 'they thought it would be applied towards payment of the accruing interest without their intervention', *The Times* reported. 'One heard these lame explanations with almost as much anger as pity . . . There was the money, their very own, which might have been had for the asking. It would have satisfied the mortgagee's claim twice, nearly three times over. Yet they did not ask for it, and the mortgagee knew nothing of such a fund.'

By autumn 1874 the communal fund had ebbed to a dangerous low. Living beyond their means, it was as if capital were wreaking its prosaic revenge on the Children of God. In October, three months after the latest instalment of interest was due, the mortgagee served a writ of eviction. Yet Mary Ann remained defiant. 'All who bought and sold', she said, 'would receive the mark of the Beast, either on their hands or foreheads'. And if she bore the wounds of the Lord, then they would bear the mark of the devil.

Edward Horatio Moore, the sheriff's officer, and later town clerk of Lymington, then aged seventy-three, would describe the whole business as 'one of the most disagreeable he had had to conduct'. He was stung by allegations about the ruthlessness with which his office had acted. On 5 December, Moore advised Mary Ann to pack up their possessions and find somewhere else to live. Her reply was that 'the Lord would protect his people'. The sect still believed that its account was in credit, and that the money owed to it covered the debt (although it seems that the stubborn, or possibly deluded, Julia Wood had apparently refused to accept the surplus when offered to her). It was not an unreasonable presumption, and in hindsight it seems that the mortgagee, the bailiffs, and the solicitors acted all too strictly within the letter of the law, and with a degree of disingenuousness in which could be read a determination to rid Hordle of its troublesome tenants. Up to the last moment, the Girlingites believed that the Lord would stay the due process of law; but His attention was elsewhere that day, and at 11 am on 15 December, forty men – 'a posse of sheriff's officers and helpers' – began their work.

SIX

The Dark and Trying Hour

> We bought, but we did not sell – Christ did not sell. We have no marriages or giving in marriage. We never close our doors at the service, or wish to keep people out. We have no secrets and defy the world to say we have not lived in purity.
>
> Mary Ann Girling

Above the forest road, against a sky turning from violet to the colour of cocoa, the wind was beginning to catch the black tangle of trees, each swaying as though reaching up for what remained of the light. Ahead lay the Lodge, its chapel overflowing with the faithful. In the lamplight their faces were animated and glowing, warmed by their hymns. Through windows coursed with rivers of rain they watched as branches bent this way and that until it seemed they would be torn into the air and crash to the roof. Inside, the men were going about their work efficiently. Bundles of clothes bound like papooses were unceremoniously heaved through the door. Strong-armed and stupid-faced, the gang looked forward only to the rest of their reward as they carried out chairs, desks, tables and stools; five were required to manhandle the piano, its veneer splattered with rain, the soft felt of its hammers strumming a discordant glissando as it was dumped at the side of the road.

To saddened observers, this pathetic drama was the work of a hard-hearted world, and they looked to history for a precedent. It was 'a scene probably without its like in England during the present century', claimed the *Hampshire Chronicle*; to another newspaper 'no Irish eviction was ever equal to it'; while another considered that it was 'conducted like a Highland clearance'. These were emotional comparisons: the Irish Famine of a generation earlier and the Scottish enclosures of a century before evoked the arrogance of one class over another, and in doing so cast this Hampshire pogrom into the shadow of imperial intolerance.

Gathered in the chapel and its upper room were twenty men, fifty women and sixty-six children. From their dormitory loft with its fifty beds, they watched as their possessions were tumbled through the trap-door like coal into a cellar. 'The men who were clearing out the effects made all the noise they could in knocking about the iron bedsteads, and dancing to drown the Shakers' singing.' The process was all the more painful for the fact that it had taken all day: even as the men carried out their work, the faithful ate their last supper of boiled carrots, potatoes, turnips, onions and pumpkins, 'having been living on one daily meal of vegetables for some time past'. Onlookers described their features as pallid from malnutrition, yet 'their eyes were sparkling with unearthly brightness; all seemed joyous and happy, as if a fete was in progress'. It was as though they embraced their calamity as a portent of things to come. Some sang hymns, some danced, others were on their knees, praying that 'the Lord might forgive the poor men who had been employed to rob them of their homes', while their elders watched, occasionally shouting, 'Praise Him', 'Praise His name', and 'Blessed be Christ'. One stout and elderly woman danced for two hours, spinning round and round.

It seems both ironic and cruel that an audience was admitted to witness this drama, a pantomimic replication of the Girlingites' earlier performances. Thirty or forty locals came into the chapel, singing their own songs, abusing the colonists and imitating their dancing, 'but however irritating their remarks or actions, they could not solicit one angry word or even a remonstration from any one of them'. And so it proceeded, like some mad opera played against a lithographic backdrop: the praying and dancing Girlingites; the chorus of hissing peasants; the mechanicals moving the scenery; and at the centre of the storm, Mary Ann, a consoling messiah as their Eden unravelled. Like common paupers unable to pay the rent, their belongings were turfed out into the lane, shamefully exposed to public view, a catalogue of attempted Utopia: 'furniture, equipments of grocery, tailors', shoemakers', and carpenters' shops, contents of outbuildings, farm produce, potatoes, a

THE LYMINGTON "SHAKERS:"

stack of beans, one of barley straw, oat straw, &c', all 'deposited at the road-side, near the lodge, in two lines, each over 150 yards long.'

The scale of the removal made for a sensational spectacle. 'There were 77 bedsteads, beds, and bedding, and other furniture in proportion. To complete the removal, 40 men were employed, and four waggons and teams. Several of the Hants Constabulary were present, but took no part in the proceedings.' As their beds were shoved over the hedge or through the gate, the Girlingites made

CTMENT FROM NEW FOREST LODGE.

no effort to save or protect their possessions; instead they said, 'It is the Lord's! He will provide!' At five o'clock it was their turn. The crowd were ordered out – apparently in an attempt to protect the dignity of the sect – and the Girlingites were asked to leave. 'This, however, they refused to do unless they were led off, and the sheriff's officer now had a difficult task on his hands . . . with the assistance of the police, he quickly escorted them into the road in the midst of their furniture, taking the "mother of the flock", Mrs Girling, first.' An easterly wind blew through the trees as they came tumbling out, greeted by gawpers who hung about the gate. The Children of God ignored their jeers, gathered around Mary Ann and resumed their hymns, 'whilst the crowd kept time by singing songs', until rain set in and sent the persecutors scurrying home.

The nation thrilled to reports from the scene. *The Pictorial World*'s artist drew a screen of conifers planted between the Lodge and the road, imbuing it with a sense of secrecy. Under snow-laden trees, the bailiff's men haul articles into the lane while women and children huddle at the verge; the reference to the Great Hunger was plain. Towering over the group is an enormous, pathetic pile of bedding, while the stark gothic Lodge is lost behind the trees, as though the forest itself were repossessing it. One man balances a dining room chair on his head. An orator declaims to the crowd, calling on God to witness this injustice. Black-caped policemen represent law and order; they and the secular observers – ladies in rich dark gowns, gentlemen in sleek top hats – stand to one side, finely drawn in close-hatched lines, while the sectarians seem more faintly sketched, fading into the wintry landscape like peasants out of a novel set on the Russian steppes.

Near the Lodge gates the Girlingites set up a temporary shelter. Some children were given refuge in a neighbouring cottage and one sick woman was taken by her husband to a place of safety, but other offers of help were rejected. Edward Clissold arrived on the scene and, assisted by the parish schoolmaster, carried several children into an adjoining barn – only for their parents to fetch them out again.

'Would I accept shelter from those very parties who have been the most earnest in persecuting me, and who have done their utmost to injure me?' asked Mary Ann. 'Besides, under what condition was the shelter offered? That only the women and children should come in; that the men should stay out and perish for aught they cared. Any that wished may have gone; but no – no one would leave us – we will not be parted.' She would never leave her Children, and they would never leave her, and so they stayed on the road all night, 'singing and praying by turns; or, when moved by the Spirit, dancing after their manner'. 'They may be strange people and have strange customs,' acknowledged one reporter, 'but all those I saw were animated with one spirit of unbounded faith and love towards Mrs Girling, their "Dear Mother".' And in an echo of the threats made to her in Walworth, he added, 'I doubt not any of them would gladly be burnt alive if she had told them it was her wish.'

By now a gale was blowing from the east, and heavy rain gave way to sleet and snow. The sect took shelter behind the hedges, standing in ditches half full of water, where it was feared many would succumb to exposure: 'In this state a terrible night was passed, the sound of singing and praying mingling at intervals with the howling of the storm.' Later, Mary Ann would compose a hymn to mark their dark and trying hour:

Ye friends of Jesus, remember
the fifteenth last of December,
In eighteen hundred and seventy-four,
A people turned out in number six score.
    And yet they sang
    'We'll swell the song
    That Jesus will come
    And take us home.'

As in the road they all did stand,
No shelter had this little band,
Their hands were linked together in love,
And their hearts were cheered by Jesu's love
    And yet they sang, etc.

From half-past five that night were seen
Storms of snow and heavy rain,
And falling upon that helpless band
As in the road they all that night did stand
    And yet they sang, etc.

It was no 'The Wreck of the Deutschland', but it said much about the steadfast Family and their indefatigable Mother. They would go on singing and dancing for some years yet.

At dawn the next morning, Vaggs Lane presented a sorry sight. Strewn along its verges was the human debris of the night's perfidy: clothes hung in hedges like ghostly figures; makeshift tents of sheets provided paltry shelter from the snow. Damp blankets draped over branches had frozen stiff, turning the trees into sepulchral monuments hollow to the sound of their inmates, now beginning to resurrect with first light. Over an open fire a kettle boiled, and stalwarts were trying to prepare breakfast for their fellows, for whom the memory of yesterday's disaster was vividly renewed by the ruin that lay around them; it was as if some giant's hand had delved into a human ant nest and dashed out the contents over the forest floor. Meanwhile, half-seen in the veil of mist, the spectral figure of Mother Girling quoted Scripture to console her stranded sheep.

Reporters, who had spent the evening comfortably in the Bell Inn, returned to the scene to record the next instalment for their readers. They found the Girlingites cold but defiant 'and sturdily refusing to leave the spot, saying they were in the Lord's hands and He would do with them as seemed to Him best'. There were those who were tempted, however. A young man 'of respectable appearance' was offered money by friends to pay for his journey home; others defied Mary Ann to work in a local brickfield. One story pointed up the pathos of their predicament: 'One little fellow, a sick boy of nine years of age, named Elkington, was brought into the Lymington Union by Dr Adams on Tuesday evening, and is being carefully attended to.' His father had joined the community, bringing 'everything he had – tools, household furniture, &c', only to find that he had 'exchanged plenty for poverty and starvation'. Having left his wife and children to look for work, he had read of the eviction in the newspapers and returned for his family. His wife refused to leave, 'but suffered him to take the children'.

To the disgust of their brethren, other apostates arrived to reclaim their possessions. One blacksmith hauled off a huge bellows, vice and anvil, as well as a chest of drawers. 'The only time I have seen any of their number at all to lose their habitual meekness and good temper was on this occasion when two brethren attempted to resist the seizure of bellows &c', wrote a reporter. Complicit in this bitter retrieval, the police were instructed to allow any former member to take whatever he claimed, 'in spite of the assurances of some of the faithful to the contrary. This action . . . has created great dissatisfaction among the Shakers, who state that the law is on one side only, and that they are oppressed and persecuted.' The scavengers contrasted with sympathisers such as Mr Palk, a local farmer, who brought the Girlingites bread, cheese and milk. But as night fell, another snowstorm blew up. By eight the snow was falling fast, and around eleven o'clock, Sergeant Simpkin of the local constabulary persuaded the sect – under threat of removal to the Lymington workhouse – to seek shelter in a nearby barn on Silver Street. Four brothers were deputed to patrol their possessions lest any further attempts were made on them. A day or so later, another farmer offered to store their piano, harmonium and good furniture, said to be valued at £1,000.

Mr Beasley's barn, twenty-five by fourteen feet, now housed seventy men and women. Next door, an even smaller cob-walled cottage served as Mary Ann's headquarters during the day and a dormitory for ten by night; the children, their teachers and the elderly were billeted with outside brethren. Asked what they were living on, one Girlingite said, 'We had "prayer" for breakfast, boiled swedes for dinner, and "prayer" for tea'; a spiritual diet 'washed down with a great deal of tea'. The same drug which had fuelled the long hours demanded by the industrial revolution and which had sustained Mary Ann during her perorations in the railway arch, now succoured the sect as they shivered in the fields which their peers had deserted in favour of towns and mills. It was a vivid illustration both of their impractical hopes, and of the exigencies of the age; their rural predicament was worse than the back-to-back slums of the city they had left behind.

Apart from the discomfort of their situation, there was the question of hygiene. Men and women had to wear the same clothes day and night as they huddled together – unable to change for decency's sake – with no light save that which came through the barn door, and only straw to lie on. The weather continued to freeze, but they were resolute. 'If we are turned out of this barn we will go together into the road again,' said Mary Ann. 'If they take us to gaol we will go there, but all together. The spirit of the Lord will preserve us, as it did on that bitter night, when, although drenched to the skin, no harm came to us.'

Like some nineteenth-century narrative painting – Ford Madox Brown's *The Last of England*, perhaps – the Girlingites' predicament had captured the national imagination. One reporter, who would telegraph his story from Southampton that night, encountered 'half-a-dozen women and girls in the road amongst the wreckage. All wore petticoats no lower than the knee, and the trousers of the other sex with a triplet of scalloped work at the bottom. Their hair hung loosely and somewhat wildly down the back; otherwise they were dressed as well-to-do artisan folks.' Even the voices of these strangely-dressed people seemed foreign: 'Two or three I should have set down as Americans, but they assured me that every member was English'.

'Let the law take its course, they have thrust us forth, and here we will stay. What is the use of Christianity if it does not give strength to bear affliction? We are the Lord's, and He is ours,' said one elder. 'The Lord called me, and I went!'

'Ah, that you did,' echoed his fair-headed, consumptive-looking son.

'We are in Christ's fold,' said his father.

And the young man, shivering with cold, touched a broken roller with his foot and replied, 'We are so.'

These born-again, proto-hippies seemed to be figures of derision, but their earnestness and philosophical language 'forbade a smile. An intellectual-looking brother, who, like the rest, wore his hair pretty long behind his ears, and was plainly and comfortably dressed in a wide-awake hat and cloth garments, had no objection to my seeing Mrs Girling, but drove me to the barn, where, with Miss Wood and the rest of the women, she has taken up her abode in a little mudwalled cottage.' Accompanied by two sisters – 'who looked in their peculiar costume more like men' – Mary Ann, dressed in long skirts, came down by the cabbage patch and into the cottage. As she entered the room, someone held up a small paraffin lamp.

'Mother dear, please sit with us.'

Mary Ann took her place in the corner by the chimney.

'What shall we do next? Ah, we do not know. We only live a moment at a time, and cannot say what a day may bring forth. We never wished to keep our proceedings here a secret, and we defy the world to say we have not lived in purity. The moment a member joins us all natural relations cease – the wife is no longer a wife, and the husband no longer a husband, except in the sense that we love each other with a holier love.'

'They have called us many names,' said one brother as he pointed to their smashed and muddy furniture, 'but Shakers is, perhaps, the best, for some persons will shake for their wickedness and illegality.'

The sect still suffered the after-shock of that fearful night, yet there was worse to come. In another echo of Ann Lee's tribulations, and three days after the eviction, Mary Ann was threatened with confinement as a lunatic. With Isaac Osborne and Julia Wood at her side, she told the reporter of her trial:

'Isaac told me that a police sergeant and two constables, with the relieving officer, Mr Marshall, had come to take me for a ride. I asked where to and with what object, and then they told me I was to go before Dr Adams to be examined as to my sanity. Dr Adams had spoken to me at the Lodge previously, and he went away and pronounced me insane. I did not fear them, and was quite willing to go – in fact, I was rather amused at the idea. Previous to our leaving, the children all assembled around us, and we had a prayer in the garden.'

Robert Seymour Adams, the doctor who had taken the Elkington boy into care, had decided that Mary Ann was endangering lives, an opinion encouraged by men such as Reverend Spackman, who thought that 'if the mother were removed, about whose state no educated person having once seen her can have much doubt . . . the community would be at an end' and 'they all will go into the Union quietly'. Adams signed a certificate to the effect that Mrs Girling was 'not *compos mentis*', and she was taken by carriage to Lymington's workhouse, where she was examined behind the boardroom's closed doors.

'There were three of them and a lawyer. They inquired about the circumstances connected with our being turned out, and asked me why I had acted in the way I had in staying out all night in the open air. I was also asked if it was really true that we expected some strange phenomenon to take place, or that a covering would come down from heaven to shelter us, to which I answered that we never had such a thought.'

Mary Ann was told that she had been brought to the Union as she would be 'more comfortable than at the barn'. She was then asked if she thought 'some strange power would appear and move all the things back into the lodge?'

'To this I again answered No. He then inquired why I did not remove, and I answered that I had had nothing to do with putting the things there, and that therefore I had nothing to do with taking them away. I gave him the explanation about the seizure of our property in the spring, and then he asked how much of the Lodge belonged to us, and I replied fully three-fourths, and that I had spent two thousand pounds there.'

Dr Adams had asked what she was doing 'with that poor girl the other day, making her dance in that fantastic manner'.

'I told him he ought to know what it was, as he was a physician, and then he said that I practised mesmerism upon them, making them dance in that frightful way, and putting them to all kinds of suffering. I positively denied that I had anything to do with it. I said that I read the word of God, and that it was caused by the Spirit of God. A few words were then addressed to me by the magistrate, who said he was sorry I had been called up under such circumstances, and asked me what I was going to do. I claimed and mean to have religious liberty and justice. The magistrates treated me very politely and kindly, and I was then driven back here again.'

As they listened to this story, the faithful were relieved – and perhaps surprised – to hear their leader laugh off the incident. To some, such self-awareness pointed to her fraudulence, but *The Times* was inclined to give her the benefit of the doubt: 'She speaks with perfect good humour of the charge of insanity . . . Admitting that the world probably thinks her an imposter, she received with equal good humour the suggestion that she might be one of those unconscious imposters of whom religious history is full. As she herself allows, she is a woman of no education, and her attempts to justify and establish her position owe whatever success they command to her perfect confidence in herself and her mission.'

No, she did not claim to know the precise time of Christ's Second Coming; 'all that she declares is that, whenever it may happen, she will be present in the flesh'. And as the newspaper noted, the Bible said this could happen at any time: 'How, then, can you prove her wrong in saying she will live to see the day?' While the police patrolled Vaggs Lane to prevent the sect returning to the Lodge, and as Lymington ran rife with proposals as to what ought to be done, others considered 'that the Shakers . . . have been very harshly treated . . . Religious fanatics they undoubtedly are, but that is no reason why they should be persecuted; and indeed, to persecute them would be to give to their beliefs an importance that they otherwise would not have.' Victimisation had made Mary Ann a martyr – and set Girlingism on the national agenda.

At eleven o'clock on the Sunday after Mary Ann's apprehension as a lunatic, a service was held to celebrate her return. The public were excluded, although members of the press were allowed to attend. 'The barn has no windows; two small lamps were used to light it,' noted the *Daily News*. Although her mission was reduced to an airless barn strewn with straw and strung with washing, her words had a tenor beyond the expectations of a town hall, railway arch or rural hovel; an elliptical typology, ever the same, but always changing, offering a new age gospel.

> She saw Christ in the clouds, and from Him received a revelation that she should not see death till He came, and also a commandment to preach this to all men. Addressing herself pointedly, she said, with arm and finger extended – 'As clearly and surely as I see you and your features, so clearly did I see the form and face of Christ the Son of God. You may think me crazed or what you like. I care not; but I know as surely as I stand here that my body shall never enter the ground. I do not say that Christ will be here to-day, to-morrow, next week, or next year – for I know not when; but I do know I shall be alive when He comes.'

Mary Ann struck a Shaker stance, her outstretched arm a spiritual dowser, as she uttered yet more extraordinary claims, as if emboldened by her release.

> I have preached the truth to millions of people, and with God's grace will still preach the same to-night. Amongst you,

> my friends, are doubtless married men. I do not say you are wrong . . . but being sons of Adam all your bodies must see death. Our bodies are already quickened by the Holy Spirit and will not see death . . . I have experienced many miraculous cures before the revelation of Christ – total paralysis of the body, blindness of one eye, a mouth all drawn on one side – all was cured in a marvellously short space of time.

She might say that she knew how crazy she sounded, but hearing her hyperbole in Beasley's barn, others may have agreed with Dr Adams: that this was a woman suffering from acute delusions. Yet in the wake of Wilkie Collins' *The Woman in White*, and with newspapers running other stories of 'inconvenient women' incarcerated in abusive asylums, public sympathy was a powerful force; one which both Mary Ann and her more influential supporters would manipulate to their own ends.

Reporting on the eviction, the forward-looking *Pall Mall Gazette*, which treated 'the Community of Shakers' with a certain sympathy, noted that, close to Harmony Hall, Robert Owen's 'celebrated experiment in Socialism . . . the latest attempt of the kind in England seems in a fair way towards collapse'. In its following issue, the *Gazette* published a letter from 'An American' which compared the Girlingites with the Shakers, drawing on John Humphrey Noyes' *American Socialisms*, a history of 'the most successful and influential of American fanatics' and their spiritualistic influences, 'possessed of the spirits of Indian "squaws"'. 'I will not fatigue you with further particulars, but, seeing that the Shakers are celibates, and therefore all converts, or perverts as one may think, their numbers are somewhat striking. Perhaps if Mrs Girling and her friends had been possessed with the spirit of Rufus, who had some connexion, I believe, with the New Forest, they would not so obstinately have rejected offers of shelter the other bitterly cold night.' But as *The Times* compared her treatment to earlier persecutions – 'Two hundred and fifty years ago they would have burnt her as a witch. The modern equivalent seems to be imprisonment as a lunatic' – the notion of Mary Ann being confined on account of her beliefs stirred the conscience of one local nobleman; a man of principle, and not a little eccentricity himself.

He may have had a distinctly different upbringing, but the Honourable Auberon Edward William Molyneux Herbert, the third son of the third earl of Carnarvon, had intentions remarkably similar to Mary Ann's. Herbert, who had arrived at the nearby manor of Ashley Arnewood as the Girlingites came to Vaggs Lane, was particularly attuned to their aspirations – not least because, as Liberal MP for Nottingham, he had sponsored Frederick Evans' Shaker lecture at St George's Hall in 1871.

Herbert's interests lay in the problems of 'oppressed peoples'. As a young army officer, he had entertained thoughts of fighting for Garibaldi in Italy, and extended his sympathies to the British working classes – although he eschewed socialist demands for the nationalisation of land and industry in favour of 'Individual Liberty' and 'the rights of Self-Ownership', a notion given piquancy by the fact that his family estate, Highclere Castle, was a vast pile designed in high gothic style for Auberon's father by Charles Barry; its cupboards would later contain relics from Tutankhamun's tomb, recovered by the foredoomed fifth earl.

Now aged thirty-five, Herbert was also an amateur archaeologist, but his fascination lay in the pre-history of his own country rather than in the Valley of the Kings, collecting artefacts from forest tumuli. He was also interested in the theories advanced by John Ruskin, although his visit to Denmark Hill in 1865 underlined the critic's strange reclusion in the south London suburbs: 'His life is unhealthy, he scarcely ever leaves his room . . . His is genius, one-sided, vivid, creative, as opposed to the much healthier cleverness or ability . . . He looked with almost loathing upon the

Americans – fit to breed to increase, but to make a beautiful thing, to advance science or art, they were useless.' If such notions were the obverse to Shakerism's ambitions, then Herbert's role in Mary Ann's story reflected his own utopian notions. He too would be drawn to the forest, as though its residual paganism exerted an irresistible force. As part of that process, this liberal aristocrat became the link between the Girlingites and the esoteric circle convened on the other side of the forest at Broadlands, the home of William Cowper – to whose niece, Lady Florence Amabel Cowper, Herbert became engaged on 22 May 1871.

Florence's diary gives a vivid picture of their courtship. At Easter 1871, she was waiting for Auberon at Broadlands, having received a copy of the republican speech he had just made in Nottingham, and which left her feeling 'as if I had been sitting for a week at a dentist's waiting room'. He arrived the same day as Ruskin, and spent his time engaged in 'amusing "Utopia" discussions' with the critic, who 'evidently has a fancy for him', observed Florence, as they listened to Ruskin reading from Thomas More. An intimate family friend of the Cowpers', Ruskin was pursuing his own utopia – as well as a hopeless love affair of which his hosts were all too well aware. Florence, however, was more concerned with her own relationship. Feeling anxious and 'rather afraid I had said and done too much last night', she joined the house party on a drive to the forest for a 'droll walk down to Rufus Stone'. They cut an eccentric sight. 'Very sloshy. Aunt Jenny in galoshes, long silk slip. Ruskin in polished slippers and high hat, hopping together over ditches. A. H. and I more at home in that sort of ground.' She and Auberon walked deep into the forest, talking passionately. 'All he asked was true friendship if that didn't bore me. Liked his face so much as he was talking to Ruskin. Ruskin so dear this time and warm-hearted and kind.'

Two days later, as they listened to a friend reading poems by Walt Whitman, Florence felt 'overwhelmed at the *utter* unselfishness of A. H.'s devotion' to his cause. It was a turbulent time in which to fall in love. That summer Florence read of the violent end of the Paris Commune: 'Paris burning, set fire to by insurgents as Versailles entered . . . the whole city like Pandemonium.' In the wake of Charles Dilke's notorious anti-monarchical speech to the Commons in November, Herbert continued to pursue his own republican ideas – to Ruskin's disapproval: '. . . I see with consternation, that even one of my own personal friends, Mr Auberon Herbert, rising the other day at Nottingham, in the midst of great cheering, declares that, though he is not in favour of any immediate change, yet, "if we asked ourselves what form of government was the most reasonable . . . he had no hesitation in saying the weight of argument was in favour of a Republic".'

Nonetheless, Ruskin welcomed the news of Auberon and Florence's marriage in the New Forest in August 1871. The following year Florence – whom Auberon nicknamed 'Hawk' – gave birth to a son, Rolf, and spent the summer at Julia Margaret Cameron's house while Herbert campaigned in Nottingham. She told Mrs Cameron: 'We are both (Rolf and I) . . . advertisements of Freshwater air. I am quite amused to see my ruddy cheeks when I come back to pale inland people.' She added that on a brief visit to Broadlands, she had found her aunt 'in high delight'. Aunt Jenny – she of the galoshes and silk slip – was the kind of woman to be often found in such a state, as others would attest.

Living so close by, the Herberts were well aware of the Girlingite commune, although at the time of its eviction, they were staying at Wrest Park, the Bedfordshire stately home of Florence's parents, Earl and Countess Cowper, where she had just given birth to a daughter, Clair Mimran. He may have been sequestered in aristocratic grandeur, but Herbert's conscience was stirred by the image of the religious refugees turned out on the road. Having read of the events in Vaggs Lane in the *Pall Mall Gazette*, he wrote to *The*

Times, protesting that he knew from 'personal observation ... that however hopelessly impracticable were the principles of the Shakers, and however certain to lead sooner or later to a catastrophe, they themselves were a quiet harmless folk, leading blameless and happy lives, and believing with a tenacity like that of the early Christians ...'

In this heroic reading, the Girlingites assumed a sense of innocence lost to England, one which some Victorians sought to reclaim. Through *The Times'* letters page, Herbert appealed to his peers in their hidebound gentlemen's clubs to forgo their prejudices and sympathise with 'an honest, industrious and remarkably happy set of people, who were only worse than their neighbours in this – that they had the misfortune to believe absolutely in what they professed'. The arrest of Mrs Girling – 'only mad ... on the religious side' – seemed to him 'to savour of that insolence which is still to be found in some squires and squireens towards what they dislike', and he announced his intention to question Dr Adams' action, warning 'there is more danger in identifying superstition with madness than some suspect ... for it may be difficult to find sane people to judge the madmen'.

Others agreed. *Vanity Fair* declared that 'Mr Auberon Herbert has done rightly in calling public attention to the attempt to treat Mrs Girling, the Shaker lady, as insane ... the doctor who signed a certificate of her lunacy should be subjected to a few interrogatories for the benefit of the community. One would like to know how much liberty is actually left one in the land of freedom ...' But on his return to Hampshire, Herbert discovered it was too late to restore the Girlingites to their former home. On 22 December – only a week after the eviction – New Forest Lodge was sold by auction at the Nag's Head Hotel. In a suspiciously speedy progress from evacuation to disposal, Mr Herbert Guillaume of Botley offered £1,340, a low price which 'seemed to give the impression that the estate had been bought in for the mortgagee'. Two days later, on Christmas Eve, it was reported that Auberon Herbert's offer of 'a larger and more convenient place of shelter' had been accepted by the homeless sect.

As Bob Cratchit-like clerks beavered away in newspaper offices, the sentiments of the season served to heighten the plight of these lost souls cast out in the wilderness. Perhaps the holiday also gave gentlemen pause for reflection as they perused their newspapers, all but pervaded with the smoke of cigars and suffused with port fumes. The *Daily News* thought there were greater issues at stake: 'It is quite simple to call her mad, but the whole strange affair has too many relations with events of great importance to be settled in this offhand way. These people may be very foolish, but what test have we to distinguish their folly from the enthusiasm of St Francis and of St Theresa?' Francis of Assisi was of particular interest to Victorian Christians, and the newpaper compared the Girlingites' plight to a group of English Franciscans recently driven from their property in Abingdon. 'The difference is that the Franciscans had no alternative, whereas the Shakers have borne the snow and wind for no other reason than that love of martyrdom which the early Christians came to recognise as over-strained, and which the writers of the empire call *livido moriendi*, the passionate desire of death.'

The day after the commemoration of Christ's birth, *The Times* published a three-column account – a diverting tale for those able to enjoy a day off. Quoting Mary Ann on the tenth anniversary of her visions ('It was vouchsafed to me to see a face as distinctly as your own – to hear a voice telling me plainly that I should live to see the Second Advent'), it reported that the Board of Guardians were about to turn the sect out of Beasley's barn on grounds of overcrowding.

> Such a proceeding would be indefensible. These people are quite able to take care of themselves. Whether they should be helped may be a moot point, but they ought not to be worried

> and harried. That all of them are monstrously deluded there can be no question; that many of them would do well to return to their friends is also probable; but looking to their well-cultivated land, the work apportioned to each, and their harmless, and not wholly aimless, lives, one cannot help regretting the blunders and muddle-headed perverseness by which their little freehold has become forfeited, and their home broken up this Christmas-tide.

Such sentiments extended the English love of the underdog to this seemingly helpless case. On Christmas Eve the sheriff's officers had arrived at the barn to offer Mary Ann £70 from the sale of the confiscated livestock of the previous spring. 'How the balance has got itself reduced to this sum I do not know,' wrote *The Times'* correspondent, 'nor why the money was only tendered to the community so long after it was due, and after the mischief was done and irreparable.' Ironically, it was also the amount which would have saved them from eviction, and from all the ills that followed.

'Why did you not bring it before?' asked Mary Ann, frustrated and suspicious – perhaps rightly so.

'Because we did not know to whom to pay the money,' replied the factotum.

'But you knew whose goods to seize,' remarked a brother, bitterly.

The twelve days of Christmas had proved to be a far from festive time for the Children of God. On New Year's Eve the Lymington Board of Guardians served notice 'to abate the nuisance caused by over-crowding, in other words, to turn three-fourths of them out. Mr Beasley, it is said, refuses to act on the notice; and, considering the present dreadful weather, to do so would be one of the grossest acts of inhumanity possible.' Yet when Herbert offered them shelter, he was threatened with a similar notice. It seemed to *The Times* that there was 'a determined attempt to root them out of the place'; but the newspaper also noted that the Girlingites 'had an offer from persons high in position who sympathize with their hard fate, to have a proper residence rented for them'.

The identity of these mysterious benefactors soon became clear. On 4 January 1875 the paper published a fierce defence of the Girlingites by William Cowper – former minister of state, MP for South Hampshire, and uncle to Florence Herbert. Cowper was also an aspiring utopian and practising spiritualist, and at Broadlands, he and his wife Georgiana – Florence's galosh-wearing Aunt Jenny – played host to beliefs at least as strange as those practised in Hordle. Indeed, even as Mary Ann's story gripped the nation, the Cowpers were joining hands around the seance table to summon the departed spirit of Rose La Touche, the object of Ruskin's obsession and, in his eyes, a kind of saint.

PART THREE

Arrows of Desire

MEMORY • TRUTH • SACRIFICE • LIFE •
OBEDIENCE • POWER • BEAUTY

JOHN RUSKIN, *Seven Lamps of Architecture*

SEVEN

The Sphere of Love

Her eyes were deeper than the depth
Of waters stilled at even;
She had three lilies in her hand,
And the stars in her hair were seven

D. G. Rossetti, *The Blessed Damozel*

As he stood at the start of the sweeping gravel drive, Edward Clifford was deeply struck by the sight that lay before him. The young vicar's son, now a budding painter, had arrived by train at Romsey station, and here, just outside the little county town, he had came to a pair of gates which seemed to admit him to heaven.

Ahead, through the trees, the view opened onto a landscape from an eighteenth-century painting. To one side, close-cropped grass rolled down to the limpid, fast-flowing River Test, filled with twisting emerald weed and nacreous-glinting trout. To the other, a Palladian mansion looked out through its grey portico with quiet self-satisfaction, framed by mature beeches and the hills of Hampshire. To an aspiring artist it was a world away from a penurious existence eked out in London. Edward's luck had changed the day the Cowpers had walked into his dealers' gallery, asking for any Pre-Raphaelite works. The couple had chosen an oil of St Anthony, whose struggles with the temptations of the devil fascinated the young artist. That chance encounter had led to this invitation – and as for many others, his experiences at Broadlands would change the course of his life.

'Low windows looked on a lawn which sloped down to a winding river,' Clifford would recall, many years later. 'Silver and grey are its lights and shadows always . . . To the left is a cluster of beech trees of holy associations. In the distance one sees hills and field in long stretches and the beginning of the New Forest.' It was an almost sanctified vista; and Edward was even more struck by its occupants. As he arrived, William and Georgiana were taking their customary late breakfast – 'their wise habit being to preserve a great bit of the morning for quiet before the business of the day began' – and were 'talking and sunning themselves at their breakfast table . . . Mrs Cowper was a vegetarian, and instead of the debris of food one usually sees, there appeared on their breakfast table chiefly fruits, vegetables, and flowers amidst choice china and silver.' Georgiana, Clifford discovered, 'could not endure the idea of beasts being killed for her food'.

Under the Cowpers' occupation, Broadlands had taken on a rarefied air. While their neighbours were devoted to hunting animals and eating them to the accompaniment of a fine burgundy, William and Georgiana drank water and dined on fruit and vegetables. Their home was a haven for 'all those movements for individual physical and moral purity . . . such as temperance, homeopathy, vegetarianism and . . . anti-vaccinationism', and they wrote almost obsessively about their health, with William entering remedies ranging from belladonna to electro-homeopathy in his oilcloth notebook. Yet to some the Cowpers' pursuits seemed essentially dilettante. Philanthropy was seen by the 1848 *Communist Manifesto* as a conscience-salver and means of social control, and to its authors, the Cowpers stood guilty of 'Conservative or Bourgeois socialism . . . philanthropists, humanitarians, improvers of the condition of the working class, organisers of charity, members of societies for the prevention of cruelty to animals, temperance fanatics, hole-and-corner reformers . . . desirous of redressing social grievances in order to secure the continued existence of bourgeois society'. What Edward Clifford was presented with at Broadlands, and what Mary Ann would see as a source of patronage, was a paradoxical mixture of aristocratic hauteur and spiritual renewal – a duality amply exemplified by the Cowpers' multifarious beliefs.

Born in Hertfordshire in 1811, William Cowper was officially the second son of the fifth Earl Cowper of Wrest Park. However, his true father was probably Henry John Temple, Lord Palmerston, with whom William's mother Emily had conducted a discreet affair for some years, and whom she would marry on her husband's death. To observers, such behaviour was hardly unusual in this family: after all, Emily's brother was Lord Melbourne, Queen Victoria's first prime minister and confidante, whose own wife, Lady Caroline Lamb, had conducted a disastrous and highly public affair with Lord Byron.

Given such an elite and intimately-connected background, William's progress from Eton to the Royal Horse Guards, where he became a dandy officer, was an irresistible one. In his youth he toyed with a vocation, but found that 'I still love the world, its pleasures, its vanities, its idols', and became a politician instead. He rose quickly through the Liberal ranks, from Melbourne's secretary to Member for Hertford and a succession of governmental posts: Lord of the Treasury, President of the Board of Health, Vice-President of the Board of Trade, and Chief Commissioner of Works. William's interests were not conventional, however. As Chairman of the Committee on the Enclosure Acts, he helped preserve open spaces and granted allotments to the poor, ameliorating the effect of enclosure on the landless. He went to Paris to observe French methods of planting, 'and it is to him', noted *The Christian*, '. . . that we owe the laying-out of our parks with flower-beds and shrubs'. But it was not only London which which owed its landscape to William Cowper; he was also the man who helped save the New Forest.

The forest had been under threat since the 1851 Deer Removal Act effectively denied its status as a royal preserve and prepared for the hunting of its deer to extinction, a prelude to the enclosure of large areas of the forest for the growing of timber and the 'industrialisation' of the area. The act was contested by many people, from landowners such as Lord Henry Scott of Beaulieu, to commoners, who saw their grazing rights at threat. Auberon Herbert was among the vanguard in the fight, as was William Cowper. Then, in 1871 the Treasury introduced a bill for the Disafforestation of the New Forest, thus reversing the process accomplished by William the Conqueror eight hundred years previously. The struggle for green spaces, and perhaps for England's identity, was a current one. While the Girlingites were being evicted from their Lodge, the *Pall Mall Gazette* had noted: 'The townsman of the middle and lower classes in this day takes a rather stagey view of the country, having for the most part confined his imaginative reading to the works of DICKENS, but he attaches a prodigious value to the few places accessible to him which still retain a look of their primitive wildness.' As the sect discovered to its cost, land was ever bound up with class and power; and as Cowper fought his anti-enclosure campaign – influenced by Ruskin – to preserve England's ancient wood, he battled with his neighbours who had a vested interest in its development. But Cowper won, and in 1877 the New Forest Act recognised the spiritual as well as the financial value of wilderness. It remains in force today.

Gladstone would declare that he saw in William Cowper 'the stamp of purity, modesty, gentleness . . . in a peculiar degree', while William's mother Emily complained that her son always seemed to be running: 'he runs to Church and runs back. He runs before breakfast and runs after . . .' Yet he was no puritan: in 1844 Cowper had been criticised by more 'serious-minded' friends for appearing in the *Illustrated News* 'in the frivolity and worldliness of a *bal costumé*' at the Queen's Fancy Ball, and for his general taste for 'going out in the world'. And where Auberon Herbert was the first man to ride a bicycle in the New Forest, William Cowper was the last gentleman to ride about London on a horse. Described as slender and active even in middle age, with 'very beautiful Vandyke-like hands, light blue eyes, and a delicate skin', Cowper would always appear younger than his years. Perhaps the glow of good deeds flushed his complexion: convinced of the need 'to bring to the poor the social justice of the Gospels', he had become a Christian Socialist. But in 1843 his smooth progress through life was suddenly interrupted. On 27 June he married Harriet Alicia, the beautiful daugher of Mr Daniel Gurney of North Runcton, Norfolk. Two months later she was dead. Distraught, William kept their love letters – including a

miniature sky-blue envelope containing a lock of Harriet's hair carefully tied in a pink ribbon – along with the black-edged letters of condolence. She would remain 'a holy and lovely memory' for him, and her loss would colour his spiritual aspirations.

In the meantime, Cowper pursued utopian ideas. During the 'Hungry Forties' he was persuaded by John Minter Morgan to present a petition to Parliament calling for the setting up of 'self-supporting villages', resembling the Chartist schemes of Feargus O'Connor. 'Men of England sleep no more; the day of your redemption has dawned, and onward is now the watch-word of the world,' said Morgan, claiming that his was 'no untried theory, but a *system* that has been in practice for more than sixty years among a people called *Shakers*'. Cowper took this campaign into London itself. In 1844 the Society for the Improvement of the Conditions of the Labouring Classes displayed examples of 'planned dwellings' in Bloomsbury, Drury Lane and Hatton Gardens; precursors of the Peabody estates, they were garden cities within the metropolis. In an echo of the Diggers and their allotments, Cowper compared these ambitions to 'people digging in a field for a treasure which we believe to be somewhere about, but know not exactly where'. But the *Illustrated London News* condemned the dwellings as 'dooming men to an oyster-like level of morals and manners' and looking 'more like a lunatic asylum than the ordinary abodes of rational men'.

The newspapers saw Cowper's pursuits through the filter of political disappointment – yet more so when he took to holding meetings in the New Forest, speaking 'from a cottage window, or a cart, so anxious was he to bring all within his reach to the blessedness of the knowledge of God'. 'There is a refuge, it would seem, for the politically unsuccessful man,' *Vanity Fair*'s columnist declared. 'Mr Cowper-Temple, heir to Lord Palmerston [who had died in 1865] and whilom Commissioner of Works, has now . . . taken to preaching on religious topics to bucolic audiences. I can imagine that this sort of life must have its charm, if only for the sake of taking rank with Lord Radstock and other of the minor prophets.'

Not even his own family could understand William's motivations. 'He is a very sincerely religious man but partly believes in Mahomed, Vishna, Buddha, the Pope, the Patriarch, at least he has a large charity for them all,' observed his sister-in-law. 'He loves high, low and Broad Church.' He even believed in miracles. But perhaps she was to blame – as if her son's unconventional birth freed him to pursue an eccentric agenda. Certainly the contrast between his utopian aspirations for the working classes and his own situation could not have been greater. When Emily died in 1869, Cowper inherited the Palmerston family name, Temple, and estates in County Sligo and Hampshire.

Broadlands was close to the former Owenite colony of Harmony Hall, but a world away in what it represented. Originally a manor within the lands of Romsey Abbey, in 1767 Lancelot 'Capability' Brown had improved the grounds and remodelled the house in fashionable yellow brick, adding an Ionic portico. With interiors embellished to designs by Robert Adam and Josiah Wedgwood, Broadlands presented an elegant if overpowering sequence of marble, plaster and gilt, classical statuary and fine paintings – including a Tintoretto over the fireplace 'on which Ruskin loved to expatiate'. It held dominion over the lush river valley, the very image of an enlightened landscape. Yet it was a deceptive picture: William, now Cowper-Temple, had inherited his mother's social salon, but under the influence of his second wife, Georgiana, the estate became 'suffused with heavenly light, divine grace, and similar celestial luminescence', as if its new owners had impressed their esoteric beliefs on the land itself.

Georgiana Tollemarche was born in 1822, the youngest daughter of Admiral Tollemarche. Hers was the typical upbringing of her class, but like her husband she had a decidedly liberal attitude: she was a woman who 'could never grasp the difference between right and wrong; when no cruelty was involved she could not see why people should not do what they liked'. William had first seen her in church, 'and, without knowing who she was . . . haunted her till she was won'. The couple were unable to have children, instead adopting a daughter, Juliet. In many ways Georgiana herself remained childlike. The love the couple shared was almost adolescent: if parted, they wrote to each other every day, with William scribbling notes from the House of Commons addressed to 'Blessed Jenny', 'My Precious Darling'. Now in middle age, Georgiana was 'extremely stately and upright. She seldom bent, but met her friends at her full height, with a radiant smile. Her golden hair as it gradually silvered had always the look of a halo. Her eyes were of a very light warm grey colour – mystic eyes, not without severity.' Since her youth she had been addicted to hospitals, 'always at the beck and call of sufferers, and would spend days and nights in the stifling atmosphere of cancer or consumption', while other titled ladies would complain that she was seen 'giving rosaries to the Roman Catholic patients!'

To the impressionable young Edward Clifford, it seemed that this aristocratic angel was transformed by her acts of grace: 'After one of her nights with the dying, I would see her face flush with youth, all the wrinkles and the pathetic look would go, and there was the rose where the lily had stood. I never saw a face change so. Her hands were very characteristic . . . Green was her colour, and her dress had generally some look of costume. It was always beautiful, but never very costly. She had a necklace of little silver cherubs with a tiny ladder . . .' It was in this ethereal guise that he painted Georgiana, wearing what Ruskin saw as a 'black and white sort of nun's dress with a silver chain', complete with crucifix. An open book, doubtless some esoteric tract, lay in her lap, while a purse of entwined serpents hung from her châtelaine. It was a vision of pseudo-religious bohemia at its mid-Victorian peak, and while he admitted that Georgiana's thin lips and aquiline nose did not conform to the 'Burne-Jones' ideal, Clifford nonetheless portrayed a certain feyness in this aristocratic priestess who was herself a patron of the Pre-Raphaelite Brotherhood.

Founded by Dante Gabriel Rossetti, John Everett Millais and William Holman Hunt in 1848, the year of European revolution and the *Communist Manifesto*, the PRB was itself a kind of aesthetic utopia, cast from a romantic, mystical England of twilight, purple and gold, yet adhering to Ruskin's exhortion to go to nature, 'rejecting nothing, selecting nothing'. Like their medieval exemplars, the Brotherhood intersected with the aristocracy in circles of mutually beneficial relationships, and Georgiana boasted of intimacy 'with that rare genius, Mr Rossetti'. They had probably been introduced by Ruskin, who regarded the artist as his best friend, and in August 1866 Rossetti dined at the Cowpers' London house, 17 Curzon Street, for which he recommended a new décor of

William Morris wallpaper and Burne-Jones stained glass. 'As soon as we had a little money to spare, we asked him to let us have one of his single figures, and so we became possessed of that beautiful picture . . . "Beata Beatrix".' And Rossetti was pleased to sell it to them: 'I am glad Mr Cowper . . . is to have the *Beatrice*', he told his mother, 'as he and his wife particularly, are very appreciative people, and it is pleasanter sending a poetic work where it will be seen by cultivated folks than to a cotton-spinner or a dealer.'

The painting, a copy of which Clifford would paint for the Cowpers, depicted Rossetti's wife, Lizzie Siddal. A native of the Elephant and Castle, she had become a Pre-Raphaelite icon, immortalised in Millais' *Ophelia* as the watery suicide entangled in weeds and willow, and in Holman Hunt's *Light of the World* as a beatific Victorian Christ (reflecting the bisexuality which the Girlingites saw in God). Muse and poet, saint and sinner, Siddal seemed haunted by her sensual mortality, as if to embody the Swedenborgian belief that sexual congress was an echo of the union of two souls in Heaven needed to form a single angel. In *Beata Beatrix* she had become that angel. The painting was freighted with an almost perverse occult symbolism. Rossetti's preparatory drawings show his lover with her hands at rest and her eyes open. But in 1862, Siddal overdosed on the laudanum she used to stave off the pain of consumption, and the work took on a remorseful, memorial air as Rossetti saw his wife as Beatrix, the young girl with whom his namesake, Dante, had fallen in love, but who had died aged twenty-four.

In the finished picture, Lizzie's eyes are closed, her body taut and her hands clasped, as though her physical beauty had become a heavenly ecstasy; the votive pose sets her on another plane of existence, evoking the littoral state in which it was created. In 1871, Rossetti wrote to Georgiana in terms which expressed the painting's transcendence: 'It must of course be remembered, in looking at the picture that it is not at all intended to represent Death . . . but to render it under the resemblance of a trance, in which Beatrice seated at the balcony over-looking the city is suddenly rapt from Earth to Heaven . . . whilst the bird, a messenger of death, drops a poppy' – a symbol of the means of her death – 'between the hands of Beatrice. She sees through her shut lids, is conscious of a new world, as expressed in the last words of [Dante's] *Vita Nuova* . . .'

This figure emerges through an eerie greenish light, as though filtered through water or the semi-luminescence of dawn. The painting's crepuscular, unfocused quality would be compared to Julia Margaret Cameron's photographs, which Rossetti admired and which themselves seemed to share the diffusion of spirit photographs. Others saw its dreaminess as an evocation of Blake's visions and his own spirit drawings, as though Lizzie/Beatrix were some kind of oracle or medium.

In his grief, Rossetti too had been drawn into the world of spiritualism, and *Beata Beatrix* was an extension of the seances he was attending. Symbolists such as Rossetti and G.F. Watts sought images of clairvoyance, 'some union of strange and puissant physical loveliness with depth and remoteness of gaze', as Frederic

Myers would write. Myers' Society for Psychical Research reported on 'Vision with Sealed and Bandaged Eyes, Experiments in', while the New York spirit artist Wella Anderson worked with her eyes bandaged at her studio on West 11th Street; and from her converted Freshwater greenhouse, 'dressed in dark clothes, stained with chemicals', Cameron told Anne Thackeray, 'Why does not Mrs Smith come to be *photographed*. I hear she is *Beautiful*. Bid her come, and she shall be made *Immortal*.'

And if photography was 'this death in which his gesture will embalm me', then the unearthly power of spirit photography and Rossetti's secular icon seemed to beckon the viewer into another world; a half-imaginary place in which Broadlands and *Beata Beatrix* connected with the spire of Lyndhurst's mother church, under which wooden pillars surmounted by angels seemed to bring the forest itself inside. It was here, in 1864, despite objections to its papist overtones, that Frederic Leighton had painted a mystical fresco depicting the New Jerusalem from the Revelation of St John, lit by Burne-Jones' exquisite stained glass. And from here it was but a short step to the island-within-an-island of West Wight and its luminous white cliffs, in whose shadow Watts, Cameron and Tennyson lived, visited by Lewis Carroll and Alice Liddell – whose own remains would be interred in Lyndhurst's churchyard.

In 1862, Rossetti had laid his lover in Highgate cemetery together with the manuscripts of his poems – only to regret the gesture, and with her approval from beyond the grave, had Lizzie's body exhumed in order to retrieve them. *Beata Beatrix* was a symbol of that attempt to move between worlds, 'the face of one whose heart's desire is fulfilled beyond the reach of hope'. The artist himself seemed beyond hope: in the wake of Siddal's suicide, he became dissolute, addicted to chloral and fearful of blindness and insanity; he too attempted self-murder, swallowing a phial of laudanum, and for two days lay between life and death.

As he regained his health – and while conducting an affair with

William Morris's wife, Jane – Rossetti followed *Beata Beatrix* to Broadlands to stay with 'these most excellent and devoted friends', as he told his mother. 'Mrs Temple is simply an angel on earth, and, though her husband is less radiantly such, he is no less so in fact.' Their home was a spiritual and creative solace to him that summer (even though he complained that the heat made his bottom stick to his chair). 'Of course the house is a most splendid place, but I confine myself almost entirely to a very quiet corner of it. The estate is extremely large, and . . . indeed the view of the whole from an eminence overlooking it is perfectly surprising. The Isle of Wight is quite visible in the extreme distance on a clear day; having the aspect of a cloud . . . floating above a halo of light – the sea.'

As he worked on his latest painting, *The Blessed Damozel*, Rossetti was nursed by Georgiana and Mrs Wagstaffe, their personal physician. 'Waggie' was a homeopathic clairvoyant, wife of an allopathic doctor from Leighton Buzzard, and as Augustus Hare reported, 'She comes up to London if desired, and works wonderful cures. *In* her trances her conversation is most remarkable, but out of them she is a very ordinary person. She never remembers when awake having seen any one (with her eyes half-open) in a trance, but meets as a perfect stranger the person she has just been talking to for half-an-hour.' This suburban sibyl suggested mesmerism as a substitute for chloral to help Rossetti sleep, and in gratitude to Georgiana he made a chalk drawing of 'my most womanly and most queenly hostess', portraying her 'Christ-like character'. He also gave the Cowpers a study for *The Blessed Damozel*; with its predella drawn from Broadlands' holy beeches and its winged babies sketched from local infants, this star-wreathed angel joined *Beata Beatrix* as a symbol of the couple's own esoteric beliefs.

When her mother died in May 1861, Georgiana was disconsolate. In a memorable, darkly gothic image, she compared her grief 'to one of the mourning women standing on the brink of a colliery where there had been an accident, seeking some sound testifying to life in the depths'. She detected that echo in spiritualism, having been introduced to the belief by Mary, wife of William Howitt, poet, radical, and sometime gold prospector, author of *The Mad War-Planet, and Other Poems*, and then at work on his *History of the Supernatural* in which he lamented the abandonment of the doctrine of miracles. But miracles seemed possible in that new age, and the Cowpers sought them in seances with English and American mediums. Theirs was a quest to contact the spirit of their loving dead – William's natural father, Lord Palmerston, was among those who 'came through' – but their experiments also reflected the fashion for this unorthodox faith.

Since the antics of the Fox sisters, spiritualism had burgeoned in America, where it now claimed 450,000 registered adherents, served by their own churches and newspaper, the *Spiritual Telegraph*. In 1854 the US Senate received a petition of 15,000 signatures to investigate the phenomenon scientifically. By that time, it had crossed the Atlantic, with the first woman medium arriving in England in 1852. Mrs Hayden – who claimed to have converted Robert Owen by introducing him to the spirits of Benjamin Franklin, Shelley and Napoleon – was later exposed as a fraud, but in her wake came others such as Daniel Dunglas Home. For the next fifteen years, the Cowpers would play host to these glamorous transatlantic magicians. During one session, the renowned American Charles H. Foster manifested the names of the dead in red letters on his limbs like typographical stigmata ('a spasm seized him & he told her he had a second name on his arm'). At another seance, the yet more famous Home addressed Georgiana, 'How I wish I could tell you who this beautiful spirit is standing close to you. She shakes her head & will not give her name . . . you could not bear it before strangers but she says you know who she is & that she will communicate with you when you are alone, quite alone . . .'

William Cowper's files, which once held state papers, were now filled with stranger communications. There were letters from a religious visionary in Alexandra claiming, 'The Lady expounder of the feminine Word in the Heavens reappeared to me 3 days ago, surrounded by an ovale circle of opaline pearls, carrying a rolled book (the Word) under her right arm . . .'; wads of spirit messages and one long scrawl ('with Planchette, Ap 1869') – '*MydearMr . . . onwardandupward . . . kissforyou . . .*'; notes on Broadlands stationery from his dead father – 'Shaftesbury did not approve of giving up chambers . . . much happier than when on earth'; and one particularly extraordinary drawing of an ark-like ship 'seen in vision, April 14th/69', surrounded by serpents and medieval whales and with a psychedelic flower sprouting from its bow as though a parable had been retold under the influence of an hallucinogenic drug.

These fantastic worlds were thrown into sharp relief by the rational architecture and man-made landscape of Broadlands, now an Elysian Fields of alternative belief, a place where the prophet Thomas Lake Harris lobbied for support, even to the extent of suggesting the Cowpers join his American commune at Brocton. 'No one I think ever attracted William more,' wrote Georgiana of Harris. 'He particularly interested us by his belief that the kingdom of Christ was soon to be set up on the earth, and that we might all help in its unfolding.'

'I think there is a period approaching when womanhood shall again be used to have born of her the word of God,' Harris told Cowper, adding, '*time is ended for me*, as it must be at no far off period for all flesh . . . all things announce that the end cannot be far . . . It is awful to behold, as I have, the vast vortices of white electric light that hold these elements in suspension . . .' William recorded it all in his notebooks under such headings as 'Evolution', 'Magnetism' and 'Regeneration', and gave Harris Clifford's painting of St Anthony (then asked the artist to paint a copy).

Harris, born in England but raised in New York, preached an admixture of Swedenborgism and spiritualism accompanied by his own 'mysterious rappings'. With his long white beard, deep-set eyes and propensity to speak in strange riddles, he struck a biblical figure, leading his Brotherhood of the New Life to the banks of Lake Eyrie, where he taught the bisexuality of God and practised *Sympneumata* – an immortal respiration – both of which referenced Shaker and Camisard beliefs. Harris told his followers that 'the more frequently one loved different partners the more perfect life on earth became', but he also warned America that it was 'literally perishing morally and physically from obscure causes resulting from the entrance of the occult world into the bodies and the minds of mortals'.

Harris was lecturing in London 'on the coming Millennial Age' when Cowper and his fellow MP, Laurence Oliphant, fell under his spell. Oliphant – a thirty-five-year-old writer, traveller and diplomat – sold his possessions and went to live at Brocton as 'a sort of hermit'. There he was not allowed to talk to anyone, and lived 'in a sort of temporary encampment which I built myself of vine boxes in a sort of large shed', as he told William. To such circumstances, not unlike those in Vaggs Lane, Harris also hoped to lure the Cowpers, even supplying texts of his interviews with God 'by His permission. I should say that you will hardly be able to understand *how* some things in it can be; but when the time comes they are as demonstrable to the sense as the scenes are on your giver or the pictures in your drawing room. It is all real! real! real! most real. The Bridegroom has come.'

It is a measure either of Harris's power or their gullibility that the couple entertained such ideas – but Oliphant was about to discover the prophet's true nature. When his new wife, Alice Le Strange (whom he had married from the Cowpers' Mayfair house), arrived in Brocton, she was told by Harris: 'Go bathe in the earth. Perhaps you can become fit to dwell among us, if the right means are used. We shall see.' The hapless woman was then buried in soil up to her neck for several hours. On his return to Brocton, Oliphant discovered that Harris had taken Alice as his 'Lily Queen' to Santa Rosa, from where her husband was outlawed – even though the new Californian colony, where Harris evoked 'electro-vital form' on his piano and practised 'Conjugial love', had been set up using funds provided by Oliphant and the Cowpers.

To some, these bizarre goings-on reflected those in the New Forest. 'Any one who is familiar with Laurence Oliphant's writings, or has at all studied the strange phenomenon of American Shakerism, will be sufficiently cognizant of the general drift of doctrines which underlay Mrs Girling's teachings,' noted the *Pall Mall Gazette*, to whose correspondent Mary Ann herself had 'detailed . . . the whole mystery of the fall of man, and a very curious one it was, but one which oddly enough coincided in its main details with that which is set forth in that enigmatical book "Sympneumatics", which many have seen but few have read'. Soon enough, Girlingism would take its place in the Cowpers' crowded library of interests. William 'saw nothing incredible in spiritualism, as he believed in the great cloud of witnesses circling the world', wrote Georgiana, and together they read 'the almost forgotten writings of Swedenborg'.

William continued to fill his red morocco books with notes on lectures by Emma Hardinge – 'Spirits form & appearance of hands by chemical transmutation . . .'; snatches of seances with a medium named Julia Leaf – 'I see a bright light & just now an angel was blessing us – I see y[r] heads in the light . . . my guide tells me I must come back & I can't see'; 'I saw you enveloped in a cloud'; 'I see you in a film – something around you that intercepts light'; Waggie's musings – 'Guardians are generally not human spirits, the guardians change at different times of our life & in accordance with our development'; remarks from fellow travellers such as Frederic Myers, William Crookes (himself obsessed with the young Florence Cook) and Mary Rosina Showers, the psychic daughter of an officer in the Indian Army; and accounts of ghostly dogs. It is disconcerting to look at photographs of Broadlands, with its terraces arrayed in a faded Victorian sun, an innocuous scene which one can hardly imagine populated by spirits. Yet behind its curtained windows, learned men and women gathered to solicit messages from beyond the grave.

As William and Georgiana continued their seances with the teen-aged Miss Showers who, like the equally precocious Florence Cook, could summon a veiled face in a cabinet; and as they listened to Charles Edward Williams' spirit guide – a 'pre-Adamite' man fond of singing Canadian boat songs – Broadlands was rapidly becoming the kind of psychic college James Burns could only have dreamt of. And when Georgiana introduced a pair of under-graduates to William Stainton Moses – the Anglican minster and medium who, as William Cowper recorded, 'felt a presence of a spirit by means of a coldness down his back' – an entire new era of spiritualist research began.

Frederic Myers and Edmund Gurney were, like Edward Clifford, both vicars' sons. Myers, born in 1843 and brought up in the Lake District, was a poet and essayist; he was also the first Englishman to swim the river below the Niagara Falls. Gurney, born in 1847, had been a delicate child, but at Cambridge became a great athlete.

Frederick Myers and Edmund Gurney

He was also extremely handsome: George Eliot had based the character of Daniel Deronda on him, having been 'so struck with his good looks that for several days she could think of nothing else'. In May 1874, Edmund's uncle, Russell Gurney – the Recorder of London and a family friend of the Cowpers via William's first wife – invited Frederic and Edmund to Broadlands. There they met Stainton Moses, who described how he received automatic writing from spirits so celebrated that he declined to publish their names 'lest their teachings be received with incredulity'.

The young undergraduates were convinced. Inspired by the minister's 'manifest sanity and probity', they would found the Society of Psychical Research, and together with their friend, Frank Podmore, compiled *Phantasms of the Living*, an examination of 'all transmissions of thought and feeling from one person to another, by other means than through the recognised channels of sense', a process which Myers called telepathy. But the project owed most to Gurney, who had a personal investment in its enquiries.

A year after his visit to Broadlands, Edmund's three young sisters died in a freak boating accident on the Nile. Distraught, he wrote on black-edged paper from his house in Brighton to tell Georgiana the terrible news: 'They were sailing with a steady & not at all dangerous wind, when a squall of extraordinary suddenness & violence came on them: my brother was on deck which saved him: for my sisters in their cabins there was not a possibility of escape as the boat sank instantly . . .' Now Edmund's state of mind became 'almost obsessively sombre'. He left Cambridge to train as a doctor at St George's Hospital, but found he couldn't bear 'the sights and sounds of the dressing room', and became a lawyer instead – all the while pursuing his speculations on mesmerism and its revelation of the 'subliminal self', a sense of multiple layers of human consciousness which would influence Freud. But his experiments ended abruptly on 23 June 1888 in the Royal Albion Hotel, Brighton. That morning, the door of his room was broken in, and Edmund was found dead in bed. 'He lay on his left side, his right hand holding over his nose and mouth some cotton wool covered by a sponge bag. A small empty bottle stood nearby.'

Myers tried to explain his friend's death by saying that he had used chloroform as an analgaesic for 'face-ache'. Yet it seemed that Gurney had hidden his own subliminal self. He had been conducting telepathic tests with George Albert Smith, a flamboyant mesmerist, showman and pioneer film-maker who sported an orchidaceous button-hole, luxurious moustache and long curly hair. Smith would later admit he and a local journalist had used code to trick Gurney. Faced with evidence of this deception and the prospect that both his reputation and his work were ruined, Gurney took his own life. But the story was more complicated than that.

Two years previously, Gurney had told the psychologist William James (who, as he admitted to his brother, the novelist Henry James, had himself taken an overdose of chloral as a young man suffering from depression) that Smith was 'blameless & acute . . . & excellent at tracing impostures'. Yet after Gurney's death, stories began to circulate that he was involved in a homosexual clique centred on the working-class Brighton youths whom Smith referred to as 'Mr Podmore's young men'; and that this revelation may have been the 'catastrophe' which Gurney faced. These rumours would be influenced by the subsequent scandals of the Cleveland Street telegraph boys and the trials of Oscar Wilde, while homosexuality had been psychologically categorised as 'intersexual' or a 'third sex', as if it too were some kind of in-between state. It seems clear that there was a Uranian undertow to Victorian spiritualism. Many members of the Society for Psychical Research were homosexual: men such as Frank Podmore; John Addington Symonds (sometime Ruskinian and now proselytiser for what Edward Carpenter called 'homogenic love'); Arthur Sidgwick, brother of the Society's president; and the Honourable Roden Noel, son of the Earl of Gainsborough and a man 'handsome, feminine in manner, and inordinately vain' with whom Symonds succumbed to liaisons with soldiers in London parks.

At Cambridge, Myers had read to Symonds from Whitman's 'Calamus', verses extolling the love of boys which were excised from subsequent editions of *Leaves of Grass*. It was also suggested that Myers and Gurney were lovers at college, although both later married. With his handsome face, his loosely-knotted tie and unbuttoned coat, Gurney struck an aesthetic figure, not unlike that of Edward Carpenter; one can imagine followers gathering round this charismatic pioneer of psychical research. In the British Library copy of Gurney's synaesthetic study on *The Power of Sound*, a florid hand on the title page announces that the book belonged to Spencer Shelley, 1881; below it is a brief, sad note of its author's demise – 'Died 23rd June 1888 aged 41' – the kind of inscription which elsewhere might have been added to a family Bible, but which here became a secular tribute to a lost hero of the movement.

Myers was shattered by Gurney's death. 'For fifteen years, we had been as intimate and as attached to each other as men can be,' he told Lady Battersea on 4 July 1888; 'every part of our respective natures found response by comprehension in the other. But I will not say more of that.' Later, he would sum up his friend's 'complex nature, with all its conflicting gifts and impulses' which 'bloomed at its freest in this intimate, this fugitive flower . . .' Gurney was, it seems, a manic-depressive, and had told Margot Asquith, among others, of his desire to 'end all things': while in a striking analogy, Myers wrote of the confinement from which Edmund's troubled soul, haunted by the death of his sisters and whatever other emotional burdens he had to bear, was free at last: 'He beat against the bars of our earthly prison-house, and he had forced a narrow opening through which we seem to breathe immortal air.'

'What hours of spiritual nurture have I lived through in the long dining rooms,' Frederic Myers recalled of his visits to Broadlands, 'from which beyond estrade and portico the broad lawns sloped in sunlight down to the Test's crystal flow!' And it was in 1874, the summer of Myers' and Gurney's visit, that another intriguing couple came to experience this aristocratic utopia.

Robert and Hannah Smith were American Quakers who could trace their faith back to William Penn's Pennsylvania, but who were now living in Paradise Row, Stoke Newington. Robert Pearsall Smith was a glass manufacturer, although the couple's literary friends included Walt Whitman, and each were preachers in their own right. At Broadlands, they described to their hosts the evangelical camp meetings they had attended in America, 'amid primeval forests or by the shore of some mountain lake' (and accompanied 'by hysterical outbursts in which the Chosen People would scream and dance and roll upon the earth', according to their less reverent son, Logan). These 'holy jubilations', with their echoes of eighteenth-century Methodism and the modern spiritualist camps reported in *Human Nature*, fascinated the Cowpers, who promptly decided to throw open their estate to a similar event that summer.

The first Broadlands Conference was convened from 16–21 July 1874. Delegates were sent instructions telling them to avoid topics of conversation which might distract them from the conference's spiritual aims, and gathered the night before in the house or, as it was 'filled to the attics', in Romsey's inns. After a service in the abbey, the day began in a beech grove, where a rostrum and seats were arranged like an arboreal cathedral. At this nineteenth-century new age festival, religious performers spoke to the crowd in meetings which continued, 'with intervals for feasting and converse', until nightfall. 'We sat in the shade under the beech trees, with sun and sky shining through the branches, and the cooing of the wood-pigeons sounded around us,' wrote Edward Clifford. 'The sense of a Divine Presence was wonderfully felt, and probably it was a crisis in the life of nearly everyone present.' Transported by the communal, proto-Woodstock experience, it was, wrote another delegate, an 'atmosphere of prayer and Christian love, which seemed to make supernatural things natural . . .'

It was also a contrast to the circumstances at Hordle. One religious newspaper noted, scathingly, 'We are informed that the noble host's income is not less than £30,000 a year.' Where the Girlingites were forced to practise in a field surrounded by the debris of their dispossession, an elective Eden was recreated on Broadlands' manicured lawns. And as the Children of God invested birds with a holy spirit, at Broadlands, when Juliet, the Cowpers' adopted daughter, was asked the whereabouts of Rab, the family collie, she replied, 'He was at the meeting, I think.' Evangelists consorted with canons and more unorthodox believers, among them Amanda Smith, 'the negress . . . the only person I ever met who claimed to be freed from the power of sin, and of whom I could in any degree accept the claim', as Clifford wrote. 'Her tall figure, her gleaming teeth, and her resonant florid hymn singing can never be forgotten.' 'I feel like a princess in disguise', she said, as she 'told her thrilling story with the strange weird pathos which long years of oppression have wrought in the negro's voice . . .'

Thronged with Quakers and Plymouth Brethren, mesmerists and homeopaths, Broadlands' visitors included Mary Ann herself, glimpsed by Clifford as she sought sanctuary in this deluxe asylum. 'A humble east-end worker, a working-man socialist, and a budding theosophist came dressed in their best to behave nicely with lords and bishops, and lo and behold there was Mrs Girling, the shakeress, being rescued from starvation, or Rowena Cassidy, the ex-slave, being taken in to dinner by the host, while a countess brought up the rear. Dante Gabriel Rossetti, George MacDonald, and Timmins, of the Universal Mercy Band, might get on happily together . . . there would be no clash between General Booth, Père Hyacinthe, Laurence Oliphant, and the Bishop of Truro.'

It is intriguing to imagine Mary Ann's tall figure in bonnet and gown, striding across the terraces, explaining to a churchman the principles of her creed; or being taken in to tea by William Cowper and presented to other delegates at these 'strange gatherings . . . where the saints seemed to walk under trees of Paradise by the crystal river': 'Thither came the High Priestess of the Shakers when she was evicted from her dwelling for refusing to pay the rates . . . and Burne-Jones . . . and vegetarians, and clairvoyantes, and "spiritual wives".'

Even in such eclectic company Mary Ann must have been a remarkable sight: an ambassadress from a colony which was living out the ideas her fellow guests merely talked about, and who had been punished for her impertinence.

EIGHT

The Storm-Cloud of the Nineteenth Century

> Is there but one day of judgement? Why, for us every day is a day of judgement – every day is a Dies Irae, and writes its irrevocable verdict in the flame of its West. Think you that judgement waits till the doors of the grave are opened? It waits at the doors of your houses – it waits at the corner of your streets; we are in the midst of judgement – the insects we crush are our judges – the elements that feed us, judge, as they minister – and the pleasures that deceive us, judge, as they indulge.
>
> John Ruskin, *Sesame and Lilies*

In 1840, at the age of eighteen, Georgiana had been taken by her parents to Rome in order to broaden her mind. By coincidence, John Ruskin was there too – for rather different reasons. Then a twenty-one-year-old undergraduate, he was thought to be 'going into a consumption', and 'many people, myself included, thought I was dying'. Ruskin was indeed coughing blood like Keats, but he was also suffering from unrequited love for Adèle-Clotilde Domecq, his 'Spanish-born, Paris-bred, and Catholic-hearted mistress', who had disdained his attentions. Now he found a new object of adoration, 'a fair English girl, who was not only the admitted Queen of beauty in the English circle of that winter in Rome, but was so, in the kind of beauty which I had only hitherto dreamed of as possible, but never yet seen living: statuesque severity with womanly sweetness joined'.

A remarkable change came over the young man that Christmas. Suddenly he was keen to accompany his parents to St Peter's 'to see the show', not for reasons of musical appreciation, but to catch a glimpse of Georgiana. His family were staying in the same building as hers, and Ruskin would follow Georgiana down the street – although he never succeeded 'in getting nearer than within fifty yards of her', able only to catch 'mere chance glimpses of her far away . . .' And if he saw this beauty as an unworldly focus for his affections, others would agree: with her 'bright waving hair', she seemed 'so slight and spiritual that people said it seemed as if a wind might blow her away'.

It was characteristic of Ruskin to romanticise Georgiana from afar, for his entire life would be filled with frustrated passion. Back in England, he met Euphemia Chalmers Gray, known as Phemy or Effie. She was then aged just thirteen. They were married seven years later, in 1848 – the same year in which William Cowper wed Georgiana (having also first glimpsed her in church). Yet while the Cowpers' love would be lifelong, Effie left Ruskin for John Everett Millais, Southampton-born founder of the Pre-Raphaelite Brotherhood which Ruskin had championed. And like so many events in Ruskin's life – more especially as recorded by himself – fate took another turn when he met Georgiana again in 1854, the year in which he and Effie were divorced. Ruskin's appearance in society was therefore an uneasy one: seated next to each other on their host's sofa, the two apparent strangers chatted politely.

> After a pause, I was rude enough to repeat her words, 'Christmas in 1840! – were you in Rome *then?*'
>
> 'Yes,' she said, a little surprised, and now meeting my eyes with hers, inquiringly.
>
> Another tenth of a minute passed before I spoke again. 'Why, I lost all that winter in Rome in hunting *you*!'

Ruskin was by then no callow youth, but an international celebrity acclaimed for works such as *Modern Painters* and *The Stones of Venice*, in which he made a science of aesthetics and determined the art of his age. He was a recognisable figure, not only for his Scottish burr, his tall, thin frame, red hair and whiskers, but for his customary velvet-collared frock coat and bright blue cravat which reflected the colour of his eyes, their intensity an intimation of his intellectual power – and a hint of the neurosis which accompanied it. Ruskin read the Bible every morning, and quoted Revelations in his rage against the destruction of ancient architecture. He feared republicanism for its threat to this inheritance, yet was passionately concerned with inequality. He was a man torn between life and art. Champion of Turner and the Pre-Raphaelites, teacher, reformer, geologist and naturalist, he was a visionary whose 'gleaming eyes', as one contemporary wrote, '. . . bore within them a strange light, the like of which I have never seen except in his'. But then, Ruskin had ever been aware of his place since his father had told him, 'You may be doomed to enlighten a

People by your Wisdom & to adorn an age by your learning.' In that mission, Ruskin had sought the mystical, as he wrote in *The Stones of Venice*: 'I do not mean to deny the actual existence of spiritual manifestation; I have never weighed the evidence upon the subject.' Now he was to attempt precisely that assessment.

Ruskin's beliefs had changed radically since he practised his parents' evangelism. He saw his spiritual nature as a butterfly emerging from its chrysalis, and no longer believed in the Fall of Man, telling his father, 'every man is his own tumbler'. Science, and specifically geology – erosion presented a particular fascination for the Pre-Raphaelites – threatened Christianity in a time of the 'melancholy, long, withdrawing roar' of the 'sea of faith', as Matthew Arnold wrote. On visits to Switzerland, the time-stilled flow of glaciers and larva gripped Ruskin's imagination as an aesthetic and a spiritual metaphor, and it was in Lucerne, the Alpine town clustered at the edge of the lake under cloud-like, snow-topped mountains, that he received what he called his 'third call from God, in answer to much distressful prayer. May He give me grace to walk hereafter with Him in newness of life . . .' Yet Ruskin was also fascinated by the supernatural, and once dug a hole in search of a Swiss ghost, 'a woman dressed all in black'. In 1843 his college friend, Charles Somers Cocks (later to marry Julia Margaret Cameron's sister, Virginia), told Ruskin that he had 'heard much of Mesmerism lately – from some one of strong mind who used to laugh at the whole affair mercilessly, and now believes in every thing – reading through walls &c'; while his own wife Effie had 'seen a good deal of Mesmerism'. Her doctor, James Simpson, the introducer of chloroform, attested to spectral illusions among his patients, including one woman who shrieked to see the head of her dead sweetheart appear behind a dinner guest, shaking itself at her. Such scenes resembled those reported by Barclay Fox in 1844, of

> ... a remarkable mesmeric patient, a boy of 12 belonging to Bradford, who possessed in the state of 'Coma' the marvellous facility of clairvoyance. His organ of vision seemed to be the tip of his thumb, with which he was able to see a person who rang the front door bell & could describe his dress & appearance ... But the most remarkable of his gifts ... was that of seeing your interior organisation & prescribing the remedy for what he saw amiss. His mode of doing it was to put one thumb in the patient's mouth & one on the pit of his stomach.

When Elizabeth Barrett Browning tried to persuade Ruskin to see the celebrated medium D.D. Home, the critic replied that he 'did not laugh at the subject', adding that in his youth, he had 'felt on more than one occasion a direct response to prayer'. Spiritualism – to some a re-enactment of biblical miracles – was by no means exclusive of Christianity; indeed, it might yet prove angels existed, and Ruskin saw no contradiction in his interest. Dismayed by the materialism of the age, he yearned for miracles: 'So far from seeing any difficulty or essential fallacy in them, I long for them, need them – feel that all is mystery and loneliness without them. But I *can't* get hold of any good evidence of them.' The Cowpers would provide him with the proof he needed.

Over the years, Ruskin's intimacy with William and Georgiana developed to the point where they had pet names for each other. He was 'St Chrysostom, the Golden Mouthed', after St John Chrysostom of Constantinople, renowned for his eloquence; Ruskin bestowed mythological titles on Georgiana: Egeria, Phile, and Isola. It was a friendship bound by faith – or the lack of it. Accepting her 'pretty' invitation to discuss spiritualism, Ruskin told Georgiana that he was 'adrift on the certainty of the immortality of the soul'. 'Don't tremble', he said; 'if I can be of use to you at all, it will be in casting out all Fear. If I hurt you it can only be in crushing an uncertain hope . . .' When Georgiana gave him a spiritualistic text, Ruskin read it 'with much pain', saying, 'I suspect you will find me interrupt all Immaterial proceedings, – not from incredulity: but from stupid Solidity'; and claiming to be a 'fatal Non conductor – I can neither see nor feel my way anywhere just now'. Yet slowly, inevitably, the way was being prepared for his adventures in the other world.

Ruskin would attend his first seance at Mrs William Gregory's salon in Mayfair. She was the widow of William Macdougall Gregory, a professor of chemistry and an expert on animal magnetism and clairvoyance. Where her fellow hostesses might be renowned for their French chefs, Mrs Gregory was known for the finest mediums, and Mary Marshall was one of the best. Then in her sixties, Mrs Marshall satisfied William Cowper's requirements for a good medium: 'sh^{d} be all-powerful as regards material & mental & spiritual vigour'. She would lure Ruskin into the charmed circle; indeed, she may have set her sights on him, aware that his conversion would be as great a triumph as that of Robert Owen a decade earlier. The psychic world sensed Ruskin was not unfavourably disposed to such matters: even before he had reached the seance table, the spirits beckoned him, and the instrument of this entrapment was a yet more incongruous figure: Captain Alfred Wilks Drayson of the Royal Military Academy, Woolwich.

Drayson was a fine example of Victorian polymathy, a professional soldier who had served throughout the Empire, but whose interests ranged from astronomy to mesmerism, and whose books included *Tales at the Outspan, A Manual of Military Surveying* and *Common Sights in the Heavens*, as well as countless articles in *Every Boy's Magazine* and the *Boy's Own Paper*. He was also an expert billiards player. Drayson had been a confirmed spiritualist since 1857, when the sixteen-year-old medium Annie Andrews had contacted his dead brother. He had since witnessed fresh eggs, fruit and flowers descend from the ceiling of his Woolwich quarters, a phenomenon which must have surprised his fellow officers. He also told William Cowper that he had once contacted a spirit who did not know he was dead, and who was surprised his friends could not see him, and spoke of a naval captain who 'often came & amused himself by rapping *Rule Britannia*. He was asked to go to Canada to see how a relative was & it took him 4 minutes . . .'

In later life Drayson would retire to Southsea, where he introduced Conan Doyle to the spirits. But on 11 February 1864, in Mrs Gregory's curtained drawing room on Grafton Street, this military finger guided the planchette to raps summoned by Mrs Marshall, and the ivory object transmitted words from beyond the reality of that winter's afternoon.

You will become a faithful Spiritualist
But whom did it mean?
St John
Would the spirit enlighten them further?
I am your guardian spirit. I will impress you with holy knowledge
The spirit spoke of love, and was asked what relationship it bore?
Mother
Pressed further, Drayson traced, '*Margaret Ru*', then declared,
All is well
Ruskin's name was then spelled out, with the pronouncement,
You have a crown this night placed on y^r head it is spiritualism

With that the piano played a jig and 'the table did a double shuffle in perfect time', and to the sound of departing footsteps and a final salutation – *Dear earthly friends good night* – the seance ended.

When told of these messages, Ruskin thought 'Margaret Ru' must have referred to his grandmother, since his own mother was still alive. Intrigued, two weeks later, on 23 February, he attended one of Mrs Gregory's seances, as if summoned by the spirits themselves. That afternoon, Mary Marshall was assisted by Annie Andrews, now at the peak of her powers and able to summon spiritual music as well clairvoyant visions and spirit writing, 'moving her fingers when she was in a state of trance'. Such phenomena appeared independent of human agency, like an autumn leaf spinning at the end of a spider's thread, the connexion lost in the movement so that no one could detect it was there at all. This was Annie's magic – or her deceit – and she would prove that the spiritualist crown was indeed intended for Ruskin's head.

Joining Mrs Gregory, Mrs Marshall, the Cowpers and Captain Drayson in the circle, Ruskin waited to hear what the spirits had to say. At first there was 'a message of common place character', as Cowper recorded, '. . . the name c[d] not be well spelled out, & the word paper was given'. Then Annie asked them to think of a friend's name. She wrote 'John R', only to change the second word to 'Bull'. She said, 'I've not come through correctly', then said the spirit was 'Honesty', or 'St John', Ruskin's 'Counterpart' (William explained that this was the spiritualist equivalent of a guardian angel). The faintly disappointing session concluded, like a Girlingite service, with a compensatory display of 'spirit over matter' – only here it was the furniture which moved. As the guests lay their fingers on two tables, 'the large table danced in time to a country dance & the little table rose & being suspended in the air the feet be[in]g about 1 foot from the ground & it rapped against the edge of a sofa . . . it also heaved as if at the top of a wave & tilted to the side'.

Afterwards Cowper stuck into his notebook the piece of paper on which Ruskin's name had appeared, investing the scribble with a reliquary importance. 'I am very grateful to you for having set me in the sight and hearing of this new world,' Ruskin told Georgiana, as though she had led him there by the hand. 'I don't see why one should be unhappy, about anything, if all this is indeed so . . . But that story of the grapes pleased me best of all. I believe it on Captain Drayton's [sic] word – and it is all I want – a pure and absolute miracle, such as that of the loaves . . .' Even then, he was not without a little self-deprecating irony: 'Am I not stupid at these seances?' he wondered. But he was soon to witness other miracles, courtesy of the most potent medium of the age: a man able to float out of first-floor windows and to play an accordion without visible use of his fingers; to produce books, flowers and disembodied limbs, and summon phantasms of light and scent; to destroy pagan idols and handle fire without being burned.

Daniel Dunglas Home was born near Edinburgh in 1833, but grew up in Greeneville, Connecticut, where, two years after the Rochester Rappings in neighbouring New York State, the sixteen-year-old heard 'noises at the bottom of the bed', as he told William Cowper: '. . . When he came down his aunt saw his paleness & questioned him & when he sat down to his coffee loud raps were heard . . . She said – "Here's a pretty thing, you've brought the devil into the house".' By the age of nineteen Home was an itinerant psychic, a thin young man with 'flushed cheeks and red hair – frail yet possessed of unaccountable powers'. At one seance in Hartford he summoned up a hand, 'white as marble, and not visibly attached to any arm', which yielded itself up to his host's examination like some trapped animal or the beast with five fingers in W. F. Harvey's Freudian ghost story. As Home sat in a trance and out of reach, the thing 'turned itself over and back' in Mr Burr's grasp, opening and shutting its fingers for his examination: 'It was a perfect human hand, but white as snow, and ENDED AT THE WRIST.' The doubter pushed his finger through its palm '*till it came out an inch or more, visibly, from the back of the hand*', and as he pulled it out, the hole closed up, 'much as a piece of putty would close under such circumstances, leaving a visible mark or scar'. And with that, the stigmatic ectoplasm vanished, 'quick as a lightning-flash'.

Through such sensational phenomena, Home's fame soon spread to New York, which rivalled London as a venue for mediums and spirit photographers; but at the same time, consumption spread through the psychic's lungs. Advised that a voyage to Europe was 'the best hope of prolonging his life', Home arrived in London in April 1855, and found himself the cynosure of English society. Lords Brougham, Lytton and Dunraven were among those who invited him to their drawing rooms; Tennyson was 'more inclined to believe than to disbelieve', while Anthony Trollope was convinced that these phenomena were 'not produced by any fraud, machinery, juggling, illusion, or trickery . . .' Inevitably, Home was consulted by the Cowpers, as his wife noted: '. . . a lady who was a distinguished ornament of English society . . . Mrs G. Cowper, saw a great deal of the manifestations in 1861'.

Home's unique ability was to work in brightly-lit rooms. In his experiments with Home, William Crookes concluded 'that when the force is weak a bright light exerts an interfering action on some of the phenomena. The power possessed by Mr Home is sufficiently strong to withstand this antagonistic influence; consequently . . . *everything which I have witnessed with him has taken place in the light*.' Home's seances followed a set routine. As his guests rested their hands on the table, they felt it 'quiver and tremble as if instinct with life . . . often the floor and walls also shook. Some have compared the vibrations to the beating of a pulse . . .' One young girl leapt up and said, 'Oh, papa, there's a heart in my chair!' At one seance in imperial St Petersburg, another psychically sensitised city where he was given 'rich presents' by Tsar Alexander II, 'Mr Home presently declared that he felt himself being raised. He took, as he was lifted, a horizontal position, with his arms crossed on his breast; and in this reclining attitude was transported by invisible means into the middle of the apartment. After four or five minutes, he was carried back in the same fashion to his old place at the table.' It was as if the medium were able to enter the same ecstasy in which saintly priests were said to levitate over their congregations.

But there were also rumours that Home was not all he claimed to be. He was said to have ordered a fur coat in the name of a client and left him to pay for it (Home was more than something of a dandy, sharing his fellow countryman James McNeil Whistler's taste in extravagant moustaches and flamboyant costumes); while some saw him in Browning's satire, 'Mr Sludge, the Medium':

> 'Now don't, sir! Don't expose me! Just this once!
> This was the first and only time, I'll swear . . .
> 'Well, sir, since you press –
> (How you do tease the whole thing out of me!)
> Now for it, then! . . .
> 'I cheated when I could,
> Rapped with my toe-joints, set sham hands at work,
> Wrote down names weak in sympathetic ink,
> Rubbed odic lights with ends of phosphor-match,
> And all the rest –'

although the poet, himself a Swedenborgian, was probably attacking fake spiritualists in general. Other forces were more darkly arrayed against Home. While in Rome, returning to his rooms late at night, he was knifed by an assailant and only saved by the dandiacal defence of the folds of his fur coat; later he was also stabbed with a stiletto on Jermyn Street in London. Home claimed that the Roman assassination attempt sapped his power; in fact he had been ordered out of the city after being accused of sorcery by the Vatican police.

Wan and drawn from the recent death of his first wife and bouts of consumption, Home was now at a low ebb, described by William Cowper as 'listless & exhausted whenever not under spirit influence – & lies over an arm chair like a rag'. Yet the thirty-one-year-old still struck a colourful figure, with his 'melodious voice', tapering fingers and hair falling in ringlets over his high forehead; Rossetti claimed that Home's blue eyes were 'little phosphorescent lights that come together and dart away again'. Ruskin was equally impressed: introduced to Home by Anna Maria Hall, the wife of his publisher, he told Georgiana, 'I've found out such a grand cloudy nest of spiritual people . . .', adding, 'I like Mr Home himself exceedingly and he says he likes me.'

Home had been sitting to the Cowpers since 1861, with William recording their seances in a notebook decorated with a gothic S cut out from some letter heading. Inside are accounts of 'idols being pitched down violently with a dashing noise, while . . . music was played . . .', and scraps of pencil scrawls in ghostly hands, eerie marks from another world. In Cowper's mind there was little doubt about their authenticity. The levitating medium seemed able to suspend disbelief. Doubtless there was trickery and deception at work; but by force of will, something else was in operation as Home's audience gathered round a three-legged oak table and watched it dance. The fact that his talents were not infallible made them more believable. In one session with the Halls, 'absolutely nothing happened all night', Ruskin reported; at another, only the potted ferns trembled – claimed to be 'the results of spirits moving about the room'. But then there were more remarkable episodes when the flowerpots flew – along with the table – into the library, where a book appeared over Georgiana's shoulders which, when opened, revealed a story by Captain Marryat. Georgiana merely said, 'Oh, that is George again', identifying a recently-deceased nephew. At another gathering, the spirit of Robert Southey dictated a poem and Ruskin replied with George Herbert's 'Dialogue', all to the accompaniment of levitating tables and a clanging sound.

Ruskin professed amazement at the 'manner and triviality' of these manifestations: 'I mean to ask, next time, for the spirit of Paul Veronese, and see whether it, if it comes, can hold a pencil more than an inch long,' he joked to Georgiana. And yet he seemed almost pathetically grateful to Home: 'It is so nice of you to like me! I believe you are truly doing me the greatest service and help that one human being can do another in trusting me in this way, and indeed I hope I so far deserve your trust . . . do please write me a line to say you are safe in America' – where civil war was in progress – 'And come to see me the moment you come back . . .' Anna Maria Hall crowed, 'Only fancy Ruskin being convinced! *But he does not wish it talked about.*' Friends were amazed: Holman Hunt told him, 'When we last met, you declared you had given up all belief in immortality!' What was Ruskin doing, caught up with these airy illusionists; could he really believe in their hovering tables and disembodied hands?

Home was much in demand in those years of spiritualist boom, and had returned from his latest trips to Paris and St Petersburg exhausted and worried about money. As a gesture of support, his friends, including Dr Elliotson and the Halls, installed him as resident secretary of the newly-created Spiritual Atheneum in Sloane Street, an upmarket version of Burns' institute, advertised as 'a rallying-point for spiritualists and their friends, and where seances, under judicious arrangements, should be regularly held'.

Subscribers, who had the use of a library 'and refreshments at a moderate tariff', would pay an annual fee of £5.5s; a brochure, bound in satin and white calf with gilt lettering, was sent to Queen Victoria and Napoleon III (although neither took advantage of the facilities, it was said that the French emperor had intrigued the Queen with 'spooky stories about "Mr Hume"'). The club opened in January 1868 with a lecture by Home and an exhibition of drawings done by Miss Houghton under the guidance of the Angel Gabriel. Whether Ruskin visited these premises is not recorded; Rossetti certainly did, and engaged Home for seances in a 'lordly pleasure-marquee' in his Chelsea garden, a decadent counterpoint to the Girlingites' forest tents.

Another visitor Home received at the Atheneum was a Mrs Lyon, although he came to wish he hadn't. Jane Lyon was a rich widow in her seventies who was told by the spirits to settle £24,000 on Home, a beneficence which caused much gossip on both sides of the Atlantic. One American journal quipped, 'The natural effect of this incident has been to cause spiritualistic stock to rise considerably', while *Human Nature* reported that 'Mrs Lyon, a wealthy lady, had recently "adopted" Mr Home, the celebrated medium, and conferred upon him a large fortune. He has accordingly changed his name to D.D. Home Lyon.' The gossipy Mrs Hall contributed her commentary, telling Home, 'All the town is ringing with the story – giving it, of course, various readings – but all your old friends are full of rejoicing' and adding, 'Mr Ruskin called here to-day ... If you could meet him here? – or at the Atheneum? ... He rejoiced for you – but oh! he is looking so worn and ill. We had such a long talk on Spiritualism.'

However, when she learned that he planned to leave England, Mrs Lyon had her erstwhile son arrested and began an action for the recovery of her money. Lyon *versus* Home was in effect spiritualism on trial. Unfortunately for the sceptics, their surrogate plaintiff was not the most rational of women, and courtroom exchanges resembled lines from a play by Wilde. 'Did you ever kiss Mr Home?' Lyon was asked. 'Well, I once just put my lips to his forehead,' she admitted. 'But only once. You see, I am not so fond of kissing.' Home complained, 'I was a mere toy to her, I felt my degradation more and more with every day that passed.' The judgement flattered neither party: Home was ordered to repay the money, and spiritualism was declared 'mischievous nonsense, well calculated, on the one hand, to delude the vain, the weak, the foolish, and the superstitious; and, on the other hand, to assist the prospects of the needy adventurer'.

As if in response to this upset, Home began to exhibit yet more extraordinary effects, elongating his body by six inches while in a trance, as if stretched on a spiritual rack. To Ruskin, such circus tricks 'bore ... the aspect of the basest imposture'; this was either fraudery or the devil's work. His 'earthly master', Thomas Carlyle – whose rough-hewn Scottishness seemed refined in his disciple's features – told Ruskin that this was 'real witchcraft, and quite wrong'; and Ruskin himself reminded Georgiana that the book of Revelations predicted such 'deceptive signs and wonders', and that 'those who have "familiar spirits"' would precede the Second Coming.

> I have no doubt it is your duty at once to abstain from all these things . . . to receive what you *have* seen of them as an awful sign of the now active presence of the Fiend among us, – . . . and at once therefore to lead such a life as the daily expectation of the coming of Christ would compel in all earnest souls – that is to say of the simplest and sternest practical doing of good. I want you and M[r] Cowper to take a quiet walk with me, through some of the streets of London, chosen by me, and to talk of these things here – in broad daylight.

'I will enquire into this spiritualism . . .' he added, 'but it must henceforward be *only* among well educated and assuredly true & dear persons . . . Come and take the walk with me . . . S[t] C.'

Just as he had envisioned the dining rooms of the rich to suddenly part and admit 'the nearest human beings who were famishing . . . pale with sickness, horrible in destitution, broken by despair, body by body . . . laid upon the carpet', so Ruskin intended to take his friends through London's streets like the Ghost of Christmas Past, to witness the city's dispossessed. Their misery made it impossible for him to enjoy his own life, and he declared, 'I will endure it no longer quietly.' He would form his own company to assist food production in benighted areas and teach workers and landowners alike new economies; he would concern himself with 'the life that *is*', although he would remain open to the life to come. His was a quest manifest in the heavens themselves, which seemed to portend both apocalypse and his own instability: 'For the sky is covered with grey cloud; – not rain-cloud, but a dry black veil, which no ray of sunshine can pierce . . . And everywhere the leaves of the trees are shaking fitfully, as they do before a thunderstorm; only not violently, but enough to show the passing to and fro of a strange, bitter, blighting wind . . .' It was an augury to which he would return, in a Turnerian response to the changing climate and the unfolding drama of his own emotions.

Soliciting William Cowper's political support and Florence Herbert's secretarial skills, Ruskin set out his plan to save the world from its storm-clouded doom. On 22 May 1869 he told Georgiana, 'I see the corruption and horror of modernism . . . and that it can only be met by entire rejection of its companionship and infection. I shall ask whosoever will join . . . in a resolute effort to recover some human law and dignity of purpose, and I shall soon write out the series of laws which they must promise – to the best of their power – to keep.' It was, in its way, a reflection of Mary Ann's efforts to rewind the past through the future; yet while his words were prophetic, Ruskin was determined his aims should be practical. Where Thomas More had imagined his 'best state of a commen welth', Ruskin saw More's fantastic isle as a philosophical state, 'infinitely foolish and infinitely wise'. Reading Thomas Lake Harris on the subject, he wrote, 'Mr Harris is strong and clear on this, – but I do not think he is right in having no servants. The great human relation between master and servant is one of the most precious means of help and affection between persons of different ranks in character.'

Staying at Broadlands, Ruskin resumed his utopian dialogue with William and Georgiana, then in the midst of Harris's campaign to lure them to Lake Eyrie. 'The sheets you have sent me are full of interest,' Ruskin wrote. 'I cannot judge of the view they take of sources of strength – but we all of us see darkly and little . . . you will find some still more singularly close coincidences about Inspiration – or as Mr H calls it *res*piration . . .' 'I should like to meet Mr Oliphant better than almost anyone,' he told Georgiana, and when he did he reported that Harris's disciple 'told me wonderful things. Please – cancel all I said about Mr Harris's imperfect writing. I understand it now.'

Given the ultimate venality of Harris's beliefs, it is remarkable that they should have provided inspiration for Ruskin. 'I want to see Mr Harris more than he can possibly want to see me,' he told Georgiana. 'I'll make my way across the country to you on Saturday evening, somehow, and stay till Tuesday morning . . . I don't in the least believe you'll come to Utopia, so you needn't pretend you will . . .' He suggested that Georgiana should 'take an acre of ground, make it lovely, give what food comes of it to people who need it, and take no rent of it yourself', and warned her that 'the Foundations of Society are rotten with every imaginable plague, and must be struck at and swept away, and others built in Christ, instead of on the back of the Leviathan of the Northern Foam . . .'

Ruskin's ideas were also intimately linked to his explorations in Switzerland, whose history, as well as its geography, fascinated him. At Brunnen on Lake Lucerne, sheltered by massive Alpine peaks (where, two years later, mad King Ludwig would order alphorn-blowers to play to him while he sat in a small boat at midnight; and where, a year after that, Richard Wagner would move to a lakeside villa), Ruskin saw the possibility of a new history of Europe. Across the water in the hallowed meadow of Rutli, Switzerland's forest cantons had been confederated in 1291. Named the *Eidgenossen* – 'comrades bound by oath into a co-operative', but corrupted, after the Swiss reformation, to the French 'Huguenot' – it was an act which, seven hundred years later, influenced the shape of his ideas for a new European republic.

If Ruskin envisaged his own lakeside colony in which that plague could be swept away, then his new northern abode would have been the perfect place. Having given up the idea of living in Switzerland, and with his ties with London about to be severed by the death of his

mother that December (buried in a coffin which her son had painted sky-blue), in 1871 Ruskin bought Brantwood, a house on the eastern shore of Coniston Water. In the lingering presences of Wordsworth and Coleridge, the Lake District was an English wilderness; set on a tree-shadowed ledge over the lake, Brantwood was invested with Ruskin's love, and fear, of nature. As he saw microcosms of creation in the minerals and shells he collected, so Ruskin's estate – running steeply up to the dark woods above, and down to the dark water below – became a powerhouse of his imagination.

On the banks of this Wagnerian lake, traversed by its own golden steam yacht, the *Gondola*, the quest for a Victorian utopia might be realised. Ruskin worked with his environment, hewing trees, shaping the land like some gigantic rockery – just as his road-building, crossing-sweeping and moor-draining schemes were public performances with symbolic, covert meanings; he even created an automated waterfall to greet visitors at his door. He illustrated his theories with giant plaster models made of flowers, feathers and oak leaves, as if in memoriam of a mythic England, peeled from the face of a medieval Green Man, while students at his lectures saw 'the strange *afflatus* coming and going in his eye'. He filled Brantwood's vitrines with intricately labelled, jewel-like geological specimens, and his grey pocket books with exquisite sketches of gothic architecture and microscopic, alien-like plant forms, obsessively indexing his experience.

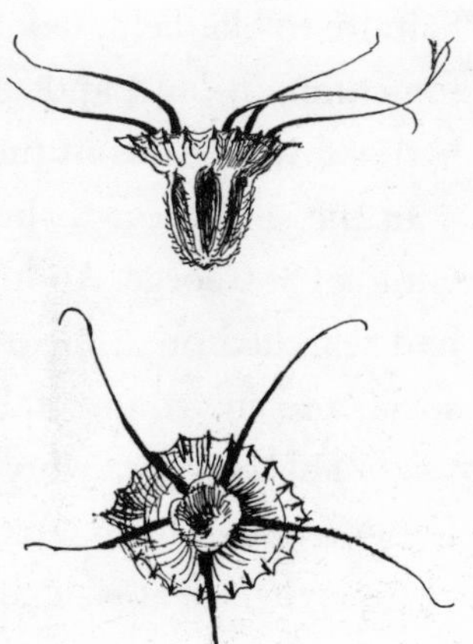

As his house expanded like some aesthetic laboratory, Ruskin saw each object – from minute lichens to lofty fells – invested with the entire power and beauty of nature. Brantwood came to epitomise the sacred struggle of good versus evil; man against machine; nature versus supernature; a Manichean battle meteorologically manifest in skies polluted by Manchester's Cottonopolis and Bradford's satanic mills. To Ruskin it seemed that a new Dark Day was drifting north, tainting clear waters with a grey reflection; a man-made miasma pervading limpid air and overwhelming his dreams. The imperial sway had cast a permanent gloom, and 'the Empire of England, on which formerly the sun never set, has become one on which he never rises'. It was the same apocalyptic storm which had accompanied the eviction of the Girlingites; the same harvest-wrecker which Hardy's Michael Henchard is told to expect by the weather-caster he consults, ''Twill be more like living in Revelations this autumn than in England.'

And as the New Forest was the southern locus for such mysticism, so in the north Ruskin's beliefs merged with the imaginings of the mid-century: a Pre-Raphaelite dreamscape populated by Angel Guides and female messiahs, where the spirits of the dead walked and talked with the living; a Zion for England's green and pleasant land. Modern Britain had erupted with utopias, from

Saltaire to Sheffield, from Lanarkshire to Hampshire, in a struggle for common land and uncommon beliefs; and here in the long-hymned wilderness of the Lakes, Ruskin reigned as its prophet.

In the same year as he acquired Brantwood, Ruskin began his Guild of St George. Another echo of the Eden for which the Diggers had searched on St George's Hill in Surrey, it called for spiritual, social and environmental renewal in the name of England's patron saint. This new fraternity would be financed by the sale of Ruskin's London house, from which he would donate £1,000 (within twenty years of their deaths, he had spent £153,000 of the £157,000 left to him by his parents) and a tithe of one-tenth of its participants' income. Ruskin set out his plans in *Fors Clavigera* – 'fate's nail' – his monthly newsletter to the working man. *Human Nature* approved:

> MR RUSKIN'S GIFT TO THE PEOPLE . . . This is his scheme as to what is to be done with it: – '. . . The money is not to be spent in feeding Woolwich infants with gunpowder [a reference to the enormous munitions factory in south-east London]. It is to be spent in dressing the earth and keeping it – in feeding human lips – in clothing human bodies – in kindling human souls . . . As soon as the fund reaches any sufficient amount, the trustees shall buy with it any kind of land offered them at just price in Britain, rock, moor, marsh, or sea-shore – it matters not what, so it be English ground, and secured to us. Then, we will ascertain the absolute best that can be made of every acre.'

Medieval in references, modern in its ambitions, the Guild would apply Ruskinian principles to all England in a kind of extension of his earlier exhortation to the Pre-Raphaelite Brotherhood to 'go to nature in all singleness of heart, and walk with her laboriously and trustingly, having no other thoughts but how best to penetrate her meaning, and remembering her instruction; rejecting nothing, selecting nothing, and scorning nothing'. It was a mission rooted, first and foremost, in the land: 'We will first examine what flowers and herbs it naturally bears; every wholesome flower that it will grow shall be sown in its wild places, and every kind of fruit-tree that can prosper; and arable and pasture land extended by every expedient of tillage, with humble and simple cottage dwellings under faultless sanitary regulation.' Labourers would be paid 'sufficient, unchanging wages', and their children educated 'in agricultural schools inland, and naval schools by the sea', where they would be taught to ride or sail, spin or weave, 'and at a proper age to cook all ordinary food exquisitely'. Music and morality would be taught equally, along with 'gentleness to all brute creatures, finished courtesy to each other, to speak truth with rigid care, and to obey orders with the precision of slaves'. Ruskin was aware of how fantastic this scheme might sound (if not to the readers of *Human Nature*), but his determination was absolute: 'Now, to what extent I may be able to carry this plan into execution, I know not; but to *some* visible extent, with my own single hand, I can and will, if I live.'

The first issue of *Fors Clavigera*, dated New Year's Day 1871, stated the position clearly enough. Ruskin described an empire 'afraid of the Russians; afraid of the Prussians; afraid of the Americans; afraid of the Hindoos; afraid of the Chinese; afraid of the Japanese; afraid of the New Zealanders; and afraid of the Caffres . . .' His Guild would provide an alternative to this global cloud of unrest, 'the Kakotopia and its curse, which we had seen actually fulfilled'. In contrast to the disastrous Paris commune, Ruskin's colonies would live and work together, with intellects fed by literature and art, even as other needs were satisfied: 'That there be no taxes to pay; that everybody had clothes enough; that everybody had jewels enough; that everybody had as many books and pictures as they could read or look at, with quantities of the highest quality in easily accessible libraries and galleries'. Ruskin believed that a love of art was necessary for good government. Machinery would be banned 'where it supersedes healthy bodily exercise, or the art and precision of manual labour in decorative work'; he saw steam engines as good only for 'cutting icebergs in the frigid zones and for blasting rocks to provide more land on which people could live'. 'Gunpowder and steam hammers are the toys of the insane and paralytic,' he wrote in the prospectus sent to William Cowper, who had agreed to be consul to the Guild.

'It is *not* to be *Communism*: quite the contrary,' Ruskin stated. 'The old Feudal system applied to do good instead of evil – to save life, instead of destroy . . . as the system gets power, I hope to see it alter *laws* all over England . . .' Some friends reacted positively to his ambitions. Watts promised a tenth of his annual earnings, even though he didn't quite know how Ruskin's scheme would work: 'I know nothing about that, perhaps it is entirely Utopian. I don't care, it is a protest against Mammonworship, and the giving-up of everything in the desire to "get on" – characteristics of the age I cannot but deplore.' Others were more sceptical: Carlyle told the poet William Allingham of Ruskin's 'wonderful folly at times! The St George's Company is utterly absurd. I thought it a joke at first.'

At Broadlands, Ruskin made a cryptic summary of the Guild's spiritual dimensions –

> A. First article of St G[eorge's] Creed. Believed in Almighty, ie in a Law, ascertainable as the will of a Governor. Compulsion according to that is a duty. They who refuse to compel confess they know not God. All is of a piece. Duke of Argyll. Automata.

– to which he added later thoughts, 'Of Art – not to be paid – and idolatry, all the precious chapter read today: Sap.13. Of Mythology: Pegasus drinking to be given of waters in Malham Cove.' This English paradise was already populated by fantastic beasts. More practically, Ruskin's Eden encompassed a tea shop which he opened in Marylebone ('where nothing but the best tea was sold at a fair price'), to be managed by his lover, Rose; and a museum in Sheffield, set on a steep hill so that 'the approach to it may be at once symbolically instructive and practically sanitary'. Nearby, over the county border in Derbyshire, Ruskin established St George's Farm at Totley, 'a little piece of England given into the English workman's hand, and heaven's.' Here, as the Girlingites attempted their commune, Ruskin tried to establish his own, but 'in a very short time they were hurling anathemas at each other's head', as Edward Carpenter wrote, '. . . and the would-be garden of Eden became such a scene of confusion that Ruskin had to send down an ancient retainer of his (with a pitchfork instead of a flaming sword) to bar them all out'. Later, the Guild leased the land to Carpenter's young protégé, George Pearson, and 'another, less voluble and more practical, body of Communists'.

Yet for all its faults, Ruskin's nowhere had a certain purity, aspiring to a philosophical state in which he wished 'to leave this one great fact clearly stated':

THERE IS NO WEALTH BUT LIFE.

He would direct his operations from his Brantwood study, where he sat in his crimson campaign chair, the fire to his left, the lake to his right, while around him the room stood littered with the stones, seeds and shells of his gathering: some in tiny wooden cylinders like miniature Shaker boxes, carefully catalogued by the same elegant hand which sought to paint, with photographic realism, the incomprehensible beauty of nature. We see nineteenth-century England through Ruskin's eyes as he crouches down to a granite crag to scrutinise some scarlet-flowering moss with the acuity of a child on a summer lawn focusing on the blade of grass in front of his face. 'To think of the quantity of pleasure one has had in one's life from that emerald green velvet.'

But beyond the detail of these botanical and geological studies, there is a hauntedness to Ruskin's art which belies his truth to nature. Closer to Blake in his prophecies – just as he looked like a relic of the Romantic era in his greatcoat and blue stock – Ruskin's thoughts would darken at Brantwood. Secluded within his distrust of the modern world, he extended his domain with turrets and terraces, as though adding clerestories and cloisters to his monastery, and had a corner cut away from his bedroom to be replaced by a latticework oriel the height of a man. Here he could stand, held out over earth and water in this gothic lantern, the landscape above and below and beyond endowing his isolation, ennobling his mind and transporting his soul. Like a figure by Caspar David Friedrich, Ruskin faced the vast expanse of which he was both a part, and from which he stood apart. Here he was confronted with his destiny – even as the glaciated fells and silent tarns awaited his imminent descent into the unknown, hand-in-hand with the spirit of his beloved Rose.

NINE

The Names of Butterflies

. . . a wreath of wild rose is not so easily disentangled . . .
Rose La Touche to John Ruskin, 14 July 1862

For nearly twenty years, the fleeting, beautiful, benighted figure of Rose La Touche had been the one specimen Ruskin had been unable to collect. Just as he could not bear to pierce a butterfly for display – being sensitised, like the Cowpers, to the pain of animals – so for Ruskin physical union would be almost sacrilegious in this fraught relationship. And although he offered himself as a man pure of heart and pure of body, this sense of innocence was also corrosive – not least because when he first met her, Rose was barely ten years old.

In January 1858, Rose's mother Maria (who had her own artistic and literary pretensions, and had published two novels) had asked Ruskin, whom she knew through a mutual friend, to become drawing master to the family. That first encounter, at the La Touches' house in Mayfair, would burn itself into Ruskin's memory. Rose came into the room, 'quietly taking stock of me with her blue eyes'; she offered him her hand 'as a good dog gives its paw, and then stood a little back'. Rose was 'neither tall nor short for her age; a little stiff in her way of standing. The eyes rather deep blue . . . Lips perfectly lovely in profile . . . the hair . . . graceful in short curls round the forehead.' Later, at Denmark Hill, she 'walked like a little white statue through the twilight woods, talking solemnly',

evoking an innocent, Pre-Raphaelite image. But there was also an element of Lewis Carroll's relationship with Alice Liddell – both of whom Ruskin knew – in the troubled attraction he felt for this young girl.

Born in 1848 to a County Kildare family of Huguenot descent, Rose La Touche possessed a beauty which 'neither camera nor lover could suggest'; Ruskin would sketch her obsessively throughout her brief adulthood, only to find that the more he tried, the more elusive her image became. Ruskin taught the young girl about art and literature and took her to the British Museum to hear his friend Richard Owen, discoverer of dinosaurs, after which she called Ruskin 'Archegosaurus'. 'Oh St Crumpet I think of you so much & of all your dearness to me I wish so very much that you were happy – God make you so', she wrote, '. . . I am ever your rose . . . You *must* see how we think of you & talk of you – rose posie.' And he thought of her too, as he stood over the river rushing through Lucerne by moonlight. 'Tower and steeple, chiming sadly' her name as 'O'er the Alps the clouds lie loose,/Tossed about in silver tangles'. As he watched Rose grow up, Ruskin thought how children changed like clouds and marvelled at their unconditional, innocent love; qualities which, in his own way, Ruskin himself still possessed. Yet there was already something eerie about their bond, as Rose told Maria, 'I think he wants to see me, Mamma', before Ruskin arrived.

As she grew, both in years and in his imagination, Rose became a kind of alter-ego for Ruskin, his Catherine Earnshaw. Her own mother wondered if Rose would ever be a civilised being: 'She is out in the dew at break of day – and all day long she is in and out let the weather be what it may, and not one single thing that girls do does she do – except a little music when she pleases.' In an episode which might have come from Emily Brontë's imagining, Maria recalled an incident in Scotland when Rose was lost 'and with her accustomed intrepidity she captured a boy to show her the way. For miles she walked over the heather with her captive. She told me of her talk with him, and how *very* kind he was to her, helping her in rough places. He told her *he* wouldn't be out after dark for the world and was surprised that she didn't mind. When they came to a house he said, "I hope there's no gentry here to see *you* walking with a dirty lad like me!" '

In those years after the Great Hunger, Rose was intensely conscious of her family's wealth, as was Ruskin when he first visited their 11,000 acre estate in Harristown; and like Georgiana, Rose sought to minister to the sick and the poor, a concern which bound her still further to Ruskin. Yet such empathy affected her psyche, too. Increasingly removed from reality as she connected with such suffering, the young woman refused to eat, and in October 1863, at the age of fifteen, Rose's fragile world fell in on itself.

> *Everything* hurt me . . . I seemed to *think through my head*, and every thought hurt me. I was only comfortable when I was not thinking . . . To talk I had to think and think in words and it was dreadful to me. Light hurt me. Food hurt me (not my head). Sometimes I was hungry but had such terrible pain after eating. Everything hurt me. I can only say again – I seemed to hurt myself . . .

Modern medicine might diagnose an eating disorder, yet the demands of Ruskin's love and the pressure of her father's fervent evangelism seemed to sunder Rose's subliminal self; there was even a suggestion that she had suffered abuse at John La Touche's hands. Her otherness became manifest in her rejection of sustenance: perhaps, like Sarah Jacobs, the Welsh Fasting Girl, Rose absorbed nutrition from the air, or, like Bernadette, she might resort to eating earth. Or perhaps her body was consuming itself, a lovely suicide by self-neglect. To her mother, it was clear that in her strange condition, which puzzled her doctors, Rose had developed 'the most extraordinary powers of clairvoyance'. And as in the crises of Ann Lee and Mary Ann, consumption was a mechanism in that state: the act of foregoing food and drink could reject the world of men and refine female spirituality. Nor was it coincidental that in an age of a consuming society, the prevailing disease was *consumption*, from which Rose was said to suffer, and which could induce an ethereal air. Thus this saint-like girl reacted to trauma with psychic phenomena of her own, able to see both 'spiritual & earthly things . . . to tell beforehand any little thing that would befall her thro' the day', wrote Maria, as out of her sleep, her daughter awoke with 'an infant's mind, . . . & an entire oblivion of all acquired knowledge, & of every person & thing not known to her eleven years ago'.

An anguished Ruskin had no idea how to face Rose's adulthood, let alone her mysterious illness: '. . . And now she's got to be fifteen there's no making a pet of her any longer – and I don't know what to do.' In an age of idealised women, Ruskin idolised Rose to a disastrous degree. It was a mystification which would propel them both into the darkness. While Rose laboured under the oceanic pressure of her parents' demands and her suitor's desires, it is hard to imagine – although his letters and diary entries convey a little of it – the horror which Ruskin felt as his beloved was struck with 'some strange complaint of the brain', leaving her unable to think, read or write for long periods, and rendering her limbs as white as marble, as if she had turned into a medieval statue. His barely living Rose assumed a sanctity in Ruskin's imagination; an icon incarnate for an industrial age, 'tall and brightly fair, her face of the most delicately chiselled beauty – too severe to be entirely delightful to all people . . . and of a strange beauty – so that once a stranger seeing her for the first time said "she looked like a young sister of Christ's"'.

As Rose moved through her inexorable cycle of physical illness, spiritual struggle and suppressed sexuality, the affair took on the air of a tragedy, one which was witnessed by two couples: William and Georgiana Cowper, whose London house was in the same elegant Mayfair street as the La Touches'; and their friends George and Louisa MacDonald, who lived in bohemian disarray in West London.

George MacDonald had been a Congregationalist minister, but now wrote fantasy novels for children. His *Phantastes*, published in 1858, the year of Rose's birth, was set in a Pre-Raphaelite forest – later illustrated by Arthur Hughes – in which a young man 'advancing towards a second midnight' meets a country maid who tells him which trees he can trust: 'the Oak, and the Elm, and the great Beech . . . But shun the Ash and the Alder; for the Ash is an ogre – you will know him by his thick fingers; and the Alder will smother you with her web of hair, if you let her near you at night'. The adventure ends in a temple of yews, where druid-like figures surround 'a youth gorgeously attired beneath his robe of white, and wearing a chaplet of flowers on his head'; the boy is an intended human sacrifice, and in the struggle that follows, the hero dies – only to wake from his dream. MacDonald's work, which would influence C. S. Lewis and J.R.R. Tolkien, was filled with such magical transformations. *At the Back of the North Wind* (1871) tells of an airy spirit which carries off a little boy called Diamond: 'I should have been astonished at his being able even to report such conversations as he said he had had with North Wind, had I not known already that some children are profound in metaphysics.' The boy dies in the tower in which North Wind visited him: 'A lovely figure, as white and almost as clear as alabaster, was lying on the bed. I saw at once how it was. They thought he was dead. I knew that he had gone to the back of the north wind.'

Influenced by symbolism and mysticism, MacDonald's books were a more ethereal version of *Alice in Wonderland*; and indeed Charles Dodgson was encouraged to publish his story by the

MacDonalds, who were his close friends. They lived with their eleven children and no servants in a riverside house in Hammersmith, surrounded by paintings by Rossetti and Hughes and unbound by Victorian convention; when Georgiana's sister died, George's letter of consolation – 'Come and see us. Our thoughts will not jar with yours' – was a contrast to the stiff formality of other condolences.

The MacDonald children were not shut away in the nursery (not least because there was no nanny to look after them), and they delighted Dodgson, who teased six-year-old Greville as he modelled for the sculptor Alexander Munro, saying, 'he had better take the opportunity of having his head exchanged for a marble one'. Greville – in his velvet cap and coat, the image of Diamond – solemnly declined on the grounds 'that a marble head couldn't speak'.

This knowing little boy – to whom Ruskin had refused to be godfather, on the grounds that 'first, I'm a pagan', and second that he had too many godchildren he didn't care about – would become another observer in the story; another pair of eyes watching the arrivals and departures of his parents' friends from half-open doorways, and sensing, as only a child could, an atmosphere inexplicably charged with emotion. Even sixty years later, Greville MacDonald felt the need to set matters straight about the scenes he had witnessed. Writing in 1932, as an eminent surgeon, he recalled the rumours that still circulated around Ruskin: that Rose was 'one of his mistresses'; that he had committed 'an unpardonable folly' for which he had to pay 'an unmentionable price'; that he was, in fact, 'an immoral man'. In his account – coloured both by his adolescent remembrance and his adult pathology – Greville MacDonald saw Ruskin's attitude to women as indiscreet – but only in that 'his innocent if endearing letters to charming girls' were misunderstood. It was as if Ruskin were unaware of the effect of his affection; as if he were unable to judge its power. Questioned about his marriage to Effie, Ruskin would tell George MacDonald that he had been persuaded to marry a woman whom he hadn't loved; and because he hadn't loved her, he was unable to consummate the union.

The events of that abortive wedding night came to haunt Ruskin. Effie would testify that her husband 'was disgusted with my person'; Ruskin claimed that 'there were certain circumstances in her person' which 'completely checked' his passion. Neither of these statements would ever be explained. 'Such notions may perhaps seem incredible to most men', Greville MacDonald wrote, tactfully, 'yet the fact of incompatibility of sentiment occasionally standing in the way of completed marriage, even with those quite normal, is fully instanced in the annals of medical jurisprudence.' But there were other moves to discredit Ruskin, and they went beyond mere gossip.

When Ruskin first met her, Rose had been like one of the characters from MacDonald's books; a faerie child – in the way children can regard you as if from another world entirely – and yet mortal and therefore fated to betray that innocence with their physical reality. And this was the situation Ruskin had to face.

Rose's parents were examining her marriage prospects, and a man in his late forties whose first marriage had been dissolved in disreputable circumstances was hardly a contender for their list of potential suitors. Ruskin must have known this, and yet his heart could not accept it. Nor had he expected the intervention of his former wife. From Effie Millais – as she now was – Maria La Touche learned 'malicious disparagements' about Ruskin's private life, in the light of which, she believed, she was right to dissuade her daughter from a marriage which was not only undesirable, but 'possibly quite wrong'.

On 2 February 1866, a month after her eighteenth birthday, Rose declined Ruskin's offer of marriage – but said she would reconsider her decision in three years' time, when she turned twenty-one. Her parents were aghast, not least because of their daughter's physical condition: left frail by her illness, Rose's adolescence had been arrested. It was one reason, writes Ruskin's most recent biographer, for her unearthly air: Rose had simply not become a woman at all. And in that physical state she seemed to be an equal match for Ruskin, who if his wife's insinuations were to be believed, was impotent. Neither, it appeared, could be bound to each other, and it was in precisely that celibate state – elsewhere celebrated by the Children of God – that they were paradoxically bound until death, and beyond.

At first Ruskin seemed placid in the face of fate, telling Georgiana, his confidante, 'she will not engage herself in any way without telling me about it first . . . (while her mother *will* always treat her as a mere child)'. Ruskin encouraged Georgiana to befriend Rose as a go-between; he even asked the Cowpers to go to Ireland to put his case, without success. His letters to Georgiana were filled with heartfelt fear and self-justification:

> . . . They may say – the mere contingency of my winning her is not to be endured by them – but why this? If they either of them believed one word of the one calumny abroad against me – they ought never to have let me *speak* to their child. If they do not, what else is there so dreadful in me? – I am old – (older now, by ten years for what they have done to me) – but many a youth is indeed older yet, and contingently nearer the dominion of the shadow of death. No human creature can say I have injured them. – Thousands can say I have aided them – I am pure-hearted – pure-bodied – many – both young & old – love me – the young most – and I love their daughter & have loved her – as few men ever love – young or old.

Not even Georgiana could console Ruskin, caught as he was in a state which ranged from rage to self-pity and whose vocabulary was violent melodrama. He saw himself 'lying wounded – bleeding to death' and Rose 'withheld by her father from coming to bind the wound . . . Every hour of this pain takes more life out of my soul . . . making my heart cold and my hair grey . . .' Exhausted, the great man of letters had run out of words: 'I cannot write of these things – it is all terrible to me – and words are useless . . .'

Yet between Georgiana and Rose words continued, in letters equally threaded with guilt and pain. The young woman wrote from her Harristown bedroom on tiny sheets of notepaper with accounts of arguments with her mother, whose behaviour seemed more immature than her daughter's: 'Last night she said I need never come into her room, that there could be no affection between us (but that *she* could not change). I slipped off to bed, tired and sad – it was such a comfort to be alone . . .' In a drama of correspondence withheld from, or in one case purloined by Rose, she lacerated herself with reproach. When Effie wrote with details of Ruskin's impotency, Rose threatened to burn the letters which 'totally misconstrued . . . St C' – 'oh it was so horrible to hear them calling him "dishonourable"' – then retreated, pathetically,

> I was very wrong in taking them – And for all the unhappiness I have caused everybody. I am very very sorry – for they are just the people I like to make happy – & will try – & it is not St C's fault – at all. Dearest Phile you will make him happy – I wish he had all the love that makes *always* happy & God bless you all. Your loving Rose.

These heartbreaking missives continued to arrive from Ireland. On the eve of her nineteenth birthday, Rose recalled that 'Mama said, long, long ago, that I was born in the depth of winter & called Rose, that I might brighten the winters & the wintry years. I wish Phile it was true –'. While the rest of the family went to church, she retired to her room with a headache to paint a biblical scene for Georgiana – 'I chose *blue* (some of St C's ultramarine) because it is the deepest most abiding colour'. Religion and morality tore at Rose's conscience, in scenes of Hardyesque pathos: '. . . I have found a poor man who lives in a bog near here, with cancer in his eye. It is in the last stage & gives him such pain – Is it not horrible to see pain you *cannot* help? . . .'

'. . . ah Phile – you do not know how unhappy I am,' she mourned. 'Life seems to grow harder every day . . . I should not mind it *only* for the pain, only I know it is not right . . .' Then, at midnight, sitting at the wide open window of her room, watching the ink-night evening, Rose saw a shower of meteors shooting across the sky 'in the cold starlight . . . The whole heavens seem moving – oh Phile they are so beautiful! . . . My hands are stiff with cold, but I must wait up & see them & I shall think about you, & what you said, when the starlight gets too cold – Your loving Rose.'

In February 1867, the La Touches returned to Mayfair where, by painful coincidence, they were neighbours to the Cowpers, and from where Rose was forbidden from seeing or writing to Ruskin. The tortured critic came to associate Maria La Touche with an evil serpent, while he saw her daughter as an immaculate conception, 'not born . . . of womankind', even claiming that her visits to ailing friends had produced miracle cures. Ruskin was reduced to walking the city streets, visiting theatres where she had been, even chasing after carriages which he thought contained the object of his obsession.

Waiting for Rose's answer to his proposal, Ruskin marked off the days in his diary like a prisoner telling his sentence on a cell wall. The forty-seven-year-old seemed to be regressing into an unlived youth, his attachment to Rose a means of regaining his own lost past: 'I wish we *were* all children,' he told Georgiana. It was a sentiment resonant not only with his love for the young girl he had first known, but with other Victorian relationships with children: Dodgson and Alice Liddell; the MacDonalds and their family; Julia Margaret Cameron and her goose-winged angels; William Crookes and Florence Cook; even the Girlingites and their orphans; as if, by its proximity to the beginning and, often, the end of life, the child embodied a sense of mortality, a half-worldly spirit caught between innocence and knowledge. But Rose and Ruskin were adults (although neither seemed to see the other thus), and in this conflict of emotions their affair took on a Shakespearean air. Through Georgiana she sent St C rose leaves; he dried her flowers, 'only one can't press massive rosebud and pink – so they will be withered at last into dark clusters of frankincense'.

Ruskin had come to realise that Rose was psychologically unstable even as, in a shocking revelation, he discovered that Effie had provided evidence of their failed marriage: 'He is quite unnatural and in that one thing all the rest is embraced.' Any relationship with a woman would now be impossible for Ruskin. Little wonder that he regarded Maria – who had shown her daughter the letter – as a poisonous snake.

In turn, Rose saw Georgiana as a surrogate mother: '. . . I should like to tell you how sorry I am for all this unhappiness & how as a child I want to do right – Let me be Your loving child Rose' and it was Georgiana to whom she turned when her sister Emily died suddenly in 1868. 'Phile write me a kind word, for my sister is dead. We expect her husband & her little children to-morrow. She died at sea coming home to us. It is not difficult to think of her as an Angel.'

Nor was it hard to see Rose as a grievous angel, suffering for others even as she suffered for herself, trapped between portents and potential disgrace: 'I am not hard but must say that the suffering of "another" [Ruskin] at this time, I cannot pity – Every day brings to my ears more of the *untrue* & altogether in excusable thing he has said of me. He has broken all laws of honour . . . All Dublin is roused & my name is in every one's mouth.' Rose seemed to be suffering from a kind of manic depression, and even intimated suicide: '. . . I never had such intense pain in my head. Oh how gladly I would close my quarter century . . . But I with my strong vitality have such terrible power of bearing & feeling suffering . . . and I must stop now I find as it is dressing time . . .'

Where the spirits were confined to curtained rooms, Rose and Ruskin's drama now burst out into public space. At noon on 7 January 1870, Ruskin stepped into the hall of the Royal Academy, and saw Rose standing there. He had not set eyes on her for four years. Stunned, he took the letters she had written to him – which he kept pressed like precious botanical specimens between thin gold plates in his coat pocket – and offered them to her. The encounter was described by Ruskin in a letter to Georgiana the following day:

> She tried to go away as soon as she saw me, so that I had no time to think – I caught her, – but she broke away so that I could not say more than ten words – uselessly.
>
> She then changed her mind about going, and remained in the rooms apparently quite cheerful and undisturbed. Having looked at her well, I went up to her side again, and said, 'I think you have dropped your pocketbook,' offering her her letter of engagement between the golden plates. She said 'No.' I said again – No? enquiringly. She repeated the word. I put the letter back into my breast and left the rooms.
>
> She is usually as quick as lightning but I am not sure that she saw clearly what it was I offered her. She might have thought it was only an endeavour to give her a letter. I am so *brisé* that I can hardly move or think, to day.

Emotions swung back and forth between them like a planchette, as Rose turned cool and hot then cool again. At one point she rebelled against her parents and seemingly offered herself to her suitor. On 23 February 1870, Ruskin told Georgiana (for whom, 'as storms assailed him', he had devised a new name, Isola), 'She has come back to me. She will not leave me any more. "If love is any sunshine to you take it – & keep it".' And like sunlight forced through cloud, for an instant his life was brighter. But then, the La Touches launched a new investigation into his marriage. It was the final blow to Ruskin's hopes.

In that momentous summer of 1871 – as Frederick Evans and Mary Ann arrived in London – Rose's father, recently baptised by Charles Spurgeon in his Metropolitan Tabernacle pool, began their inquiry into Ruskin's marriage to Effie. The La Touches were concerned at the legal position of Ruskin's annulment: if he married Rose and had children, the annulment might become invalid, and their daughter's marriage to him bigamous. This was one reason why Rose was shown Effie's correspondence, in which she cruelly accused Ruskin of abnormality. Now, as a result of this stress, of the interrogation by lawyers and the abuse of his emotions, Ruskin suffered a nervous collapse – the first frightening augury of the madness that would engulf him.

He had gone to Matlock Bath, the Derbyshire spa, which he had known since childhood, and where the Cowpers went to comfort him. Ruskin had written to Georgiana, pathetically, '. . . Would you come and nurse me . . . only to want some orange juice and things?' Now, having seen Clifford's portrait, he told her: 'This semblance of you is very pleasant to me, in the character of Nurse, to which I owe so much.'

'My dear William,' Ruskin wrote in July, almost unbelieving of the fact, '*Was* I so very ill, really? when you saw me first? . . . Everybody thought I was acting in mad or foolish whims of sickness, but I could have written you a medical statement of the case . . .' It was no coincidence that it was at Matlock, in that eventful summer of 1871, that Ruskin first diagnosed the 'plague-cloud' which over-lowered his madness – and that of the modern world.

With William's help, Ruskin sought legal advice and was told marriage was possible. But that summer it seemed that neither Ruskin nor Rose were in possession of their senses. Rose was unable to eat the forced strawberries and cream served at the family table while the Irish poor were starving – as though, like Ruskin, she imagined their emaciated bodies hovering over her shoulder. One London surgeon told Ruskin she was suffering from *hysteria*, a condition 'most prevalent in the young female members of the higher and middle classes . . . persons easily excited to mental emotions, of sensitive feeling, often delicate and refined', in whom the mind 'appears to exercise some mysterious or occult influence . . .' History would have other diagnoses: in the 1930s, Greville MacDonald claimed, 'To-day we should give her malady the name of psychastenia, and . . . should have cured her'; while modern commentators discern anorexia nervosa, which arrests development (as if the mind were rejecting the body's changes), rejects parental will and concentrates obsessively on the self. Still others cited consumption or cardiac disease but whatever the truth, Rose's was a fatal disruption of the heart.

She told George MacDonald that she could not trust Ruskin and must take her parents' advice; yet when they met at the MacDonalds' house in Hammersmith, 'both were for a few days supremely happy'. For the first time in six years they were able to talk freely. 'It is these days that bring back to me the great man and the fragile girl, as if in living presence,' wrote Greville MacDonald, recalling Ruskin's care-worn 'grandeur of face, his searching blue eyes, and his adorable smile', contrasting with 'the frail Rose, so amazingly thin yet with such high colour and her great eyes, with the tenderest of smiles possessing so readily her exquisitely red lips . . . I was astonished at her being alive', he remembered through his young eyes, 'seeing that, I well remember, her dinner once consisted of three green peas, and the very next day, of one strawberry and half an Osborne biscuit! She was too frail to sit at table, of course.'

To Ruskin they were 'days of heaven, which I would have very thankfully bought with all the rest of my life', and they resumed in the liberated environment of Broadlands, where he and Rose walked and rowed and where, on the placid Hampshire lawns, she allowed him to kiss her, and he vowed his loyalty to the death. In his room that night, Ruskin wrote a note to his hostess: '. . . I do not believe that ever any creature out of heaven has been so much loved as I love that child . . . she was so good and so grave, and so gay, and so terribly lovely – and so merciless, and so kind . . .', although he feared that 'her entire soul is being paralysed by the poisoned air'.

Rose was caught between a mother who 'said I was a baby instead of a young woman of 24!', and a lover old enough to be her father, to whom she was 'the only living thing in the world'. Such tensions would be hard for the most worldly woman to bear, but for Rose they were insufferable. Withdrawing into her faith, she began to invoke weird reveries: 'I who believe in a day to come when the Great White Throne shall be set . . . and our secret sins shall stand in the light of His countenance . . .', exhorting Ruskin to 'Hear His Voice whose love you have rejected . . .' She also asked him to join her in Cheshire, only to reject him herself, violently, shouting at him on the train.

Beaten back to London, Ruskin retreated penitentially to the Euston Hotel, which he hated, telling friends that Rose was dying,

and writing a letter to the *Pall Mall Gazette*: 'I assure you sir, insanity is a tender point with me. One of my best friends has just gone mad and all the rest say I am mad myself.' Should that be the case, he requested 'that I may be immediately shot'. It was as if he felt the need to make his personal trauma public. That autumn Ruskin drew Rose, but her profile seemed focused only in two dimensions, receding into the ether. This wilful Rose lacked the physicality of *Beata Beatrix*, and her own eyes were closed in a sad, ghostly insubstantiality, as if she was slipping away, having existed only in her lover's dreams.

Yet Ruskin put faith in his dreams, and even proposed to give up Brantwood to live in 'the first cottage of George's company, for Rosie and me – in the New Forest', a personal utopia for his innocent bride, even as the virgin forest sheltered the celibate Girlingites. But Rose wandered from Hastings boarding houses to modern hotels in Tyburnia, a new district of London named after its site of martyrdom; and while Ruskin must have been aware, since his days at Denmark Hill, of the strange trajectory of Mary Ann's story, he was too busy dealing with his dying Rose and her own mania to have much appetite for the dilemmas of the Children of God.

Throughout these years of frustrated love and mental instability Ruskin had one particular outlet for his emotions as well as his creativity. *Fors Clavigera* was a self-published work-in-progress: cyclical, unclassifiable, discursive; as wide-ranging as James Burns' *Human Nature* and as doomy as Frederick Evans' pronouncements on the modern world or a Camisard tract from the previous century. It was aimed at 'the working man', but the addresses on its mailing list ranged from Winnington Hall, the Cheshire girls' school in whose pupils Ruskin had a vested interest, to Windsor Castle, where the Queen's son, Prince Leopold, was a confidante in the critic's crises over Rose. The *Daily News* declared it 'notorious as a curious magazine of the blunders of a man of genius who has travelled out of his province', and even Ruskin acknowledged its 'desultory and accidental character'. 'To read *Fors* is like being out in a thunderstorm,' wrote his acolyte Collingwood; and its pages resounded with the Lear-like rant of a fifty-one-year-old prophet in the wilderness.

Fors Clavigera was haunted by the spirit of Rose, and encrypted in its serendipitous, grandiloquent texts were messages from a spurned lover, as Ruskin switched from sardonic critique of Rose's evangelism to deep empathy with her pity for the poor. Snatches of autobiography and art critique (it was in *Fors Clavigera* that Ruskin would accuse Whistler of 'flinging a pot of paint in the public's face') alternated with polemics on the perfidious state of Britain, contrasting its dispossessed poor with the materialism of its '"rising" middle classes'. In these fire-and-brimstone sermons for a machine age, Ruskin set newspaper reports of families starving to death against scenes from London's popular culture: Gustave Doré's pictures (which Ruskin regarded as vulgar to the point of blasphemy) on show in Bond Street, and around the corner in the Egyptian Hall on Piccadilly, the performing 'illusionists and antispiritualists', Maskelyne and Cooke. Presenting these to his readers like images from a magic lantern, Ruskin delivered a breathtaking commentary on the corruption of the modern world:

> Nor are we without great and terrible signs of supernatural calamity, no less in grievous changes and deterioration of climate, than in forms of mental disease, claiming distinctly to be necromantic, and, as far as I have examined the evidence relating to them, actually manifesting themselves as such. For observe you, my friends, countrymen, and brothers – *Either*, at this actual moment of your merry Christmas-time, that has truly come to pass, in falling London, which your greatest Englishman wrote of falling Rome, 'the sheeted dead do squeak and gibber in your English streets,' *Or*, such a system

> of loathsome imposture and cretinous blasphemy is current among all classes of England and America, as makes the superstition of all past ages divine truth in comparison.

It was a vicious indictment of the era; a vision of western civilisation in thrall to decadence and necromancy – even as Ruskin himself delved into the world of the unseen.

> *One* of these things *is* so – gay friends; – have it which way you will: one or other of these, to me, alike appalling; and in your principal street of London society, you have a picture of highly dressed harlots gambling, of naked ones, called Andromeda and Francesca of Rimini, and of Christ led to be crucified, exhibited, for your better entertainment, in the same room; and at the end of the same street, an exhibition of jugglery, professedly imitating, *for money*, what a large number of you believe to be the efforts of the returned Dead to convince you of your immortality.
>
> Meantime, at the other end – no, at the very centre of your great Babylon, – a son leaves his father dead, with his head, instead of a fire, in the fireplace, and goes out himself to his daily darg [work].

There was an apocalyptic, gothic horror to Ruskin's discourse, a sardonic sensationalism which dwelt on road casualties and a 'Shocking Parricide in Halifax', where an eighty-six-year-old man was attacked by his mill hand daughter: 'She struck him on Monday with a rolling pin, and on the following day tore his tongue out at the root at one side. He died in the workhouse, of lockjaw.' At times the melodrama lurched into the truly bizarre. Discussing the existence of souls, 'and if ever any of them haunt places where they have been hurt,' Ruskin declared, 'You may laugh, if you like. I don't believe any one of you would like to live in a room with a murdered man in the cupboard, however well preserved chemically; – even with a sunflower growing out at the top of a head.' It was a surreal, obscure nightmare caught somewhere between Jeremy Bentham's mummified corpse in University College, the psychic ark of William Cowper's correspondent, and some dark corner of Wonderland. But perhaps most arresting of all was the edition which deliberated on 'an inquest on a woman found dead with her child in her arms in a cellar' and the habit of 'narcotising young children that they may be more conveniently laid aside when more lucrative occupations present themselves than that of nursing the baby'. Citing a recent report that 'excessive infant mortality' was the result of 'hundreds of gallons of opium in various forms' sold each week in manufacturing districts, and conflating this terrifying fact with a discursion on hunting, Ruskin put forward a Swiftian proposal for saving on 'maintenance and education': 'Why not shoot babies instead of rabbits?'

Ruskin was reckless in the manner in which he charted his emotional life in *Fors Clavigera*, and never more so than in January 1875, when he revealed that 'the woman I hoped would be my wife is dying . . . Nevertheless, I have . . . bought a piece of land on which I could live in peace; and on that land, wild when I bought it, have already made, not only one garden, but two . . .' His hope of taking Rose to that Eden was futile, however; she was now living, as he told Carlyle, 'chiefly [on] sugar almonds', and seemed to blame him for her illness. She told his cousin Joan that she was 'quite sure that there's no disease either in her stomach, or her breast, – but gave . . . broad hints that it was all because she hadn't *you*, that she was ill!' How cruel this consuming insanity must have seemed. A month later, Ruskin saw her for the last time –

> *Of course* she was out of her mind in the end . . . raving violently till far into the night; they could not quiet her. At last they let me into her room. She was sitting up in bed; I got her to lie back on her pillow, and lay her head in my arms, as I knelt beside it.

> They left us, and she asked me if she should say a hymn. And I said yes, and she said, 'Jesus, lover of my soul,' to the end, and then fell back tired and went to sleep. And I left her.

– and in a recently identified drawing, he sketched her once more, her hair splayed over the pillow, her wild eyes staring out of her emaciated face, the would-be lover holding her inamorata and eternity in her last focus, *livido moriendi*. It is a frightening contrast to the portraits of the younger, living Rose, and it must have stayed with Ruskin for the rest of his life as an image of their unfulfilled passion.

Taken back to Ireland, Rose died, demented, at the age of twenty-six, in a Dublin nursing home on 25 May 1875. 'The last solemn promise she made me make to her, lying in my arms, after that fit of torment, was that I will never let her stand between me and God,' Ruskin wrote in the final chapter of a story which echoed that of Dante and his beloved Beatrice, whom the Italian poet met when she was eight years old and who died when she was twenty-four. 'He saved others, himself he could not save; and she who held his salvation in her hand could do nothing, it is very clear, but die for love of him.' The skies had darkened over Ruskin, and it was no coincidence that in *Fors Clavigera* that month, he first published his thoughts on 'The Plague-wind of the Nineteenth Century'; or that the July letter concluded with an etching of a tomb sprouting with roses.

She might be dead, but like Beatrice, Rose still walked with Ruskin, a shadowy guide to that world beyond. And as they had been unable to live together in life, so Ruskin could not accept Rose's absence in death. Broadlands had been the site of their last happy union on earth, and it was there that Ruskin was drawn to reclaim her spirit.

In November 1874, as Rose was entering the final phase of her troubled life, Ruskin had renewed his interest in spiritualism, prompted by a meeting with Frederic Myers (himself fresh from his life-changing encounter with William Stainton Moses at Broadlands just six months before). The two men were introduced by their mutual friend Prince Leopold, who had sent Ruskin a volume of Myers' verse. Leopold, then an Oxford undergraduate whom Ruskin had taught, was a gentle figure whose haemophilia – in January 1875 he would come close to death with a severe haemorrhage – served to focus his interest in the other world (although he was the Queen's favourite son, he would also rebel against his mother, at one point declaring his intention to become a radical politician). Between them, the two young men reawakened Ruskin's interest: 'Dined with the Prince, and heard from Mr Myers, things wonderful and most precious, much strengthened and awe-struck by what I heard yesterday of the advance in spiritualism.'

Now, five months after Rose's death, Ruskin went to stay with the Cowpers, seeking solace in their embrace. Georgiana spoke poetically of 'adopting' him, like Juliet: 'it is so precious to me to be thought of as a child, needing to be taken care of . . .' Ruskin replied, and addressed her as 'darling Grannie', signing himself as 'your loving little boy'. He arrived at Romsey station on 6 October 1875, with his Swiss valet Klein, and from Brantwood summoned his gardener, David Downs, for whom there was work to do. William had offered the Guild of St George some acres of land, along with a cottage on his estate – the same cottage around which Ruskin had woven his fantasy of marital life with Rose. In the wake of her loss, Ruskin considered carrying out his plan of living in the New Forest as an alternative to Brantwood. But the damp Hampshire autumn echoed the decay of his emotions, and his visit took on a melancholy air.

> October 9th. *Saturday*. Grey with soft mist. Y[esterday] walked up hill toward Southampton, after picking up sticks with Juliet, and sweeping grass in morning with gardeners . . .

Like a Wordsworthian figure in a twilit landscape, Ruskin lost himself in the gathering of wood as kindling for the poor, a task in which he enlisted his fellow guests, relishing the fact that 'the Recorder of London' – Russell Gurney, Edmund's uncle – 'and MP for Southampton, with his wife, Mr and Mrs Temple, the Duchess and Miss Munro' were 'all making faggots with me . . .' But as the clouds lowered, so did his mood – '. . . Utter blackness and misery, after rain all night . . .' – and under a lurid sunset, he and William walked to the old cottage 'where I had my last Broadlands walk with R[ose]'. He fell prey to a 'curious violent attack of sickness . . . with faintness and cold fingers' after 'much excitement and successful brain work on glaciers', which he modelled in the Cowpers' kitchens out of egg-white. Ruskin's overstimulated mind could not rest, even as he slept, and the next day he recorded a vivid dream which seemed to come from some future modernist poem via a medieval apocalypse.

> An entirely graceful lady began dancing a minuet to quick music, for a lesson, in company, all standing by to see, and it was pretty for a few moments; and then in her quickest motion she staggered, and one of her legs seemed to break, and we saw it was a wooden stilt, tied on with blue ribands, and she had to limp away to mend it, only in a tumultuous wild way the whole.
>
> Then of crossing a bridge and seeing that what I thought were weeds in the water were large green serpents; and I called to Crawley to look and he wouldn't come, and then the serpents came out of the water and on the road to meet me, but I saw they were harmless, and they turned and glided beside me, with large blunt heads, like dogs.
>
> Then of a most grotesque fight, between two large snails, rearing up like seahorses, and one biting the other like a weasel, covering it with blood.
>
> Then of a dinner where I was talking a great deal and forgetting to see people who were close to me; and at last talking so fast that a bit dropped out of my mouth into a dish that was handed to me, and the kind waitress only seeing and pointing to me where it was, so that I could take out . . .

'What a time it takes to write all this!' bemoaned Ruskin, 'Morning half gone already; it dark, and I tired. But had all manner of most useful plans and ideas given me, in wakings between this broken, half mended, half stilted nightmare.' His haunted exhaustion was caught in a photograph taken that summer by Charles Dodgson, who, 'with some difficulty', persuaded Ruskin to sit for him in his leather armchair. It might as well have been a dentist's chair for the pain in his face. Ruskin's dreams of serpents and dragons would recur throughout his half mended life, as did other perfervid images – a proto-Freudian sequence of swimming and wading, a surgeon dissecting himself, cancer in the mouth, his foot diseased, losing himself in a vast hotel, being shut in a dark cellar, having holes in his hands, saints rising from their tombs, a woman with duck-billed feet – metaphysical stigmata bearing witness to his martyred love. By night Ruskin was living out the uncanny of the age, as though, freed from the day's critical rationality, his dreams returned to signs and wonders, and in the process assumed a visionary state.

From episodes of pagan belief, Ruskin was being drawn to another extreme: an idiosyncratic, self-invented Catholicism. On a visit to Assisi he stayed in a cell just yards from St Francis's grave, identifying so completely with the saint – whose relics he had been allowed to handle – that he felt he was becoming him, experiencing apocalyptic revelations. After two months of anxious wandering, Ruskin returned to Hampshire, where his hosts hoped Broadlands would prove balm to their friend's bruised soul. Accompanied by Klein and his pet Turners in their leather carrying case, Ruskin was installed in a new extension dubbed the Bachelor's Wing. Here his regime was fixed and solitary. He would read and write throughout the day, breaking to join his friends for lunch at two, taking tea alone in his suite at 7.30. Occasionally he left his aesthetic nest to collect sticks with Juliet or walk with William in the country lanes. 'Bright at last', he recorded, ever weather-aware, 'after a very lovely vermillion sunset yesterday, clear on the river and sweet woods, as I walked towards Southampton.'

But Ruskin was not the only guest at Broadlands that winter. Under Georgiana's nun-like mien, the house had acquired a mystical and overwhelmingly feminine air; and just as mesmerism was said to be 'peculiarly exercisable by ladies' by virtue of their 'nature and . . . Christian education' and their talents as 'ministering angels in sickness and suffering', so mediumship and healing was accredited to sororial hands joined across the seance table. In one respect, it was an empowerment for these women; in another a connexion with the *hysteria* which was a symptom of Salem, Niskeyuna, Walworth, or even Rose's own psychic abilities.

At Broadlands, a veritable coven of female mediums assembled, among them Annie Andrews (now Mrs Edward Acworth, after her marriage to a Brighton doctor). Having amazed Tennyson by causing his study table to heave 'like the sea', Annie demonstrated her *apports* for the Cowpers, materialising 'distinct but very small pearls . . . seeming to grow like mushrooms on the table cloth' and announcing, like Harris, 'I come to consecrate you to a larger work, & to prepare a people for the Messiah to reign over. They are preparing in the West & the time of preparation will be short . . .' She also claimed that she 'often left her body to transverse the spheres'. Annie was joined at Broadlands by the redoubtable Waggie, who was thrown into a trance by Georgiana to diagnose Ruskin's ill-health (blamed on 'a long life of variously mismanaged digestion'). After 'another bit of witchery', Georgiana 'waved her victim awake in ten seconds!' The mystic circle was completed by Annie Munro, sister to Alexander Munro and governess to the Cowpers' daughter Juliet, and, characteristically in this esoteric household, also 'gifted with second sight'.

Suffused as he was with the memory of Rose, it was almost pre-ordained that Ruskin should seek her spirit among these sybils; and the talented Annie – known as 'Love's Messenger' – duly obliged. This 'Spirity lady sees all manners of ghosts about the house', and had seen a spirit standing by his side 'dressed in daisies' –

> December 14th. *Tuesday*. Heard from Mrs Ackworth, in the drawing room where I was once so happy, the most overwhelming evidence of the other state of the world that had

> ever come to me; and am this morning like a flint stone suddenly changed into a firefly, and ordered to flutter about – in a bramble thicket. Yet slept well and sound all night.

– and in a letter to his American friend Charles Norton, Ruskin made an even more astonishing claim for that day's events:

> Broadlands, *14th December 1875*
> . . . I have heard wonderful things this very afternoon. I have seen a person who has herself had the Stigmata, and lives as completely in the other world as ever St Francis did, from her youth up . . . she had the wounds more than once, but on one occasion conveyed instantly by a relic of St Catherine of Siena. And I'm as giddy as if I had been thrown off Strasburg steeple and stopped in the air; but thing after thing of this kind is being brought to me . . .

The identity of this stigmatic remains a mystery; she was just another of the strange figures with whom the Cowpers had contact. Such scenes were all the more strange for the celebrated personality who bore witness to them; perhaps it was just as well that they took place behind Broadlands' drawn curtains. Confused by grief and confronted with the evidence he had sought, Ruskin felt 'quite crushed' by the brooding, unreal atmosphere, and 'overpuzzled' by the contributions of Miss Munro – 'Actually everything we had thought nonsense turning out true. Ghosts – witches – magicians – even fairies' – while Annie had seen 'little wingless angels' as a child, 'and *now* she's exactly like St Francis, who had tame butterflies! and makes them know their names!'

Such psychic taxonomy took its toll on a man who himself felt in communion with St Francis, 'And am this morning – bewildered . . . Dark all day yesterday. Dark this morning . . .' He fell ill with a 'heavy, horrid cold', as did the rest of the household, communally burdened by their penumbral experiments. Three days later, Ruskin recorded, 'Increasing anxiety about illness, and more and more wonderful or sad things told me, unfit me much for my work . . .' The sky itself seemed to lower as final revelation beckoned: 'The mornings always dark; no vestigate of dawn ever coming to comfort me. Fire and candle only . . . Again, first through Phylae and her friend, then, conclusively, in evening talk . . . the truth is shown me, which, though blind, I have truly sought so long.' He was reaching an epiphany, and he saw it in the evening of the shortest day.

> December 21st. *Tuesday*. Actual starlight, last night . . . In afternoon, the trance-teaching, and the reading of *Marmion* with companions . . . Mr MacDonald came; and Mrs Ackworth came up with me in the evening and told me what to trust and hope, in all deed and thought.

Ruskin had asked Annie if she had seen any spirits lately.

'Oh yes', she said, 'there was one close to you as you were talking about men and women, last night.'

'And what shape did it take?' asked Ruskin, with apprehension.

'Fair, very tall and graceful – she was stooping down close over you, as if she were trying to say something.' She had seen the same ghost earlier that day, next to Georgiana; the woman was unmarried. 'I think she has not been long in the spirit world – not a year perhaps.'

As if summoned by the stars, this grey shape out of his imagining could not be mistaken. George MacDonald told his wife that Annie had 'seen and described, without ever having seen her, Rose whispering to Ruskin. He is convinced.' The knowledge came like a physical blow: his lover was here, in the lee of the forest in which he had imagined they might live out their earthly lives.

That Christmas, Ruskin took away from Broadlands and its strange house party something he held as close to his heart as Rose's letters, or the lock of her hair and her photograph which he carried about in a rosewood box. For a man who had searched for truth all his life, it was nothing less than astounding to be confronted with evidence of another plane of existence, here in a Hampshire mansion.

At the end of January 1876, Ruskin came back to Broadlands, as if ineluctably drawn to this place of spirits. This time he found Edward Clifford and Frederic Myers as fellow guests, and together they undertook further explorations into the unknown; the unknown of their subconscious, their collective hopes and fears. In her diary for Saturday 29 January, Georgiana records that Annie had told Ruskin 'that she had . . . a spirit she believed it to be Turner . . . "That's very wonderful to me" said St C.' Then, on 2 February, on the tenth anniversary of his proposal to Rose, Annie saw her 'looking quite happy'.

In his letters to Charles Norton, Ruskin attempted to rationalise these experiences: '. . . At Broadlands, either the most horrible lies were told me, without conceivable motive – or the ghost of R. was seen often besides Mrs—, or me.' He believed he was 'being brought every day now . . . whether I will or no, into closer contact with evidence of an altered phase of natural, if not supernatural, phenomena . . . To me, personally, it is no common sign that just after the shade of Rose was asserted to have been seen beside Mrs T and beside me, here, I should recover the most precious of the letters she ever wrote me, which, returned to her when we parted, she had nevertheless kept . . .' But Frederic Myers saw the dangers of this revelation 'as of a longed-for meeting of souls beloved in heaven, – a vision whose detail and symbolism carried conviction to Ruskin's heart. While that conviction abode with him he was happy as a child; but presently he suffered what all are like to suffer who do not keep their minds close pressed to actual evidence by continuous study . . .'

A year later in Venice, Ruskin felt he no longer had need of mediums. In Assisi he had been in communion with St Francis;

now he felt that he was being guided by St Ursula. Venerated in Venice and often portrayed holding the banner of St George, Ursula was a Dark Age British saint whose myth Ruskin retold in *Fors Clavigera*: 'She came into the world wrapped in a hairy mantle . . . only God in Heaven knew how the rough robe signified that she should follow holiness and purity all her days . . . And because of the mantle, they called her "Ursula", "Little Bear".' Promised as a bride to a Gaullish prince, Ursula requested three years' grace to lead a ship-borne pilgrimage of virgins (some said eleven thousand, some just eleven) to the shrines of Christendom – only to be massacred by Huns on their arrival in Cologne.

In Carpaccio's painting, and Ruskin's copy, Ursula lies asleep as an angel holds a palm, a symbol of the saint's martyrdom. It is a strange, stilled scene of heavenly visitation: Ursula, bundled tight in her linen like a Buchanite, lies in effigy, eyes closed but head cradled in her hand as if dreaming, while her remarkably solid-seeming visitor stands in the doorway in the early morning light: 'So dreams the princess, with blessed eyes, that need no earthly dawn.' Blasphemously, Ruskin yearned for immortality, that he might meet Rose again, like Dante greeting his lover's ghost in paradise.

And as *Beata Beatrix*, now installed at Broadlands, was the reincarnation of Lizzie Siddal as Beatrice, so in Ruskin's imagination Ursula assumed the image of the saintly Rose, as if to effect their unconsummated union in heaven. He even dedicated a feast day to Rose, on the anniversary of the date which she had fixed as his 'period of probation', and in *Fors Clavigera* he made his veneration public, as if daring the world: 'It is eleven years to-day since the 2nd of February became a great festival to me: now, like all the days of all the years, a shadow; deeper, this, in a beautiful shade.' Yet that same shadow was a herald of Ruskin's fate, for it was in Venice, in the Christmas of 1876, that he went mad.

*'There she lies, so real that when the room's quiet –
I get afraid of waking her!'*

In that fearful, fantastic time, his waking hours were suffused with symbolism, as if his haunted dreams had begun to take over his conscious life as he wandered the city's darkened streets, seeing a gondolier with bloodshot eyes as the devil and a Venetian girl as a saint. For two weeks, Ruskin received 'teachings' from Rose and St Ursula: 'Meaning was everywhere, as though the past, present and future worlds were joined together by a system of symbols that were occasionally revealed in brilliant light when the clouds of mundane knowledge parted.' And as an accompaniment to his departure from the rational world, Rose sent Ruskin flowers from Heaven, just as Shaker instruments had received psychic blooms.

Eventually the madness subsided, 'and leaving the unseen world in its old sad uncertainty, he went back to the mission which was laid on him,' – as Myers saw it – 'that mission of humanising this earth, and being humanised thereby, which our race must needs accomplish, whatever be the last doom of man'. Ruskin's spiritualist experiments left him more convinced of the need for change, both in his utopian Guild of St George whose banner Ursula bore, and in his expectation of the life thereafter. Spiritualism was part of those metaphysical explorations. Through his friendship with Myers, Ruskin was enrolled as an honourary member of the Society of Psychical Research – joining Tennyson, Watts and Dodgson, among others – and corresponded with Oliver Lodge, scientist, spiritualist and discoverer of radio waves.

In October 1879 Ruskin returned to Broadlands for further seances, still trying to tune in to the world to which Rose had gone. Although friends pointed out that Annie Ackworth had been involved in a scandal which threatened to expose her as a fake, he countered that the revelations he had received had restored his faith in God. At Broadlands, the manifestations had diminished – 'the only *definite* thing I felt this time', he told Prince Leopold, 'was a quiet natural guidance (in all ways) in right directions'. To Ruskin, spiritualism was a vindication of his love for Rose, and of his skittering, elusive faith. Like his friends, the Cowpers, he sought belief as a harbour in a stormy, changing world. But across the forest at Hordle, the Girlingites found no such solace in a faithless age which even now conspired to deny them refuge.

PART FOUR

The Countenance Divine

As a living soul, I am the very contrary of History, I am what believes it, destroys it for the sake of my own history . . .

Roland Barthes, *Camera Lucida*

TEN

This Muddy Eden

Monday, Corfe Castle; Tuesday, Poole; Wednesday, the Rhododendrons; Thursday, Rufus Stone; Friday, the Shakers (Hordle)

Charabanc programme, 1878

Through the forest's tangled roots, the psychic circle was joined in nature and supernature, a sense of heightened reality as seen in the hyper-real stilled lives of the Pre-Raphaelites, where the representation of a fern or branch might frame the drama of parting lovers, the passing of Christ's earthly presence, or the transcendence of an angel. In close-up focus and in the vast sweep of time, the Victorian utopia abided in an imaginary region between reality and faith. From Broadlands' grand plaster salons to the Girlingites' makeshift tents, the same dilemmas which preoccupied Ruskin and the Cowpers inspired Mary Ann in her quest. And as Ruskin joined William and Georgiana in that year of seances, his hosts' sense of social justice and religious freedom was drawn towards the events at Hordle. Here, on the borders of the forest William had sought to protect, a new utopia was being attempted. Mary Ann and her rag-tag communists may have been a world away in class and intellect, but in spiritual intent they were as brothers and sisters, and geographically, they were camped out on the Cowpers' doorstep.

In these affinities, two worlds met in a mutual search for answers in an age of questions, and as the plight of the forest sect pricked the nation's collective conscience, the voice of William Cowper rang out loud: 'The pitiable conditions of the Shakers in the New Forest is traceable to cruel illegalities committed in the name of the law.' To him the sect were victims of their own Christian generosity, and the lack of it in others. Although Gladstone's liberal government, in which he had served, was now out of office, Cowper's concern was an extension of his duty as Member of Parliament for South Hampshire. But for William, it was also a personal matter. Not only was his niece married to the Girlingites' great defender, Auberon Herbert, but he and Georgiana saw another common cause with Mary Ann. Her mission had already been identified with spiritualism – as visits of spiritualists to her Chelsea chapel indicated – and the Cowpers seem to have made the same connexion. In his seance notebook, William had written that

> . . . The Shakers in America amounting to 3000 are Spiritualists, the younger ones who have been brought up in the institution have communications but are considered uninteresting mediums by the rulers, prejudiced as they are by love of authority . . . Their theory is that Christ has come & is to be manifested thro' them to the world. The peaceful harmony in which they live & their restraint from the flesh are evidences in their favour but their government is cramping.

The Cowpers' private papers reveal the depth of their sympathy for the Girlingites. Georgiana had already announced her intention to pay the rent 'of any house large enough to shelter them'; her diary entry for Boxing Day 1874 begins: 'Meant to visit the Shakers, but it was *impossible* to drive.' Instead, they telegraphed to ask Mary Ann to send someone 'to receive the food that we had for them'. That evening Isaac Batho arrived at Broadlands, 'a very thin looking man with a beautiful heavenly air – & a quiet gentle manner'. William and Georgiana listened as he told them the story of how '140 were turned out – without a penny. Slept the first night under hedges in a snow storm – but they were preserved from harm . . . They think Mother Girling is in communion with the Lord . . . He speaks of her as a real good loving woman. Unhappily they have no one apparently who knows anything of the world of business.'

The following morning Hampshire was still snowbound, and Batho was forced to stay on and enjoy his hosts' hospitality. 'We like our Shaker friend very much – He seems very simple – honourable & heavenly minded,' wrote Georgiana. 'I took him for a walk in the afternoon.' That evening, Batho sang hymns and the couple joined in. 'We talked with him of the Coming of the Lord. They believe it to be very near . . .' Batho left the next day, 28 December. That evening the Cowpers had eighteen guests to dinner.

On New Year's Day 1875, with the weather lifting, William and Georgiana drove across the forest to see the state of the sect for themselves. They found the Girlingites spread out between Beasley's barn and four rooms, a wash-house and another barn in the Herberts' grounds. The aristocrats' arrival in Hordle was itself an extraordinary scene, as they picked their way through the mud to meet the elders like some colonial deputation. After a long discussion, William decided to appoint a solicitor to act on the sect's behalf. The following day, he sat down to tell *The Times* the facts as he saw them; he wrote as the drama of the eviction was still raw and as the rime of winter lay on the dispossessed, and his stern words put the nation on notice. 'Their furniture was thrown by those who acted under the orders of the Sheriff on the high road and neighbouring fields, and, to a great extent, was damaged and destroyed. The Shakers had to pass a frosty night under the hedges in a snowstorm, and they must have perished from the cold of the last fortnight but for the shelter of the barns of Mr Beasley and Mr Auberon Herbert.'

Cowper appealed to those gentlemen who raised the morning's broadsheet over their breakfast tables. Surely no Englishman could condone such injustice? Far from the special pleading of a do-gooder with a bizarre belief in table-tapping, this pragmatic assessment was pitched between an accountant's tally and authentic moral outrage:

> Their houses and land, worth £2,000, which had cost them, inclusive of additions more than £3,000, were sold immediately by auction for £1,350. Their eccentricities and strange opinions could not justify the harsh treatment they have received. They are pure in morals and anxious to do what they believe to be right, but are ignorant of the law and inexperienced in business.

It was a rational argument couched in the cool terminology of a former minister of state – albeit one who had helped introduce allotments and social housing to England. They might be 'peculiar people', but the Girlingites deserved the defence of British law as much as any grand landowner. '. . . I have put them into communication with an able solicitor, who will take steps to obtain for them some redress as the law may provide; and I invite the co-operation of those who may sympathise with the helplessness and sufferings of these poor people. Contributions to enable them to obtain necessary food and clothing are received by Mr Henry Doman, at Lymington, and may be paid to his account at the Hampshire Bank, at Southampton.' Doman was Lymington's resident poet and publisher; his support would prove valuable in the days to come. 'Since the publication of Mr Cowper-Temple's letter,' *The Times* noted, 'a considerable sum has been sent for their relief and assistance.' Within a few days the appeal had raised £66.2s, including a substantial donation of £20 'for the poor creatures' from Samuel Morley, another MP, and £5 each from Mr Henry Gurney – Edmund's brother – and Mr De Burgh, both well-known names in the world of spiritualism.

* * *

The solicitor's report was bleak. 'On the facts which are before me it is impossible to determine in whom the property is,' wrote William's man in the Temple, London.

> If partly in Miss Wood, partly in Mrs Girling, and partly in Leonard Benham, it is difficult to see what right the Sheriff had to seize the ppty of Mrs Girling or Benham, and they might bring action for an illegal seizure – If the property belongs to the Community at large all must be joined as Plaintiffs – I should think it most probable that the deed of gift *did* include the goods, & that such Goods are vested in the Trustees – I need scarcely add that in such uncertainty an action would be a *perilous* proceeding and I cannot advise it.

Isaac Batho had been back to consult with the Cowpers' agent, and there now followed a series of letters from Batho to both William and Georgiana, asking for help, criticising the legal assessments, and justifying the sect's holy mission. They are remarkable documents, for they constitute the only extant records written by the Girlingites. Batho, as a former postmaster, had been deputed as amanuensis, and in his large, naïve hand, in sepia ink on cream paper, the first letter, headed 'Ashley Arnewood' and dated 15 January 1875, addressed William as:

> Hon Sir
> My visit yesterday to Romsey was in consequence of having recd from Mr Potter a request for a personal interview. Mr Potter informed me that he has made enquiry respecting the sale of the property, and has concluded in his own mind that New Forest Lodge is to all intents and purposes passed out of our possession, which we at present do not credit. We still lay legal claim to the property, and feel a silent indignation at the unjust treatment of the whole matter, can it really be possible, that there is to be such an awful sacrifice?

Batho said that they had spent £3,000 on 'first purchase, two years of hard toil, and hundreds of pounds spent on the place'. Now the lot had sold for £1,340,

> ... something to me, so dreadfully devilish on the part of those who have plotted our ruin, and who has so far as they now see, effected their purpose but I think you know, kind Sir, that our God will arise and avenge his own, who cry night and day to Him? Oh yes I know He will! praise His dear name. while I am penning these lines, the 37 psalm is by the spirit made very blessed to me. how good, how kind and how mindful is God to His dear children. my whole being seems permeated with the soothing influence of the Holy Spirit of God.

Even as Batho called on the Lord, he argued against Man, saying the community,

> ... would never have gone to law about it, but as you kindly offered to employ y[r] solicitor, and defray the expenses, as you kindly observed 'To see us righted.' We have every confidence in you, that you will act in accordance with the law of God so leave the matter fully in your hands to decide, and arrange as you deem best. Be pleased Hon Sir to accept my earnest thanks, the thanks of Miss Wood Mrs Girling and all our Community for your great Kindness to us. Our prayers are still, that you may be preserved by His power, piled with His Love, guided by His spirit into all truth; and at last reign with Him in Glory.
>
> I am yours in Christ Jesus
> I Batho

This was followed by a letter to Georgiana, who had forwarded a challenge from a 'Revnd Gent'. Batho's response, interlarded with chapter and verse, was fiercely defensive. 'No Dear Madam We are not following a cunningly devised fable ...'

> We know what we have received is of God and from God, and that we are not in doubt in the slightest degree as to the Salvation of our souls, or Redemption of our bodies, I trust

> you don't think me an egotist for it is with grateful feelings to [our] arisen Saviour that I can affirm He has given us the power to become Sons & daughters of God (John 1.c. 112 verse), and through Him (& I Peter 4.c. 5 verse) and Him alone are we kept, and by His power, do we live holy, and pure lives (Ephesians V. 27.v Peters 2 c.14.v) all praise to His Holy name.

He closed with a statement of their Edenic intent:

> Oh how pure was Adam and Eve, prior to their fall, and how soon lost, but we praise God it is regained in Christ . . . Trusting you are still reposing on the love of Christ and . . . trusting his word
>
> I am Hon Madam
Yours in Christ
I. Batho
>
> Hon Madam I wrote this letter on Saturday, but was too late for post.

It was as though the Cowpers were receiving communications from some seventeenth-century sect. The aristocrat philanthropists may have come to regret their offer of support, as ever-longer epistles from Hordle, in Batho's unmistakable hand and declamatory vocabulary, continued to appear in the Broadlands post-tray. Two days later, William took delivery of another missive which ascribed 'villainous and base designs' to the Girlingites' persecutors, while providing their own accounts –

> . . . I believe I explained to you Sir that previous to the seizure we had been offered £70 for one horse and £60 for the other but would not sell them the two amounts make 130.0.9
and the 3 cows in their
condition more surely
worth £20 each, making 60.0.0
190.0.0

> The Writ was for £40.0.0
> and I should think ten pounds,
> an ample allowance for serving
> [it] making expenses   £ 50.0.0
> the balance to us would be   £140.0.0

– and concluding:

> Hon.d Sir
> I thank you for condolence, and sympathy expressed in y^{r} letter, and also for y^{r} earnest advice. We feel no condemnation for past occurrences, but everything that has transpired will surely work together for good to us we having committed our ways to God and we know He will bring to pass that which we are praying and believing for . . . God will surely deliver us, and take us to our home again
> Wishing you every spiritual blessing
>
> I am Hon Sir
> Yours faithfully
> I. Batho

And with this last sermon, William put away the letters and left the Girlingites to Auberon Herbert's more patient care.

While the Children of God sought such aristocratic patronage, Edward Clissold remained their implacable enemy. He even seemed to suggest, in his own letter to *The Times*, that Mary Ann was deluding the Cowpers and the Herberts. 'Whether by fanaticism or, as I have strong ground for belief, by mesmerism, the leaders of this society have brought under their control men and women of considerable means, and by their ignorant management, as well as by their indolent habits, have involved all in general ruin . . . I do not feel disposed to subscribe to feed young men and women under 21 years of age who would be much better at home or at work, than trying at such an age to work out a religious and social experiment.' However, for Auberon Herbert, it was precisely that sense of utopian aspiration which attracted his sympathy. After his protest to *The Times*, he had continued to receive letters and money in support of the Girlingites. Florence Herbert, then at Wrest Park, told her sister-in-law that Auberon was 'at Ashley Arnewood, with the Shakers, a good deal troubled about them as you will have seen by the papers – it is an unfortunate affair, and a nasty, tiresome thing to be mixed up in'. Indeed, her husband's sympathies were about to be severely challenged.

Dark rumours still circulated about the Girlingites, 'obscene stories . . . as to their religious dances and secret rites', although no one could prove any of them. Concerned at their persistence, Herbert interviewed Mary Ann, expecting to hear her refute them. To his amazement, she denied directing her Children in such behaviour, but admitted that in the excitement of the spirit, clothing might be cast off.

Herbert was shocked. 'Sir, – I have an unpleasant task before me', he told *The Times*, 'but one which I cannot rightly avoid. A statement of facts has been made before me which I do not think I have any right to withhold from that part of the public who are interested in the Shakers.' He recalled earlier visits to the community at the Lodge, when

> . . . we were allowed to make a thorough inspection of the buildings and all arrangements for living and sleeping. Everything was clean, orderly, and decent. The men and women slept in separate rooms, and everything bore witness to Mrs Girling's account of that strict morality on which the community was founded . . . I asked if there was any truth in the statement that the men and women bathed together in the sea. She assured me there was none, and, as far as her own knowledge went, I believe she spoke truthfully.

But now he saw 'another side of the picture'. At Yeatton House, Clissold produced an apostate Girlingite who 'on several occasions . . . had been witness of naked dances, in which both the men and the women took part. One would begin to throw off his clothes, and others would follow his example. Some remained conscious and others were unconscious of what they were doing.' Herbert acknowledged that the witness was biased, but believed 'the substantial truth of what he deposed'.

It is impossible to know the truth of what happened within the Girlingite encampment. There may have been elements who took matters to an extreme, as had the early Quakers, with whom Mary Ann had claimed affinity. A 'trustworthy correspondent' had reported that on the night of their eviction, one Girlingite, possibly Leonard Benham, 'got so excited (just before the public were allowed to come into the chapel) that he exclaimed, "they take my coat, they shall have my garments also", and immediately divested himself of his clothes and danced amongst the others, who did not even express the slightest surprise, but took it quite as a matter of course. One of the elders, however, made him don his garments.' Later, Lymington magistrates were told 'that the men and women, in presence of their children, danced together in perfect nudity'. These stories were coloured by reports of Girlingite rituals written by male journalists seeking salacious copy: 'Off started another, and then another – oh! but she feels it warm; first she throws off her hat, then her jacket, and I began to feel a little queer, for I fully expected to see her dress come off. Now there were two more, and then two more – altogether there were seven dancing at once. One would fancy himself at a Jack-in-the-Green meeting rather than at one to praise God.'

Yet the reference was apposite: there was more than a little of the maypole and the Green Man about these rites enacted on the forest's edge. And on this question, as on others, Mary Ann proved elusive. Back in Walworth, when asked about followers taking off their coats and boots, she had struck a Blakean stance, saying, 'Did not David dance naked before the Lord?' Indiscriminate hugs and kisses between both sexes served to encourage such notions.

Perhaps in their ecstasy the Girlingites did dance naked; perhaps – as Clissold was so keen to prove – they were beguiled into rituals which, with their white robes and trance-like states, echoed those of mediums such as Florence Cook, who was said to have part of her clothing removed as she was floated over the seance table, her psychic *alter ego* clad in loose white sheets revealing glimpses of her young flesh.

Whatever the truth, Mary Ann's admission irrevocably undermined Herbert's moral defence. Although he still felt 'much pity' for the people who occupied his farm buildings, he now withdrew his support: 'There are many children and young persons in the community, and, if only for their sakes, I cannot wish for them a life where, to use the mildest expression, delusion is no longer harmless.' Yet he acquitted Mary Ann 'of any sensual purpose', and ended his letter with a hint of his own eccentricity:

> As regards myself, I do not pretend to any very strong prejudices on the subject of clothes. No person who has lived in a very hot climate can keep them in their full strength. But, if ever the experiment of living decently without clothes is to be tried, I should wish it to be done by those who know exactly what they are doing, and not those who are in a state of religious delirium.

Herbert's public admission in the press elicited yet more colourful editorials. 'This nondescript tribe has had notice to quit Mr Auberon Herbert's property even before the expiration of next month as agreed, and that the next encampment will be pitched near Christchurch,' reported the *Hampshire Advertiser*. It painted a portrait of a sect scarcely less offensive when fully clothed: 'The men in black leggings and the women in a bad imitation of the Bloomer costume, with short scanty skirts, long tubular trousers, as rigid as cast iron, and untidy hair falling rather than flowing over very high shoulders, have been for some days spying out the land and now "The Lord be Praised" they seem going westward for the Milton parish. If they only creep on far enough in pursuit of the setting sun, so very emblematic of their plight, they may reach that paradise of follies and monstrosities on the other side of the Atlantic.' It was another indication of contemporary anti-American and anti-liberal feelings: 'To express it as delicately as possible, we may say that the *nuda veritas* has been discovered, proving Shakerism to be both indecent and immoral; and it is high time that Mr Herbert, who, with his relative, Mr Cowper-Temple, MP for the county, maintained the contrary, thought of publicly apologising for the great wrong done, or endeavoured to be done, to Dr Adams in threatening to prosecute him for holding an opinion that Mrs Girling was mad, or hopelessly crazed . . .'

On 12 January, Herbert had asked Mary Ann to sign an undertaking: 'I hereby promise that I will use my whole influence and all the means given to me to prevent any dances without clothes taking place among any of the brothers, sisters or children of our community for the future.' This was an extraordinary statement, all the more so for the fact that Mary Ann agreed to it (privately Herbert thought that she was 'a very clever woman' who did not believe in her own miraculous power, although she 'seemed to understand that to influence others, she must show no doubt or hesitation'). It was also a telling example of the way in which Mary Ann was used, as much as she herself used. In this controversy – in which Herbert saw 'that instead of the dances being really founded on the extinction of the sexual passion, they were grotesquely allying themselves with it' – proscribed sexuality emerged as the key to their ecstasy, part of the unseen power that held the Family together. Herbert found its members 'weak, dreamy, impressionable' and considered Clissold's belief 'that they lived under mesmerism was partly true, though made use of unconsciously'. Yet for all this, there was an essential innocence to the Children of God; and as for their dancing naked – well, that was part of the protest. A century later, when the pacifist Doukhobors were tried for their naked demonstrations against the decadence of their age, they told a Canadian court, 'When a man takes off his clothes he mortifies everything fleshly. He stands naked before God – in his pristine purity. How were you dressed when you were born?'

Mary Ann could be all things to all men or women: mother or mystic, shaman or show-woman. Her lack of literacy made it tempting to put words into her wry mouth, as if to force exegesis out of it. Even her naïvety was deceptive; and if Ann Lee had been called a 'grand actress', then Mary Ann was more than a match as her understudy. Like a character in a Victorian pantomime, her performance convinced her Children. And yet just as the allure of theatre fades as the house lights are turned on, so her power is lost to us. The reality of what Mary Ann was still seems concealed by her public persona and self-myth; consciously or not, she created an identity which echoed seeresses of earlier ages, yet which was reproduced a thousandfold by the new media, whose editions were carried across the country by rail and road, disseminating this local affair throughout the nation. On Saturday, 9 January 1875, for instance, *The Graphic* devoted its entire front page to 'The Shaker Settlement in the New Forest'.

In a kind of strip cartoon following their sensational debut in the *Illustrated Police News*, *The Graphic* presented the further adventures of the Girlingites, from their bleak-looking premises of New Forest Lodge – resembling, in the artist's compressed version, Dickens' Satis House – to the oddly domestic interior of the stable-chapel in which Mary Ann is seen ministering to her flock. A couple dance with abandon – albeit in a more decorous manner than their previous portrayal, their frenzies seemingly abated by their rural retreat and reduced to the harmlessness of Morris men. The women pose in their bloomers, while their leader sports a

THE GRAPHIC

AN ILLUSTRATED WEEKLY NEWSPAPER

VOL. XI.—No. 267] Regd at General Post Office as a Newspaper] SATURDAY, JANUARY 9, 1875 WITH EXTRA SUPPLEMENT [PRICE SIXPENC Or by Post Sixpence Hal

1. New Forest Lodge, the Recent Home of the Shakers, Hordle, Hants—2. Interior of the Chapel: The Prophetess addressing the Community—3. The Dance—4. Barn at Batchl Farm, the Shakers' Present Abode—5. Mrs. Girling, the Prophetess—6. Exterior of the Chapel—7. Scene on the High Road upon the Night of the Eviction—8. Off for Walk—9. The Shakers' New Hall, built of Unburnt Brick, and now Falling in Pieces.

THE SHAKER SETTLEMENT IN THE NEW FOREST

ridiculously small straw hat and a muff palpably inadequate to the elements. There are scenes from the black night of their eviction; a group going for a walk, looking like Tolstoy peasants; and the final dilapidation of their 'New Hall', its sagging roof and decrepit walls 'built of Unburnt Brick, and now Falling in Pieces'. The accompanying text seems to have picked up the flavour of the productions advertised next to it – *The Babes in the Wood* at the Theatre Royal, Covent Garden, and *The Black Statue: or, The Enchanted Pills and the Magic Apple Tree* at the Britannia Theatre, Hoxton; Victorian fables of loss and transformation.

THE 'SHAKERS' OF THE NEW FOREST

> . . . The personal appearance of these strange people is by no means prepossessing, they are mostly of the lower class, and have a half-starved, epileptic look which excites commiseration. Miss Wood is a meek, gentle, little lady, with a sadly, pensive expression, but Mrs Girling, the 'prophetess,' is a tall, thin, keen-eyed woman, who has been warned that attempts will yet be made to prove her insane. As to their religion, it is difficult to say what it is. There is a strange mixture of fervour and devotion, with the wildest expressions and ejaculations. During the singing and preaching many of them, sometimes with closed eyes, dance until they fall exhausted. The dance differs from that of the American Shakers, in that there appears to be no system or arrangement, each devotee gliding and whirling about, according to his or her own fancy.

Like the Extra Supplement included with that issue – a print of 'The Poor Orphan' – this portrait was partly sentimental, partly sensational, partly charged with charity. But for all its artistry, *The Graphic* failed to grasp the essence of the prophetess. Like the unlit moon, her substance remained hidden. And just as she has no voice – only secondhand reports of one – so Mary Ann's 'true' image exists only in one verifiable photograph.

With its COPYRIGHT stamp – as if to market the Children of God – the reproduced commerciality of the image sits somewhat disturbingly with its subject's mission. It invites analysis, and rejects it. Fulfilling the demand for a likeness of the phenomenal Mrs Girling, this new Shaker icon would have provided phrenologists with a fascinating case study; yet in its thin veneer, stuck down on pasteboard like the spirit photographs inserted in *Human Nature*, it arouses scepticism, too.

In the picture, taken at the high street studio of Lymington photographer Richard Hughes, Mary Ann leans over a gothic pew, as though to underline her religious respectability. She might be a preacher from the future Salvation Army, or a village teacher in her Sunday best – or an actress playing the part. Her hat is not a puritan's plain poke bonnet, but the embroidered lace confection of a faintly vain woman, firmly tied in a fulsome bow beneath her chin, her hair falling in heavy curls behind. Her gown, probably self-made, is heavily fringed and imparts a western feel, a prairie echo of the transatlantic influence claimed for her, while around her neck hangs a dark chain, fettering her to the Lord. Or perhaps, like Georgiana's châtelaine, it held the key to another world. Unlike other such studio shots, there is no semblance of Victorian domesticity, no aspidistras in jardinieres, no context of its subject's modern existence. How else could the daguerrotypist immortalise a saint? It would be like photographing the Virgin Mary.

Or perhaps the inhabitant of an asylum, for the fixed expression – the deep-set eyes, the tightened cheeks, the drawn lips – also recalls the physionomical portraits taken in 1881 by Galton and Mohamed, which sought to diagnose disease in the faces of the criminal, the destitute and the mad. 'But since all these patients still look at me, nearly a hundred years later,' writes Roland Barthes, 'I have the converse notion: that whoever looks you straight in the eye is mad.' Was this then the photograph of a lunatic, ready to take her place next to Richard Brothers and other deranged visionaries, 'gone

Mary Ann Girling,

"Mother" of the Shakers.

mad for Pity's sake'? Mary Ann's story has its resonance in sensational novels of incarcerated women, while her promise of immortality has its echo in other gothic fictions such as Mary Shelley's *Frankenstein* and Bram Stoker's *Dracula*, with their revivification of the dead. It was an age of new monsters, and Girlingism, like galvanism, seemed to be born of both the sacred and the profane.

Messiah or mad woman, the wry twist of genius or charade is explicit in Mary Ann's mouth, a kind of oral punctum of her unseen stigmata which lay concealed in her clasped, gloved hands and stiff-booted feet. Taut, as though held in the photographer's brace, the withheldness of the picture is part of its impact, even as its historical effect is impossible for us to comprehend. Perhaps young Richard Hughes saw the Mother of the Shakers as a lucrative subject to sell in *cartes de visite*, to be ordered at five shillings a dozen; Mary Ann, like Elder Evans, may have seen it as a useful dissemination of her mission. Yet this is her only photograph: perhaps, like some noble savage, she feared her power would be diluted in the transition from real to still life. Or perhaps her reluctance to be photographed had more to do with vanity and the fact that her terse expression was the result of her lack of teeth, rather than any lingering effect of visionary paralysis.

Despite her vicissitudes, Mary Ann's fame – or notoriety – continued to spread, sometimes by word of mouth from her own followers: '. . . One of the Shakers, who brought £300 and two horses into the community, travels the country sharpening saws, and endeavours to prove to anyone who will listen that Mrs Girling is the woman alluded to in Revelations . . .' But in January 1875, as the frost and snow returned, a new tragedy overcame the Girlingites. The death of fifteen-month-old James Benham – an illegitimate child and therefore the innocent product of knowing sin – challenged their tenets of celibacy and immortality. The infant's demise also provoked questions about the colony's attitude to medicine and the care of their children ('An eye witness states that several of the children in that place [Herbert's barn] look very ill, and that some are suffering from whooping cough,' noted the *Hampshire Advertiser*), and invited comparison with their erstwhile cousins, the Peculiar People, themselves no strangers to controversy. In 1872, the south London sect had been accused of wilful neglect when two of their children had died of smallpox after their parents refused to have them immunised. The right to resist medication was a debate familiar to readers of *Human Nature*; and was counterpointed by the notion that the working class could not be trusted with their children, an idea echoed in Ruskin's reports of opiated babies. Others saw baby James's death as a divine judgement on his mother's sins; some even claimed that the child had been murdered, either to dispose of this reminder of moral transgression, or as a ritual sacrifice – just as witches were accused of killing their own or other children.

Before Leonard Benham and his family had moved to New Forest Lodge, his eldest daughter Ellen had been engaged to a blacksmith, James Todd – son of Thomas and Agnes Todd of Parham, who had come to the Lodge as part of the advance party in January 1873. Leonard disapproved of the match and had persuaded Ellen not to marry the young man, but a fortnight after the Benhams arrived at Hordle in March 1873, she told her father there was 'something the matter' and she could not stay there. She left for London in April, and gave birth to a son, named James after his father, on 17 September 1873. Ellen then returned to Hordle where, on the night of the eviction, Levi Macey and his wife had taken pity on her and her baby and offered them shelter in their Silver Street cottage. Some accounts claimed that when James Todd – who had been expelled from the community – had read about the eviction, he came back from London to claim her as his bride, only to be rejected. Soon afterwards the baby succumbed, aged fifteen months.

'Ellen Benham is a young woman, in stature rather short, with dark features and an intellectual capacity above the average of the artizan-girl. Her answers to questions put were well chosen and concise; her narrative compact, her general manner cool to indifference.' The jury of Lymington coroner's court questioned her. Had she been out all night during the eviction? No: she had accepted the offer of shelter around midnight, and had been with Mrs Macey ever since; she had not rejoined the sect, due to the existence of her illegitimate child, but 'now that obstacle was removed, she had no doubt she would return'. But this did not address the question of culpability for the baby's death. Was Ellen to be blamed for her blind faith? Or Mary Ann, for her mesmeric deceptions? Or those who had permitted their eviction on that dark and wintry night?

Such metaphysical questions were beyond the jurisdiction of the inquest, which returned a verdict of death from natural causes; while the *Daily News* saw the sad affair as a warning: 'The professed immunity from death on the part of the Shakers has received a stern disclaimer by the death.' It was one which would be fulfilled by the morbid fate of the Benhams. Ellen's sister Emma died of consumption on 20 April 1877, aged nineteen; their mother Martha died a year later, on 8 June 1878, aged forty-nine; and Ellen died on 26 June 1880, of the same disease. All three would be buried at All Saints in Hordle, leaving Leonard – who had given up everything to join Mary Ann – a widower with only three of his children, Arthur, twenty-six, George, fifteen, and Mary, fourteen, still in the care of the Family.

As pathetic as it was, James Benham's demise had the effect of reawakening interest in the Girlingites – not least in James Burns' *Medium and Daybreak*. With its quasi-religious masthead – a bearded sage confronted with an array of angels emitting auroral rays from their foreheads – this best-selling spiritualist journal dedicated itself to such subjects as spectral messages written in 'the hand of the infant boy of Mrs and Mr Jencken, aged 5 months and 15 days' – a peer of James Benham, perhaps, or the ectoplasmic children in Mr Hudson's spirit photographs. 'I love this little Child, God bless him advise his father to go back to London on Monday by all means Susan', ran the shaky scrawl, recorded at Lansdowne Terrace, Brighton, 'the pencil used having been placed in the right hand of the infant by invisible means'. Elsewhere in the half-penny paper, a spirit Dr Forbes denounced vaccination, and Joan of Arc retrospectively solved the mystery of her visions ('She had been a physical medium, and spirits were able to address her in the spirit-voice'), while a correspondent wrote sardonically, 'I say friend Burns, here's a pretty go! Have you insured your life? Here's the end of the world coming, in what our American cousins term "everlasting smash" at least so far as you and 15, Southampton Row are concerned.' Strangest of all was an illustration of a 'semi-light seance', as though transmitted through a badly-adjusted television screen.

As a weekly, *Medium and Daybreak* was able to publish more up-to-date reports than the monthly *Human Nature*, and in early 1875, having been alerted to Shakerism by Evans' mission, its readership seemed determined to claim the English version for their own.

> HELP FOR THE SUFFERING SHAKERS
>
> Mr Burns has handed us the following post-card, which came addressed to him on the 6th January, 1875: –
>
> Dear Sir, – I received last night yours with Mr Watson's 21s. for the poor Shakers. I have acknowledged receipt to him. Am glad to see your active hand at work again. –
>
> Yours faithfully,
>
> 21, *Francis Terrace, Victoria Park, E.* A. Glendinning.
>
> Further sums will be gladly reserved.

Andrew Glendinning was a well-known spiritualist and later editor of *The Veil Lifted: Modern Developments in Spirit*

A WEEKLY JOURNAL DEVOTED TO THE HISTORY, PHENOMENA, PHILOSOPHY, AND TEACHINGS O

SPIRITUALISM.

[REGISTERED AS A NEWSPAPER FOR TRANSMISSION IN THE UNITED KINGDOM AND ABROAD.]

No. 296.—Vol. VI.] LONDON, DECEMBER 3, 1875. [Double Sheet—Price 1

Semi-light Seance at Newcastle, showing Spirit and Medium at the same time.

Photography. Affronted by the treatment meted out to the Girlingites, readers' feelings were running high:

> THE NEW-FOREST SHAKERS
>
> Mr Editor. – Dear Sir, – If the last monstrous outrage on the poor and, I fear, in some respects, foolish New-Forest Shakers, should lead to any combined effort to see them righted, I shall be glad to contribute a small sum to a fund started with that object. The details of the last outrage impel me to ask earnestly the friends of Spiritualism whether they will longer stand unmoved witnesses of deeds that recall the cruelty and bigotry and lawlessness which characterised the age of witchcraft.
>
> – Yours truly, F. N. Broderick
>
> *Ryde, I. W.*, March 2, 1875

Broderick was a young photographer working in Ryde, where he knew the Girlingites Henry and Charles Knight (also photographers, like his own father). Nor was it a coincidence that Broderick was a keen supporter of Frederick Evans, who noted, in his 1871 diary, the receipt of a letter from Broderick and that he was 'one of the committee who invited . . . me in London & staid so late, he resides in Isle of Wight'. How far Mary Ann was aware of spiritualistic support from such figures is unclear – there is no record of contact between her and James Burns – but she was pleased by the general reaction and wrote to her local paper, thanking the press for 'the sympathy and kindness shown to them in their troubles'.

In her remarkably shrewd relations with the newspapers, Mary Ann was represented by Henry Doman, her Lymington supporter. Thanking Doman for his help in the publication of an earlier defence of accusations that her brethren had mistreated the evicting bailiffs, she now asked 'that you will obtain for this epistle the same honour'. Written 'in a bold, clear hand' (although other letters, to the editor of the *Secular Review*, indicate only a rudimentary literacy), dated 5 February and addressed from 'The Barn, Ashley, Arnewood', this epistle provided colourful copy for a letters' page. Mary Ann protested that she had been accused of 'fraud, craftiness, immorality, cruelty, hypocrisy, licentiousness, indecency, and deceit . . . without the slightest CHARITY being manifested to us'. Her argument was clever, if not sarcastic: 'Now if any clergyman knows my soul to be subject to all these diseases, his pity as a physician of such souls should have led him to make every effort to save me . . . Depend upon it, had he done so, I should have been a very fine fish in his net.' For the likes of Edward Clissold, there was even a suggestion of supernatural threat – 'the time will come when my enemies will be ashamed of having spoken evil of me . . . These statements I make to the world . . . for the sake of that truth, which I love and keep, and also for the Hon. W. C. Temple's sake, whose kindness has been manifest to many and very beneficial to us . . . We do not desire to live on what is called charity,' she concluded. 'No, we are willing to work for our own living, but it will be on our own land. This command we have from God.' Thus she set out utopia, and signed off, 'Restoration, ah, blessed word. At first proclaimed by Christ our Lord.'

But at night, mice and rats ran over their faces, preventing any thought of sleep; the weather was tempestuous, and their muddy surroundings frightful. A quarter of tea was being made to serve one hundred and seventeen people at a time, donations had slowed to £10 a week, and the sect's very presence in the area was increasingly problematic – not least for the parents of nineteen-year-old Harry Burdon from Portland.

Portland stands out from the Dorset coast, barely connected to the mainland by Chesil Beach, a sea-washed isthmus along which each stone is graduated in size, ground to a scale so that, it is said, a mackerel fisherman can tell exactly where he has landed, even in dense fog. This semi-island is famous for two things: its stone and its convicts; and in the nineteenth century, Victorian efficiency married the two by employing prison labour in Portland's quarries. By reputation, Portlanders are a race apart, isolated from the rest of England; but to visitors, their monochrome isle seems strangely familiar, for the same grey hue dominates London's buildings of worship and governance. These limestone cliffs are the womb of metropolitan magnificence, its monumentality seen here in architectural absence, in the negative space left behind by imperial construction. There are still stones at Portland marked by Wren for St Paul's but rejected by the builders. And so too Harry Burdon felt rejected, until God called him.

Friends described Harry as a 'very respectable well-grown fellow, of fair education, and prepossessing appearance'; but somehow he had been caught up in the Girlingite whirlwind, and his family lamented his loss. That February, encouraged by the eviction, Mr Burdon engaged a detective, Mr Pearce, skilled in the rescue of 'deluded friends' from the sect – a practice so well known that it had acquired its own term, 'cutting out' – and together with Harry's brother, the Portlanders arrived in Hordle to set up camp at the Bells Inn. They had been told that the Girlingites slept in Herbert's barn, which, being close to the gentleman's own house, presented a difficult target. However, the men took their meals along the lane in Beasley's barn, and passed the Bells on their way. While Harry's brother and Mr Pearce patrolled between the two barns, Mr Burdon stayed at the inn: he'd been to Hordle on earlier rescue attempts, and as his face was known there, it was feared he might alert the sect to their intentions. Just at that moment, they saw a dozen Girlingites coming down the road – with Harry among them.

The Burdons rushed to get him, but the brethren resisted, and Pearce pushed one into a ditch. As another muscular Shaker ran at Harry's brother, Pearce used a rope to lasso their quarry, tying the lad's wrists together with a cord with a stick at each end, like a bucking steer. Villagers stood on their doorsteps as the Portlanders dragged Harry down the road to the house of Mr Cole, an ex-Girlingite, followed by the brethren, shouting kidnap. The rescuers managed to get inside and bolt the door, but having got this far, they decided to demand the return of Harry's clothes and possessions. It was a foolhardy move. As soon as they made their way towards the encampment, they were set on by thirty brethren 'like a tribe of savages', and had to retreat to Cole's farmhouse, to which the Girlingites then laid siege, waiting for movement from within.

I will not come! I will not come, I tell you! My mother is Mary Ann now, no other; my brothers and sisters are here, in these fields. I am no longer the man I was, for I have been reborn in Christ, and I expect His Coming.

You will come with us, my boy, and you will thank us. God is your Father in Heaven, and I am your father on earth, and your duty lies in Portland; its stones are your home. Aye, lie quiet and give in, for old Harry's cords here can tighten, and no amount of shaking will set you free. You are ours again.

A constable from Milton arrived, and not liking the look of things, sent to Lymington for reinforcements. Three more officers came, and warned the Girlingites not to intervene. But Auberon Herbert also appeared, accompanied by his steward.

'If your son refuses to leave the community you will be breaking the law if you take him,' he told Mr Burdon.

'All right', replied Burdon, but added, 'Mr Herbert, mind you prevent any violence on the part of the Shakers.'

Herbert then addressed the young man himself: 'Do you wish to go home with your father or do you wish to stop with the community?'

'I want to stay with them,' replied Harry.

'You go back then,' said Herbert, but Harry's brother and Mr Pearce held the lad tightly by his shoulders.

'That's violence,' declared Herbert, 'I shall hold you responsible.'

The rescuers said that they knew the law as well as he, whereupon Herbert set off for Lymington for legal advice, and was told that the Burdons had no right to use force. Armed with this judgement, he returned to Hordle, but before he could get there, a fast cart had drawn up outside Cole's house and Harry was bundled into the back of it and sat upon to keep him there. Brandishing a club like a Zulu knobkerrie alternately over Harry's head and at the Girlingites – who, despite warnings from the police, rushed towards the cart – the Portlanders drove off at speed through the farm gates, leaving Herbert and his sergeant powerless to stop them.

Racing up the road to Holmsley station – a quiet country halt more used to genteel visitors detraining for Bournemouth and Christchurch – the kidnappers were pursued by a cartload of fifteen Girlingites, the trees swaying in their passing draught. Despite Harry's squirming, the rescuers paced ahead. They had bribed a labourer with sixpence to give the Girlingites false directions, and making a sudden turn to Ringwood, they left the brethren thinking they were still bound for Holmsley. The Burdons arrived at Ringwood station just in time to catch the down train, and manhandled their trussed-up trophy on board. Within the hour, Harry was back in Dorset and in sight of home.

On 11 February 1875, the Lymington Union Rural Sanitary Authority instructed Herbert that his barn was overcrowded. Although Herbert offered to allow the women and children to stay, the Girlingites refused to be parted, and so, two weeks later, the Family began another exodus. At 9 pm, with the snow thick on the ground, the infants, the aged, the infirm and twenty 'Shaker teachers and parents' moved back to Beasley's barn, where the floor was covered with beds. For the rest, eighty adults, the only home now was the two-acre field next to the Lodge. Here they

'These singular people still cling with extraordinary pertinacity to the neighbourhood of the New Forest Lodge . . . The encampment which they now occupy . . . is situated in a field adjoining Vaggs Lane, belonging to a Mr Draper, of Dorchester, and which is leased to the Shakers for a term of seven years, about two of which have already expired.'

constructed rough shelters by throwing carpets over a few poles, with a screen of furze, under which they could barely stand upright; nor was there room for them all to lie down in this little ease, so they slept in relays. Miss Wood, now in her sixties and described as 'our blessed benefactor . . . a lady of good manners and address and of evidently higher breeding than the strange people by whom she was surrounded', took a small cottage nearby. Meanwhile, Mary Ann had been warned 'that attempts will still be made to prove her insane, and that she must be on her guard'. In the event, it was not she who would be incarcerated.

On 26 February a man said to be Julia Wood's nephew arrived in Lymington to persuade her to return home. In fact W. Muskerry Tilson was a legal advisor to her family, and the next day – together with Dr Adams, Dr Maskew from Lyndhurst, a nurse and two policemen – he arrived at Vaggs Lane, where the *Manchester Guardian* took up the story.

> Dr Maskew entered the field singly, and made his way to the tent. At the entrance he was met by Brothers Isaac and Harry, who demanded his business, when he replied that he was a friend of Mr Cowper-Temple . . . He was then admitted to the tent. Most of the Shakers were sitting round the stove, some reading books, while one young person, evidently the hairdresser of the community, with a round stick and a brush was engaged in curling the hair of her sisters. In all about 70 persons were present in a tent measuring about 20 ft by 10 ft.

Having gained entry under false pretences, Maskew said his wife had plenty of money; would they rent a place if she bought it for them? Then he introduced the name of Miss Wood: 'By the by, how is Miss Wood? I do not see her. Where is she?' Mary Ann told him she was in the habit of visiting their brethren in the neighbourhood, and could not say where she was at that moment. Just then, a policeman walked in with Mr Tilson, 'who was known to the Shakers [and] the plot was thus "blown"'.

Although Maskew tried to protest that he'd come alone, and this was an accidental meeting, his party had to retreat. With the Children of God spread throughout the area in cottages and barns, they faced an impossible task, but the local constable sent them to Bashley and the cottage of an 'outsider Shaker', Mr Knight, a hawker and chimney-sweep, where they found Julia Wood, along with James Haase and several female Girlingites. Recognising her pursuers, Julia ran upstairs, followed by Maskew and Tilson. Mrs Knight invited the *Guardian* in to witness what was happening: 'Mr Haase, a Shaker of gentlemanly address, the cottager Knight, and seven women were present, Miss Wood being seated in the smoky chimney-corner, clad in her accustomed bloomer costume. Beyond the excitement consequent on such an event, Miss Wood seemed perfectly sane to an inexperienced eye.' As the warrant was signed by the two doctors,

> her removal was at once attempted. Mr Haase placed himself before her and repeatedly urged them to show their authority for removing Miss Wood. Dr Maskew refused to do so, saying 'he was the authority.' The police-sergeant was called, who took Haase by the arms and threw him back. Mrs Knight next placed herself before Miss Wood, but in vain. Half supported by Dr Maskew and her nephew, her gray hair streaming in the wind, she was placed in the carriage, calling on the representatives of the Press to bear witness that she was being taken away against her will. The carriage was then driven to Lyndhurst, *en route* for Laverstock, a private asylum near Salisbury.

Female incarceration – for reasons ranging from illegitimate births to religious mania – remained a contentious topic, and on 2 March C. S. Perceval, Secretary of the Commissioners of Lunacy, the board which regulated Victorian psychiatry, had to issue a denial that Miss Wood had been apprehended under their authority. Meanwhile Tilson told *The Times*: 'Those poor suffering New Forest Shakers have ruined Miss Wood. She is now absolutely penniless and dependent on her friends, who have acted solely with the view to remove her from a scene of filth, privation, and squalid misery . . .' As to her mental state, 'It will suffice to say that Miss Wood was pronounced insane years ago, and was a patient in a lunatic asylum for a considerable time during and since which period her disease has exhibited itself in other forms besides that of mere religious hallucination, as can be testified by every member of her family.'

The Penny Illustrated Paper, took a more colourful line, however. In an editorial – printed beneath advertisements for Maskelyne and Cooke's *Psycho*, Nella Davenport's nightly SPIRITUAL FLIGHT ('being bound with ropes and firmly corded in the casket'), and Miss Dollie Dumas, the 'celebrated Mexican wonder and indescribable Phenomenon' with her 'most extraordinary light séance' – it noted that Miss Wood 'appealed to members of the press to witness she was being taken away against her will – but what can the press do? What can anybody do?'

> Two doctors have declared her to be insane. Her relation takes charge of her as legal custodian, and consigns her to a madhouse . . . Probably none of the visiting magistrates who periodically inspect the asylum hold Shakerian tenets, possibly none of the Commissioners in Lunacy have a tendency that way – so the chances of her liberation may be remote. Of course, if the said commissioners and magistrates were to find themselves amidst a Shaker community – and be it remembered that there *is* a Shaker community in America – they might incur suspicion, if peculiar views of religious formation constitute insanity . . . It becomes a question, of course, where the line is to be drawn. At present we have not heard of anybody being shut up by dear relations because of practising the vagaries of so-called Spiritualism . . .

The enraged Girlingites, meanwhile, pronounced their patroness's abduction to be 'the crowning act of a shameful conspiracy', and pointed out that if Miss Wood had been examined by the same board of magistrates as Mary Ann, she too would have been liberated. Moreover, they claimed that Auberon Herbert, 'who has had many opportunities of judging, declares his belief in the sanity of Miss Wood'.

It was doubtless through Herbert that the nation's debating chamber was alerted to the affair. In the House of Commons on 8 March, L.L. Dillwyn, the member for Swansea, registered continuing public disquiet about the events in the New Forest. Dillwyn's own interests were indicated by the other questions he had tabled that year – from petitions on women's suffrage to 'the removal of lunatic paupers' from Devonport Military Hospital to Westminster Union Workhouse. He now asked the Home Secretary, Assheton Cross,

The Penny Illustrated Paper.

SATURDAY, MARCH 6, 1875.

Topics of the Week.

THE SHAKERS

are still out in the cold, and are exciting more public attention, because of what they doubtless regard as persecution, than they ever attracted by their strange ceremonies and eccentric doctrines. The other day one of their number, the son of a farmer, was "rescued" by his friends, who adopted the remarkably simple expedient of seizing upon him, binding him hand and foot, and driving away with him in a cart, after a sharp scuffle and a hot pursuit on the part of some of the more energetic members of the community, with whom he had lived for some time.

Mrs. Girling, the "mother" of the colony, has been declared to be insane; but it seems that nobody is sufficiently interested in her to cart her away, or even to shut her up in a lunatic asylum. With Miss Wood, the lady who built—or at least paid for—the New Forest Lodge, the case is different. She has an affectionate nephew, who, with Dr. Masken, of Lyndhurst, and a female nurse from the Laverstock Lunatic Asylum, went for his aunt—Dr. Adams, of Lymington, joining in the chase, while a party of police "in a trap" followed to render official assistance. The unfortunate lady was tracked to a cottage at Bashley, about two miles from the Shakers' barn; the two doctors signed the papers which, it appears, entitle any individual to shut up another on medical evidence; the police, the nurse, and her relative then forced Miss Wood into a carriage and drove her off to the asylum.

Mrs. Girling is herewith sketched by an Artist who interviewed the Shakers last Sunday.

Whether his attention has been called to the case of the recent arrest on the New Forest of Miss Wood, a person alleged to be a lunatic; and, if so, whether such arrest was made on the ground that she is dangerous to herself or others; and whether such arrest is legal and justifiable?

The minister rose to answer.

Sir, my attention was called to this arrest. I immediately put myself in communication with the Lunacy Commissioners. I ascertained that the certificate which had been given did not warrant a detention in a lunatic asylum, and that it might have been amended within a period of 14 days under the statute. I further communicated with the Lunacy Commissioners, and directed that an inquiry should be made, in order that Miss Wood should be released, if they found no necessity for her detention. I am happy to say that this afternoon I have received a note saying that she has been discharged.

Miss Wood was duly liberated – only to be reimprisoned two hours later under another certificate of lunacy. Back in the Commons, Dillwyn asked the Home Secretary,

Whether the attention of the Government has been called to the rearrest of Miss Wood, a member of the Shaker community, and whether they considered that the fact that she was arrested, set at liberty, and rearrested within a few hours, was in accordance with the law?

Assheton Cross drew to his feet again and, mindful of the farce of Miss Wood's release and recapture, told the House that there had been 'no interference on the part of any one in order to secure her release . . . But the attention of the Commissioners in Lunacy has been specially called to her case, and I am promised that a report respecting it will be made in a few days . . .'

The report was never made public. But down at Hordle, a letter arrived from Laverstock and was released to the press. In it, Julia Wood related how, on her brief discharge, she had been taken by

Tilson and her nephew to 'two young doctors' in Salisbury who had 'separately examined her touching [on] her religious views'. She was 'struck with their want of scriptural knowledge, and thought they were very unfit persons to conduct a religious examination'. They signed a new certificate 'to the effect that she was suffering from "religious hallucination"', and Julia was returned to Laverstock. 'She speaks very highly of the kind treatment of Dr Manning, the principal of the asylum, and says she is very comfortable, but considers it most ignominious that she should be confined as a mad woman. She is most anxious to rejoin the community, and prays for a speedy release' – as did her Family at their eleven o'clock Sunday service, when one man shouted, 'Oh, Lord, shake down the prison walls!'

Laverstock, Wiltshire's oldest asylum, was a large private institution with a staff of thirty to look after its eighty inmates. Julia's fellow patients were of a certain class – the famous cricketer, Charles Lister, had died there in 1873 – and their circumstances were certainly better than those at the military asylum at Netley (where, that January, one inmate had been found in the bathroom, having cut open his stomach with a razor, left by a careless workman, and had incised a four foot section of his intestine, thereby accomplishing that to which Fruitlands' Samuel Hecker had only aspired).

However, since their early uproarious days in Suffolk, many had thought that the entire Girlingite sect belonged in Bedlam. Their lowly origins encouraged notions of inbred degeneracy – criticisms later aired in the *Daily Telegraph*, which published a letter suggesting that 'the Shakers are mad', while another hostile voice wondered if they were 'fanatical monomaniacs, in a state of mental weakness approximating to imbecility'. In response, the paper felt moved to remark that 'We are not urging that they should be sent to Hanwell or Colney Hatch' – the two large suburban asylums serving London – 'their heads shaved, and ice applied to their spines. It is not the proper business of the State to set up as a mad doctor upon a large scale . . .' Nevertheless, many regarded religious mania as a psychiatric condition (while a generation later, in 1908, the Hampshire polemicist Arnold White would comment, 'There is no hard-and-fast formula for the neutralisation of the unfit, but the process of wise sterilisation will begin on the day when the British public insists on the break-up of the concentration breeding-camps of the insane').

Whatever Julia's experiences at Laverstock – or whatever further attempts were made to free her – she would languish there for seven years. On her release in 1881 she was probably reclaimed back into the security of her own family; she died ten years later, on 13 April 1891, aged seventy-six, never having seen Mary Ann again.

In the light of recent events, a defiant new communiqué was issued from Hordle. 'As to the assertions men make in reference to our sanity, or insanity . . .' averred Mary Ann, 'it is but a few weeks since Doctor A— pronounced me insane, but God in His mercy allowed me to be brought before a bench of honesty-hearted magistrates, who gave me my liberty . . . Our present position is one which I never desire to see or hear of its like again, but what could we do when turned into the road?' She struck an apocalyptic note to rival *Fors Clavigera*: '. . . you will only quench one fire to light a larger one, and thus every effort to exterminate us will prove futile . . . And soon the world will know whether I speak the truth or error.'

As Mary Ann published her challenge, Ruskin was lecturing to the London Institution 'on the simple dynamic condition of Glacial Action among the Alps', using daguerrotypes ('the most marvellous invention of the century') of ghostly but immense rocks worn by frozen water. 'There were three great demonstrable periods of the earth's history,' he said. 'That in which it was crystallised; that in which it was sculpted; and that in which it was now being unsculpted or defaced . . .' His faith too was being eroded, and his elemental eschatology had its echoes in the events in Hampshire, where the Girlingites were battered by 'the noise of rain and wind, and the roaring of the sea . . . a south-west gale is no slight matter at Hordle . . .'

Pitched on the high road, their sailcloth tent resembled some ocean-going vessel bracing itself against the elements, with Mary Ann at the helm. Inside, the faithful crouched around two stoves, using the forms rescued from their old chapel as seats by day and beds by night. They continued to pray that the Lodge 'might soon be recovered from the hands of evil men', and even inquired about buying their former home – but were told they would be charged £2,000, a sum which would have made the new owner a profit of £660 within the space of little more than a month. This was either property speculation or a ploy to price them out of the district. However, Mary Ann's claims that she had made £2,000 worth of improvements were not substantiated by *The Times'* own survey: 'A visit to the Lodge will help to explain its remarkable depreciation in value. For all purposes but their own, the Shakers have injured the property instead of improving it.'

> A large stable has been altered into what looks like a chapel. Overhead is a loft, which has been used as a dormitory. One outbuilding had been opened as a small store for supplying the neighbourhood with small wares; another was fitted as a blacksmith's forge; another was a workshop. There was a schoolroom, and a new and larger chapel was in the course of building [but] unfortunately, the Shaker workmen failed conspicuously in brick-making. A deep pit, now full of half-frozen water, showed where they had dug clay. They then moulded this material brick-fashion, dried it in the sun, and built their walls of it, sometimes giving it a coat of pitch. Naturally, the rain and frost have played havoc with such walls. A touch now crumbles them. Some have bulged out,

> some are bulging in, and roofs well finished with bought tiles or slates now rest on tottering supports, which the first high wind will level low.

This was evidence of the sect's sadly abandoned ambitions, a visible indictment of intolerance. 'Much of the land is unsown, and the general aspect is one of dreariness and desolation.' Worse still, the crops which they had planted – 'turnips, parsnips, onions, broccoli, cabbages (all sorts), swedes, carrots, &c . . . 'the Shakers, it must be remembered, were to a considerable extent vegetarians' – were now being harvested by Mr Cole, their former supporter, and his sons. Camped opposite the Lodge, the sect watched as if their eviction was being re-enacted – on their produce. It was all the more galling that the house stood empty, its new owner, Herbert Guillaume, never having taken up residence. To the Girlingites, this was a daily reminder of injustice, and now, aggrieved and hungry, they took matters into their own hands.

On 10 June 1875, they crossed the lane and attempted to reoccupy their home. Unable to gain entry, they took up position in the stable-chapel and refused to leave. Through the afternoon and evening they sang and prayed, as if to resanctify the space; for those few hours they had regained their Zion. On being told of the situation, Guillaume telegraphed his agent, Mr Colborne, who arrived that night with a large party of men and constables, and the squatters were re-evicted as, once again, a sizeable crowd of some three hundred assembled to witness the scene. A month later the Lodge was sold to a Mr G. T. Mason, and with that transaction the Home receded even further from its former tenants.

In July, more bad news reached the Family: the land on which they were now encamped had been sold, and although their lease still had five years to run, it was likely the new owner would evict them. It was reported that the colonists were living 'ankle-deep in mud . . . It is evident something must be done and that speedily, to alter a state of things disgraceful to our age and country.' Some even suggested that a place be found for them overseas. It was not an unusual idea; they were, after all, already refugees in their own country, and emigration had ever been a resort for the dissenting and the dispossessed (just as it was, like the threat of asylum or the workhouse, a means of social control). What was extraordinary was that one of those who proposed it was Frederick Evans, whose visit to England had foreshadowed Mary Ann's own mission.

In the *Shaker and Shakeress*, Evans declared that 'we, the Shakers of America, sympathise with those sincere, desolated enthusiasts . . . ruthlessly . . . turned out into the highway'. Although concerned to point out their theological differences – 'as to who and what Christ is – and in the time and manner of his second coming' – he stressed 'important elements of union': 'Respecting the ownership of land, in large quantities, and the monopoly of life elements – holding that community of goods is a Christian virtue, [and] the Shakers and Bible Christians are at one . . . Both agree that the dead are raised, and may reanimate their physical bodies, if not too much decomposed for their reparation, under the laws of materialisation.' He even seemed to envisage a future alliance:

> The Marriage of the Lamb and Bride will be effected through Spiritualism. It will be a union between the Jewish Pentecostal Church, in the Heavens, and the Gentile Pentecostal Church on Earth . . . Could the English Shakers, some of whom have visited us, see things in this light, *good homes* await the whole ejected company. And what appeared to be their total ruin, may thus be turned to their temporal and eternal gain.

It was a fantastic idea: a spiritualist utopian binding of Girlingites and Shakers which would fulfil, in the most circuitous and extraordinary manner, Evans' earlier mission to the mother country. But this communion would never take place. In October 1876, a disappointed Evans said he had corresponded with 'the Girling woman', and that her group were 'the most orthodox of all sects'. Two years later, Elder Giles Avery of New Lebanon stated that the Society had 'no relation to or connexion with' the Girlingites; while one visitor to Vaggs Lane, who suspected that 'this very clever lady is well made up in the life and proceedings of a certain Hannah Leece [sic] . . . the foundress of Shakerism in America', remarked, 'As to the woman in the Apocalypse . . . Mrs Girling, pointing towards herself in a way not to be misunderstood, said, that *she had already come!*'

Yet the idea of leaving England was encouraged, it seemed, as a convenient way of dealing with one hundred homeless religious communists, and the Girlingites were visited by 'emigration agents . . . asking many questions respecting their mode of life'. One newspaper suggested 'that they should move away into lands where farms can be had at a nominal figure, and where the climate does not debar dancing and singing in the open air in the depth of winter'; while a 'resident of Southampton, who discerned that Mary Ann 'has more personal influence over her community than Brigham Young ever had over his' (Young had led his persecuted Mormon Saints from Nauvoo to Utah) proposed a similar hegira. 'I recommended her to consider the desirability of emigrating to New Zealand, but she replied, "Sir, I thank you sincerely; but God has placed me here, and nothing shall induce me to leave this place. My destiny is *here*, and if even an angel from heaven told me to go, I would not."'

Like their American cousins, the Girlingites were also the focus for day-trippers newly liberated by the railway, the charabanc, and shorter working hours. At first they restricted access to 'four or five visitors from Lymington' – doubtless apprehensive of the fellows who 'congregated in the road outside, and strove to annoy the worshippers' – but realising that they were denying themselves a source of charitable donation, they now admitted the public. It was a risky move. Soon enough their services attracted 'fast, loudly-attired young men' who had to be met with 'firm, though respectful, denial'. Nevertheless, many visitors made donations which the Girlingites 'gladly accepted, and even seemed to expect': 'They say that God sends them money, but the devil brings it,' noted one tourist.

They might have sensed other attractions, too. In the mid-1870s, all Hampshire seemed alive to evangelism. At nearby Sway, for instance, the 'true' Bible Christians were playing host to revivalist preachers from London, their chapel 'crowded to excess' as it resounded to sermons on the virtues of abstinence and hymns from 'Sankey's handbook'. (The American evangelists Moody and Sankey were 'regenerating' sinners on their tour of Britain, reports of which, appearing alongside the Girlingites' story, encouraged new allegations of transatlantic influence.) Meanwhile, Primitive Methodists were holding 'revivalist open-air camp meetings' at Alresford; and at Cadnam, William Cowper took the precepts of the Broadlands conferences to the forest, founding a 'People's Hall' which 'could bring together 300 people on a dark rough night', united 'in pulling Satan's kingdom down'. Next to such gatherings, Girlingism could look almost tame. However, holiday crowds flocked to Hordle, and 'The roadway near their tent presented the appearance of a fair, and the landlord of the Bells had a roaring trade.'

These were scenes worthy of *The Pickwick Papers*. 'On Thursday last, the day being consecrated to the "early closing" movement, and the weather all "smiles and tears", a large wagonette left [Bournemouth] Arcade . . . bound for the Shakers; so pleasant a party indeed, that long ere the tattered canvas at Hordle was reached, in anticipation of the curious manifestations in the store, the whole wagonette, so to speak, repeatedly shook its sides with laughter.' At Ashley Arnewood, the Herberts found that their country home had become a less placid place: 'Such char-a-bancs just passed, come from the Shakers,' Florence told her mother. 'Oh, dear! The man at the public [house] close to them has made a fortune and had a huge waggon of beer every Saturday night and Monday morning.' By September 1875 the police were being called upon to manage Sunday crowds of up to five hundred, many of whom behaved 'most improperly . . .' On one occasion, drunken 'roughs' chucked stones at the community's tents, a frightening episode for the children inside. Such threats made the need for a permanent home, and the money to fund it, yet more pressing. Mary Ann had a remarkable solution: she would take the Girlingites on tour.

The *Southampton Times* announcement was aptly set between a letter on 'The Primitive Church' and a report on William Cowper's address to the town's Guildhall on 'the treatment of fugitive slaves who had sought the protection of the British flag' – a response to recent incidents of these nineteenth-century asylum-seekers. Under the headline, THE SHAKERS, it was noted that Mrs Girling was to appear in the town. The storms that autumn were particularly fierce, and having been marooned when their coach broke down on the way, eighteen Girlingites finally arrived, armed only 'with a hymn book, composed by various members of the fraternity'.

The first date on their tour was determined by the fact that Mary Ann had engaged a Southampton hotel keeper, Mr Thompson, as their promoter, and the Drill Hall on St Mark's Road was packed with Sotonians keen to see the prophetess for themselves: 'a spare woman . . . with rather a florid complexion', wearing 'a plain black stuff dress, with white collar and cuffs' and 'a small red cap trimmed with a white frill'. Her female acolytes wore white muslin or stuff dresses, their curls 'kept back from the forehead by a plain black comb'. Having been introduced by Councillor Purkis, Mary

Ann began by repudiating American influences and 'the name of "Shaker"' ('she had never been there and she knew nothing about them'). Then, after a hymn, *Awake, awake*, she detailed 'the reason she was not going to die'. This was greeted with 'loud cries of "Nonsense"'. The women then began 'a measured kind of hop . . . accompanied by gesticulations and continual bending of the body. One feature of the dance is that the "Shakers" hold up the forefinger of each hand during the time it is continued, their eyes being more frequently closed than open'; but from the moment they began until the meeting was broken up, 'the hall was the centre of a scene of excitement the like of which has probably never before been witnessed in the town'.

It was a discouraging start to the tour, made worse by the appearance of Southampton's resident mesmerist, Sergeant-Major Millin, who challenged Mary Ann 'to a contest on Friday evening, when he would take the hall, and bring several persons, and there produce the same results as she did upon her followers'. Millin would dog the Girlingites, following them to Bournemouth where he gave 'mesmeric entertainments' 'with a view to exposing the Shaker swindle at Hordle', entertaining audiences with 'humorous recitals and ridiculous experiments' in which victims shook and danced (although he himself would be exposed when a father revealed that his young son had been paid to perform feats while supposedly mesmerised). And when the Girlingites arrived at the Portland Hall, Southsea (sponsored by the United Kingdom Alliance, not because they endorsed Girlingism, 'but because the object in holding the meeting was to procure funds for the erection of a wooden shed to shelter the community in the winter'), Mary Ann felt the need to declare that she had been 'charged with influencing her followers by means of spiritualism and mesmerism, but it was not so. God did not make known himself by means of chairs and tables' – although, as the events would show, their opponents did.

On 9 December the tour reached Exeter, where the service-cum-lecture, 'The life and aims of the community at New Forest', was interrupted by Mr Carroll, a commercial traveller, and Mr Rose, a town councillor, who stood up to denounce it as a 'blasphemous farce', while a restive crowd brandished sticks and called the Girlingites 'Yankee adventurers'. With a second meeting planned in Exeter's Royal Public Rooms, magistrates ordered that tickets should be issued and go on sale for just two hours – and they promptly sold out. When the Girlingites appeared on the platform, Mary Ann invited requests. Would the audience like to hear from the young women, or should she speak for them? The crowd decided 'unanimously' on the former. Eliza Folkard spoke in a 'firm and rather melodious voice' of her conversion; and when Mary Ann introduced the youngest member of the group, someone shouted, 'And very pretty too.'

'The poor girl had to tell her story amid a running fire of compliments on her good looks', noted the *Hampshire Independent*, somewhat protective of its adoptive children, 'and when she came to relate how . . . she ran away to Mrs Girling's camp without wishing father or mother "good bye," there were ironical cries of "shocking," and "very bad".' As she sat down, someone shouted, 'Let's have some shaking.' Mary Ann said they could not shake when they liked, although she herself had danced in the presence of thousands.

'I tell you, I never felt any desire to reject it, it is so good. I am happy now, but that is intensified happiness. It is something like the children. When they are eating bread and butter, they say, "This is very good," but if you put a little sugar on it, it is much better.'

This was greeted with more laughter.

'Ah, but it's a living salvation,' she rhapsodised. 'The salvation we have got doesn't make us unhappy. We don't go about sanctimoniously . . . I tell you, the grand secrets of life are, be good, and do good.'

Such beatitudes were lost on her audience. As the Girlingites left the auditorium, there were 'groans and expressions of dissatisfaction that no dancing had taken place'. Instead, a gang of lads got up onstage and began throwing bags of flour which they'd brought along in the hope of using them on the Girlingites. In the square outside, a thousand-strong crowd waited until 10.30 pm to witness the departure of Mary Ann and her followers who, despite a police bodyguard, 'were roughly pushed about on their way from the rooms to the public-house where they had obtained lodgings'.

The tour continued through the winter, making few converts, although the merchandising, in the form of their hymn book, 'a very curious composition', sold in 'large number'. On her third visit to Bristol – where it seems a satellite sect was underway – Mary Ann appeared at the Colston Hall in front of a crowd of two thousand – and found herself at the centre of another riot, 'during which the chairs, tables, and other property were broken up and heaped in the middle of the hall'. The ring leader, a young cigar merchant named Augustus Wilson, was charged with afray, and magistrates heard how he had used a heavy stick to smash the table and its water-bottles. But they also criticised the hall's owners for having rented out to Mr Thompson, 'it being evident to them that the affair was now being taken up . . . merely as a speculation to make money by'.

The Girlingites' turbulent West Country progress is redolent of James Naylor's blasphemous ride into Bristol on a donkey; or, perhaps, the Sex Pistols' 'Anarchy in the UK' tour of 1976, which faced the ire of local residents and the resistance of councils. And just as punk was a reaction to a 1970s Burnt Over Region of industrial disputes and a modern dystopia – 'When there's no future, how can there be sin?' – the 1870s was an equally uncertain age, as *Fors Clavigera* testified, with a grieving queen clad in black bombazine whose reclusion led to calls for a British republic, and war and revolution raging in Europe and around the Empire. At such a time, the Girlingites might have been regarded as the enemy within, as their American equivalents had been in the 1770s.

Mary Ann had become a catalyst for the release of irrational emotion. With the erosion of traditional belief and the biblical past restocked with strange new dragons, Girlingism was an act of deliberate regression: blasphemy, faith, deception and myth all combined in one woman, her body branded with the devil's marks or saintly stigmata. Fraudsters or mystics, communists or lunatics, the tour had become a holy, chaotic sideshow, and failed to do much good for their brethren back in Hordle. Yet there was a hopeless romance to their story which was paralleled by another event dominating the headlines that winter. In the early hours of 7 December, the S.S. *Deutschland* had foundered in a snow storm off Harwich – the site of Camisard revelation a century and a half earlier, close to Mary Ann's own Suffolk birthplace, and to the port from which Turner sailed strapped to a mast to experience another tempest. Among the sixty passengers and crew who perished were five German Franciscan nuns fleeing punitive anti-Catholic laws and bound for America; they drowned together, holding hands as their leader, 'a gaunt woman 6 ft high' called out 'O Christ, come quickly!'

For Gerald Manley Hopkins, the scene was enough to stir him from a seven-year silence to write 'The Wreck of the Deutschland', eliding the nuns' watery martyrdom and their founder, 'With the gnarls of the nails in thee, niche of the lance/his/Lovescape crucified'; St Francis's stigmatic body as a landscape of Christ's love. Hopkins blamed England for the women's death (it was said that boats stood by waiting for the ship to break up to pillage it, and that bodies washed ashore had been stripped of their jewellery). So, too, the Girlingites saw themselves as refugees marooned in the storm, fleeing persecution while their 'prophetess towered in the tumult, a virginal tongue told', her followers 'Loathed for a love men knew in them/ Banned by the land of their birth'.

The Girlingites' tour had raised enough funds to enable a new fifty-foot barn to be built and a children's festival to be held, but Mr Henry Knight remarked on the low takings of the venture in contrast to the Isle of Wight group of which he was Father, where 'a great increase in numbers is prophesied' and where 'a house at Swan-more has been taken for a Shaker house'.

In contrast to the remote bohemia of West Wight over which Tennyson and Julia Margaret Cameron presided, the east end of the Island had a more commercial air, as a correspondent to *Fors Clavigera* remarked: 'the Isle of Wight . . . is very pretty, but all over-builded. It threatens soon to become a mere suburb of London.' When she first left London, Mary Ann had stayed on the island – following in Mary Toms' footsteps – and in Ryde, its largest town, had made converts of the Knight family. Henry Knight was a 'dealer in Marble Ornaments' in the Royal Victoria Arcade, as well as being a town councillor and a commercial photographer, as were his two sons, Henry and Charles – although the latter was also described as 'a young man who had been in Chichester studying for the Church' and said to be 'in rather ill-health . . .'

In January 1876, it was announced that Henry Knight, town councillor of Ryde, had been accepted as a Girlingite having taken 'the greatest interest both in the religious belief and moral conduct of the community' since their recent visit to the town. The 'Shaker Camp' at Hordle – where Knight underwent 'the usual examination as to fitness, &c.' – celebrated their prestigious new recruit 'amid a scene such as it would be impossible to describe . . . The proceedings lasted till a late hour, to the astonishment of the natives . . .' Knight, it was said, intended not to live in the camp, 'but has undertaken the duty of agent his ultimate object . . . being the restoration to the community of their old residence, Forest Lodge'. To that end, Mr Knight arranged for the Girlingites to appear at Ryde's Victoria Rooms, duly advertised in the local press.

Initially, it looked like one of their most successful engagements, so much so that they extended their residency. 'Mrs Girling, and the "Heavenly-Looking Girls", have, by their "shaking", &c., drawn such crowded houses nightly at the Victoria Rooms, that it has been resolved to prolong their stay during the past week', it was reported. But the meetings also met with progressive antipathy, from ridicule to riots. During one, the back doors were broken open and a free fight ensued, with tables and chairs flying, and a stone ginger-beer bottle was thrown at Mr Knight. 'Mrs Girling and the whole of her party escaped unhurt', having run across the street to the house where they were staying, opposite the Yacht Club. 'For some time afterwards the streets were crowded with roughs, yelling and howling.' The young Girlingite women were not immune to this violence: at the bottom of West Street, 'to the eternal disgrace of some fellows, they very roughly treated some of these girls, getting in front of them, pushing them up against walls, &c . . . Stones were thrown at a very quiet, harmless, male shaker called "Uriah", [Isaac Batho] whose hat was knocked off . . . One of the poor girls who had been jostled about suffered from heart disease, and the roughs may be thankful no serious consequences ensued . . . The windows (plate-glass) of the house were smashed, potatoes being thrown from opposite! Mr Knight addressed the mob, requesting them to leave, and pointing out that the landlord would have to pay for the broken windows – not Mrs Girling.' 'We fear bad will be the result of the meetings', warned the local newspaper, which could only account for the 'large attendances . . . on grounds of curiosity and devilry'.

But it was clear more organised forces were at work. The culprits were summonsed, 'and the evidence showed that the storming of the Victoria-rooms on Monday night was a pre-arranged affair, in

VICTORIA ROOMS, RYDE.

"Holiness, without which no man shall see the Lord."

MRS. GIRLING will (D.V.) go through the Book of Revelations, with other parts of the Bible, in the course of a series of LECTURES, every evening at 8 o'clock, and afternoons at 3 o'clock, until further notice. Doors open half-an-hour previous. On some occasions the proceedings will be interspersed with Music.

The Lectures will consist of the Revelations of Christ made to her regarding the Coming of the Lord Jesus, and the Truth of the present Bible; and during her stay at Ryde, Mrs. Girling will attend at the Victoria Rooms every afternoon from 3 to 4.30, and will also be prepared to meet any Christian or Christians for a Bible Class, and for proper questions. No questions or interruptions will be allowed at evening meetings, as all disturbers will be removed. All are invited.

Should there be manifestations of the Spirit of God, such as Dancing, or Speaking with Tongues, or Songs of Praise, according to the working of the Spirit, the audience are earnestly entreated not to mock or jest at what they may hear or see, for it is the Spirit of the Living God.

Admission, Sixpence each, to all seats in the building; but those who are disposed to contribute more are requested to place their contributions in the box at the door.

Mrs. Girling is visiting Ryde by request, so that she and her teaching may be thoroughly understood, and as the Community have no means of paying expenses, a charge for admission is necessary; the proceeds go to benefit the Community. No charge will be made, however, to attendants at any of the Bible Classes, to which all Christians are cordially invited. As there is no charge made for the Bibln Class, Voluntary Offerings can be made in the box at the door.

NEW TOWN HALL, RYDE.

MESMERISM

VERSUS

SHAKERISM.

SERGEANT-MAJOR MILLIN, MEMBER OF THE LEGION OF HONOUR, WILL GIVE

THREE ENTERTAINMENTS

Introducing experiments in the above Hall, on MONDAY, TUESDAY, & WEDNESDAY, March 6, 7, and 8, 1876.

Admission—Front Seats, 2s.; Second ditto, 1s.; Back ditto, 6d.

which many of the tradesmen of Union-street were concerned'. One of the accused testified that 'afterwards he went to the Conservative Club smoking room', where a Mr Beasley 'was speaking of Mrs Girling and said he didn't mind spending a sovereign over the affair . . .' Even William Mew, the verger of the parish church, was accused of assaulting Henry Knight. But worse than sticks and stones were to come. A month later, the unwelcome figure of Sergeant-Major Millin reappeared on the scene to confront Mary Ann with acts of mesmerism in what was advertised as a kind of challenge match. Millin appeared at the New Town Hall, as the Girlingites performed that same night at its rival venue; his show was designed as a damning exposé of Mary Ann. It was perhaps the most virulent attack she and her faith – and its followers – had yet faced.

> Sgt-Major Millin, a member of the Legion of Honour . . . explained the 8 or 9 medals he wore, and then proceeded to lecture, to show that what Mrs Girling terms the pure Spirit of the Lord was mesmerism . . . On one visit to the Shakers, Mrs Girling, preaching from the 1st chapter of Genesis, used expressions which he as a married man and father of a family could not utter – it was something disgusting – something filthy. He noticed a girl in bloomer costume – trousers and tunic – go off very much like mesmerism: he brought her round, and he brought a man to his sense two or three times. Mrs Girling admitted hers was mesmerism and asked if he didn't think she was putting it to a good use for she got people to be teetotallers and then showed them the way of Salvation. That make [sic] his blood run cold.

Millin's evidence had the benefit of being highly-coloured, if not entirely circumspect; in his words, Mary Ann becomes a coquettish fraudster, emaciated and toothless (as if in reflection of her reduced power in comparison to his). 'He told Mrs Girling it was nothing but a mockery of religion and she was an imposter. She turned on her heels and said, "You're a wicked man."' Millin told his thousand-strong audience that when he first knew her – having gone to New Forest Lodge in the autumn of 1873, he claimed – Mary Ann was 'much stouter. Was it not reasonable to say that if God permitted one member of her own body to decay he would others? Some of Mrs Girling's members had decayed and others were decaying – for she hadn't got above 3 or 4 sound teeth in her head.'

This assault on Mary Ann's physical status – the obvious signs of human ageing – was met with applause, even as it portrayed her as some kind of witch-hag. Millin maintained that Mrs Girling used her hands in 'magnetic passes' to mesmerise her victims, and proceeded to demonstrate, on volunteers from the audience, how they might be made to squirm with invisible fleas, or sob with tears having seen their dead relatives in heaven. In these performances, Millin showed himself to be hardly less moral than the woman whom he accused, and when he offered to make his grief-stricken victim – a bill poster by the name of Coombes – pray, 'the audience forbad it'. He concluded with an admonitory anecdote concerning a solder who had been mesmerised in an officer's room in an Aldershot barracks. 'They excited the bump of destructiveness, and told the man he was a mad bull, and he did £40 worth of damage, and remained in that state three days, till a professor who had been telegraphed to come and brought him round. It was dangerous to mesmerise unless one understood phrenology.' Even Millin's science resorted to esoteric belief.

When Henry Knight heard of Millin's pronouncements, he proposed that Millin and Mary Ann should meet, 'on the challenge of the latter', the following afternoon, at the Victoria Rooms. 'A large company assembled, Mrs Girling and party occupying the platform.' Millin protested that he hadn't had enough time to gather his witnesses, but maintained all his accusations about Girlingism were true. Mary Ann began the meeting with a prayer, thanking God that 'they had the privilege of answering for themselves, knowing that the assertions against them were falsehoods . . . They freely forgave the Sergeant, and prayed that mercy be extended to him.'

Millin treated the occasion like a court of law – with Girlingism on trial. He said that he had 'heard from an ex-Shaker, a lad of 19 years of age, that a child had been born at the Lodge' – presumably the doomed James Benham. The lad's name was Kitcher, and the father of the child – James Todd – was a friend of his, 'and the child was doing well at the time'. Kitcher 'felt the influence of Mrs Girling upon him so strong that he had an inclination at times to leave his work and go back to her'. He also said later that 'Mrs Girling never admitted anyone without they were prepared to put down a certain sum, but he said they had nobody to shoe their horses and that was the reason they had him and his mate.' His friend and landlord, Mr George, a greengrocer, had come to Millin at Southampton, 'and asked if he could mesmerise a lad who had been under Mrs Girling's influence'. Millin did so, 'and after making a few magnetic passes over his body, the lad began to shake and tremble. Without taking his senses away, he asked him if he felt the same as when under Mrs Girling, and he replied – exactly the same . . . Next day the lad leapt from his chair and jumped about the room', and told Mrs Millin 'that Mrs Girling led her people to believe that she was the wife of the Lord Jesus Christ'.

Millin explained how he had subsequently attended the Girlingites' first meeting in Southampton 'at the public request', and that Mrs Girling had threatened to have him 'locked up', and had denied that the lad, Kitcher, had ever been at the Lodge (he said he was there for six months). Millin's accounts of his visits to Hordle fluctuate wildly in the numbers he apparently encountered there – he took sixty people with him on one occasion, when there were '200 or 300 persons' there from Southampton; on another, 'nearly 9,000 people were in Hordle that afternoon', he claimed. In one confrontation, Mary Ann had declared, 'You're a wicked man', and he had been shaken by one of the Girlingites, before his friends formed a protective circle around him. Then, 'whilst they were arguing, a tall young man, with a white frock on, such as farmers used, began to dance'. The battle of wills continued.

Millin said, 'To further prove it's mesmerism, let me go and bring him round.'

'No, God has not thought it right,' said Mary Ann.

'Fetch him to if you can, soldier,' said someone else.

At that Millin took the lad by the wrist and arm 'and immediately the young man fell on his seat'. He asked Mary Ann what she thought of the 'pure Spirit of the Lord then'.

'Does mesmerism come from God?' she said, rhetorically.

Millin believed all things did, 'but they had power to put things to good or bad purposes'. It sounded as though they were discussing witchcraft. 'To prove it could be put to a good purpose, if any of her people had the tooth-ache or head-ache he could take it away.

Mary Ann replied, "So can I: and cure rheumatism too."' At which point 'someone called out that the young man was off again'.

Millin claimed it was not only Mary Ann who had the power to mesmerise; Isaac Batho could, too: 'directly he went opposite him the young man got up and began to dance again'. One of Millin's Southampton friends, Mr Butt, contributed his own observations: that Mary Ann seemed to pray with her eyes open (evidently suspicious). 'He watched her while they were singing: she kept beating time – "throwing it about". He believed the influence against her was too strong for a long time', and when he talked to her and said he believed in the Lord Jesus Christ, she had said, 'You're my brother.' But 'he would not have anything to do with her: her God had got a black face'.

Later, Mary Ann had tried to stop Millin attending her services, so 'he disguised himself by putting on a pair of spectacles, and walking behind a stout gentleman, Lieut. Guard, of the Volunteer Artillery, Southampton', and got in. It was another farcical scene – albeit with unsettling hints. 'Unfortunately, when sitting down, his spectacles fell off: then the Shakers recognised him, and began touching each other and looking in his face with a sort of smile.' He gave up his disguise and began to sing from one of the hymn books, 'for he was very fond of good sacred singing', and after her sermon was over, he invited Mary Ann to come to Southampton, as if he were an ordinary member of the public. 'Someone then called out, "That's Sergeant Mullin." [sic] She then stepped back, pretending – that was a strong word, but he meant to say pretending, for she had seen him a number of times – she didn't know him.'

As Henry Knight and Sergeant Millin fought this war of words in the Ryde meeting rooms, Mary Ann rose to say that the public should be allowed to make their own judgement. Millin implied that she had moved the service inside to avoid him, but she said that they had held open-air meetings only three or four times in the summer, and that day the wind had been 'so boisterous' that they had been obliged to shelter from the dust: 'It was dark when she saw Sergt. Millin at the Lodge, and she should not have recognised him again. She had no knowledge whatever of his spectacles falling over. After the meeting, there were about 500 in the meadow . . . she didn't say that Sergt. Millin was of the devil, but the practice was. (Laughter).' The next time she'd seen him had been in Southampton – where she had gone 'on the invitation of Mr Budden and others' – when not only she, but Councillor Purkis had forbade Millin from taking the platform.

> If he wanted to prove that the influence he used was the same as *he* said she used he should have 120 people together, be turned out of house and home, as they were, into the road, and have no more shelter, food, raiment, sympathy or money

> than they had, and should go through all they had gone through, going without food 48 hours at a time, and that not once but 40 times. Many weeks they had only four meals a week, and that only dry bread without even a cup of tea, and one meal in two to two and a half days, and many a week she had not a farthing. For 18 nights they had not their clothes off, having nowhere to lay their heads, and no shelter. His 120 should vary as they did from 5 to 75 years of age, and if at the expiration of the same time, now about 18 months, there was no more sickness or death than with them, and the people were found in as healthy and happy a condition as they were, then she would say no more about mesmerism.

It was a heart-felt, passionate piece of rhetoric – with not a little justification, if some exaggeration – and with it, Mary Ann seemed to settle the matter; still more so when a Mr Davis told the meeting that Coombes the bill poster's father had been paid to perform his grief-stricken act. 'He (Davis) had seen as much show life as any of them. It was all humbug and rot. Mesmerism was all trickery.'

A few days later, the Girlingites held their own inquest on the matter in the Victoria Rooms – for which the venue was 'converted into a sort of Court House', chaired by Mr Broderick, the Ryde photographer, while at the table was 'a young man whom some might have taken for a rising young barrister . . . This was Mr Charles Knight.' Knight, relishing the drama of the situation, called various Girlingites to testify, denying that Kitcher was a member of their community, or that there had been a birth at New Forest Lodge, 'not even amongst the married ones. They wound up by recounting how after hearing Mrs Girling they realised their sins were forgiven, thanked God for it, prayed for the Holy Spirit, and were sure they received it – in most cases when Mrs Girling was miles away. They were positive it was the Spirit of God, and not mesmerism. Father Bathel (Uriah) [Isaac Batho] said his wife and family were also at Hordle. The "Counsel for the Defence" evoked much laughter by asking one of the girls, "Did Kitcher ever sleep with you?"' – and other witnesses said that when Sergeant Millin had touched Harry Buttles and Anna Knight, they merely went on dancing.

Charles Knight then contributed his own testimony, saying he and a fellow tradesman had made an anonymous visit to Hordle, where he found the brethren 'at work, building their new house', rather than 'laying around on the grass with their arms round each other's necks'. He also produced a letter from Moses Kitcher, father of the boy, which stated his son had never stayed at Hordle 'and was always back at the hour he told him to be . . .' But the uproarious events in Ryde ensured that the reign of Girlingism on the Isle of Wight would end in ignominy; and when Charles Knight was accused of extorting money from a Miss Ann Taylor, who kept a boarding-house with her sister in Southsea, Mary Ann's island cult was on trial for a third time.

Mary Ann had stayed at the Taylors' house, Glendore, on The Circle, Clarendon Road, during her tour in January and February 1876. The house was a substantial, gabled semi-detached Victorian villa, and afterwards, Charles – who attended the Hordle camp as an 'outside Shaker' – continued to visit the sisters there. Ann Taylor complained that the young man had 'forced himself upon them', even when he was suffering from 'an infectious disease'. We may imagine what went through the court's collective mind at this point. It transpired that this 'dreadful' disease was 'the itch' – scabies.

'Is that a complaint peculiar to the Shakers?' asked the defendant's counsel.

'I believe I really caught it sleeping at Hordle,' replied Charles.

Ann Taylor said she was surprised by Henry Knight's enthusiasm for 'the Shaker religion' (he was 'like an old hermit, constantly looking into the Bible to see what it said about Mrs Girling'), and claimed that the Knights had spent at least £200 on their beliefs and were overdrawn because of it. But when she lent Charles some money, instead of paying it back, he 'denounced terrible judgement on her sister, and said that she had been seen by others when in the spirit'. This development was greeted by laughter in court.

'Ah, you don't understand it,' said Ann. 'If you could have been there! He said that one should be taken and the other left. He was looking for the coming of Christ, and one was to be taken to Him, and the other left here in this wicked world!'

Charles Knight alleged that the Taylors had wished to become Girlingites themselves, and his letters to Ann Taylor are a rare insight into the venality to which the cult could lead.

> My very dear sister in the Lord Jesus Christ, – It is now past 11 o'clock . . . but I must write you a line, though so late, lest Satan should have told you I had forgotten you. I know you would not believe him, but it is difficult to tell him sometimes for he comes as an angel of light, and I think more often as such as a roaring lion, and as he is disguised sometimes we fail to recognise him until some pain has been inflicted by him with his fiery darts . . . I have been . . . making mention of you morning and night in my private prayers, as we also have at our private meetings lately . . . All are well save a cold or two, and all send their best and fondest love. As to those in the tents they are all well except Lottie, who is better; they kindly enquired after you, but all I could say was that I had not seen you for a long time. Goodbye. Your loving brother after the spirit, CHARLES KNIGHT.

Ann denied having become a Girlingite, but under cross-examination admitted that she and her sister saw visions, although they declined to elaborate: 'What we heard or saw is between God and ourselves.' Pressed for details about being 'in the spirit', Ann snapped, 'What are you talking about? Don't make such remarks, sir', to which her sibling added, 'Confine yourself to what you understand.' These weird sisters of Southsea were not to be mocked. 'Don't trifle with such things,' warned Ann as the court was told that her sister had seen herself floating down a river and heard a voice shriek, 'My sins! My sins!' At this evidence both Taylors cried 'Oh!' in unison, and Ann pronounced, biblically, 'We don't know whether we were entangled in a lying wonder or not.'

Another bizarre figure now entered the story: a tramp-like young man named Davis who claimed to be a prophet, foretold the destruction of London, and said he had a revelation from God. Addressing Charles and his friends in the Knights' studio, Davis – who had been living rough – announced that Henry Knight would receive the spirit of laughter, another the spirit of kneeling, and that Charles was to be 'head and chief over all'. The group convened in a house in the upper town until the neighbours complained about the noise, at which Davis revealed 'that they were to take a house in Swanmore-road, called Claremont Villa'. The Knights rented this suburban version of New Forest Lodge, and installed Davis as its caretaker. One Sunday Charles Knight took Davis across to Southsea to call on the Taylors. 'Davis was very dirty,' recalled Ann, who fetched a bottle of eau de cologne to empty over the prophet and gave Knight two sovereigns to buy clothes for his filthy friend. When she asked how he came to be so unclean, Charles said, 'Because he did not wash himself, I suppose.'

With such ludicrous characters in charge, the Ryde Girlingites collapsed into acrimony. The Knights turned violently against the sect, said Ann (who was disgusted to learn that Charles had married the nineteen-year-old daughter of a yacht captain from Ryde), and Henry no longer spoke to his son. Indeed, it was Henry who suggested that the Taylors take Charles to court. Faced with this farrago of distrust, the bemused Newport magistrate concluded 'that the only spirit which the adherents of Mrs Girling seemed to possess was the spirit of talking'. The case was found in favour of the defendant, and as the Misses Taylor left the court, they were heard to say, 'What a shame' and that his Honour was 'every bit as bad as the Knights'.

With the opening of the summer season, the Girlingite tour resumed at Bournemouth's Town Hall, where the colourfully-dressed crowd overwhelmed the doorman; many got in free, although the genteel paid a florin to enter by a side door, their money taken by a brother 'of lath-like and cadaverous appearance'. As Mary Ann described how the Holy Spirit had come down to her, some local youths who had climbed onto the roof threatened their own descent through the skylight, and the Girlingites were driven offstage by hollering hooligans who tore up their hymnals and stole the women's shawls. It was the kind of behaviour which would discredit a 'manufacturing district' said the local paper. Only with a strong escort to their farmer's waggon could the party escape to the safety of the forest, where Mary Ann expressed indignation 'at the harsh treatment she and her people received at Bournemouth which, she says, far exceeds the outrages at Exeter'. Or, indeed, the Isle of Wight.

The Girlingites may have slipped from national attention, but they had not been forgotten by their spiritualist brethren. In August 1877 *Human Nature* turned its attention to 'the Shaker community in Hampshire' in a piece introduced by none other than William Stainton Moses, who had been sent an account of the Girlingites by 'a friend'. For Stainton Moses, Mary Ann had her place 'in search of the one great Cause', and he thought it

> very striking to notice how all great ideas of spiritual advancement find external expression in self-abnegation ... the anchorite retires to his cell to meditate in lonely isolation while he subdues the flesh ... and fasts on herbs and roots; the nun to her cloister, and the monk to his monastic round of penance and prayer, equally with Mrs Gurling [sic] to her

> Hampshire hedge-side and her life of stern simplicity and self-esteem . . . Let me therefore take the reader with me to the Shakers' camp at Hordle, near the coast overlooking the Isle of Wight.

Interviewed in her 'own little private tent', Mary Ann described, in greater detail than before, how Christ 'had challenged her to abandon all carnal desire', and on successive visits had taken her above the world to witness 'a vista of ages . . . This translucent soulical body showed her what her resurrection body would be like when she left the earth.' Given a sympathetic hearing, she warmed to her theme: 'She believes, and has been told by the Spirit repeatedly . . . that she is the *last* of the Gospel Dispensation', and that the apocalypse was 'very near, for that the present war between Russia and Turkey was the sign of his coming as the king omnipotent, through the conflicts of two struggling nations'. Mary Ann may have become a kind of martyr to the greater cause of spiritualism, but other visitors found her colony an altogether more dispiriting place. An Irish Jesuit, Edmund O'Reilly, holidaying in a nearby town, took a charabanc tour to the encampment, where he found 'two or three women . . . sitting listlessly on chairs; we were told they were sick, and, in truth, they seemed to be in a dying state'. Indeed, one young female Girlingite had recently died, but rather than 'admit that her doctrine is wrong', Mary Ann had merely assured the faithful 'that the girl's death had been caused by disbelief . . .'

The shadows of hunger and mortality hung over the sect: another brother, Henry Dance, had been convicted in Lymington 'of leaving his wife chargeable to the parish of Hordle, and also of neglecting to supply his three children with sufficient food and nourishment'. In an awful echo of anchorites and Buchanites, the Welsh Fasting Girl and the Peculiar People, Dance's young son was brought from the workhouse, his famished body testament to the consequences of religious mania. 'The boy was terribly emaciated,' *The Times* reported. 'Though ten years old, he weighs only 51 lb.' Dance, who had already served a sentence on a similar charge, was sent to Winchester prison.

Throughout the winter of 1877–8 there were more departures, among them the once stalwart Isaac Batho. A journalist reported, 'After a four or five years' trial he has left quite *disillusioné*, and as I was assured, starved almost to a skeleton, the serjeant of police here [in Lymington] being in receipt of a communication from him, asking the aid of the authorities to try and recover some of his goods'. It was a sad end to Isaac's once loyal stewardship, now reduced to bickering over possessions: he had wanted to take away an oil painting which, although Mary Ann claimed it to be worth £50, was sold for £7 to pay off their debts to local tradesmen. That sale, enforced to satisfy a county court judgement, saw Mr Moore auctioning items ranging from a cake crusher, for £8, 'a strong and useful chesnut mare', sold for £15, despite being worth £40; and 'a useful pony, but with a very bad temper', which fetched £6 6s. They even sold their precious piano – which had 'lost all tone' in the process of eviction – for six guineas. The Girlingites profited by £9 from these transactions, but the *Lymington Chronicle* concluded 'it cannot be long before Shakerism in England will become a thing of the past'. Meanwhile, other families tried to reclaim their loved ones. One 'London lady' on O'Reilly's charabanc was making her third trip to persuade her brother to return with her. 'He was always most pious', she told the priest, and recalled that he was 'eighteen or nineteen years of age when he joined the Shakers, and *was never known to tell a lie*'; she believed 'that he would have come away with her, only he was afraid of Mrs Girling!'

It seemed that like the Israelites, the Children of God were condemned never to be at rest. They had just finished their breakfast on Monday, 19 August when, as if from nowhere, a crowd of six hundred spectators began to gather. At 11.30, Edward Horatio

Moore, accompanied by the bailiffs, came to read out his warrant. Moore had faced many such situations – although he had never been told that it was the Almighty Himself from whom he was claiming a bad debt.

The Girlingites were dressed and ready to leave, but as if to make their point, had not packed any of their things; not even their beds were made. From their wooden chapel were trundled tables and bibles, pianos and pictures. Then came Mary Ann's mahogany bed, dressing-table, sofa and armchair, a domestic scene complete with stove and chintz-lined walls, 'making . . . what a Scotchman would pronounce quite a snug cosy corner'. As their interior lives were suddenly exposed to the light of day, her flowery bower contrasted sharply with the men's dormitory, 'really a disgusting place' due to its lack of ventilation and damp earth floor. Tidier was the children's schoolroom, with its makeshift wallpaper of illustrated periodicals and religious pictures. Meanwhile, the bailiffs chased geese, ducks and hens, one duck getting as far as the pond and freedom before she was eventually captured and carried, quacking loudly, back to the roadside to which the Family were once more relegated. Behind them they left their wooden shanties and flowerbeds and vegetable plots: a sad little allotment of untended cabbages and summer fruits, wilting witnesses to this muddy Eden.

That August, the nation was reminded of the Girlingites' plight by a pair of panoramas published in the *Illustrated London News*. Mary Ann, wearing the solar topee of a colonial explorer, converses with two gentlemen whose demeanour suggests sympathy; her hand is held out in supplication or perhaps desperation. Her Children go about the business of living in the open like Gypsies – a scene made more extraordinary by the piles of furniture dumped along the verges like the remnants of some gigantic jumble sale. Knife-grinders and mangles, bedsteads and barrels, armchairs and trunks tumble over each other as though in the act of eviction:

THE SHAKERS' ENCAMPMENT AT HORDL

THE SHAKERS' ENCAMPMENT AT HORDLE

The scene in Vaggs Lane is wretched, as well as absurdly strange; the roadside n
chairs and tables, beds, chests of drawers, sofas, and other furniture, arranged a
blankets, counterpanes, and shau

·TON, HAMPSHIRE: SCENE IN VAGS LANE.

GTON, HAMPSHIRE: DWELLINGS OF THE FAMILIES.

ass and ditch, on either hand, for a length of one hundred yards, is covered with : be to form a little shelter for each of these miserable family parties, with n them from the wind and rain.

so often exposed to the elements, these household goods must have already begun to warp and decay, their chaos a counterpoint to the cottages in the background, with their ordered lives and respectable tenants.

Below is a tidier picture, drawn before their latest exodus, a kind of up-ended utopia, a parody of Victorian domesticity – as though the contents of a terrace of houses had been turned out neatly into a field. Trunks fit together like leather building blocks to create walls and doorways; mattress and canvas roofs are held down by baskets and pans; an open umbrella perches as if blown there by the wind. In their luggage caverns the Family sit drinking tea and curling one another's hair, while their children play decorously in the lane. All this is rendered in the *Illustrated London News* house style: forensic yet sentimental, conveying contemporary news through the filter of nineteenth-century certainty: on other pages we see natives in the Congo, the Austrian occupation of Bosnia and Herzegovina, sea-monsters off Zanzibar and other images from the imperial project; anthropological documentaries, glimpses of other worlds, a codex of Empire. Here, much closer to home in the New Forest, was the obverse to orthodoxy, the anarchy which ensued when order was abandoned. It was a powerful parable for a modern age.

In September 1878, the Girlingites' bedraggled camp was electrified by 'a visit of the Spirit'. Without warning, Mary Ann burst out from her boudoir, her arms outstretched, eyes shut and 'gesticulating somewhat alarmingly'. Surely revelation was at hand? Stumbling about and at times requiring support, she declared through shut eyes and with tensed muscles that she was a special messenger of the Holy Spirit, 'to whom she stood in such rank that she could see the Saviour'; dissenters would be punished by eternal damnation. Like Beatrix, she *could see God* through her closed eyes. Resembling some pagan revenant or a Shaker instrument, Mary Ann was a symbolist sybil, blindfolded yet sentient, moving ever closer to the appointed time. This new communion, conducted in the semi-public of an open service, drew 'uncouthful expressed disgust' from the crowd, and at one point violence threatened.

Such hubris aroused strong feelings. One commentator declared Girlingism 'repugnant to the instincts of civilised humanity', and fulminated against the 'sentimental twaddle' written about the sect. 'They grievously offend against the social regulations under which English people live, and their whole life is, in very many ways, at variance with those instincts of propriety which English people have a pride in, and which they rejoice to see in their children.' Here was their real threat: 'Shaker communism is as opposed to the social conditions under which British life is regulated as is the Shaker interpretation of Scripture writ to the usually accepted truths of Christianity.' The Clerk of the Highway Board, Mr Jackman, expressed his own view quite clearly: 'If Mrs Girling was sent to Winchester [gaol] for sleeping out in tents, it would do her a deal of good.'

Afraid that this fate might befall its leader, on the morning of Friday, 13 September – their latest unlucky date – the sect removed most of its roadside possessions to Henry Moore's barn. With no hope of meeting the demand to have the highway cleared before noon the next day, they were rescued by George Veal, a landowner from Barton Common, who allowed them to use a field at Tiptoe, half a mile north of Vaggs Lane. Their 'moonlight flight' provided dramatic new copy for reporters, who arrived the following morning to find two female Girlingites, who had spent the night at an 'outsider's' cottage, wondering, like Mary at Christ's tomb, where their leader had gone. But brethren 'had not yet departed for another world'; they had merely regrouped up the road, behind 'the prickly impenetrable hedges of Mr Veal's little fields opposite the Baptist Chapel'.

Their new home faced the Mount Jireh Chapel, an 'odd looking structure' built in 1825 by a Baptist called Torquand. Behind a dilapidated thatched cottage with concrete walls, the sect set up camp again like an army on manoeuvres: a stove was constructed from old meat tins and breakfast served from a 'field kitchen' of trestle tables; barrels became cupboards; mattresses rolled up to form seats. The Girlingites' arrival can hardly have been welcomed by the inhabitants of Tiptoe, an even smaller settlement than Hordle, this field suddenly filled with eighty religious communists, their shambolic tents, their weird rituals and their strange costumes, attended by journalists, gentry, spiritualists and well-wishers – some with surprising proposals.

That September, Mr W.P. Warner of the Welsh Harp Fishery, a pub in Hendon, offered the sect the use of the grandstand and other buildings on his racecourse at Kingsbury. He and Mary Ann exchanged letters. *The Times* announced that the grandstand had been converted into a temporary hotel, and Mr Warner raised £80 from 'like-minded gentlemen' to pay the Girlingites' train fare to Kingsbury (at the same time denying that he intended to 'make a show' of the sect). Yet the crowd which assembled expectantly at the Welsh Harp were to be disappointed. Back at Tiptoe, sipping tea in her makeshift drawing room formed from chests of drawers with a carpet roof, Mary Ann said she had decided not to go to Kingsbury. She preferred to stay close to New Forest Lodge, 'where all things were to be accomplished'.

But seven Girlingites now lay in Hordle churchyard, their graves marked by an evergreen tree to symbolise their immortality. Their first eviction had marked the slow beginning of an end racked by hunger, disease and death. Of the seven interred in All Saints by 1878, at least four were young women. Mary Ann Miller, known as Polly, had died on 3 May 1876, as the local newspaper announced: 'a young woman aged 22, died suddenly last Wednesday morning in the Shakers camp at Hordle, to the great consternation of Mrs Girling and her community. A doctor was sent for, but life was extinct before he arrived . . . This is the first death of an adult which has occurred amongst the Shakers.'

Mary Ann's young women were felled by tuberculosis – then responsible for a quarter of the deaths in Britain – its infection ironically exacerbated by their communal living, poor diet and exposure to the elements. Polly Miller's death was followed by Emma Benham's, from the same disease, in April 1877; and a month after that, on 4 May, Charlotte Chase, thirty-twoyearold wife of Cornelius Chase, passed away, having suffered from consumption for fifteen months. Agnes Todd, wife of Thomas and mother of the errant James, Ellen's would-be husband, died aged fifty in September 1877; while Martha Eliza Cooper, daughter of John Cooper, the Dallinghoo gardener, died on 31 May 1878, aged just twenty-four years old, another victim of tuberculosis; her passing was recorded, like those of her sisters-in-faith, by Doctor Robert Stevens of Sway. Martha Benham died in June of that year, aged forty-nine, followed two years later by her daughter Ellen's death, at the age of twenty-nine. It was a terrible price to be paid by Leonard Benham, who had given his all to join Mary Ann's mission, only to lose both his daughters and his wife within two years.

Reduced by this tragic tally, depleted by disease and apostasy, in their retreat to Tiptoe – away from the gaze of passersby – the colonists had sealed their fate. It seemed that their story was moving to its sad but inevitable conclusion. Yet even as the future in which they had placed their communal trust now seemed so uncertain, a new kind of folly was rising in the forest sky.

ELEVEN

Mr Peterson's Tower

> There must be no lightheadedness in your noble tower: impregnable foundation, wrathful crest, with the vizor down, and the dark vigilance seen through clefts of it . . .
>
> John Ruskin, *The Stones of Venice*

In his new life at Arnewood Towers, Andrew Peterson had proved an eccentric character. Roaming around his high-ceilinged concrete rooms, he gave names to his furniture – one Indian armchair was called 'Eternal Peace' – while on the train to London, he took his tea in a baby's bottle to avoid spilling it, sucking it through a rubber tube. Although married, Peterson was a solitary man, used to ordering things his own way. Like Edward James, the millionaire surrealist who would create his own concrete follies in the Mexican jungle, this bearded figure bore an aura of benevolent dictatorship, using his wealth to pursue his whims and directing operations himself to ensure his instructions were carried out – no matter how odd they might seem. It was said that one winter he employed labourers to sweep the snow from the road to Lyndhurst so that he could visit a lady friend there. This may have been mere gossip, but 'the Judge' did have a mistress: a dressmaker, Catherine Johnson, living in Deptford, who in 1878, at the age of thirty-four (when Peterson was sixty-five), bore him a daughter, also named Catherine.

Politically, Peterson supported Gladstone – perhaps because the statesman believed that psychical research was 'the most important work being done in the world today'. Indeed, in 1885, the year after Gladstone made his pronouncement, James Burns would publish Peterson's *Essays from the Unseen*, one of the most extraordinary texts to emerge from the spiritualist movement. Between its gold-stamped boards were accounts of fifty-eight 'controls', 'delivered through the mouth of W. L., a sensitive, and recorded by A.T.T.P.' – Peterson himself, portrayed in its frontispiece as the very image of psychic jurisprudence.

These controls constituted an historic cast list – from Aristotle and Jesus Christ to John Knox and Jonathan Swift, taking in Mohammed, Martin Luther and the Duke of Wellington along the way. But of all the great men summoned from beyond the grave, the most significant was Tom Paine, whose spirit had already inspired mediums such as Charles Hammond and Elder Evans. Peterson's book featured a spirit image of Paine, an icon so radiant that it seems impolite to disclose the fact that this other-worldly work of art is identical to a postcard sent to me by a friend from Paine's home town of Thetford in Suffolk – barely twenty miles from Mary Ann's own birthplace – displaying George Romney's 1792 portrait of Paine, then aged fifty-five and very much of the earth.

Yet the distance between these two images – implicit in the halo which Paine has acquired in his translation – was the same gulf which Peterson sought to bridge. His *Essays* boldly declined to

apologise for 'giving the Public my experiences on such an unpopular and thoroughly derided subject as MODERN SPIRITUALISM', whose phenomena he declared 'facts beyond either denial by, or cavil of, those who are too idle or too prejudiced to investigate . . .' The author was certainly neither of these. Peterson had been a Deist – like Paine – then a Unitarian, then a Materialist, but it wasn't until he encountered Mary Ann that he began to explore the survival of the soul; and it was her 'strange doctrines' which set him on 'the first step towards Spiritualism'.

By the 1870s, spiritualism was firmly established in the public imagination, promoted in the memoirs of figures such as D.D. Home, J.W. Fletcher and J.J. Morse, often under Burns' imprint and issued in deluxe editions to satisfy the carriage trade, illustrated with frontispieces of their celebrity subjects: Home with fey moustache, Fletcher in pristine evening dress, Morse with his handsome, vaguely feminine face – theatrical images which spoke of a sense of performance.

Morse's *Leaves from My Life* told a typical story. From lowly birth and early tragedy – his mother's death, and life in his father's pub in Bunhill Row – Morse recounted the day he called at a haberdasher's shop in Bishopsgate and overheard the proprietress extolling her son's mediumship. From there he was led to a Whitechapel seance where he experienced sensations 'of a peculiar and indescribable character . . . my brain felt as if split in two halves, and into the cavity thus created a shovelful of burning sand seemed to be poured . . . I tried to rise up and shake the feeling off, but, to my horror, I was a fixture. My eyes had closed and were proof against my most powerful efforts to open them.' Morse feared he was about to be admitted to Colney Hatch, but, guided by J. M. Peebles, he became resident medium to a Dalston homeopath and went to America, where his experiences inspired him, on his return to London, to open a 'spiritualist hotel'.

In his own journey towards spiritualism, Peterson read papers by the eminent scientists Alfred Russel Wallace and Sir William Crookes. Crookes had discovered cathode rays, and conducted investigations into the cattle plague, the profitability of sewage, and the nature of diamonds. At first Crookes thought spiritualism 'might prove to be a trick', but after sittings with Morse and Mrs Marshall and experiments with D.D. Home 'in a strong light', he became a believer, enough to invite Florence Cook, the attractive young medium from Hackney, to lodge in his house for three weeks in 1874 to enable him to investigate the 'materialisation and dematerialisation' of Katie King. This theatrical spirit, whose hand Maurice Davies had squeezed and with whom it was said Crookes had a more than passing physical interest, duly appeared in the laboratory, to be 'frequently photographed . . . by the use of electric light on one side and magnesium light on the opposite side to soften shadows. On several occasions five cameras were simultaneously employed, giving the features and form from as many different points of view . . .' As Conan Doyle was convinced by the Cottingley fairies, so Crookes invested explicit belief in these multi-dimensional miracles, like ghostly images from the X-ray machines whose invention he had enabled, and whose own mysterious rays he thought might play a part in the telepathic process (while ironically it was claimed that his discovery of thallium had poisoned him, thus explaining his 'irrational' conclusions).

Alfred Russel Wallace was an equally important scientific figure, having described, with Darwin, the theory of natural selection. But on youthful visits to the Hall of Science off Tottenham Court Road, Wallace had been introduced to the work of Owen and Paine, and undertook his own investigations into psychic phenomena. Given such eminent voices (even Darwin drew up to the seance table), Peterson concluded that these men could be neither 'dupes' nor 'rogues', and that spiritualism was worthy of his enquiry. And so, while staying in his Gray's Inn chambers, he paid a visit to Burns' Spiritual Institution in nearby Southampton Row. There he bought a few books, took out a subscription to *Medium and Daybreak*, and asked where he might experience a seance for himself. Burns, who had an eye for affluent patrons, supplied his visitor with contacts from his 'Register for Mediums', and told Peterson that he was 'half a medium already, and before long you will accept Spiritualism thoroughly'.

Having rejected 'the cocoa-nuts, canaries, and sweet-smelling flowers of the fashionable and non-professional medium', Peterson settled on Eliza Olive, who lived in Kentish Town 'in a small street near "Mother Shipton's tavern"' – a suitably spectral-sounding location. A frequent advertiser in *Medium and Daybreak* –

> **Mrs Olive**, Trance Medium for test communications from Spirit Relatives and Friends; also, for the Cure of various diseases by Spirit-Magnetism and Prescriptions.
> – 49, Belmont Street, Chalk Farm Road, London, N. W.

– she was renowned for her black spirit guide, Hambo, with its 'guttural negro laugh', a lisping Red Indian woman called Sunshine, and the anti-vaccinationist spirit doctor, Forbes. One evening Peterson found himself crowded into a tiny suburban room with a dozen other visitors. Mrs Olive, 'a lady-like, rather good-looking woman', entered a trance and began to speak in the 'Scotch accent' of Dr Forbes, who proceeded to diagnose the medical complaints of the entire group. Shortly after, Peterson began to suffer frightening pains in his chest. On returning by omnibus to Kentish Town, he experienced another attack, vomiting blood, and was taken in by Mrs Olive. Dr Forbes diagnosed 'heart derangement', and as she began making passes over him, Peterson

> . . . felt as if a long skewer had been drawn through my chest . . . in my agony I pushed the Medium violently backwards from me, and she staggered backwards and fell against the mantel-piece and on to the fire-grate, but she jumped up as nimbly as a young goat, and in a strong decisive male voice said, 'Ye must be more patient . . . in five minutes ye will be free from pain altogether.'

As indeed he was. Forbes assured him that for three guineas – Mrs Olive's fee – he had been 'cured of a complaint that, under ordinary treatment, would have cost you ten times as much'. Assured of this spiritualistic bargain, Peterson and Forbes struck up a dialogue on Reichenbach's theory of the 'electro-positive' qualities of the sun's rays, and the effect of coloured glass on hothouse fruit (an experiment which Peterson appears to have carried out at his Hampshire estate). And as they talked, a physical change seemed to overtake Eliza Olive, a vision to rival Mary Ann's sibylline stare: 'The Sensitive came in front of me, and looking at me fully with nothing but the white eyeless orbs, said, "You are entirely negative to the moon's rays; no moonlight will ever hurt you".'

With Eliza's aid, Peterson began to develop his own powers of healing. One Sunday morning, setting off from London Bridge station, he met an elderly man afflicted with rheumatic gout, whom he decided to try and treat. After a quarter-of-an-hour of 'passes' – doubtless to the surprise of fellow passengers in the waiting room – the man was cured. Then, in the autumn of 1875, on a trip to his home town of Wakefield in Yorkshire, where spiritualism was practised in blackened brick terraces far from London's fashionable salons, Peterson operated on a mill worker named Cooper, who'd had his leg amputated and was suffering from abscesses. The 'intellectual looking', emaciated young man was lying on a bed in the sitting room being nursed by his aged mother. Following Forbes's instructions, Peterson placed his hand on the man's groin, and felt a lump 'the size of a pigeon's egg, quite hard when I first put my hand on it, but which gradually got softer, until I was ordered to desist from operating further . . . and get back to my inn and go to bed as quick as I could'. There his own legs swelled 'as if I had *Elephantiasis*. I had evidently imbibed the poison from Cooper's body'.

Peterson now left on a world tour, taking in Egypt, India, Australia, New Zealand and America; in Vermont he visited the 'well known Eddy family', and in New York he consulted other mediums who told him 'much that was astonishing'. Back in England, he decided that to conduct a truly rigorous experiment of his own, he needed a 'Sensitive . . . entirely to myself, and one who, without my permission, would not sit with any one else'. He was in the reading room of the British Association of Spiritualists in Great Russell Street, Bloomsbury, one day when a 'pale-faced, shabbily-dressed and rather emaciated young man' came in. Peterson was told he was a medium named Lawrence who was being prosecuted and who had come to apply for financial assistance for his defence. At that moment, the young man suddenly went 'under Control', came up to Peterson's table and asked, 'in very good Hindostanee', how he was. He then described a Calcutta street scene. If, like the mediums who conjured up Rose La Touche for Ruskin, Lawrence had set a trap for this wealthy sympathiser, then it was well laid.

Peterson seemed to have an eye for such young men, and whether by luck or design, Lawrence fitted his requirements perfectly. He had been a porter in an East End auction room, where 'he had a very good character, but . . . used to "go off queer at times"'. He now lived in Heath Street with his young wife and family. Burns reported that Lawrence's technique was unusual: 'The medium will be sitting entranced – eyes shut, so that he cannot see anything; or he may be walking about the room in a similar condition, and so situated that he could not see what the Recorder writes even if he had his eyes open. Under these circumstances the Recorder will be writing down the wrong word, when the spirit will at once stop him and give the correction.' Lawrence would remember nothing of what he had seen in his clairvoyance, during which 'his very face seems changed . . . he seems as if he had the power of projecting, as it were, his soul into space . . .'

In these strange, semi-ambulant states, Lawrence often returned to India, describing horrific scenes from the Mutiny of an officer 'tied by one leg to a tree, and by the other to the top of a stout sapling bent to the ground, and which, being let go, tore him in pieces'. But of all the voices he was able to produce, it was Tom Paine's which most impressed Peterson: 'Men like Paine, Cobbett, Holyoake, and others like them were the real pioneers of thought for the masses,' he declared; and in return, a message came through to his Gray's Inn chambers: 'You are right; we are the pioneers of public opinion; the masses follow us, because we speak to their hearts; they understand us, and will in the future understand us more. I have long been attempting to get near you, and to claim my position as your guide, but hitherto conditions have not been suitable. I have been your Spiritual guide from your earliest infancy.'

This was an extraordinary revelation. Peterson had been chosen by Paine, who maintained he was 'highly favoured in Spirit Land

. . . and that in all probability he would be appointed the Angel Spirit of a new Dispensation'. Like Mary Ann, Peterson had received his own visionary mission, and under Paine's patronage he would be impelled to yet more extraordinary experiments – although not before a decidedly temporal hitch.

In January 1877, Lawrence was brought before Clerkenwell magistrates charged with having 'unlawfully and falsely pretended to James Hulbert that he had power to communicate with the spirits of deceased and other persons . . . and also, that he had produced and summoned to be present in the place where he was such spirits in a materialized and other forms . . . and with having thereby obtained one shilling'. Hulbert had seen an advertisement in *The Medium* –

7, Northey-street, Church-row, Commercial-road, E.
(back of Limehouse Church).
Messrs. W. Lawrence and Chandler, with other mediums,
hold *seances* for physical phenomena and materialization, on Monday,
admission 1s., at 7 for 7.30 pm.
Developing circle for trance test and psychological manifestations on Tuesday;
admission 1s.; at 8 for 8.30 pm.
Friday for physical phenomena and materialization;
admission 1s., at 8 for 8.30 pm.

– a spiritualist playbill to rival those of nearby Wilton's Music Hall, deep in the East End, where the glitter of the imperial city met its dark docklands, and the warehouses where Lawrence had worked were piled high with ivory and opium. Hulbert, himself a denizen of Limehouse, accordingly arrived at Northey Street, enquiring 'if this was where *seances* were held?' Lawrence hoped 'that he was not coming with the idea of discovering any trickery'. Hulbert promised to return on Sunday night with his brother.

In a dimly-lit room, they found the audience sitting in two circles around a table. As they joined the outer circle, Lawrence 'went into contortions, closed his eyes and kept his head raised towards the ceiling', during which he delivered a spiritualist oration, 'asserting that it would take the place of all religions'. It was a performance which recalled Mary Ann's evocations – as did the commotion which ensued. With the lights out, Lawrence and Chandler performed a double act of hymns by Moody and Sankey, and Lawrence spoke in 'a negro minstrel's dialect' – another representative of the racial other. The room then erupted in phosphorescent sparks; unseen hands rang bells, twanged a banjo and banged a tambourine. When the lamps were relit, it was discovered that the paper and watercolours which had been left on the table had produced a spirit painting. As the company gathered at a bay window curtained to create a 'cabinet', a turbanned Turk's head appeared 'amid sounds of groans and struggling . . . his face covered with some white material, which hid the features'. The spirit's name was Tonto.

On returning the following Friday, Hulbert was whacked on the legs with a three foot long cardboard tube, presumably in admonishment for his scepticism. 'I see a light, some one is breaking the conditions,' complained the spirit. 'I'll break his head. I broke somebody's last Tuesday.' But as the apparition came out of the cabinet, Hulbert rushed at it, shouting, 'Up boys and at them.' After a scuffle lasting some minutes, the lights went up to reveal a coatless Lawrence 'roaming about as if trying to get out of the room'. He was grabbed by one of Hulbert's mates, who said, 'Hollo, Tonto, I've got you', to which Lawrence replied, like Mr Sludge, 'Don't expose me; think of the children.' This was damning testimony, and the judge duly delivered his verdict:

> It almost surpasses belief that any person of fair understanding could be deceived by such palpable and preposterous delusions . . . but it is well known that the profession of supernatural power has a peculiar attraction for many people. There may be little sympathy for the dupe, but the law

> punishes the fraudulent imposter. There is no power to impose hard labour on you. You will be imprisoned in the common gaol as a second-class misdemeanant for three months.

Lawrence served his sentence in the grimly-named Coldbath Fields in Clerkenwell. As A.T.T.P. noted, it was a bad time for spiritualism: 'the same spirit, that lighted the faggot at Smithfield, or applied the thumbscrew of the Inquisition, shows itself when it gets the chance'. Faced with a country of wandering magicians, it seemed that the authorities were joining a cycle of persecution which had begun with the stoning of the 'spiritual vagrants', Ira and William Davenport, when their spirits failed to perform in Newcastle; continued with the prosecution of Dr Slade and Francis Monck's imprisonment 'as a rogue and vagabond' (the former Baptist preacher was staying in Huddersfield when he was discovered to have a pair of false hands in his bag); and culminated with the jailing of Susan Wills Fletcher, the wife of American medium John William Fletcher, who was charged with false pretence at the Old Bailey and who was seen as a martyr of a 'modern Babylon . . . dead to the inner life of man . . .'

On his release, Lawrence returned to Peterson as his personal medium, assuming the personae of such figures as Plato, Rameses, Walter Raleigh and Oliver Cromwell, while Peterson made notes in a shorthand of his own invention. Sometimes 'tears rolled down the cheeks of the Medium' as he brought back accounts of the dead, although these encounters, with their native guides and historical spirits, recall nothing so much as Noël Coward's *Blithe Spirit*, and one half expects a grey-Molyneux-gowned Elvira, summoned by Madame Arcati, to drift into mischievous view. Yet there were dangerous episodes, too. Having prepared a darkened chamber, Peterson had 'scarcely been sitting in my cabinet ten minutes, when the Sensitive went under the control of a Spirit, who in strong and decisive terms ordered me out instantly, telling me to light the lamp at once, unless I wished to kill myself . . .' On another occasion,

Lawrence was possessed by 'the Spirit of a fanatical Ranter' and 'with a scream fell like a dead body on the floor, and it was some two or three minutes before I could restore him to his normal state'.

In late 1877, Lawrence began to produce 'Spiritual drawings' via William Blake, 'who on earth was ridiculed as the Spirit Artist', and who sent Peterson to a shop in Golden Square for paints, brushes and paper, with the instruction that 'the same Spirit Artist, Benvenuto Cellini, who had guided his hand in earth life, would guide that of the Sensitive whose body he was occupying . . .' Blake's technique of copper etching, in which acid dissolved the 'apparent surfaces' of rationality to reveal 'the infinite which was hid', had been taught to him by his brother Robert's spirit after the latter's death in 1787. Now the mystic became psychic tutor to Lawrence, along with other dead artists such as Henry Fuseli, whose own perfervid paintings depicted uncanny scenes.

When Peterson published these sessions in *Medium and Daybreak* in early 1878, sceptical friends suggested that Lawrence might have paid someone else to paint the pictures for him. This was possible, Peterson admitted; but as he didn't pay for these extra manifestations, what was there for his Sensitive to gain? Not only did Peterson have complete faith in Lawrence, but like Robert Owen, he had a utopian belief in these experiments and their importance: 'Spiritualism will teach men that their future depends not on their faith but on their works.' Peterson asserted that 'unknown to themselves', many in the past had been Sensitives – 'I would refer to Mary Barton, [Elizabeth Burton] the Maid of Kent, in the time of Henry the Eighth, and to Elspeth Buchan, the founder of a sect called Buchanites, in the latter end of the last century.' Victims of demonic possession in the Bible were likely to have been 'ill-developed Sensitives'; while 'many others nearer our time have been consigned to lunatic asylums, owing to being, by nature, mediumistic, and not being properly developed, they have become the sport of earth-bound Spirits'. Peterson even suggested 'that half-a-dozen well-developed Sensitives, employed in our Country Lunatic Asylums, would do more good in curing so-called Lunatics, than twice the number of medical men and the warders employed'. It was a connexion between madness and mediumship made manifest a century later at R.D. Laing's anti-psychiatry institute, Langley Hall in Bow, east London, where personalities of the day came to see Mary Barnes, a former nun given to visions, making 'spiritual paintings' with her own excrement.

But the central text of Peterson's *Essays* was Paine's 'Universal Prayer'. This new testament promised 'freedom to men, freedom from fear' and eternal life: 'Immortality is known to us, make it known to men on earth . . .' It also evoked apocalyptic visions worthy of Richard Brothers – 'Let Thy name be a guide and counsellor to stay the course of Northern ambition; let it not run riot in bloodshed and robbery. Direct Thy mercy, O God, to the down-stricken people of the East, whose hecatombs appeal to Thy aid. The ravages of disease are thinning its populous cities and decimating their numbers' – and called for 'the sacred liberty of inferior races'. The *Essays* came to a close in the dark, empty days between Christmas and New Year, an interregnum suited to communion with the dead. On that gloomy winter's afternoon, Tom Paine invoked the other world as if gathering its souls at the year's end: ancient philosophers in their gowns, esteemed generals in their greatcoats, maharajahs in their turbans. Speaking through Lawrence, he told Peterson, 'I, your guide, could not let the old year pass away without giving you a strong assurance, although I have ever been near you . . . you are now master of time . . . It is now your soul's capital, and you can trade with it for life eternal or worldly pleasures here . . . Good night!' Like Mary Ann Girling, Andrew Peterson was charged with an immortal mission; the difference was that he had the means to accomplish it.

* * *

Sometime in the late 1870s, Lawrence channelled a new control for his employer. 'You are thinking of building a tower,' declared the spirit of Sir Christopher Wren.

'Now A.T.T.P. had not whispered one syllable to that effect to his medium . . .' wrote James Burns. '"Ah! mind-reading," someone will exclaim. But was it mind-reading when the control, adopting the knowledge and manner of a practical architect, began to advise the Recorder as to the basis needful to render such a superstructure safe?' Eyes closed, Lawrence delivered the plans which would cause the skyline of the forest to be changed.

'What breadth will your foundations be?' asked the spirit of Wren.

'Well, I was thinking of making it twenty feet – a tenth part of the contemplated height, that is, two hundred feet.

'Had you not better make it twenty-four feet?' added the spirit, at the same time giving reasons for the recommendation.

Wren had built St Paul's from Portland stone; now, under his ghostly guidance, Peterson would use Portland's dust to create a monument to Paine and the Enlightenment ideal of a progressive future. And where it took Wren half a lifetime to complete London's mother church with its great dome and towers – one of which was intended as an astronomical observatory and laboratory – Peterson would achieve his feat in five years.

For all his peccadilloes, Peterson was well liked in Hampshire, not least because of his generosity to its dispossessed and his concern for the forty men or more in his employ. An 1875 return had ennumerated one thousand two hundred and seventy 'outdoor paupers' in Lymington and the New Forest alone, and with 'the shadow of the evil days of the Eighteen-eighties . . . lengthening', Peterson's labourers were paid 14 shillings a week – two shillings more than the going rate (thus annoying local farmers whose workforce were outpriced). '[T]he poor-rate has fallen in a gratifying manner,' Burns reported. 'The principle of the Recorder is to encourage local talent, and avoid the blunders of professionalism. He has brought no skilled workmen from a distance, but given men in the locality an opportunity to distinguish themselves and better their position.' Among those thus employed was Tommy Ackland, an outside Girlingite, wheelwright and coffinmaker who became Peterson's head carpenter.

Foundation work had commenced in 1879, but Peterson's Order Books for the construction of his tower begin on 11 September 1881. Discovered a century later in an old suitcase in one of the Arnewood outhouses, mouldy and half-eaten by rats, the books survive as essays in Peterson's ambition. Bound in now-cracked oilcloth and filled in sepia and purple ink, they contain diagrams, calculations and graphs, details made dream-like by the folly they record in imperious tones: 'Note – This Book is to be on my table without fail when I return from London'. Peterson wrote out tasks for each day, and his instructions veered from the practical – 'Shingle & sand must be hoisted on to each. It need not be too fine save & except what floor is required to be coloured' – to the impetuous – 'I *cannot* listen to any suggestion it cannot be done'. Occasionally they even verged on the manic: 'I have not to *request* but to order that you go up *once* a day without fail & see with your own eyes that my orders carried out . . . as written in this book. I can not admit the excuse of no time.'

Black-clad bibles to be obeyed by the likes of Tommy Ackland, the Order Books were practical counterparts to Peterson's *Essays from the Unseen*. They also charted the rise of his staircase tower, rising alongside: '1/3/82 . . . The small and big tower must be carried out simultaneously . . .' Peterson used a technique he had witnessed in India. Sand, shingle and cement were mixed together and hauled up in boxes by a derrick fitted to the top of the building, with the ropes drawn through pulleys by horses circling below – just as he had seen Indian bullocks draw water from deep wells. Once in place, the mixture was rammed into wooden frames. As each 'lift' set, another was added, and so the towers grew, layer by layer, like a concrete angel cake. Where windows were required, moulds were inserted and the mix poured around them; blocks for pillars, steps and landings were made on the lower floors and hoisted upwards. The supply of materials was a constant concern ('I hear there is some very good small shingle from the beach'), and to ensure employment for his workforce, which some said included other Girlingites wheeling the barrows of shingle, Peterson paced construction of the staircase 'or I shall have no work for winter'. By September 1882 his tower had reached the height of 150 feet 9 inches, and a new problem.

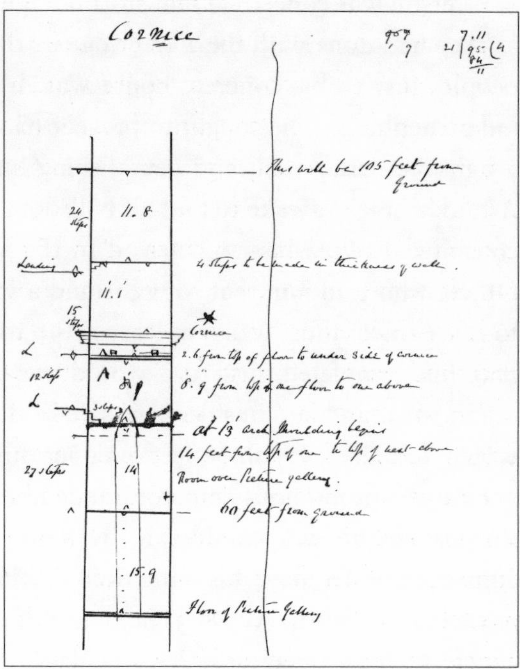

Wind Pressure.
A question arises as to whether there will be weight in the Tower to resist the maximum gust I am likely to get. Rollo Massey calculates the force of the winds at 56 lbs per foot
He takes the weakest point on the west side which will give
A face of Tower 20ft
Hexagon 7.8
∴ Press will be from top to bottom –
$27.8 \times 200 \times 56 = \dfrac{27.8 \times 200}{40}$ 139 tons force of wind

Peterson was concerned that storms might topple his endeavour, as they had done with the Tay Bridge in 1879, killing seventy-five people. Just as his concrete house was fireproof and 'practically indestructible', so he sought to prevent his tower from falling like a lightning-struck oak and demolishing his home in the process. Afraid he might awake to find his ballroom full of rubble, Peterson consulted Rollo Massey, a friend in the Westminster Engineer's Office, who told him that to withstand a wind force of 56 lbs per foot the tower must weigh at least 1,390 tons. Peterson calculated that his completed structure would weigh between 1,518 and 1,870 tons, and so considered it safe (although in high winds, it would actually sway three feet in either direction).

Like an autonomous emperor, guided by his personal mage and the seances he was conducting by night, Peterson oversaw the construction by day, his attention darting from one detail to another. In February 1883 he was 'thinking of finishing the Tower with an Octagon . . .' As the days and weeks extended into months and years, the tower seasonally adjusted like the trees around it, growing in summer, falling fallow in winter, each spurt of growth recorded in the Order Books like a gardener's journal: 'Spring 1883 – Tomato House to be finished at once. Tower to recommence season 1883. Take care you are not stopped for cement.' As a man of law accustomed to being heard, Peterson despaired: 'I am afraid this book if read at all is chucked aside & nothing thought of it. I have been five days asking for it & only got it at last as I was leaving for London. PARTICULAR ATTENTION IS REQUIRED TO THE FOLLOWING . . .' Girders were set in place, cornices shaped and floors installed as the forest resounded to the clattering of wood and iron and the shovelling of sand and cement, turning this quiet countryside into a semi-industrial site.

Quite what his neighbours made of this invasion is not recorded; Peterson was not subject to modern planning restrictions, nor did he seek their consent. They might have been yet more surprised had they known the true function of this vast undertaking, for his Order Books make clear that Peterson was preparing a mausoleum for his own interment: 'VAULT . . . Inscription on plinth. I have three faces 2'0'' × 15''. In each face I can get three lines with capitals 4'' and smaller 3'' high.' Even here the practical and the spiritual went hand-in-hand: the crypt was designed so that, like the undercroft of Winchester Cathedral, it could accommodate winter floods; the pair of oblong plinths on which the Petersons' ashes would stand could rise from the subterranean tide like islands, while the waters lapped around the concrete catafalques. And yet for all Peterson's detailed directions, there was no overall plan to his tower. It seemed to take shape organically, inspired as much by the forest over which it rose as such rivals as the Portland stone column in Trafalgar Square, whose height it would exceed by 48 feet. 'I have made up [my] mind as to building up to [a] floor at 192 [feet],' Peterson wrote in October 1882, wondering, 'is it to be finished with spire, dome or cone? How much higher is it to go?' Perhaps he wouldn't know himself, until he had consulted his medium.

No sooner had the neighbourhood got used to the Girlingites' attempt at Eden than it was confronted with this concrete utopia. On Barrows Lane, Peterson built a model piggery, whose distinctive arched roofs and moulded cornices gave passersby the distinct impression of an eccentric mind at work – even as visitors encountered the strangely dressed denizens of the nearby religious commune wandering the same country lanes. Peterson was changing the topography of the land itself, with other houses such as Newhook, by the railway viaduct, and a four-storey tower and observatory rising over the hills towards the coast at Ashley Clinton; while he surrounded his main tower with high concrete walls, a North and a South Lodge, a Tower Lodge, and pairs of cottages for his workers – as much a testament to their creator's philanthropy as the gigantic structure which dwarfed them. These constructions would have looked more at home in Tuscany than in an English village; in contrast to traditional forest homes of brick and thatch, their design marked them, like the Girlingites, as alien invaders, for all that they were composed of New Forest gravel, shingle from Hampshire beaches and cement from Dorset's rockier shores.

A VISIT TO A.T.T.P.'s COUNTRY SEAT:

THE GREAT SPIRITUAL TOWER

In June 1883, Peterson invited James Burns to see his tower. 'During the summer of 1881 a height of 80 feet was gained,' the rapt editor told his readers. 'This was increased last summer to 150 feet.' 'So from the top of your shaft you can look on the inhospitable rocks of the Isle of Wight,' as the spirit of the Duke of Wellington informed A.T.T.P. Unlike Ozymandias' 'colossal wreck, boundless and bare' in the sands, this was a monument to the future. 'The most conspicuous landmark visible to the mariner as he approaches the Solent from the Channel is a Tower, rearing its top high above all other objects, and daily it still becomes higher and higher'; and in his characteristic rhetoric, Burns was at pains to defend his friend from accusations of *folie de grandeur*.

> The Duties of Life – What are they? When do they end? According to the notions of some, Wealth has no duties; it has only enjoyments and privileges . . . But this practice is regarded by another class as a great mistake. It is after the struggle for position and means has been successfully accomplished that the real duties of life – for self and others – can indeed be commenced on an enlarged and loftier plane of action. This view has been practically adopted by the gentleman of whom we write. The fruits of his efforts at his country seat, during the last dozen years, are a monument of genius, perseverance, and unstinted expenditure. The stiff, unculti-

> vated soil has been transformed into trim lawns, ornamental woods, gardens, orchards etc. Experiments are being made which may bring about results instructive to the cultivator and beneficial to the community.

Over this utopia loomed the tower itself, and as Peterson took Burns to the top, they saw a virgin view, just as Lunardi had first seen London from the air a century before. That afternoon, Peterson's folly enabled the two men to rise breathlessly over the forest in the same way as Mary Ann was transported by her visions 'into a realm far above the earth'. Here, nature and supernature met in an airy panorama, as though projected from some vast *camera obscura*.

> Looking southward the Channel is seen right in front. Towards the right – looking westward – is Bournemouth. Due south are the entrance to the Solent and the Needles of the Isle of Wight, stretching quaintly into the sea. Turning gradually to the left . . . the Solent appears like a canal or mill-stream, and the Island itself looks more like a weather-beaten model seen in an exhibition than an object in nature. The town of Lymington is almost under you, the roofs of the houses presenting themselves. On the opposite shore . . . the town of Yarmouth is seen on the coast, and on a clear day, in the eastern horizon, Spithead and Portsmouth may be visible. Inland, to the north, the vast expanse of the New Forest presents its varied features of hill and dale, wood and heath, relieved by gentlemen's residences and the spire of Lyndhurst church.

To their 'elevated eye', the two spiritualists stood as super-humans, suspended over this startling new vista as immortals of the gods, or Mephistopheles exhibiting his domain. They felt that strange sense of detachment which such views induce, as familiar landmarks were reduced to the scale of toys; from the forest's moss-like treetops, across the Solent to the seaside palace of the

Queen-Empress, command post of the imperial century. And if the Empire revolved somewhat insouciantly around Osborne, then the spirit world might have pivoted about this eyrie: from here anything was possible: the entire universe might be made manifest, and with it, the new age which both men sought.

For Burns, this out-of-body experience was beyond words: 'It must be confessed that the ordinary earth-plodding mortal cannot realise the fact of such an elevation so slenderly supported, without a sense of awe. It is a sheer descent, so that unless one looks straight down, it is easy to imagine that the room occupied is floating in the air.' He seemed gripped with another vertiginous sensation: the desire to throw oneself off. 'What a blessing it is that mankind are not forced to ascend to heaven in their clay tenements! The attraction of dust to dust is so great that it is a positive relief to know that one is again returning to the bosom of the universal mother.' Perhaps, as Ruskin had imagined falling from Strasbourg's steeple, the two men might be miraculously arrested in mid-air by an angel – or even Tom Paine himself.

Disconnected from the earth, they hung as if in the gondola of an invisible balloon, prey to the elements. 'It was also a breezy day on our visit, and the gale of wind which disported itself at that height through the open windows was something terrific. What if the solid stone would snap, and pitch its living parasites into the meadow beneath!' Burns marvelled that even at 'that giddy elevation', the construction workers stood 'on the extreme verge, beating away vigorously with their mallets, regardless of the strong breeze that makes their loose garments flutter actively'. And perhaps it was here, at the summit of his ambition, that Peterson confided in Burns his greater plans for his monument, the eager editor pressing his host for the details as he answered the readers' most obvious question, 'What is the use or purpose of the tower?'

Or rather, the spirits did: 'In recent controls which have been given . . . in the MEDIUM, allusion is made to the spirits who are associated with it' – most importantly, that of Tom Paine, to whom it was dedicated. 'At present all that is intended to set forth is somewhat indistinct, but matters unfold themselves gradually,' wrote the editor, hinting at a project grander than any attempted by Peterson so far. 'The spiritual worker must toil in faith, doing to the best of his ability that which is revealed to him day by day, not troubling himself with that beyond his present province. It is stated that such towers will become rather numerous, and that they will be Spiritual Cathedrals of the future . . .' This was an astounding example of spiritualist faith, a new wonder of the world to rival any Fourier phalanx: 'There shall be Spiritual Towers and Turrets scattered throughout the earth. They shall be spiritual rallying places, strongly built and eminent for their great height. Above Time's defilements shall be the primal combination of time-hardening stone, eternal as the mountains, and there the spirits of millions shall find rest.'

It was a vaulting, gothic vision: a dream of self-replicating towers marching philanthropically across the land – industrial-scale temples for a brave new world. Just as Wren had imagined a new city of Carolopolis to be carved from the post-apocalyptic remains of London after its Great Fire; and just as Peter the Great and Napoleon had imposed their imperial utopian fantasies on St Petersburg and Paris, so it seemed that now, new, spiritualist cities were set to arise. But Peterson's immediate plans were hardly less grand: 'In the meantime the mind of the constructor is occupied with various uses to which he intends to consign portions of it. In resemblance to the custom of the kings of ancient Egypt, he proposes that his remains find a resting place, after the ascent of his spirit, in the vault excavated beneath the basement.' Fifty years before the fifth earl of Carnarvon would order his excavations in the Valley of the Dead, here in Hampshire the chambers of an equally ambitious mausoleum would embody a new religion: 'On the first floor will be a seance room, from the windows of which it is possible that the materialised spirit may address an audience in the direct voice, on the ground below. The room above is to be used for meditation and retirement. On the third floor will be the picture gallery of spirit drawings and paintings.'

Peterson's tower was to be a spiritualist laboratory, echoing Wren's monument in Pudding Lane, completed two hundred years earlier both as a testament to the city's survival and as a giant telescope, scanning the skies for evidence of the physical universe. Inspired by the same architect, this tower would search for proof of another world; even as it reached back over time immemorial, it would look into time to come. 'A vast amount of space is yet at disposal, for the tower is really a street of houses set on one end, and it might afford lodging for upwards of a dozen separate parties.' Had they been able to see beyond their altitude through some transchronological eye-glass across the Atlantic, Peterson and Burns might have glimpsed rivetters scurrying along iron girders as skyscrapers rose over Manhattan. It seemed that A.T.T.P. had built the first tower block, from a democratic material – not Portland's stone of state governance, but an amalgam of its worked dust and commonplace sand and shingle. Like the Shakers with their clean-lined furniture and utilitarian spaces, its creator seemed to anticipate a modernist utopian aesthetic, regarding the 'plain simplicity' of his tower as 'a reflection on the gorgeous cathedral, where the soul is more engrossed in the building and its appurtenances than with prayers'.

Now, as his tower reached 190 feet, Peterson decided that it was time to allow others to view his work. In his 'hopes of making that Tower useful to the spirit still in the body', he would charge an admission fee to finance the construction of 'eight sets of double cottages' – radical spiritualist alms-houses for 'those who have lived a real selfhood, independent of priest or parish; and to whom lodging and a ton-and-a-half of coal and a nice garden may help to tide over the remaining years of life . . .' In a letter to *Medium and Daybreak* published on 17 August 1883, he wrote, 'The Tower is not in that state now in which mischief can be done; I therefore do not object to visitors, although were I to throw it open to the public, the still remaining work would be interfered with.' Peterson arranged for readers armed with issues of the periodical to be admitted, with a possibility of a more general opening later:

> My object is this: many, who would spit and splutter at the very name of spiritualism, like giving caviare to the mob, would be too glad to get a far-reaching prospect from its top, and on the journey, after they had got tired of talking, would be induced to read their ticket of admission, where they would find something to attract their attention; and might learn that the same agency which spoke through the mouth of an illiterate man, operated on the mind of myself, the designer and constructor of what, to say the least, is a curiosity.

By the following summer, however, Peterson was regretting his invitation: 'Keep the *top room locked from visitors*. The windows are . . . dangerous. In fact keep all doors locked.' He was also experiencing other problems: the all-consuming tower was depleting the county of resources, and he had to look further afield to satisfy his behemoth's appetite for aggregate: 'This shingle matter is becoming serious . . . Is there none about Milford? Where did Mr Kennard get his?' Matters were made worse by the economic depression, and it was not until 1886 that the tower was completed, at 218 feet and a cost of £30,000. It was topped off by Tommy Ackland, paid £50 for a feat no one else would undertake.

Initially Peterson had planned his edifice to be twelve storeys high, with fifty-two windows, one for each week, and three hundred and sixty-five stairs, but the finished building eschewed such calendrical symmetry in favour of thirteen storeys and ten windows. Each floor contained a room about eighteen feet square, although the tapering walls – which began at a thickness of two feet at its base and reduced to one foot at the top – meant that the

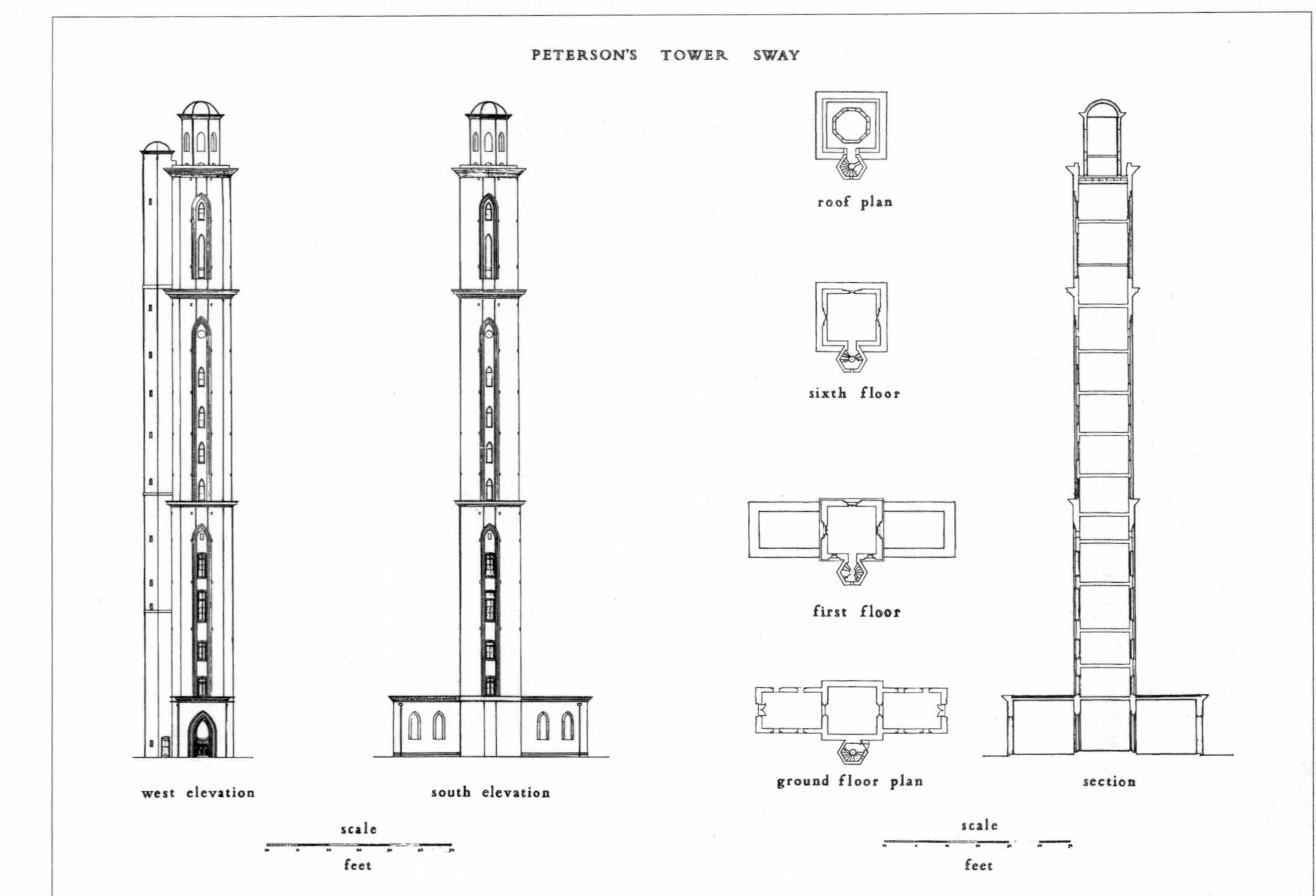
PETERSON'S TOWER SWAY
roof plan
sixth floor
first floor
west elevation
south elevation
ground floor plan
section
scale
feet
scale
feet

upper rooms were larger than those at the bottom: in an *Alice*-like inversion, Peterson's tower really was bigger inside than out, while the fairytale effect of the structure seemed to call for the spirit of the North Wind to swirl about its summit. Or perhaps this was some secular church, with its gothic porches (added at a later date) and windows framed in contrasting red-pigmented concrete. Along with its minaret-like dome, these features imparted an oriental air, an echo of the sub-continent of which Victoria had recently become Empress – just as her Durbar Room had imported a little bit of India to Osborne, and as Julia Margaret Cameron installed similar eastern flourishes to Dimbola. Calcutta had come to the forest, and Peterson's folly lacked only the sound of a sitar or the call of a muezzin.

This mystical structure was to be crowned with a final, extraordinary glory. Peterson planned to install an electric light in its lantern-like top, and an illuminated clock face in the circular holes below the second cornice; thus the tower would glow with electrical as well as spiritual power, just as Owen had planned to illuminate Harmony Hall with a 'koniophostic light'. But this St Elmo's fire would never dance over the treetops. The Board of Trade forbade the beacon 'by reason of the possible danger to shipping, for the Solent is quite clearly seen from the tower's top, and the light might prove a will-o-the-wisp to unsuspecting vessels'. Mistrustful of this spiritualist lighthouse, the authorities sought to suppress its power. Invested with so much effort and faith, the tower now stood empty and unlit, a solemn silhouette against the forest sky.

TWELVE

The Close of the Dispensation

> There is no doubt . . . that ere long the story of Shakerism in Hampshire will become a thing of the past, to be numbered among many other abortive attempts to bring about the reign of spiritualism upon earth.
>
> *Lymington Chronicle* 23 September 1886

> But of that day or that hour no one knows, not even the angels in heaven, nor the Son, but only the Father.
>
> Mark 13:32

As Peterson's tower rose over the stranded Girlingites, it seemed like a signpost on a spiritual map – the same mysterious chart which had brought the Children of God to New Forest Lodge and Ruskin to Broadlands' seance table, a mystical landscape coursed by a leyline running through southern England, an immanent, unseen circuit buried in the soil. But the realities of the modern world had reduced Mary Ann's Eden to mud, and with the rest of the country suffering from the depression, her attempts to exist outside capital meant that her sect was even more at the mercy of a failing economy. At such times, philanthropy was thin on the ground. Their one-time patron William Cowper was ennobled and entered the House of Lords, no longer a representative of the common people; while the Herberts left Ashley Arnewood – 'farming was too much anxiety to us, in these bad times' – and retreated deeper into the forest.

With the century nearing its close, new radical ideas were permeating this corner of the country. In 1880, Florence told her husband that 'gossip' had reached the neighbourhood 'that your latest political creed is "Nihilism". I do not know how that would suit the South Hants people!' In fact the southern coast had already played its part in that creed. In 1862, Ivan Turgenev had stayed in the Isle of Wight, where the rocky shore of Blackgang Chine, infamous for shipwrecks, inspired *Fathers and Children*, 'the greatest storm of any work of Russian literature, giving currency to the term "nihilist"'. The tempest-racked Children of God too had laboured under such labels as 'communists' or 'religious maniacs', but they were beyond political discourse. At Tiptoe, most of their possessions had been sold, and many members had left. Those that remained kept the faith in their shanty chapel, where only William Girling was allowed to play the harmonium. In this sanctified dance-hall in the middle of a field, they would live out their final years.

'Very little is heard or seen of the Shakers now, though occasionally Mrs Girling and Elder Isaac Osborne drive through the town,' noted a Lymington reporter. In 1881, however, the sect was subjected to an earthly reckoning as the census enumerator arrived in Hordle. Having taken down the details of the local vicar, Laurence Whigham, the innkeeper of the Bell, George Collins, and the tenants of New Forest Lodge – the Yorkshire-born Harriet Houle and her two nieces – he proceeded to record the age, sex and birthplace of each Girlingite. The Children of God joined the rest of the kingdom in due order; and in registering Mary Ann as the head of the Family, the process was a kind of official recognition, as well as an audit of her mission to date.

Hordle *The Shakers House & Tents*

Name	*Relation*	*Condition*	*Age*	*Occupation*	*Where born*
Mary Ann Girling	Head	Mar	54	Prefers to live by faith	Little Glemham, Suffolk
William W. Girling	Son	Unm	25	*ditto*	Ipswich, Suffolk
Eliza Folkard	Daur	Unm	34	*ditto*	Letheringham, Suffolk
Henry Osborne	Son	Mar	44	*ditto*	Easton, Suffolk
Eliza Osborne	Daur	Unm	45	*ditto*	Peasenhall, Suffolk
Mary Ann Osborne	Daur	Umm	13	*ditto*	Easton, Suffolk
James A. Haase	Son	Widr	37	*ditto*	All Saints, London
Cornelius Chase	Son	Widr	37	*ditto*	Newborough, Staffs
Leonard Benham	Son	Widr	58	*ditto*	Helsole, Suffolk
Arthur Benham	Son	Unm	26	*ditto*	Clifford, Suffolk
George Benham	Son	Unm	15	*ditto*	Stratford, Suffolk
Mary Benham	Daur	Umm	14	*ditto*	Stratford, Suffolk
Elizabeth M. Robinson	Daur	Unm	33	*ditto*	Dulwich, London
Emma Knuecheles	Daur	Unm	34	*ditto*	Dulwich, Surrey
Elizabeth Knuecheles	Daur	Unm	14	*ditto*	Camberwell, Surrey
Thomas L. Collins	Son	Mar	34	*ditto*	Saint James, London
Jane Bridges	Daur	Unm	22	*ditto*	Little Glemham, Suffolk
Harriet Calver	Daur	Unm	36	*ditto*	Wortwell, Norfolk
Nathan Hatt	Son	Unm	26	*ditto*	Kingsland, London
Hannah Ballard	Daur	Wid	35	*ditto*	Dover Court, Essex
Amelia Ballard	Daur	Wid	15	*ditto*	Kingsland, London
Annie Froude	Daur	Wid	42	*ditto*	East Malling, Kent
Jane E. Froude	Daur	Wid	13	*ditto*	Horton, London

Name	*Relation*	*Condition*	*Age*	*Occupation*	*Where born*
Thomas Todd	Son	Widr	60	*ditto*	Parham, Suffolk
Martha Todd	Daur	Unm	23	*ditto*	Parham, Suffolk
Ellen Todd	Daur	Unm	17	*ditto*	Parham, Suffolk
Jane Grist	Daur	Unm	25	*ditto*	Edgware, London
Emma Wright	Daur	Mar	62	*ditto*	Dalling Hoo, Suffolk
Herbert Wright	Son	Unm	27	*ditto*	Dalling Hoo, Suffolk
John Manuel	Son	Unm	53	*ditto*	Benhall, Suffolk
Isaac Osborne	Son	Mar	50	*ditto*	Easton, Suffolk
Sarah M. Osborne	Daur	Mar	46	*ditto*	London
Sarah E. Osborne	Daur	Unm	24	*ditto*	Kettleburgh, Suffolk
Hannah M. Osborne	Daur	Unm	21	*ditto*	Kettleburgh, Suffolk
Eliza Osborne	Daur	Unm	17	*ditto*	Easton, Suffolk
Ada Osborne	Daur	Unm	15	*ditto*	Easton, Suffolk
Lena Osborne	Daur	Unm	14	*ditto*	Easton, Suffolk
Mary Cooper	Daur	Mar	59	*ditto*	Wortwell, Norfolk
Cecilia Cooper	Daur	Unm	31	*ditto*	Wortwell, Norfolk
Sarah E. Cooper	Daur	Unm	29	*ditto*	Wortwell, Norfolk
Mary Cooper	Daur	Unm	20	*ditto*	Dalling Hoo, Suffolk
Elizabeth Ellerington	Daur	Mar	38	*ditto*	Stoke New.[n], London
Mary A. Smith	Daur	Wid	52	*ditto*	Hatcherton, Suffolk
Sally Smith	Daur	Unm	21	*ditto*	Hacheston, Suffolk
Alice Smith	Daur	Unm	16	*ditto*	Hacheston, Suffolk
Anna Smith	Daur	Unm	15	*ditto*	Hacheston, Suffolk
John Smith	Son	Unm	13	*ditto*	Hacheston, Suffolk
Henry Worsall	Son	Mar	38	*ditto*	Horne, Surrey

Name	*Relation*	*Condition*	*Age*	*Occupation*	*Where born*
Lucy Worsall	Daur	M	35	*ditto*	Tongham, Surrey
William Worsall	Son	Unm	13	*ditto*	Lambeth, Surrey
Caroline M. Worsall	Daur	Unm	11	*ditto*	Lambeth, Surrey
William Ireland	Son	Mar	45	*ditto*	Huyton, Lancashire
Elizabeth Ireland	Daur	Mar	49	*ditto*	Weymouth, Dorset
Gwilliam Ireland	Daur	Unm	19	*ditto*	West-Derby, Liverpool
Rebecca Young	Daur	Mar	31	*ditto*	Thornton, York
Hannah Knight	Daur	Unm	26	*ditto*	Lyndhurst, Hampshire
Mary A. Knight	Daur	Unm	21	*ditto*	Wootton Milton, Hants
George Frampton	Son	Mar	37	*ditto*	Bashley Milton, Hants
Eliza Saunders	Daur	Wid	71	*ditto*	Benhall, Suffolk
Eliza Saunders	Daur	Unm	44	*ditto*	Benhall, Suffolk
Henry Saunders	Daur	Unm	36	*ditto*	Benhall, Suffolk
Emma Piggot	Daur	Unm	44	*ditto*	St George's, London
Fred. J. Goldenworthy	Son	Unm	21	*ditto*	St Thomas, Oxford
Laviena Chase	Daur	Unm	23	*ditto*	Hadley, Suffolk

In cool facts and dry figures enscribed by the recording angel of Victorian bureaucracy, this was a memorial to the New Forest Shakers – now one hundred fewer than in their heyday. Of the remaining sixty-four souls in this Tiptoe field, more than half were from the remote-sounding eastern villages – Letheringham and Peasenhall, Kettleburgh and Dallinghoo – where Mary Ann had first preached. Entire clans had sworn to her, and had suffered their own losses: the Benhams and the Osborne families of Isaac and Henry, now depleted; even Isaac's son, pledged to be a soldier of Christ, had deserted. Perhaps most serious was the loss of Isaac Batho, Mary Ann's mediator.

Among those who stayed were local converts such as George Frampton (recently released from Winchester prison, having served a month for neglecting to pay five shillings a week towards the upkeep of his wife Elizabeth, an inmate at the county asylum, Knowle, near Southampton), and Hannah and Mary Knight, from Lyndhurst and Wootton, Milton. Then there were the Londoners: the widowed James Haase, now thirty-seven and still fighting his doubts; Elizabeth Ellerington, thirty-eight and married but without her husband, hailing originally from the dissenting district of Stoke Newington; the Worsalls from Lambeth, the Knuecheles – a strange surname, perhaps misspelt – from Dulwich. Some came with no family connexions at all. Most were married or widowed women of a certain age: forty-three sectarians were female, as opposed to just twenty-one men and boys. The seventeen remaining children were now almost grown up. What could Victorian teenagers have expected from such a life?

I feel a great sense of sadness when I read this list. It must resemble – probably more closely than I'd like to imagine – similar returns from gypsy camps or navvies' huts. This reduced roster is a final roll-call of faith. It bears testament to defeated hope, and its bare data encodes a narrative of doomed belief. At the top of the page is Mary Ann, followed by her son, William, and the rest of her followers, whose relationship to her – their 'head' – are all described as 'son' or 'daughter', as if officialdom accepted the fact that they were one big family with Mary Ann as their mother. And in the column marked 'Occupation' is a phrase partly obscured by the checker's crayon: 'Prefers to live by faith'; while below, in the spaces once filled with 'farm labourer', 'laundress', or 'carpenter', is a repeated 'ditto', like children answering to their teacher's register. They felt they were following Christ, spending their days in work and prayer in expectation of transcendence. They had left their homes to follow their new mother, abandoning everything that defined them in favour of a new identity. They deserve our sympathy, if only for the bravery of their sacrifice and separation, led into the wilderness by Mary Ann. She was responsible for all this: she was answerable to their fate; she was to blame. And what did she feel, this matriarch who had lost eight infants but had gathered a hundred more to her cause, orphans saved from the world's iniquities to be reclaimed as Children of God? A sense of power, probably; as to how far she realised her responsibility for their lives, it is impossible to tell.

It is as difficult to know who they were, these people, even though they stand only just outside memory. My great-great-grandfather, a Methodist minister in nearby Parkstone, would have heard of and perhaps even visited them. Yet as the generations separate us from their faith, so our lack of faith makes us different, and difference is a dangerous thing. Mary Ann's nearness to our age is as remarkable as her nearness to an age of magic and miracles. Her followers were ordinary people – albeit the women more suntanned than might be considered seemly, their bloomer costumes not quite respectable – it was their souls which were different. The Girlingites created their own dispensation; for them, there was no future. And as I walk through these same fields, these scrubby verges, their faith is denied by their absence and our presence. Their future was our now, and we are still waiting. They placed their trust in one woman, following her in a pioneering migration. But where their peers had left rural communities for the towns and cities, they had moved in the opposite direction, summoned, like an earlier family, to this place for census. And there they waited, as other forms slouched towards their Bethlehem.

One Sunday evening in December 1881, the Mancunian spiritualist William Oxley visited Tiptoe, and in an interview with Mary Ann, asked if she was aware that 'several others' were making the same claim to divinity. She replied, 'It was prophesied that false Christs should come, and all others are false, for besides me there is none other.' Evidently Mary Ann was aware of her rivals; equally evidently, she dismissed them, although Oxley recorded their claims, along with hers, in his *Modern Messiahs and Wonder Workers*.

In 1875, a foot soldier named James White, seeking to re-establish Joanna Southcott's 'House of Israel' in Chatham, Kent, promised his followers immortality and, using funds provided by his own 'lady of wealth', created an 'Israelite Colony' of shops, shoe factories and even a shipyard, all crowned by a central temple which would dwarf the ambitions of Peterson's spiritualist tower. One hundred and forty-four feet square, 'its *subterraneous passage* will extend for miles, while "The holy of holies" will form the topmast graft into the building, lit up by a revolving electric light. The lower story will contain twelve presses, worked by a steam engine. The second or middle story will be the great hall, seating many thousands. The upper story will be divided into dining, sleeping, and sitting rooms, kitchen, &c., for an habitation for the members who work in the grounds.' It would be a kind of nineteenth-century nuclear shelter, intended to hold 20,000 of the elect in advance of the apocalypse. But unlike Peterson's tower, White's folly was never completed, standing instead as a ruin on Chatham Hill. 'Except for the purpose it was intended for, the building – which is of *concrete* – is all but useless, and from the manner of its construction, it would not pay for the cost of its demolition,' Oxley wrote in 1889. By that time, White was dead and succeeded by his wife, who proclaimed herself to be the Woman Clothed with the Sun, 'thus adding one more to . . . the list of Woman-Messiahs and Madonnas'.

Yet Mary Ann had most to fear from an anonymous woman known as 'The Mother', who also claimed to be the Woman from Revelations and manifested stigmata – although 'they appear to have been fugitive, and not permanent like those of her contemporary rival'. She had appeared, with two female acolytes, at a lodging house in an unnamed south coast town in 1877, 'habited in plain black garb, with the appearance of a white band round the face', 'the living picture of some Roman Catholic saint', or perhaps Georgiana Cowper at her most unearthly. This sub-Virgin Mary seemed to have been commissioned to retrieve the faithful, as if Rome had become afraid of the power of other prophetesses. Preaching apocalypse and dispensing divine healing, she drew on Catholic belief but employed spiritualist techniques against the coming storm. In 1878, in another southern lodging, a violent tempest 'threatened destruction to her dwelling and herself', but she 'commanded even the raging of the sea' and 'the huge waves advancing toward them . . . while completely deluging the land on either side, were powerless before the Presence in that house'.

The Mother exceeded Mary Ann in physical reinvention. On Christmas Day that year, three female followers beheld her transfiguration, 'the *inner* body having the appearance of refined and living silver; *that* encased as in living amber; and the whole enveloped in spiritual flame of exceeding brilliancy. Thus the Birth of THE NEW DISPENSATION was signalized . . .' She declared that 'The Second Coming of The Lord Jesus is Twofold – TWO in ONE; as will be His Manifestation DUAL – HE and SHE: Feminine and Masculine in One', a divine bisexuality which echoed the conceits of Ann Lee and Mary Ann, as well as those of Swedenborg and Thomas Lake Harris. And as Oxley added, pertinently, 'It is noteworthy that in the South of England, and not very distant from each other, there were *two* women, both claiming to be the manifestation of Jesus Christ in his Second Advent in their own persons. The outside world . . . may well wonder, and ask: Who is who? and, Which is which?'

As if in response to these rivals, Mary Ann's doctrines were becoming more apocalyptic as she entered her own end-time. On 28 February 1882, Mary Ann had written a letter to the local press in which she responded to recent rumours of her 'sickness and death' and spoke of herself in the third person. 'Notwithstanding all appearances, this mysterious woman, known as Mrs Girling by name to the world, is no less a person than the re-incarnation of that same Holy Spirit of God, the Great Father of Love, that once appeared in the form of a man . . . He was made the God father, and whose *print marks* of the evidence of his former suffering in His body now appear upon *her body*, showing it is the same spirit . . . Now, why should the truth and love suffer any longer? Ask the mysterious woman known as MARY ANN GIRLING.' She now issued an extraordinary new mission statement to outclass her competitors. Resolute, triumphant, inspired or deluded, the now grey-haired prophetess claimed complete communion with God, as if the Holy Trinity had been expanded to become a quartet. Her *Dispensation* appeared at the end of a century already denying the presence of God, but her text might as well have been illuminated with medieval scenes of defecating demons and gilt-winged angels. To believers, however, it was a new age gospel, broadcast into the ether:

The Close of the Dispensation: the Last Message to the Church and the World

Children, hear your Mother's call

There was a time in the history of the world when God, the great Spirit, took a woman's body, and formed out of her flesh and blood a male child . . . From his childhood He was acknowledged to be the Son of God, and he was also the son of Woman; so that he was both male and female, but only the male form was seen . . .

From the time He took that body into Heaven until now He has only revealed Himself to the people by His own spiritual presence . . . until about 23 years ago, when . . . it pleased the Lord God, called Jesus, the Father Supreme, to take the body of a woman called by name Mary Ann Girling to be the

> terrestrial habitation for the celestial God-mother love-life to dwell in . . .
>
> She is on earth, suffering for the love's sake. As soon as she is accepted, bodily, as His bride, the Lord's Christ, Love, then He Himself will appear in His glory and glorify her . . . There will be no more war or death, the full light of the millennial reign of peace and power, the lovely kingdom of the God-mother and Saviour will be manifest, and all that was lost in Adam will be given back in Jesus Christ, the Lord God, the Father and Mother in Heaven, and all the children celestial and terrestrial . . . So long as she is refused, Christ is refused, because they are one life . . .
>
> His first appearing was in the form of a man. He now appears as a woman, yet it is the same life, the same God, the same Jesus Christ. The beginning of creation was a male; the end is a female – not to be crucified but to be glorified . . . I am the second appearing and reincarnation of Jesus, the Christ of God, the Bride, the Lamb's wife, the God-mother and Saviour life from Heaven . . . I ask the whole human family, as my children, if they have any pleasure in my suffering for them any longer? . . .

This new testament reached back to Mary Ann's earliest days of preaching in Suffolk – and perhaps even further, to Ann Lee, Joanna Southcott and other prophetesses. It also drew on St Paul's letter to the Corinthians: 'But some one will ask, "How are the dead raised? With what kind of body do they come?" You foolish man! What you sow does not come to life unless it dies . . . There are celestial bodies and there are terrestrial bodies; but the glory of the celestial is one, and the glory of the terrestrial is another . . . for star differs from star in glory.' As Oxley noted, by claiming her oneness with Christ, Mary Ann was 'greater than the Holy Ghost . . . and henceforth her followers must regard her as their God-Mother, the Bride of Christ . . . the Bible was merely the dead letter, she was greater than it'. Superseding even the Scriptures, this forest sybil in a merino gown seemed suspended from the vagaries of time and space. She also discouraged 'spirit manifestations' among her followers, for whom her new omnipotence was 'a great stumbling-block . . . for they had shared in these, but now the Mother was taking all the honour and glory to herself'.

On his own visit to that leaky hut in Tiptoe, Oxley had encountered a kind of tribal decadence, with Mary Ann all but stuck with fetishes, and her scarred hands and feet as *muti*. It might have been deepest Africa as rural Hampshire.

> There were about some sixty people present, chiefly females, very thinly clad, and deep poverty was manifest everywhere, for a more wretched and miserable place of abode and surroundings could hardly be imagined. While engaged in the singing, Mrs Girling entered and three young females (one of them very pale and emaciated) rose up, in a state of semi-trance, and commenced dancing, ever and anon bowing down to Mrs Girling and in a singing tone addressed her in these words: 'Holy, holy, holy, art thou, O King, for thou, who wast dead, art alive again; and we worship thee as the Lord our God.'

It was an authentically uncanny scene, more pagan than Christian; a rite which reached into the pre-history of the forest itself. It was also a bastardised liturgy bent to Girlingite ends. Mary Ann now assumed the appearance of the Woman Clothed with the Sun, a new Virgin Mary clad in a white robe with blue ribbon and a lace shawl ('a relic of other days'), and adorning herself with a wreath of everlasting flowers, she entered the room 'with naked feet, pointing to them, on which were imprinted the "nail-marks" of the crucified Jesus, declaring at the same time: "I am both Mother and Saviour!"' To the cynical, this epiphany was stage-managed to assert her religious dictatorship; to others, it was proof that their leader was indeed the new Christ.

Until now, Mary Ann's stigmata had remained hidden, known only to a chosen few; rumour rather than display had rendered her sacred scars more potent, part of her unifying mystery. Now, as she reached apotheosis, these marks were made manifest. Even Oxley, generally antipathetic to Mary Ann, observed that 'the evidence of their actuality has been attested over and over again by sceptical outsiders, as well as the members of the Family. I have it on good authority that the marks on the feet were permanent, while those on the hands were variable, sometimes faint, and at others distinct and plain.' Like the names of the dead on Charles Foster's forearms or the ectoplasmic faces in spirit photographs, these signs provided doubting Thomases with the proof they required. In 1937, Reverend Andress of Brockenhurst would state: 'In some extraordinary way, Mrs Girling unquestionably had the STIGMATA . . . How they came there, through design or accident, through intense devotional thought on the Redeemer's sufferings, or through other causes, I do not pretend to say. All I do say is that there is good and sufficient evidence that this was the actual fact.' Indeed, Andress would unearth an eye-witness account – from the Dundee *Evening Telegraph*.

'The Mysterious Woman (By a Holiday Visitor)' was a journalistic scoop: 'I am the first newspaper correspondent who had been permitted to witness in her body those mysterious wound prints to which she has referred somewhat ambiguously,' claimed the anonymous reporter. Like a country doctor examining his patient, he assessed Mary Ann as 'above average height, and very ladylike in her manner and conversation, though her . . . dialect still smacks of the Eastern counties . . . But as to the "marks" with which I was now more particularly concerned' – he teased his readers with the forensic details as he was about to finger the scars of a female Christ – 'It was, perhaps, a delicate matter to introduce; but my wish was gratified . . .'

> On her feet, hands, and side, are wound prints. How they came there I am unable to say, but there they are, unmistak-

> ably; and, doubtless to be seen, when the time comes for such a manifestation.
>
> The appearance of the feet favours the idea that one foot had been placed on top of the other, and a large nail driven through both, the uppermost foot having the mark of the jagged head of the nail, with a kind of second head, as if the weight of the body had caused the head of the nail to sink further into the flesh. The peculiar position and locality of the nail print wonderfully bears out, as Mrs Girling observed, the truth of the prediction, 'Not a bone of Him shall be broken'.
>
> On her hands are also similar wound marks, and on her side a large oval scar, giving the appearance of an old spear-thrust healed up. It is difficult to describe the peculiar appearance of these wound prints. They are quite clear, but seem to be under a transparent skin, white and sunken; not, perhaps, much unlike what is known as a birth-mark.

It was a pseudo-medical account as ostensibly objective as that of the disembodied hand manifested by Home in Boston, and bore its own pathological relationship to the spectral photographs first produced by Mumler in that city. In describing these 'print marks', this diagnosis saw Mary Ann's body as a daguerreotype of suffering, a holy lithograph – just as the Turin Shroud revealed the crucified Christ in a spirit photograph which had its equivalent in the cloth with which St Veronica wiped the Saviour's bleeding face.

But of Mary Ann, who defied the shroud, there was only one true portrait, and that did not display her wounds. 'Photography has something to do with resurrection,' wrote Barthes; 'might we not say of it what the Byzantines said of the image of Christ which impregnated St Veronica's napkin: that it was not made by the hand of man, *acheiropoietos*?', like an icon. And like an icon, the complex layers of image and impression projected by this medium-messiah reached through into other dimensions. The Dundee reporter affected to distance himself from the supernatural aspect of the story, but he was enchanted; perhaps he had been mesmerised by Mary Ann's magnetic eyes.

> What these marks may mean, it is not for me to say. Mrs Girling calls them her credentials – the seals put upon her, when she yielded herself to Christ Jesus, and surrendered her body for the same Holy God to dwell in her as dwelt in Him, God the Spirit. She has borne these marks, she adds, from the time she took her Lord 'for better, for worse', and became, to use her own expression, 'absorbed in Him, and He in her', when a positive exchange seemed to be made.
>
> Through all her privations and all the insults she has been subjected to, she has kept these marks a profound secret, even from those who have endured the sufferings with her. For I am assured, though evidence points to the fact that she has borne these marks for at least ten years, the knowledge of them has been kept from the whole of the members of the community until a few weeks ago. Her reason for this withholding is that they had received her for love's sake, and not for what the 'eye hath seen and the ear hath heard'.

And in that 'positive exchange', the report slipped from impartiality to faith, convinced by her holy wounds.

> Referring to the difficulty, even in her own 'family' as she calls the community, in realising that God their Father is walking in their midst under the cloud of her body, she remarks, '. . . It's been a great struggle for me to reach the top of the mountain of men's wisdom, and then to look over them at all times; so I do not wonder that my little children are a little timid as to their Father's steps.'

For this 'holiday visitor' – the byline assumes a deceptive informality – there was a sense of ambiguity to 'those marks . . . Whether Mrs Girling's explanation of the mystery be accepted or not, it seems to me to be a most cruel thing, that in this Christian land . . . men and women can look on unmoved, while their fellow-

Christians are first robbed of all they possess, and then left to starve.' And with that, the reader was left with the impression that some kind of miracle had taken place in that damp Hampshire field.

As the last days loomed, those elusive marks would appear fitfully, as if under Mary Ann's skin there lived another body entirely, one which was about to burst out on the appointed day like a butterfly from its chrysalis, its metamorphosis complete. Her stigmata were a solace for her Family, although unlike the legendary pelican plucking at its breast to feed her young with her own blood, her wounds would not succour her brood: when asked to save her followers from want, she said that would not be possible until she was accepted as Christ in a woman's form.

Meanwhile, on its appearance in the press, Mary Ann's *Dispensation* was seen as confirmation of her madness. 'This extraordinary document is the outcome of mental disease,' Oxley declared, 'and forms one of a number from others who have been, and are, afflicted by the same malady.' 'One can understand such religious dementia as this, easily enough,' wrote 'Dagonet' in the *Referee*, 'but the astonishing part . . . is that there are hundreds of men and women who accept Mrs Girling's estimate of herself.' The columnist added that 'in these days of prosecutions for blasphemy', the *Dispensation* was 'certainly worthy of attention'. Thus Mary Ann was seen as deserving of censure as any of the other medium-charlatans then subject to legal action. A century before, Richard Brothers had been committed for his prophesies, and even now asylums were filled with the religiously insane. Yet attempts to treat this prophetess in the same manner had failed; and who in the 1880s could prosecute a woman for such claims? To do so would dignify them with a gravity no rational man could admit. Nevertheless, Christians stood up in church every Sunday to proclaim their belief in the Second Coming; and if God had first appeared on earth as a man, Mary Ann's claim that He would reappear as a woman did not seem so incredible: 'The beginning of creation was a male; the end is a female – not to be crucified but to be glorified.' More difficult to accept was the idea of her divine consubstantiality: that God had reappeared within her, as if His actual presence were pushing out through her flesh, 'suffering for the love's sake'. She too was a bride of Christ impaled and suffering in the throes, just as Ann Lee had walked by night, her eyes pulled open for fear of a less sacred concupiscence.

Mary Ann anticipated her celestial re-creation, like the Virgin Mary assumed into Heaven, as if to return to the stars from which all men were made. If, in the meantime, the world accepted her mission, then her earthly presence would precipitate the end of history and a return to Paradise – 'all that was lost in Adam will be given back in Jesus Christ' – just as Blake saw Christ walking in his Felpham garden. But there was also an escape clause in this doxology, and it lay in the sin of the world; and when Mary Ann asked if mankind took any pleasure in her suffering, she seemed to anticipate further pain. Indeed, she was already aware of the signs of her own mortality.

With her white robes, her bloody scars and her eschatological pronouncements, it was clear that Mary Ann had either entered the last stages of mania, or that she was ready for the final confrontation. Like Conrad's Kurtz, she had become a demigod, worshipped here, on the forest's edge, by her starving followers. And in the penultimate decade of the nineteenth century, that was a blasphemy the orthodox world could not allow. So when, in the summer of 1883, Henry Osborne himself was accused of manslaughter, the resulting inquest was in effect a last stand for the Children of God, their leader and her lieutenant.

That July, the Osbornes' fifteen-year-old daughter, also named Mary Ann, had died of consumption, as had five other Girlingites (prompting their leader to declare that 'their deaths were due to their unbelief, and their rejection of her, as the Saviour'). But such were the circumstances surrounding Mary Ann Osborne's death, and the sect's way of life, that once more a legal enquiry was launched into the state of the Girlingite colony.

The inquest was held at the Plough Inn in Tiptoe, from where the coroner, James Druitt, led the jury to view the girl's body, still lying at the encampment. It was a macabre scene, this justice and his witnesses traipsing into the country field, and an intrusion for its tenants who rejected the rule of law here, in their anarchic bit of Hampshire. Back at the Plough, Eliza Osborne gave evidence.

'Sometimes my daughter was a little better, sometimes a little worse, so I was not really alarmed. Until Saturday morning, I had not thought she might die. I sent for the doctor, but could not get one.'

By 3 o'clock that afternoon, the girl was dead.

'She had not wanted for anything,' protested Eliza. 'She had new milk, eggs, chicken, porter and so on, supplied by the community and what neighbours were kind enough to give.'

Her sister-in-law Sarah corroborated this, as did Mary Ann, who was asked if their community had regulations against medical advice.

'No,' she replied. 'If Mrs Osborne had so wished, a doctor would have been sent for.'

It was noted that 'a great deal of unjust prejudice seemed to have arisen in the neighbourhood in consequence of the deceased's death'. The jury were local people, long exposed to stories of the cult's naked rites and murdered babies; they may have been pre-disposed to believe that the girl had died as a result of dogma, if not witchcraft. And when Druitt directed that a verdict of manslaughter was inappropriate, they countered with exactly that verdict.

Osborne was taken to Winchester, there to be charged with

having 'feloniously killed and slayed . . . his daughter' by 'neglecting to provide her with medical assistance'. As ever, Mary Ann attended the hearing, along with a band of followers – a formidable, if not intimidating presence. Speaking to the press outside, she said that 'no one was satisfied with the jury's verdict, and the doctor and coroner were satisfied with the treatment the deceased girl received'. But just as it seemed the spikes of Winchester's prison gates were about to enclose Harry Osborne as a religious martyr, or a political detainee, the grand jury rejected the charge, and he was free. Yet as Maurice Davies might have pointed out, Mary Ann had once proclaimed that her followers had neither need of doctor nor undertaker. Now both had had cause to visit her benighted Family.

In the winter of 1883–4, as Ruskin delivered his lecture on 'The Storm-Cloud of the Nineteenth-Century' to the London Institution, illustrated with sketches thrown onto a screen by limelight, the Tiptoe camp was battered by winds which blew away tent coverings, leaving beds soaked and lamps too wet to light. Perhaps it was the weather which drove Mary Ann back to London and Suffolk in a last attempt to rally support. In Ipswich, she visited her husband George and daughter Mary Jane; there were also emotional scenes as Mary Ann met former members who had deserted her, 'and many were melted to tears'. As events tumbled towards their close, it was as if she wanted to take them all with her, in a last push for power. But back at Tiptoe, the remaining faithful had fallen into a spiritual coma, left 'dazed and doubtful' by their leader's new doctrines; many deserted, 'destitute . . . and but most scantily clothed'.

In 1884 Mary Ann fell ill with a sore throat, 'accompanied by great bodily prostration', confining her to bed for three months. She recovered, but was too weak to move about, and from early 1885 she was unable to take part in the work of her household. Her intimates knew there was something seriously wrong, yet she kept her own counsel, even as she languished like an invalid child in her canvas-covered cot. Her illness declared itself as cancer of the womb: a cruel diagnosis for a woman whose crusade had begun with her stillborn: the womb that produced them was now the cause of her demise, and that of her doctrines. It was as if her mission was rewinding: the pain and loss of her dead children had initiated this sequence – implicit in the paralytic twist in her mouth and the stigmata on her hands and feet. Now, as her life came full circle, she was revisited with disability, as if in confirmation of the mortal arc.

The colony was living on weak tea, buttermilk, bread and butter or cheese, and vegetables grown by themselves. Occasionally a friend would donate some bacon, but generally they were vegetarian; the Family had killed only three pigs in the last eleven years, and for five of those years had not one joint of meat. Some blamed the ailing constitution of the communal body, and that of their bedridden leader, on this restrictive diet. They addressed the inevitable in a meeting, and decided that those who could leave should go before the winter, reserving their dwindling resources for the last, true believers. The following Whitsun a dozen members left to visit friends, and did not return. Yet still the 'excursionists' came.

• Summer Season 1886 • George H. Ames •

Riding, Posting and Job Master (*Telephone No. 28*) with Carriages and horses of every description for hire offers Char a banc trips on Mondays and Thursdays to see the Shakers' Encampment, *Fare 4/-*, via Christchurch and Hinton, returning by Highcliffe Castle and Mudeford. And on Tuesdays, Wednesdays, Fridays and Saturdays in September.

By July 1886 the community was reduced to twelve women and eight men. Their hamlet of seven huts remained, one a sickroom in which their leader lay; the others took on a derelict air. Yet in approaching starvation, the Girlingites were entering another, sacramental state: the same state in which Julian of Norwich, Ann Lee and Elspeth Buchan had their visions; the state to which Samuel Hecker and Sarah Jacobs had aspired; and in which Rose La Touche had died. In the light-headedness of hunger, a new ecstasy could hold sway. Paradoxically, in their decline, the sect seemed to attain the simplicity of their American brethren: 'There is perfect decency and perfect order but of the refinements of civilisation, or even of what a well-to-do artisan's family would consider absolute necessities, not a trace.' A shed served as a workshop where they made everything they needed, even their clothes. A stable housed a solitary pony; the rest of their livestock consisted of a pig, a few fowl, a parrot and a pet thrush. In those last few months, the colony had achieved its mission: stripped of everything but their basic needs (and sometimes not even those) and most fervent believers, they had reached their utopia.

And as Mary Ann lay, 'ill from cancer induced by cold', she still imagined great plans. She would have 'willingly united with the Baptists, Wesleyans or Congregationalists had they been ready to receive her, as the terrestrial presence of a celestial Being', she said. She even spoke of comparisons with William Booth's newly-formed Salvation Army. But now the Girlingites' services were curtailed, and the Family drew into itself, anticipating the end, yet resolute in faith: 'If I did not feel sure I was going to live forever', said one colonist, 'I would leave the camp tomorrow.' Ten years previously, Mary Ann had told an audience of her vision of Christ: 'A sight of Him was worth all the gold upon the earth, and she would willingly subject herself to persecution and torture to see Him again.' It was ironic that that was precisely what she would face in order to achieve her final sacrifice: an atonement for the world's sins.

* * *

She looked like a broken bird as she lay there on the trestle bed, overhung by bits of tatty carpet and threadbare chintz, the evening light shining through the weft. Her dress, with its semblance of lace and tailoring, clung to her shrunken form as she clung to life. Disease was eating away at her body; like her dream, both were wasting away. The night was drawing in, and the starlings scattered in spiky shapes across the sky; the dying down of the year had begun. Overhead, a lone seagull joined the starlings, swooping low over the fields.

The horror of Mary Ann's end was that that which gave life was now the source of her death. It was as if her faith had its own pathology: from stillbirth, paralysis and stigmata, to cancer of the womb; as though her flesh expressed all that she stood for, this empassioned woman, so proud and so tall and now laid so low under the star-sharp night.

'The agony and excruciating pains she endured were terrible, and while those nursing her could see but one termination, she still persisted in declaring that she should not die, and what she suffered was for the unbelief of her children.' She was put beyond hope by her hope, and her own irrational will. To the frustration of her son William, and her daughter Mary Jane, who had come from Ipswich, Mary Ann declined assistance, although she told others that she 'would not object to a medical man seeing her, not for the purpose of attempting to save her life' – of which she was assured – 'but for the purpose of easing and allaying her sufferings'. Dr Stevens arrived from Sway, but pronounced hers a hopeless case. She was nursed by her neighbour, Alice Read, whose husband Charles was the Tiptoe baker, and who would recall no stigmata on the dying woman's body: 'You have no faith, Alice,' Mary Ann rebuked her. And when some of her attendants told Mary Ann she could not get better, she burst into tears, saying, 'Why do you not comfort me in my sufferings? I shall not die.'

It was a heart-rending sight, this grown woman reduced to a

crying child. 'Mrs Girling had been in a semi-conscious state all day on Friday, but in the evening she recognised her son's voice and tried to speak to him, but failed,' reported *The Times*. And after twelve hours of unconsciousness, 'she gradually sank . . . and at seven o'clock on Saturday morning passed peacefully away, surrounded by the whole of the members, whose grief it is impossible to describe'.

As his mother died on Saturday, 18 September, William was unable to register her death until the following Monday. At Lymington, the final document in the few that record Mary Ann's life was completed by Dr Stevens with the words that had coolly disproved her teaching: 'Cancer of the womb, 10 months'. Yet few crowed at this disconfirmation; rather, Mary Ann's death was seen as a poignant conclusion. One correspondent who had followed their progress summed up the 'persecution from which these poor people suffered for years, and which only died away a comparatively short time ago . . . a Shaker, male or female, who was recognised on the public road was scarcely safe from maltreatment, their fences were destroyed, their crops stolen, their cattle let loose, and every imaginable species of petty irritation was devised against them'. Now 'the cardinal tenet of their faith has, in a moment, been overthrown', and the sect 'compelled to admit that . . . Mrs Girling must have been altogether mistaken. Deluded as these poor people have been – and no one who knows them can doubt that they were sincere in their errors – it is impossible to withhold from them a respectful sympathy in the double grief under which they are labouring. The little community is absolutely *déraillé*.'

As she lay in her tent, her coffin was made by loving hands – among them those of Tommy Ackland, who lived close by. 'Who is the coffin for?' he had asked, and when told, replied with a disbelieving, 'What!' The faithful had their explanation: 'She never would have died, only when the Lord told her to excommunicate certain unworthy members, she had not the heart to do so, and hence she herself suffered the punishment of death . . .' As her mesmeric hold was loosened, some admitted that they had given up the doctrine of immortality. They hoped to stay together, although given their debts, it was likely that the rest of their belongings would have to be sold off. Without their Mother, their utopian dream evaporated like the mist on a forest morning. 'One of the brethren . . . said they would have to break up and start life afresh, which would be a difficult matter, as most of them were old people . . . and their money was all gone. He further said so far as the experiment was tried it had failed.' In the cold light of day, *The Times* assessed their assets as though an auctioneer had arrived to value the Children of God:

> The community is reduced to 20, of whom seven are men and the rest women. The youngest person is 19 years old. There are three at 30 years, and the rest middle-aged and old. They are in poverty and in need of assistance. The grounds are about 2½ acres in extent, the garden occupies about two, and the tents and various offices fill up the remainder. The tents, though slight, are fairly well built and the interiors are beautifully clean and well kept.

But who could take on such a lot? Few philanthropists would adopt these orphans. Nevertheless, in the week after Mary Ann's death, Auberon Herbert wrote to the *Pall Mall Gazette* – now edited by the crusading Liberal journalist, and later spiritualist, W.T. Stead – lodging a new appeal on behalf of the bereft Girlingites. 'I have not at this moment a statement of their affairs, but I know there is a very large bill owing to the baker and a small amount owing for rent . . . I should be glad to share the responsibility of receiving and spending the money with some other person.' He asked for cheques to be sent to Henry Doman, 'who has always been interested in the community', and added, 'I shall send this letter to the Shakers for their approval before sending it to you.'

And yet, even now, the fate of Mary Ann remained uncertain. Was she actually dead? Like Joanna Southcott, it was said that she had asked not to be buried; that like Dr Emes of Bunhill Fields, she might yet be resurrected. 'Since her death, early on Saturday morning, there had been rumours that no funeral would take place, but that the Shakers expected the deceased would "rise again" – such expectations being probably engendered by the secrecy which was maintained, as to the day on which the ceremony would be performed.' These precautions were necessary 'on account of the anxiety of the Shakers that everything should be carried out in as quiet a manner as possible'. Reverend Frederick Fisher, who was to officiate at the funeral, made an emotional appeal on behalf of the bereaved Family to whom he was evidently acting as counsellor:

> They are a quiet, unassuming, moral and harmless people, kind and easily accessible; and . . . it is with a touching and primitive simplicity that they confess their surprise and perplexity at what has befallen them . . . Mrs Girling is to be buried to-morrow in the parish churchyard, and it is characteristic that they wish the funeral to be as quiet and orderly as possible, using the Church of England office without deviation, and only asking that they may appear in their garb of white, instead of black.

The morning of Wednesday, 22 September broke dark and lowering, with a strong north-easterly wind. At 10.15, the procession moved out of the field and into the lane. Mary Ann's coffin, made of elm but oiled to look like oak, was carried on the little chaise which she had used when driving to Lymington; it was drawn by an elderly pony led by Thomas Todd, gardener and one of the Elect who had first arrived in Hordle twenty-three years before. On top of the coffin lay a wreath of autumn dahlias and forest ferns; the mourners carried everlasting flowers and ferns. The women wore white, the men black, as they marched in pairs, led by William Girling as chief mourner; he was joined by his sister and father, who had come from Ipswich. Harry Osborne and Eliza Folkard marched behind, 'then brothers Chase, Osborne, and another, each accompanied by a sister; several sisters bringing up the rear'. Even Isaac Batho returned for the funeral.

Many onlooookers, also dressed in black, watched as the hearse moved through the village; others 'came to their doors and took a look at the last scene in the history of her whose singular life had excited so much interest'. It was as if the modern world were paying tribute to the passing of a medieval saint. Slowly, following the pace set by the lone pony, the cortège moved down Vaggs Lane, where the faithful had arrived in such hope fourteen years before. As it passed, 'several conveyances also fell in behind, the procession increasing by degrees into a long line of followers'. This silent, mournful human snake negotiated the hedgerows and the temporary railway bridge – 'Bournemouth direct line', the newspaper helpfully informed its readers – which now sundered the autumnal quietude. Here, gangs of navvies worked on the new line – ten of whom would die in its construction – living in makeshift mud huts like the Girlingites, whose otherness they shared. Fifty of their number stopped work and raised their hats, as if in augury of another rite fifteen years hence, when the Queen-Empress – also dressed in white – would be ferried across the Solent from Osborne, her own death a disconfirmation of the immortal imperial project. Or perhaps this monochrome scene looked back a thousand years, to when William Rufus's sacrificed body was carried from the forest created by his father.

As the coffin passed New Forest Lodge itself, several servants came running out to watch, but the owner was nowhere to be seen. By the time they reached All Saints Church, the crowd numbered five hundred. Four brethren bore Mary Ann's body through the lych gate and into the brick interior, where the service was conducted by Reverends Fisher and Travers Garrick. At the last, this religious renegade was reclaimed within the body of the Church, although the reading from Corinthians had a piquant effect: 'Lo! I tell you a mystery. We shall not all sleep, but we shall be changed, in a moment, in the twinkling of an eye, at the last trumpet. For the trumpet will sound, and the dead will be raised imperishable, and we shall be changed.' And in a nod to posterity, the vicar added a note to the burial register, to the effect that Mary Ann was 'The leader or Mother of the so-called sect of "Shakers" in the New Forest.'

And so the woman who said her body should never enter the ground was lowered into the earth. The sisters threw their bouquets of everlasting flowers into the grave, and afterwards spectators crowded round for a glimpse of the coffin. The plaque, 'a primitive kind of breastplate', was obscured by flowers, and so Mr Catling, a London friend of the community, read out –

MARY ANN GIRLING
Who sleeps in Jesus
September 18th, 1886
Aged 59 years

– adding, 'God grant that you and I, when we are called, may fall asleep in Jesus.' Meanwhile, the Children of God slipped away quietly, leaving their Mother behind. Now they would have to make their own way in the world.

PART FIVE

A New Jerusalem

I will arise my God to praise
Exalt the ancient King of days,
I arm myself with Gospel power,
To stand the dark and trying hour.
It was Jesus made me strong.
To sing the new Jerusalem song,
To give me power to fight
For wrong against the right.

Mary Ann Girling

THIRTEEN

In Borderland

For strange deep longing move us,
As betwixt the two we stand,
And share in the mystic meetings
And partings in borderland

Auberon Herbert, 'In Borderland'

Born in 1865, six years after his now more celebrated brother, Alfred, Laurence Housman was a product of the aesthetic movements of his age; a link between the gay decadence of the *fin de siècle* and the modern decades of the twentieth century. In his memoir, *The Unexpected Years*, Housman writes evocatively of studying art in South Kensington, where he read Ruskin and was 'carried off my feet by the strange beauty of his winged eloquence. Later I came to value chiefly not his writings on art, but his political economy. But for a short while he shared with Blake . . . my devout admiration.' One afternoon Ruskin himself passed through the room in which Housman was working. 'I rushed out hoping to catch sight of that prophet of the Lord; but I was too late, and my lamentation went up to Heaven – Why had Fate let me be in the same room with Ruskin, but not to set eyes on him?' Ruskin's spirit stayed with Housman, however: he felt 'a singularly personal affection' for the critic; and years later, 'when . . . I stood for the first time by his grave, it all came back to me, and I felt that, in some strange way, Ruskin . . . was my spiritual father'.

Housman made his name as an artist, illustrating Christina

Rossetti's *Goblin Market*, as well as a story written by his favourite sister, Clemence: *The Were-Wolf*, in which he depicted a sinewy, elegantly lupine man, in the fantastical manner of George MacDonald's stories. But he also became a well known writer and poet; when his collection of poems, *Green Arras*, appeared in 1896, they received more acclaim than his older brother's *A Shropshire Lad*, published that same year – and displayed 'introspective glimpses of his own soul of a disturbing oddity'.

Housman wrote his own fairy tales, as well as publishing a selection of Blake's writings, a series of playlets based on the life of St Francis (a similar series about Queen Victoria was initially refused a dramatic licence by the censor because of its subject matter), and a 'free rendering' of a conversation between himself, Oscar Wilde and Robbie Ross during the writer's exile in Paris. He also contributed radical tracts to the Women's Freedom League on 'The Immoral Effects of Ignorance in Sex Relations', and was a fervent supporter of the suffragettes, joining the male wing of the extremist Women's Social and Political Union. In June 1909 he was at the centre of a violent disturbance in the House of Commons' lobby, and Clemence would be imprisoned for refusing to pay her taxes as a protest. But Housman was equally fascinated by religion, and in *The Unexpected Years*, he describes how, as a child, his imagination was fed by illustrated papers, especially *The Graphic*; and how, in its pages – next to images of Queen Victoria, and the siege of Paris – he saw 'something quite small and domestic – the eviction of Mrs Girling, and her followers . . .' From that moment, he seems to have been haunted by Mary Ann: in 1886, he dreamt he had 'heard somebody say: "Mrs Girling is dead". And the next day her death was in the papers'.

A few years later, Housman was contributing to the *Universal Review*, a literary magazine published by the flamboyant editor, Harry Quilter. In its edition for 15 October 1889, the *Review* ran a long poem by George Meredith, the eminent novelist and poet.

Friend of the Pre-Raphaelites, Meredith had lived with Rossetti and Swinburne at 16 Cheyne Walk; Wilde described him as 'a prose Browning'. 'Jump-to-Glory Jane' was clearly inspired by Mary Ann and the Girlingites; Meredith admitted as much in a letter to Quilter about its verses: 'Yes, they are a Satire, but one of the pictures of our England as well. Remember Mrs Girling and her following, and the sensations of Jane with her blood at the spin with activity, warranted her feeling of exaltation. An English middle-class Blavitsky [sic] maniac would also be instructive, though less pathetic than poor Jane'. The poem was thus a sardonic comment on religious utopianism, as well as a literary reflection of intellectual attitudes to the strange narrative of Mary Ann's life. 'Its motive ... was the Mrs Girling episode ...' Quilter wrote. 'The Janeites are persecuted, laughed at, called mad after the old fashion, and they too take up their parable against the powers that be, personified here by the squire and bishop, until their founder and leader dies by the roadside, and – the rest is silence.'

A revelation came on Jane,
The widow of a labouring swain:
And first her body trembled sharp,
Then all the woman was a harp
With winds along the strings; she heard,
Though there was neither tone nor word.

In 1892, somewhat to Meredith's annoyance, Quilter took advantage of serial rights to republish 'Jump-to-Glory Jane' as a separate edition, and commissioned Housman to illustrate it. 'As I drew my pictures of "Jumping Jane" I had Mrs Girling in mind,' wrote Housman. His illustrations, which would make him famous, evoke Burne-Jones and Rossetti, as well as the direct influence of Charles Ricketts, whom he knew as a friend, and through whom he met Wilde. In graphic, elegant lines, 'Jane' is depicted as a tall, thin figure in a bonnet and shroud-like shawl and dress, remaining ramrod-straight as she leaps and inspires others to do so; an image which is as much Brothers Grimm as it is social satire.

"Her first was Winny Earnes, a kind
Of woman not to dance inclined."

In his poem, Meredith acknowledges the influence of Shakerism on Jane's leaping – 'Of late: she had a mania/For mad folk in America' – as well as the immortal tenets of Girlingism:

A good knee's height, they say, she sprang;
Her arms and feet like those who hang:
As if afire the body sped,
And neither pair contributed.
She jumped in silence: she was thought
A corpse to resurrection caught.

And as Jane's rural mission grows apace,

> It really seemed on certain days,
> When they bobbed up their Lord to praise,
> And bobbing up they caught the glance
> Of light, our secret is to dance,
> And hold the tongue from hindering peace;
> To dance out preacher and police.

But perhaps the strangest scene is that in which Jane and her jumpers confront the bishop in a tent; it might be another episode from Hardy – only here peopled with vaguely disturbing figures, surreally suspended in a bizarre confrontation with authority.

The poem concludes with Jane's demise in a shack, rendered by

"In Apron suit the Bishop stood,
The crowding people kindly viewed,
A gaunt grey woman he saw rise
On air, . . ."

Housman in a scene which echoes Diamond's death bed in *At the Back of the North Wind*:

Her end was beautiful: one sigh.
She jumped a foot when it was nigh.
A lily in a linen clout
She looked when they had laid her out.
It is a lily-light she bears
For England up the ladder-stairs.

"Her end was beautiful :—"

– while her spirit departs her body as a dove, like one of the Girlingites' mystical pet birds; or perhaps an image from Blake's *The Marriage of Heaven and Hell.*

Twelve Girlingites now lay in Hordle churchyard, where one visitor was moved to emotion; his account resembled a tribute to a military campaign, as though this row of grassy humps had some relationship to the wars which would add many more anonymous graves to the world: 'Some have died in the flower of their youth, unable to endure the hardships of camp life; others in mature age, and now, with the prophetess herself, are quietly waiting for that Second Coming they so fondly hoped to have seen with mortal eyes.' Resting under their verdant crosses, the Children of God had no need of permanent commemoration, for soon the churchyard would resemble a Stanley Spencer resurrection as 'all the children celestial and terrestrial' emerged to face the Final Judgement.

Mary Ann's power was too strong to be extinguished by death; and as her life had differing versions, so her demise produced alternative endings. Shortly after her death, the biographer of her rival, the Mother, claimed that 'This unconscious imitator of the Truth has recently passed into the world beyond. Her spirit remained in trance after death two days, and on awaking she beheld the angel Gabriel standing at her side, who, bidding her arise, brought her into the presence of the Divine Mother-Queen, whom she had ignorantly personated.' This final outrage offended even William Oxley: 'That is, Mother Girling – who at least was not ashamed of her name and her personal work and mission while proclaiming the same to the world – is made to be guided by no less than the Archangel Gabriel! to a woman whom nobody knows, except the "very few" to whom she had revealed herself, and who is said to be living now upon the earth. Seeing that Mrs Girling was first in the field, to make her an "imitator" of the later woman, is only in keeping with the rest of this "stupendous" falsity!'

Oxley's own account of Mary Ann appeared in 1889, complete with an engraving made from her photograph – a realistic contrast to Housman's rather more idealized depictions. Later, she was dignified with an entry, written by George Clement Boase (who sought 'information from Brother H. Osborne of Tiptoe, Hordle'), in the *Dictionary of National Biography*. Mary Ann also merited a mention in the *National Encyclopedia* – albeit appended to the end of an entry on the Shakers, as if, even in death, she could not escape comparisons with the American sect. This brief postscript noted that 'the only wealthy member having been transferred to a lunatic asylum, the "family" got into debt and were ejected . . . They indulged much in dancing, and lived together huddled in a hovel [and] finally dispersed after the death of their "mother," Mrs Girling . . . in 1886.' Some reports even claimed that several Girlingites – among them, perhaps, James Haase – went to America, with the suggestion that they joined Shaker families there.

Whatever mark Mary Ann may have left on posterity, her immediate legacy was debt. She died leaving liabilities amounting to £535. Herbert's appeal gained £12.16s for the sect; their property was valued at £50. By late October 1886, there were just seven members left in Tiptoe. Henry Osborne had taken out a lease on their field as a kind of Girlingite almshouse, 'providing a home for those elderly members who have no friends to go to; he wants everything to be sold to settle their debts, then intends to start anew in life'. He and his wife would remain there, still practising Girlingism, before acquiring land of their own in Ashley. But soon these villages would become suburbs of New Milton, the town spawned by the railway line that now rumbled under Vaggs Lane, and where, just across the lane and one month after Mary Ann's death, a new church was erected to serve the inhabitants of Tiptoe. This place of worship had been imported from Netley Abbey: constructed from pre-formed tin and painted green as if to camouflage it in the forest, it was now home to former Girlingites who had returned to the orthodox faith. Rehabilitated like modern cult-survivors into the 'real' world, they may have looked back with embarrassment at that extraordinary episode in their lives.

Yet many had stayed in Tiptoe, as if to keep their old community spirit alive, living in small cottages with tin roofs, or sharing larger houses, and returning to the world of trade and, presumably, ordinary family relationships. Cornelius and Elizabeth Mary Chase – and her widowed mother, Emma Robinson – lived at Rose Cottage, where Cornelius carried on his carpenting and wheel-wrighting business. Close by were Henry and Eliza Osborne, and their Girlingite friend, John Manuel (who died in 1894), Henry's occupation shifting from farm labourer back to bootmaking; his brother Isaac lived as his neighbour, working as a gardener. Thomas Saunders, gardener, lived with his wife Sarah, née Cooper, and her sister Mary, in Crabbs Lane (where the two women worked as laundresses); George Frampton, who had served his sentence in Winchester prison, would live to the good age of eighty-six; and Charlotte Knight, who made a living by hawking goods, lived with her daughter Hannah and grand-daughter Lilly (whose surname also being Knight seems to indicate her illegitimacy).

Others escaped Hampshire entirely; among them, William Girling, now thirty years old. Soon after Mary Ann's death, William returned to Ipswich, where his father's business as a general dealer (in tools and scrap metal) had prospered, and from where he left England, yet still within the bounds of Empire. He sailed for Jamaica – possibly accompanied by George, who may have visited the island during his sea-faring days – and landed at Alligator Pond, 'a Port of Entry for English and foreign goods'. From there he moved twelve miles inland to Newport, Manchester County, where he worked in a hardware store in a tin-roofed shack initially as an indentured labourer. And there he abandoned his mother's precepts, marrying Martha Todd, the daughter of Thomas and sister of James, father of Ellen Benham's illegitimate son. Joining him there in 1891, she would run her own shop selling cakes and fancy goods.

The couple befriended the local priest, Reverend Wilde, and William played the parish organ at the Bethabra Moravian church, although according to his descendants, he had given up the religious life. One photograph, now torn and cracked, survives, showing William and Martha sitting on their porch, with their teenaged son William Stanton – named after his grandfather – between them. His father is now bearded, with neat grey hair, and still handsome; his mother, Martha, has less refined features, and is tanned by the Caribbean sun; William Stanton, in his collar and tie and parted hair, appears to have inherited his grandmother's wide, terse mouth. The family were visited on a number of occasions by George Girling, who made the trip across the Atlantic with supplies such as barrels of cement and bags of rice and flour, all hauled inland on mule-drawn drays. William died in 1938, a year after Martha; they were buried side-by-side in the tropical churchyard at Newport. In 1975, their grand-daughter moved to the Cayman Islands, where she still lives, 6,000 miles from Mary Ann Girling's attempt at utopia.

For Mary Ann's daughter, however, there was a sadder ending. Mary Jane, who had married her printer husband, William Bailey, in October 1875, had watched him die of tuberculosis a year later. She had since moved in with her father at York Road in Ipswich where, in 1881, she gave birth to a daughter, Victoria, sired by a station master, William Browne, who was boarding with the family; there is no evidence that he married Mary Jane, or that he remained at York Road. Later, Mary Jane moved to Felixstowe, where Victoria, who never married, taught at a private school. In 1931, at the age of forty-nine, Victoria committed suicide by putting her head in a gas oven. The death certificate read, 'coal gas poisoning caused by the deceased while in an unsound state of mind'. There was no explanation for her fatal disturbance; and she was joined in the same Felixstowe grave by her mother, nine years later.

In 1886, the year in which Mary Ann died, Auberon Herbert moved further into the forest, to Old House at Burley, where he employed the Girlingite carpenter, Cornelius Chase, and his wife, Lizzie, and where new rumours emerged that Shakerism was about to resume in the depths of the woods. In fact, the aristocrat's utopian ambitions were even more remarkable than Mary Ann's.

Among the letters Herbert received during his defence of the Girlingites was one from a writer in Brighton who sympathised with him 'respecting the unjust treatment of the Shaker Mother', but who wanted to draw Herbert's attention 'to the fact that the Oxford Union had decided by 88 affirmative votes to admit Spiritualist newspapers into its reading room', and offered to introduce him to 'such proof positive of spirit communication that no room should be left . . . for doubt or hesitation'. Like Andrew Peterson, Herbert also had embarked on his own journey to the other world. He undertook investigations with Edward Clissold, summoning 'strange phenomena' in the seclusion of Yeatton House – set back from the road as it was, its bay windows hidden behind holm oaks and rhododendron – and discovered his own mesmeric influence over subjects, including one former Girlingite. Soon he was joining the Cowpers at seances given by Mrs Guppy, a medium who specialised in apporting scented flowers and fruit, complete with dew drops.

As for so many others, his was a personal quest. In April 1882, the Herberts' young son Rolf died, aged ten years. Florence Herbert 'never recovered from the loss', as Georgiana would write, for all the consolations of their other children, Auberon, Clair and Nan. To help Florence recuperate, the family holidayed in Italy with the Cowpers and the MacDonalds, but on her return to England, Florence was told that she had three weeks to live. In Georgiana's dark turn of mind, her niece's death resembled Burne-Jones' *Psyche* 'falling over the cliff, caught in the arms of Love'. Yet this second tragedy was to be compounded by a third, in the most upsetting circumstances imaginable. In January 1893, Clair, the Herberts' eighteen-year-old daughter, committed suicide, and in Auberon's letter to Georgiana, terse with emotion, the reason became clear:

> My dear Aunt Jennie –
> She shot herself in an act of love & renunciation – thinking that her love for Osman – was dividing the family.
> Things had gone rather wrong in the holidays – & that day I blamed her for using her influence with him so that we were splitting into two parties.
> Had I only spoken kindly it would not have happened; but I spoke harshly.
> I will send you tomorrow what she wrote.

For Herbert, knowledge of the soul's survival now seemed more necessary than ever; and as he moved towards new notions of spirituality, his politics also became more radical. In 1885, he published *The Right and Wrong of Compulsion by the State*. Reviewing it, Benjamin Tucker wrote, 'I know no more inspiring spectacle in England than that of this man of exceptionally high social position doing battle almost single-handed with the giant monster, government . . . Its only parallel at the present day is to be found in the splendid attitude of Mr Ruskin, whose earnest eloquence on behalf of economic equity rivals Mr Herbert's in behalf of individual liberty.' That year, Herbert established his Ruskinian 'Small Farm and Labourers' Land Company', its communitarian ideals prefiguring those of William Morris (whose own *News from Nowhere* would be published in 1890, and with whom Herbert would engage in utopian discussions).

The nineteenth-century search for spiritual meaning seemed to pick up speed with its *fin de siècle*. When Herbert published articles on spiritualism in the *Pall Mall Gazette*, Annie Besant (the campaigning socialist who, on Madame Blavatsky's death in 1891, had taken up the Theosophic cause) told him: 'I have had a lot of queer results, experimenting *without* "a medium", and am sure that there is at work some force we do not yet understand. *What* it is, I am at present quite unable to judge,' she said, telling him to study Theosophy: 'It *may* throw light on the darkness.' Herbert appeared to be drifting towards the limits of belief, living in seclusion at Old House in the woods east of Ringwood, an area still remote, even today. According to legend, the site was squatted by a charcoal-burner named Squa, who lived there as a hermit. In 1886, Herbert had acquired the land and built what his wife called a hut, adding 'a bed-sitting room, and then, bit by bit, as the humour took him . . . a room here or a room there until the crazy pile was completed . . .' The result was an arboreal version of Brantwood, complete with towers and look-outs.

Herbert detested fires, and rather than pollute the atmosphere, he sat in his overcoat to keep warm – although, ironically, he was forced to keep Squa's fireplace in his library, in order to retain his rights. Like the now dispersed Girlingites – two of whom he employed – or some 1960s hippie, this aristocrat, whose family lived in baronial splendour at Highclere, was in effect a forest squatter, 'for the most part a recluse, yet often enough as a hospitable host to a few close friends of advanced political and sociological thought'. Among these was Ernest Westlake, with whom Herbert discussed the establishment of a Hampshire Psychical Society, and who devised an instrument for the detection of ghosts. The two men would roam the forest in search of pre-historic stone tools; or Herbert would take one of his caravans to the nearest high point of land and live there alone. He had become a shadowy, Whitmanesque figure, greeting guests such as Sir Edward Grey with 'perfect good manners' and the query, 'And now what would you like to do? – we are reading' (an invitation which had not a little in common with Grey's future step-son, Stephen Tennant, who would retreat into his own aestheticism in nearby Wiltshire). Surrounded by his books, papers and flints which washed over every shelf and surface like an archaeological tide, Herbert slept in a different room each night. He also extended Old House upwards, with an observatory tower painted red, each of its three storeys containing a bed, as though, should the effort of ascent grow too much for the aristocrat or his visitors, they might take a rest before continuing their climb.

Yet in his forest retreat, Auberon Herbert's thoughts turned to anarchy. Anarchist bombs were exploding all over Europe and America in a wave of international terrorism at a time of depression and unrest. In 1887, even as it announced the dispersal of the New Forest's religious communists, *The Times* reported that four anarchists had been hanged in Chicago, while in Britain a second year of unemployment riots saw Marxists mixing with striking spiritualist miners. Herbert's essay, 'The Ethics of Dynamite', made clear his 'detestation of the use of dynamite by Anarchist assassins' ('We have morally made the dynamiter; we must not morally unmake him'). His sympathy lay with 'the small group of peaceable Individualist-Anarchists who are devoted to liberty and strong believers in property', rather than 'a universal system to be forced on the world by the new methods of chemical evangelism'.

This bicycling aristocrat had become a kind of prophet. In another lengthy missive to *The Times* headed 'How the British Army Captured the New Forest', Herbert described how he had been disturbed by military manoeuvres that summer. The sight of his beloved forest swarming with troops and munitions 'as in a splendid diorama' prompted him to wonder, 'Shall we wake tomorrow and find ourselves vowing eternal friendship with

C. BROWN'S SERIES. The Hon. Auberon Herbert and Old House, Berrywood, Ringwood.

Russia, or with Germany . . . or Japan, or the United States?' He believed it better 'if the big ship sailed steadily on her perilous way alone . . . as the one hope of good in this quarrelsome world of ours'. But a new century would put paid to such hopes, as other troops would move through other forests, in pursuit of more violent dreams.

Auberon Herbert died aged sixty-eight on 5 November 1906, leaving an estate valued at £19,655 17s 6d, and an international reputation as 'one of the most important and articulate advocates of liberty'. But shortly after his death, new and strange reports began to emerge from Old House, and the *Telegraph* sent a special correspondent to investigate. 'In the heart of the New Forest . . . accessible only by means of a cutting through the purple heather and green fernery', he found 'a pile of crazy buildings, entirely devoid of architectural design or even of architectural "sanity"'. To the reporter they resembled 'a caravanserai in the wilderness which has been suddenly deserted by some grotesque circus party; the home, until the forest menaced them, of clown and columbine and pantaloon'.

The house itself appeared to have been assembled, 'apartment after apartment, after the fashion of the "elastic" bookshelves which one sees advertised'. This was 'the home of a prophet . . . that great-hearted, liberty-loving, but eccentric gentleman, the Hon. Auberon Herbert . . . It was in the forest that he made his home after the publication of "A Politician in Trouble About his Soul", that he endeavoured to found a colony of Shakers, and when Mrs Annie Besant attracted the fashion of Bournemouth . . . to her lecture on "Theosophy", it was the Hon. Auberon Herbert who presided.' Surrounded by caravans on rusty trestles, and odd outbuildings with crumbling walls, the interior of the house had been left untouched. Every table and shelf was laden with 'ordinary, valueless pieces of flint, taken from the gravel pits to be found in the forest . . . arranged on the expensive porcelain among prodigious tomes and even under glass-cases just as if they were so many precious gems. Books and flints, flints and books. They have invaded every room in the house, including the music-room, the bed-rooms, and the observation tower'. From there the visitor could 'look over the multitudinous arms of the forest, or, with a turn, down to the sea where the Isle of Wight lies glittering like an emerald placed on a silver dish', while Herbert himself lay 'beneath the shadow of the crazy house, within a little clearing surrounded by tall elms and poplars', not unlike Mary Ann's own resting place.

Part museum, part junk yard, this was to be the site for a new utopian commune. In 1901, Nan Herbert, Auberon's twenty-seven-year-old daughter – 'the most independent, fearless creature in the world . . . accustomed to rough it as her father . . . roughed it before she was born' – had joined the 'Purple Lotus Mother' of Theosophy, Katherine Tingley, at her commune at Point Loma, a suburb of San Diego. Nan's primary appeal to the sect was her private income, and having served as the 'directress' of a Theosophic establishment in Santiago, she now offered them Old House. In 1907, she and Tingley travelled to England, along with a Mrs Hanson, who told the press of Point Loma's sub-tropical paradise: 'The grounds are entered through an Egyptian gateway . . . The buildings are some fifty in number. There is an Aryan temple with amethyst dome; a homestead with a green dome; and there are landscapes adorned with fruits and flowers all round.'

This five-hundred acre compound, which resembled 'a chapter from the Arabian Nights', had been established in the wake of the fantastical African utopia proposed by the book *Caesar's Column*, which had sold thousands of copies in America in the 1890s, and followed the precedent of experiments such as the Ruskin Commonwealth in Tennessee, and spiritualist communes attracted by California's climate. Like the Shakers and the Girlingites, the sect insisted on the separation of children from their parents. The 'little Theosophists' rose at dawn for a morning bath and drill – 'the girls are dressed in white, the boys in white blouse and dark blue trousers' – and breakfasted to the sound of music. Older groups then took lessons while the younger ones rode in carts drawn by Shetland ponies in this Lilliputian utopia.

The time seemed right for such ideas. A few miles from Old House, Pamela Tennant, devotee and neighbour of the spiritualist Sir Oliver Lodge, drove round the countryside with her children in a gypsy caravan, telling her son Stephen to listen to the flowers and run with the breeze; while to the south at Parkstone, the bohemian Augustus John, inspired by Fourier, set up his caravan commune, mostly stocked with his own illegitimate children. Off the coast on Brownsea Island, Baden Powell drilled his scouts; while Westlake's Woodcraft Folk camped in the forest, close to Fordingbridge.

Meanwhile, the same edition of the *Illustrated London News* which published photographs of Point Loma devoted pages to 'Dr Baraduc's Extraordinary Pictures – a Paris Nerve-Specialist Photographs Prayers', a sequence of dark explosions of ether. 'A Cataract of Curative Force at Lourdes During A Miracle' and 'A Strange Apparition from the Spirit World' resembled a cross between Odilon Redon's symbolist aliens and the Cottingley Fairies championed by Conan Doyle and the Theosophists. There was also an even more unbelievable scene: 'The Coming Trafalgar of the Air', an 'artist's forecast' of an aerial fight between flying battleships. Next to these images, the Theosophists' plans for the New Forest seemed almost practical – and as ambitious as Ruskin's Guild of St George, which also insisted on aesthetic education. (Indeed, three decades later the Theosophists would summon their own 'mighty Angel' of St George to assume 'the armour of light' and, like Arthur rising from Avalon, or Rufus from his grave, defend the country from the 'encroaching dark clouds' of Nazi invasion, exhorting their countrymen to imagine 'a great revolving pillar of white light' at the heart of England 'continually sending its vital and purifying rays out into the world'; an act of psychic defence which bore its own relationship to the Hampshire witches who would send their 'cone of light' over the Channel). But in 1907, the prospect of Arabian cupolas rising over English oaks proved impossible to comprehend.

'You contemplate the creation of some such place in the New Forest?' asked the man from the *Telegraph*, barely able to disguise his incredulity.

'Why, yes', said Mrs Hanson, 'that is, I think, Madame Tingley's intention. We are going down into Hampshire in a few days to look round and make arrangements.'

However, on revisiting Old House, Madame Tingley declared it would not do: 'Although it was splendidly located, and had a historical name, it was unhealthy,' she said. 'But I never told that to Nan; for she would not have it. The area was very small; and it was built right in a basin, in the midst of the forest; and the trees were so heavy that rarely could the sun get in through them to the ground, and there was mould and dampness all the year round.'

Instead, these impenetrable environs became a 'summer vacation spot for poor children; by now a characteristic way for the Utopian to become practical'. The spirit of Eden relied, more than ever, on the invested hope of infants.

Ten years later, on 3 November 1916, Nan's brother Auberon, now a captain in the Royal Flying Corps, flew his aeroplane over no-man's-land and its bomb-blasted trees and mud, and never returned. Aged forty, he was the third of his father's four children to die young. England's brief idyll was overturned, and spiritualism now acquired a graver meaning for bereaved parents such as Arthur Conan Doyle (himself a sometime forest resident at

Minstead, where he would be buried), Rudyard Kipling, and Pamela Tennant, whose eldest son, Bim, also died that year on the Somme. Her gypsy caravan lay empty, as she conducted bizarre 'book tests' at Wilsford with Mrs Leonard, the latest in a long line of mediums who ministered to the aristocracy.

Meanwhile, the forest was experiencing its own holocaust. Where twenty years earlier Auberon Herbert had watched army manoeuvres like boys' war games, a voracious Armageddon now sucked up every resource as the woods became a tree factory to satisfy the war's demand for duckboards and trench walls, rifle stocks and gun emplacements, packing cases and carriage wheels. The silent forest became an extension of the cacophonous conflict. Shouldering out glossy beeches and placid oaks, serried ranks of foreign pine were harvested like some gigantic crop, by imported European labour, their presence still marked by the archaeological

THE STAG HOTEL
IF LYNDHURST HAD BEEN IN BELGIUM !—

remains of the Portuguese Fireplace. One propagandist artist envisioned Lyndhurst's high street under attack from a Zeppelin, as if Lunardi's balloon had been recast as an evil flying fiery whale, discharging its destruction in a forest apocalypse and incinerating the Pre-Raphaelite interiors of its capital church.

And at Brockenhurst, where Indian troops camped in the woods, rows of war graves echoed Hordle's Girlingite interments, while the genteel Balmer Lawn Hotel became a military hospital where shell-shocked officers displayed the quivering symptoms of their end time – just as their nostrum was hypnotherapy, propounded by the anatomist of hysteria, Sigmund Freud. The rational and the irrational, the conscious and the unconscious blurred in this mayhem, and spiritualism overtook Christianity, as a poem published in *Medium and Daybreak* had presaged in 1875, eight years before Nietzsche.

> Dead, dead, stone dead! your Christianism is dead!
> O blind, blind mortals of degenerate days,
> Were ye not blind as moles are in the blaze
> Of sunlight, ye would see that it was dead!

Only now it really was a religion of the dead, a more potent solace to widows and orphans than the grey empty tombs cut from Portland's quarries.

And this was the world which Ruskin had prophesied: 'So far as the existing evidence, I say, of former literature can be interpreted, the storm-cloud – or more accurately plague-cloud, for it is not always stormy – which I am about to describe to you, never was seen but by now living, or *lately* living eyes.' It was a phenomenon he had first diagnosed at Matlock in that fateful year of 1871; his 'Storm-Cloud of the Nineteenth-Century' was the antithesis to the innocent cloud of childhood in which Ruskin had watched Rose grow. This was a mass 'made of dead men's souls'; and in his vision of 'blanched sun . . . blighted grass . . . blinded man', Ruskin saw the moral darkness of the modern world personified in the fight between St George, the angelic knight, and the dragon, a fire-spitting serpent out of Revelations, and in the monsters he drew in his pocket-books.

But it was a battle long since lost. 'I have been thinking', Ruskin had written to Georgiana in 1874, '. . . why you couldn't believe in Utopia.' William Cowper had resigned as 'purse bearer' of his Guild, unable to take 'the sword & shield of St George as crusaders against the spirit of the 19th century – Oh why did you make it impossible for us', he protested, '. . . by ordering St George to fight against interest in Capital, rent for the use of our land & against all machinery except pens & paper & kitchen utensils. Why did you give us away by trying to set up again on the wall the Humpty Dumpty of feudality, Divine right of Squires & Captains of Industry – I believe that God governs the world . . . by allowing men to fail . . .'

Ruskin had been unable to accept that reality. The sadness in his eyes had grown more intense, burnt out with memories, as if what he had witnessed was too distressing even to express in one of his perfectly-formed sentences; as if he had seen what was to come, and it gave him as much pain as his own past. At Brantwood, the engine-

room of his creation, he looked out over the slate-peat waters fed by the cataracts which coursed the fells like veins of white marble. Here, in his turret, he was caught in an anchorite's cell, unable to breech the barrier between man and nature and the land of which he yearned to be a part and which he documented so obsessively. In the summer of 1878 he had stood in that lucent little ease, and in an instant of revelation, a new madness came upon him.

It was another kind of epiphany. Ruskin saw Rose coming towards him in a white dress, with the Maid of Orleans as attendant and William Cowper as a witness; he even put his hand in the fire to see how Joan of Arc felt. On the night of 22 February 1878 his mind gave way. Like Shelley, he feared the foul fiend was coming for him, and he threw off all his clothes in the chill night. Unable to sleep, he walked up and down, like Ann Lee, 'in a state of great agitation, entirely resolute as to the approaching struggle, . . . with perfect knowledge of the real things in the room, while yet I saw others that were not there'. The next morning he was found naked and deranged. Brantwood became an asylum; restrained by burly male nurses and force-fed, Ruskin was brought to the brink of human experience, calling for 'Rosie-Posie' and crying, 'Everything white! Everything black!' as if all England were engulfed in his nightmare.

When he recovered his senses, Ruskin left his bedroom, taking with him his favourite Turners. He would never sleep in that room again, withdrawing to a smaller room as if to ward off further attacks, the solid wooden bed placed close by the wall as though for security. He seemed to be regressing into childhood. He would row out to the middle of the lake, wearing his wide-awake hat, his dog Bramble beside him, and lie at the bottom of the boat, watching the clouds. Or he would stand at the water's edge, playing his rock harmonicon, created from the stones of the fells, as if to summon up ancient forces in the struggle for nature and man's soul in this voracious despoiling age. He believed that he might lie in the lake itself for salvation, as if its sublime beauty – or some Arthurian spirit – would restore his sanity; but as his grey beard grew longer and his blue eyes sadder, he could only lie in bed, watching the demons dance on his bedpost.

Arthur Severn, R.I. H. S. Uhlrich

Ruskin's Bedroom

And yet he was able to dictate his final, defiant text, *Praeterita: Outlines of Scenes and Thoughts Perhaps Worthy of Memory In My Past Life*, before words became truly useless –

> Some wise, and prettily mannered, people have told me I shouldn't say anything about Rosie at all. But I am too old now to take advice, and I won't have this following letter – the first she ever wrote me – moulder away, when I can read it no more, lost to all loving hearts. 'Nice, *Monday, March 18th*. Dearest Crumpet, – I am so sorry – I couldn't write before, there wasn't one bit of time – I am so sorry you were

> dis$_{s}$ap^{p}ointed . . . So you thought of us, dear St Crumpet, & we too thought so much of you . . .'

– and bequeathed his last memory, of walking in Italy as

> the fireflies among the scented thickets shone fitfully in the still undarkened air. *How* they shone! moving like fine-broken starlight through the purple leaves. How they shone! through the sunset that faded into thunderous night . . . and the fireflies everywhere in the sky and cloud rising and falling, mixed with the lightning, and more intense than the stars.
>
> Brantwood
> *18th June, 1889*

It was a plaintive cry, uttered in an innocent ecstasy of lost love and beauty.

His last letter to Georgiana came from a dreary seaside resort in Kent, where he had exiled himself after another attack.

> During this last year, I have felt more and more bitterly every hour, – how I have failed to you both – Alas to whom have I *not* failed? – but to you, who have loved & given and forgiven so much – that I should become at long last – only sorrow – Oh me –
> I cannot go on. Perhaps Joanie can add more cheerful word.
> Your poor Dovie
> She will write later.

Shortly afterwards, Ruskin was brought back to Brantwood, where he died on 20 January 1900, seeing in the new century, or seeing out the old. He was buried in Coniston village, 'sunk to rest', in Frederic Myers' words, in 'the bracken and bilberries of the Lake-land which he loved' (and where, a year later, Myers too would be interred). He lay under a Celtic cross engraved with a Hindu swastika and surmounted by St George embattled with the dragon. And as this stone stood in the lakeside churchyard, surrounded by yews and backed by the fells, their hues changing subtly in the cycle of seasons he had watched from his window, Ruskin's ambitions lived on. His life was predicated on art and

faith, on memory and loss, but his legacy was felt in fair rents and free education, in the charitable Guild of St George and its eccentric museum in Sheffield, filled with his geological specimens and exquisite watercolours. Yet even now, one spirit still haunted all his dreams: the ten-year-old girl whom he had met one afternoon in a Mayfair drawing room, and who remained an angel to him.

At Broadlands, spiritualist investigations had come to an end with William's death in 1888. In old age, Lord Mount-Temple, as he had become, had assumed the appearance of a biblical scribe, albeit one with a fur-lined coat, attended by earthly angels. Nursed by Waggie, his homeopathic clairvoyant, as he lay dying, 'smiles flickered over his face, and the listeners caught broken words and broken sentences – "And Jesus was there – Jenny, Jenny – I saw Jesus –"'.

The Cowpers' eccentricities would also inspire fiction. In 1929, John Betjeman would write a gothic story whose protagonist goes in search of Lord Mount Prospect, a member of the Ember Day Bryanites, 'an obscure sect . . . founded by William Bryan, a tailor of Paternoster Row, London', who believed 'in a bodily resurrection and . . . that the sun is four miles from the earth'. The narrator pursues Lord Mount Prospect to his estate in a far-flung corner of Ireland, so remote that a company asked to deliver a stuffed rhinoceros to the address gives up without finding it. But the house is a pink stucco ruin of 'curious Gothic pinnacles', an image from a John Piper painting, with its collapsed dome resembling 'a diseased onion . . . This was a romantic and poetical finale to a beautiful story. Lord Mount Prospect did not exist. He had been caught up in a bodily resurrection to sit for ever with other Ember Day Bryanites.'

In reality, with William's death Broadlands had passed to his nephew, the Right Hon. Evelyn Ashley, Under-Secretary of State for the Colonies from 1882 to 1885, and in the process, the estate reverted to more reactionary tastes: its later master, Ashley's son, Baron MountTemple, Minister for Transport in the late 1920s, was founder of the Anti-Socialist & Anti-Communist Union and the Anglo-German Fellowship, an aristocratic organisation which held Hitler in high regard. Georgiana, meanwhile, was forced to leave Broadlands, retiring to Babbacombe Cliff, a rambling house on the south Devon coast which the Cowpers had built in 1878, some said to Ruskin's designs.

Perched on the cliffs in what is now a suburb of Torquay, Babbacombe certainly had the air of Ruskin's Coniston retreat. This 'strange, charming house' was 'full of surprises and curious rooms' – named after the flowers on their Morris wallpapers – 'with suggestions of Rossetti at every turn'. 'Wonderland', Georgiana's boudoir, named after Lewis Carroll's fantasy, had its own oriel overlooking Lyme Bay. Hung with Pre-Raphaelite paintings and decorated with medieval motifs, this chamber of meditation was charged with a particular resonance – not least because in 1892 its mistress had rented it to Oscar Wilde, Ruskin's Oxford disciple and erstwhile road-builder. Here Wilde would write under the gaze of *Beata Beatrix*; and just as Rossetti's painting was imbued with symbolist meaning, so it was witness to the *fin de siècle's* most perfervid text: *Salome*, a foreboding study of unholy lust, conducted in an anteroom of the apocalypse.

Constance, Oscar's wife, was a distant cousin of Lady Mount-Temple, but they were so close that she addressed Georgiana as 'My darling Mother'. They often discussed belief: 'Mr Gurney says that the early Christians did not all have their goods in common and that the scheme of Socialism is a wrong one. But I am quite sure that the way we live now is wrong – not the way you live darling, but then there are very few people like you in the world . . . your most loving Bambina.' Like her husband, who consulted chiromancers and Mrs Robinson, 'the Sibyl of Mortimer Street', Constance was fascinated by the occult: she was a member of the Society for Psychical Research and delved into thought transference and spirit photography. She also attended meetings of the Theosophical Society, and in 1888 was initiated into the Order of the Golden Dawn, wearing a black tunic. And when Georgiana lent her books by T. L. Harris and Laurence Oliphant, Constance told her aunt, 'I wonder that you did not become one of Mr Harris's converts and join the community; I believe I should have done!'

But Constance also confided details of her emotional life: 'I don't believe that anyone can be happy unless they marry for love,' she wrote from Tite Street, Chelsea; then from a sequence of rented country houses in Norfolk – 'The only thing I fear is that Oscar will get bored to death, but we have heaps of room and can ask people down to cheer him up'; from Surrey – 'Oscar is, I believe, up in London, and returns to Goring to-morrow . . .'; and Brighton – '. . . I very much wish that Oscar had not taken the Cottage on the Thames for a year. Things are dreadfully involved for me just now . . .' Through these letters Georgiana was witness to the pain of the Wildes' disintegrating marriage, just as she had been privvy to the disastrous affair between Ruskin and Rose La Touche.

Constance often stayed at Babbacombe, 'a place she so much loves, and where so much love has been given her', as Oscar wrote. In the winter of 1892–3, Georgiana insisted on leasing the house to the couple; perhaps, as with Ruskin and Rose, she hoped to effect a reconciliation. 'With the children of the gods one dare not argue,' Oscar wrote from the Royal Bath Hotel, Bournemouth, '. . . your lovely house will be treasured and watched over by us, and the spirit of the *châtelaine* will preside over all things.' At Babbacombe, Oscar spent his days working in Wonderland, but in the evening he itched for metropolitan hedonism, and wrote to Robbie Ross, asking, 'Are there beautiful people in London? Here there are none; everyone is so unfinished. When are you coming down?' And it was from Babbacombe that Wilde wrote the letter which would ultimately send him to Reading jail. 'My Own Boy', he told Bosie,

> Your sonnet is quite lovely, and it is a marvel that those red rose-lips of yours should have been made no less for music of song than for madness of kisses. Your slim gilt soul walks between passion and poetry . . . when do you go to Salisbury? Do go there to cool your hands in the grey twilight of Gothic things, and come here whenever you like. It is a lovely place – it only lacks you . . . Always, with undying love, yours OSCAR.

Just as *Salome* was an allegory of Wilde's fated affair with the young lord, so from Wonderland there issued another text of decadent seduction. The letter, which was used to blackmail Wilde and would be read out in the Old Bailey at his trial, summoned Douglas, who arrived – complete with innumerable trunks, a fox terrier and a scarlet morocco dispatch case ('a gorgeous and beautiful gift from Oscar') – after Constance had left for Italy. Wilde told Georgiana that her house 'has become a kind of college or school, for Cyril [his son] studies French in the nursery, and I write my play in Wonderland, and in the drawing-room Lord Alfred Douglas – one of Lady Queensberry's sons – studies Plato ... Constance seems very happy in Florence. No doubt you hear from her.' To another, Oscar boasted that he had 'succeeded in combining the advantages of a public school with those of a private lunatic asylum, which, as you know, was my aim. Bosie is very gilt-haired and I have bound *Salome* in purple to suit him. That tragic daughter of passion appeared on Thursday last, and is now dancing for the head of the English public ... Sincerely yours, OSCAR WILDE, Headmaster Babbacombe School.' In the drama to come, Georgiana's sympathies would lie with Constance (who was at Babbacombe when Queensberry left his libellous calling card at Wilde's London hotel); yet it is a mark of her humanity that when Oscar was bailed between his two trials, she invited him to visit, 'by which letter ... he was greatly touched'.

At Babbacombe, Georgiana continued to play hostess to unconventional friends such as the Quakeress Hannah Smith, who kept her informed on Thomas Lake Harris's progress in California, where he lived in an '"arch-natural" world ... a life very much like the one we live, only purified and made divine'. 'I do not accept Mr Harris's "views",' she told Georgiana; 'in fact, I do not understand them ... But he *interests* me' (this despite 'a loathsome description' Harris gave of his 'breathing' techniques with women; an uncomfortable reminder, perhaps, that Hannah's own husband, Robert Pearsall Smith, had been accused of impropriety with women, and 'exciting nature in its sexual appetites' in order that 'a higher spiritual life could be obtained').

Later, Hannah joined Georgiana at a house in Surrey to hear Laurence Oliphant speak: 'He has been living in Palestine for several years, and actually owns the plain of Armageddon! His wife died lately, and he has come over to England on a mission to propagate a sort of mystic spiritualism of a most peculiar kind . . . "Sympneuma".' Oliphant disclosed his 'secret to regenerate the world', but to Hannah 'it sounded like pure unadultered trash!' At Babbacombe, she encountered other prophets entertained by Georgiana, including 'a mysterious creature, a *man* he looked like, who is the leader of a strange sect called the "Temple"', and who told Hannah 'that he had not slept a wink for 8 years but had every night got out of his body and travelled around the world on errands of service for the Lord!! He declared that he sees angels as plainly as he sees men, and knows them all apart, and that Michael has light flaxen hair, and Gabriel dark eyes and hair, and they all live in the sun!'

Such metaphysical voyages were now the only ones Georgiana could undertake. Disabled by a bizarre accident in 1883 when she caught her foot in a coil of wire 'carelessly thrown on the road'

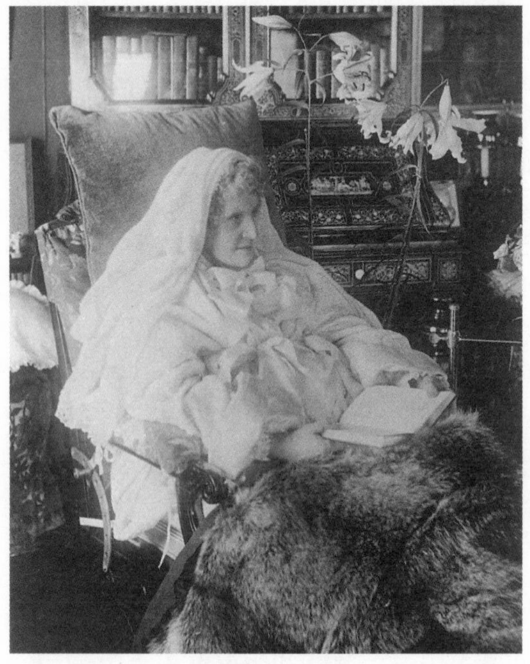

Sancta Lilias

(only discovering when she undressed that night that her body was numb), Georgiana was bed-ridden, but as she lay surrounded by lilies and propped up on a velvet cushion with a book on her fur-covered lap, her face seemed strangely unlined, as if, like Dorian Gray, she had not aged at all.

For the last ten years of her life, Georgiana did not leave Babbacombe; like Ruskin, she had become enclosed in her own home, although 'perfectly clear in her mind to the last . . .' Installed in her shrine of hooded statues, bathed in stained-glass light from its chapel-like window, she was an ethereal figure in an ever more elaborate costume of bows and veils. The aesthetic nun was now a *fin-de-siècle* anchoress, visited by the Reverend Bernard Vaughan, a socialist Jesuit whose sermons on subjects from 'The Menace of the Empty Cradle' to 'The Workers' Right to Live' brought society women flocking to Farm Street 'to hear themselves cursed and abused'; Vaughan would also testify at the infamous Black Book trial of 1918 as to the moral perversion of Wilde's *Salome*. 'He very nearly made a Catholic of her!' bemoaned Hannah Smith. 'He assured her that all her spiritual troubles arose from the fact that she had never been baptised . . .' 'I have not yet got to be a Christian,' Georgiana confessed, 'I only see it . . . far off . . . & sit myself in darkness.' She aspired to be a bride of Christ, but like Miss Havisham, she seemed to have been jilted. She raved 'against God one minute, and does not believe there is any God the next . . .', yet kept faith with spiritualism – unlike the woman who introduced her to it, Mary Howitt, who in 1882 herself converted to Catholicism and declared her former beliefs 'false, all false and full of lies. Revelations seemed to come, and they were nothing but the suggestions of devils.'

On 21 January 1900, Georgiana received 'the tidings of my beloved friend's transfiguration', Ruskin's death. She died a year later, and was laid next to her husband at Romsey Abbey, where their graves too were planted with evergreen trees. But this eccentric couple have more public memorials. In honour of her adoptive mother, Juliet gave Rossetti's study for *Sancta Lilias* to the nation, just as in 1888, Georgiana had presented the original of *Beata Beatrix* in memory of her husband – although few who pass one of the Tate gallery's most famous works could have any idea of the mysteries which lie behind the donor's name engraved on its little brass plaque.

FOURTEEN

Resurgam

> Alice laughed. 'There's no use trying,' she said: 'one *can't* believe impossible things.' 'I daresay you haven't had much practice,' said the Queen. 'When I was your age, I always did for half-an-hour a day. Why, sometimes I've believed as many as six impossible things before breakfast.'
>
> Lewis Carroll, *Through the Looking-Glass*

They all believed: from Ruskin's Guild to the Cowpers' spiritualism, from Peterson's tower to Mary Ann's colony, they all placed their trust in the power of faith. At the height of the Victorian empire, their curiosity was unbounded by science, art or religion. In 1895, Wilde wrote in *The Soul of Man Under Socialism:* 'A map of the world that does not include Utopia is not worth even glancing at, for it leaves out the one country at which Humanity is always landing. And when Humanity lands there, it looks out, and, seeing a better country, sets sail. Progress is the realisation of Utopias.' Two years later, in *Forecasts of the Coming Century*, Edward Carpenter wrote, 'We can see plainly enough the communistic direction in which society is trending.'

But the new century had replaced such dreams with a brutal new vision. In 1919, even the New Forest became part of that inexorable process: the Forestry Commission was established to ensure supplies for a future war, giving a dark tint to its peacetime role as playground to the suburbs. Yet its myths remained, even as the memory of the Girlingites passed into legend, along with the

Gypsies and the ghostly hart of the Rufus Stone, as if the trees themselves conspired to create an immemorial refuge for these restless souls.

In 1927, as interwar hikers in their sandals, shorts and long socks tramped across the forest heaths, celebrating their youth and a fragile decade of peace, the intrepid Mr Wylie of the Milford-on-Sea Record Society began his investigations. To a world caught between conflicts, the Girlingites' attempts at social justice and communitarian living seemed to anticipate the aspirations of a new generation: even down to the 'bloomers' worn by the women, 'a costume which, as we all know, was very generally adopted by land girl workers during the late War'. Wylie even found a still sprightly pair of Girlingites, Violet and Lizzie, who, in 'trembling old voices' delivered heart-rending accounts of their sufferings, and who were so overcome by their memories that one old lady jumped out of her armchair to show how they danced. Wylie's account – along with an essay on Peterson and his tower – appeared in the Society's privately-printed journal. Ten years later, the Girlingites had another, sensational resurrection when Reverend W. T. Andress, a Baptist minister in Brockenhurst, made public his own findings in the *Hampshire Advertiser and Southampton Times*. Published in serial form, its headline, 'THE INNER SECRET OF THE SHAKERS', promised something between a murder mystery and a tabloid scandal; as though, like a 1930s sleuth, the reverend was about to uncover dark goings-on in the Victorian past. The paper's readers – who included my own grandparents, living in a Southampton suburb – would not be disappointed.

Entering his own story, Andress described how, during pastoral visits in the area, he had heard 'strange disconnected accounts of a singular personage called Mrs Girling . . .' His first lead came when he interviewed a 'literary and newspaper proprietor' who 'still believed in the Mother's mission, held Shaker doctrines, and was convinced the Lord's Return was being delayed for want of their acceptance'. This was evidence that Girlingism had not died with Mary Ann, but had persisted into the twentieth century. Not only that, but Andress's contact's own wife had seen Mary Ann's mysterious print marks, 'and there was no doubt they were on her body'. The minister compared these to those of St Francis of Assisi, in whom 'the marks were carefully concealed till near the end. The Saint's body was shown to the wondering, awe-stricken multitudes after death, in contradistinction to Mrs Girling, who, while living, permitted certain privileged ones to see her marks.' Andress might also have cited Padre Pio, an illiterate Italian Franciscan who had exhibited similar wounds on his body since 1918, and was photographed saying Mass with blood staining his palms.

After years of work, Andress published the results of his research. His first article used Hughes' portrait of Mary Ann: like the iconic images of Padre Pio, it too seemed to retain some kind of power. 'If the photograph of this lady . . . be gazed at intently, the exclamation of a friend of mine will perhaps be repeated, "Ugh! That woman is getting hold of me."' Conversely, another image found by Andress, 'of a group of her followers . . . shows them to be the type of people who might be so influenced. For they have nice faces and are what the French term *spirituelle*.' In this second photograph, a group is arrayed before the camera in a characteristic Victorian composition: arms over shoulders, leaning in laps, an affectionate display of their spiritual union.

When I first saw this picture, I thought it must be a fake or misattribution. Surely these are actors, or guests at a vicarage tea party? They wear their Sunday best: the men look like curates or students in their wide-knotted ties, loose coats, narrow trousers and boots, while the women, having eschewed their workaday bloomers for virginal white gowns, would not be out of place in a genteel drawing room. But there is something more: they seem to glow with chastity, a numinous whiteness; they have a steady gaze of eyes which have beheld salvation, and smiles which speak not

Group of the followers of Mrs. Girling. Some were still living 20 years ago, when Mr. Andress was given the photograph.

of hardship but of inner contentment. Like the Oneidans of New York State, theirs is a deceptive calm: these placid, complacent figures could whirl about in a frenzy when in the Spirit, shaking and speaking in tongues.

And the longer one looks, a strange, almost sexual cohesion seems to unfurl, as if twisted in their long, loose curls and languid pose. It is disconcerting, after all this, to come face to face with the Girlingites. We cannot give them names, but these twelve must include those elders who stayed with Mary Ann since the Suffolk days. Surely the tall bearded man with quiffed hair must be Henry Osborne; but which is Violet, and which Eliza? Perhaps they assembled in the same Lymington studio as Mary Ann, for a promotional pose taken as they began their missionary tour. Was their leader behind the camera, encouraging her Children? Or is that her, on their right hand side? As elusive as ever, wherever she stands in relation to this image, Mary Ann is indisputably in control; she is its fixative. This is Girlingism at its apogee, her amative flock at its youthful, enthusiastic, almost glamorous peak. At least four female acolytes wear the same dark necklace seen in Mary

Ann's portrait: an identifying symbol of faith and otherness, a wooden rosary-chain gathering them in celibacy to their Mother; bound by love indeed. 'Let not loyalty and faithfulness forsake you; bind them about your neck', as the Bible told them. They had given everything up for their Mother: money, sex, ambition. Their rhapsody has an other-worldly air, and a vague emptiness, as if their souls were already hers. And perhaps that is why I question this subtly dramatic and ultimately deceptive image. It is like seeing the performers from a radio play, being suddenly confronted with the reality of imagined, elusory faces. Lacking discrete identities, these figures seem fated to fade back into the anonymous, yellowing volumes of the newspaper library.

'This photograph, I may add, was given on condition of discreet use, some of the persons in it being then living,' Andress wrote in 1937. 'As that was nearly 20 years ago, I trust the photograph may now be used without hurting anyone's feelings . . . however mistaken they may have been, they were pure living and in many respects estimable people. In proof of this, it is a fact worth noting that on returning to normal life they all did well.' On its publication, the picture sparked off the memories of Mr G. T. Thorne, husband of Alice Read, who had attested to the absence of her stigmata when she nursed the dying messiah. 'I remember when they were turned out of Forest Lodge, and seeing them by the side of the road in Vaggs Lane. I attended some of their meetings after they were at Tiptoe,' Thorne told the *Advertiser*, and claimed, 'An old friend living close is the only one of the community living in the neighbourhood, and the lady in the extreme right of the picture is either her or her late sister.' The following week, a letter duly appeared from 'E. M. Chase, Rose Cottage, Tiptoe' as a voice from a prelapsarian past.

> . . . I was one of those who came from London on January 2nd 1872. I was 25 that year, and lived with the community through all their joys and all their sorrows and privations. I

> have no regrets and I am not ashamed of my life there. Mrs Girling did not exercise any influence over us. We were free to go or stay. I never, through all those years, heard Mrs Girling say she would never go into the grave. But 'I shall never die'. Is that not the hope and belief of all true Christians? As a Canon of the Church of England once said: 'She is not dead.' As regards our way of worship that is between ourselves and our Father who seest and knowest the hearts of all.

It was a final, cryptic testament, speaking down the years. Lizzie would die in 1941, aged ninety-five, 'still lamenting her beloved Mother', and with her vanished the living memory of those remembered ecstasies. Yet the silence of history somehow perpetuates Mary Ann's mission, and the reason for my own search. Writing in 1937, as the *Advertiser* filled with foreboding reports from Germany, Andress had 'little doubt but that some similar religious enthusiast – male or female – will arise and beguile, intentionally or unintentionally, unwary and too confiding folk into disaster. In this eventuality, a reliable account of Mrs Girling will be as precious as rubies to those concerned.'

Between the wars, the Forestry Commission addressed the problem of the hundreds of people who were living wild in the woods. Its solution was to confine them to compounds where, like native Americans in reservations, they could be corralled within a wilderness they had once roamed at will. Forbidden from erecting any permanent structures, they were issued with six-monthly licences which could be revoked instantly, should they displease the Commission with their behaviour in these arboreal concentration camps. 'Although nobody so far has proposed to liquidate these nomads after the Hitler style, is it possible that, in his own country, John Bunyan's people have been sentenced to a lingering death?' asked Augustus John, champion of Gypsies. By the late 1930s, the population of the seven compounds had reached nearly one thousand, a figure swollen by the effects of the Depression and later by inhabitants fleeing the south coast towns and cities being bombed by the Luftwaffe, many of them evacuees who had left Southampton by night to escape its blitz, and who by day were reluctant to forsake the forests shelter for their now dangerous homes.

In 1949 there were still about five hundred living this way when Arthur Lloyd wrote a report for the *Picture Post*, illustrated with photographs by Bert Hardy. These grainy post-war pictures – the modern equivalent of the *Illustrated London News* and its lithographs – discern a sense of forlorn romance in these lost people living under canvas rags, or 'slums under trees', and the *Post* saw them: 'In the New Forest, tucked away from the bird-watcher and the week-ending stockbroker, hundreds of poor folk live in compounds, under Stone Age conditions. Some call them gypsies, some call them dirty, some call them thieves. Most of them are none of these things. Many are decent people, with a strong wish for a better life, and a struggle before them to overcome prejudice.' These were insular communities, withdrawn from the world. At one compound, Shave Green, near Minstead, the artist Sven Berlin, a friend of Augustus John, painted the forest-dwellers 'in their green underwater world of summer, moving like drowned men. . .' Soon they too would be evicted, rehoused in faceless council estates to join the rest of humanity, the memory of their forest days behind them.

That same year that the *Post* published its exposé, Laurence Housman's 'The Watchers' was broadcast on the BBC's Home Service and printed in *The Listener*. It was the product of his continuing fascination with Mary Ann Girling, and geographical coincidence. Back in 1912, he and his sister Clemence had been staying at a holiday cottage in Ashley. 'Who do you think used to live close here?' Clemence had asked him. On investigating, Housman was told that one Girlingite was still living in the sect's old meeting house, and he went to visit her. He found an elderly woman, poverty-stricken but happy, who spoke of her 'Mother' as if she were still alive. The woman – possibly Eliza Osborne, then in her eightieth year (her husband having died three years earlier) – told him of the strange events which happened in Hordle churchyard three days after their Mother's death.

In Housman's embroidered account, which evokes the graveyard scene in which Lizzie Siddal's body was exhumed at Highgate, a hundred-strong crowd, some holding lanterns, gather by a row of graves, all marked only by evergreen trees except for the most recent, which was covered in flowers. As dawn breaks, the crowd stand around it in a circle, praying. Then their leader – presumably Harry Osborne – instructs them to put out their lights.

> The elder's voice broke the silence: 'She has come!' he said; 'She is risen. But we were too weak of faith to see it'. 'But I did see it', affirmed another. 'Yes, I saw her rise!' His lips trembled, his eyes shone bright. Two others affirmed the same . . . 'Three of us saw', they said, 'though the rest did not'. Were not three proof enough of that which had so certainly been foretold?

In this romanticised retelling, a child suggests that they move the grave flowers to enable their Mother to arise. But this in itself seems an echo of Housman's illustration of Jump-to-Glory Jane's death, rather than the result of anything he may or may not have been told in Tiptoe. Housman seemed to be haunted by this woman he had never met; indeed, he had regarded that Edwardian encounter as another omen. 'The call had come', and inspired by this new, direct contact with the memory of Mary Ann, he had written a novel, *The Sheepfold*, taking Meredith's jumping Jane and expanding her life into elegant allegory. Just as his fantastical illustrations of Mary Ann had first made him famous, so Housman's sensational fictional version of her story had provided him with his first best-selling book.

Jane Sterling grows up in rural Suffolk under the joint influence of the puritanical 'Primitive Brethren' and local folklore; a weakly child whose mother rubs slugs and turpentine into her back to strengthen it and who sews her daughter into her clothes in winter as a 'cloistral internment'. Young Jane is devout but rebellious: at fourteen she looks for angels in the boughs of trees like Blake, but at the same time is attracted to a village lad – only to be raped by him. Later, using her stocking filled with stones, she murders her suitor-assailant, regarding her crime with a macabre coolness: 'Tom as he lay dead, now that she had washed the blood from his face, was a very presentable young man, broadchested, muscular, like and fit . . . she did not know why she had killed him.'

Having given birth to a son, Jane marries a farm labourer, Ben Sterling, another 'very comely youth' of 'strong physique and general favour'. But when both he and their newborn daughter die, Jane 'tramps' to London's East End, standing outside public houses with a bucket of whitewash and a brush 'to wash black sinners white'. Then, following another lover, she sails for New York and 'disappears from history . . . America keeps no trace of Jane's footprints during that seven years' pilgrimage'.

It is a part of his story which the author drew from rumours of American influences on Mary Ann, and the enigma of her early life. Housman's heroine even seems to change sex, like Virginia Woolf's Orlando or the young crewcut Willa Cather, a tomboy John the Baptist: 'Whether during that time of searching preparation she bore the name of John or of James Sterling, or some other appellation more remote, record is not to show. The wilderness whereinto she was driven of the spirit provided multitude as a covering, and the hermit cell she lived in went with her from place to place.' Jane arrives as the civil war is in progress, and becomes a builder. 'And when I left 'em, they'd done killing men on the battlefields, and was doing it on the railroads instead, to show how much the spirit of the Lord was in 'em after they'd had their way. After that they took to killing houses, so as to build Babel; and New York, being in a tight boot, was beginning to get corns . . .'

Forsaking Manhattan's crowded Babel for her 'public mission', 'Jane reverted to her own sex . . . She could still boast that she had never had a day's illness, though her body bore scars; and in her jobs at the building trade she had learned to look down from great heights.' Back in Suffolk, she gathers her 'Jokers' (so-called because 'they laughed till they fell down') in a former lunatic asylum. 'These were the days of their prosperity: before the end of the year the place had eighty inhabitants . . . The money-box stood on the Table of Testimony, and was not locked. The locking of any door, or the retention of any material privilege unshared by all, would have been a denial of the life which they sought to establish.'

Crossing counties to Hampshire, Jane embarks on her final mission; seeking shelter for the night, she sees 'a tall tower-like erection rising palely against the darkening layers of sky'. This forest skyscraper is the home of Barnaby Hebron, an eccentric who is driven about in a carriage which resembles a bathing machine.

'He don't much like people to look at him – not strangers,' his coachman explains.

'Is he so beautiful as all that?' asks Jane.

'He's the finest of his sort as ever breathed, but queer, oh, very queer!'

An amalgam of Herbert and Peterson, Hebron is 'a pleasant-looking elderly gentleman, with hair that had once been auburn now turning gray . . . On one of his well-kept hands he wore a large signet ring; and his rather *négligé* attire, soft-coloured shirt, and loose tie carried a flavour of refinement indicative of a nice choice, possibly even of a sense of beauty.' He is not a little like the author himself. Occasionally sleeping in his 'house in the trees', Hebron spends most of his time at the top of his tower, in a 'light and spacious chamber . . . square as a cube with a long window in each wall.'

'Are you mad?' says Hebron when Jane enters unannounced.

'No more than yourself,' she says, 'but we both do queer things. It's the only way to get on in a country where there's no freedom except what you make for yourself.'

Hebron warms to Jane; they discuss spiritual and social problems, which he thinks can be solved by 'a controlled birth-rate' and 'pending that, assisted emigration' – as did Housman, perhaps. Jane says she needs ten acres of land and the right to build wooden huts on it; Hebron wonders what she will do with 'a hundred and twenty helpless people', having 'led them into the wilderness with a high hand and a stretched-out arm'. Sure enough, her followers soon fall away, and shortly after, Hebron's tower is felled in a storm: he and Jane stand looking at the rubble of his own Babel-like ambition to reach heaven, now scattered over the fields. Hebron rapidly declines, lying in his bed 'in an Eastern richness of costume, but looking very frail . . . his eyes . . . without light', and his death is followed by Jane's: 'No headstone ever marked the spot . . . and the place where that heart – so faithful in its love of earth and heaven – resumed unhindered allegiance to both alike, is now unknown.'

Housman's novel is a wry comment on nineteenth-century utopias, a fey fantasy hiding its sympathies behind elegant prose and opinions which the author seems to share. His descriptions of Jane as having a stare which can see through a man, and a mouth 'as wide across as her two eyes', resonate with his personal research in Hordle and the eye-witness accounts he heard of Mary Ann Girling. But most revealing of all is the book's frontispiece, itself a pastiche of spiritualistic tracts. It is a photograph of 'Jane Sterling', looking like a cross between one of the Shaker Ladies in Hepworth Dixon's *New America*, and Mary Ann's cowboyish portrait. But on comparison with the photograph in Housman's memoirs, which depicts the author as Disraeli (and credits a theatrical firm in Parkstone for the make-up), I realise that this 'Jane

Sterling' is Housman himself, assuming a sly sexual ambivalence that elides with the gender-changing figure who still haunted him.

Complicit in the act of mystification, Housman perpetuated the process in which Mary Ann Girling was subject, victim, martyr and creator, even then, a generation after her death. Thus she achieved her immortality, even as she mesmerised her chroniclers. As for Housman; three years after he published 'The Watchers', he became a Quaker, having been a pacifist since the First World War. In 1955, his sister Clemence, with whom he had lived at Street in Somerset since 1924, died, and four years later, in 1959, Laurence himself died in a hospital in Glastonbury.

In 1889, four years after the completion of Andrew Peterson's tower, his wife Charlotte received 'a decent Christian burial' in Sway churchyard, rather than be interred in the crypt of the bizarre folly. Perhaps her disaffection in death lay with her husband's continuing affair in life with Catherine Johnson. That March, *Medium and Daybreak* announced that A.T.T.P. had been 'quite incapacitated' for twelve weeks, 'but now has had a most favourable crisis'. The nature of this epiphany was not explained, but James Burns hoped it would 'open up to him another course of useful action amongst us, which will give joy to many of our readers'.

Peterson's tower remained untenanted – apart from its use by an artist allowed to occupy the lower rooms when painting in the neighbourhood – and in widowhood, its creator grew yet more reclusive. He retreated, like Barnaby Hebron, into his house, Arnewood Towers, and its once-gracious ballroom – its walls now insulated with carpets – where he lived, according to family legend, on bowls of gruel. One of his relatives, when a little girl, recalled seeing him coming out of an hotel on Lymington high street, a bearded, Tolstoyan figure in smock and brown leather belt. In the mid-1890s, the damp climate and his failing health persuaded Peterson to hand over his estate to a cousin, Major-General Thomas Trevor Turton, and he left for the warmer shores of the Canary Islands, building a Spanish-style house in the hills above Santa Cruz. Yet he retained his Grays Inn chambers, where he continued his spiritualistic endeavours and where, on 29 November 1906, he entered the ultimate experiment: his own death, at the age of ninety-three. With this final act, his tower achieved completion. Peterson had requested that his body be cremated, and that his ashes be placed in the void beneath the tower. As Wren was interred in the vault of St Paul's, so Peterson would be interred in the crypt of his monument, while his soul would join that of his spiritual architect in the after-life.

From Westminster Bridge station, the Necropolis Railway took the coffin first class to Brookwood – the suburb of the dead and one of the few places in the country where the new process of cremation could be carried out – and from its solemn pines Peterson's ashes were returned to Hampshire. Sealed in a Doulton urn, they were carried into the chapel-like porch of the tower by four workmen, led by the Girlingite Tommy Ackland who, having topped off the building, now effected the consecration of its crypt. A hatch was opened and the funeral party descended a ladder into the square, whitewashed, seven-foot high chamber, decorated with dark evergreens and white chrysanthemums. The two concrete plinths stood as if in wait for some Roman emperor and his wife. Peterson's friend Rollo Massey watched as 'a mournful spectator, when the urn containing all that was mortal of this great and good man was reverently lowered to its last resting place . . . by the hands of the old remaining workmen who had carried out his design'. On top was laid a wreath of violets and ivy, symbols of love and eternity.

Soon after Peterson's death, his lover Catherine went to live with her married sister Lucy Robertson in Cobbett Road, Bitterne, Southampton, where, aged sixty-seven, she died of cirrhosis of the liver in 1911, ten years before my own mother was born in a nursing home in the same road. And as my infant mother was posed naked on a fur rug in a photograph which seemed to present her to the world like some Victorian trophy, in 1921 Arnewood Towers was sold at auction. It was advertised as a 'delightful freehold country property', with its seven bedrooms, its reception rooms (including billiard room, smoking room and heated conservatory), tennis court, and twenty-three and-a-half acres of land – although the elaborate estate agent's brochure does not mention the 200-foot tower next door, with its builder's ashes interred below.

The house was bought by a General Bright, but the tower remained in the possession of Peterson's family. In the Second World War, as invasion once more threatened the south coast, the Home Guard was stationed in its chambers, piling them with sandbags and knocking chunks out of the windows to enable access for their guns. In 1957, a year before my own birth in a Southampton suburb, the tower was sold to Mr J. G. Stanton for £100, and Peterson's remains reinterred in his wife's grave at St Luke's in

Sway, where a marble memorial tablet in the church commemorated his family. By now his tower had become a gothic ruin, its windows open to colonies of pigeons and its porch gates overgrown with ivy; some rooms were still filled with sand left over from its wartime occupation; some were piled high with bird droppings. In the 1960s it found employment as a 'booster station' for the local broadcasting company – in effect, a giant TV aerial – but it was feared that the tower was beginning to crack, and demolition threatened. However, along with Peterson's model piggeries, it was listed as a Grade II* building, and in 1972 was sold for £2,750 to a new owner who made the building safe – all the more necessary after the Great Storm of 1987 swept through the forest, flattening trees like crop circles and sending two of the tower's concrete blocks crashing to the ground, as if in echo of Barnaby Hebron's fated folly.

After a brief, unsuccessful incarnation as an hotel (guests staying on the twelfth floor may have balked at the lack of a lift), the tower acquired a new function – as a site for mobile phone transmitters. And as the Society for Psychical Research recently announced that the advent of the cellphone has coincided with a sharp reduction in spectral manifestations, it seems the twenty-first century has finally sapped Peterson's tower of its psychic charge.

Mary Ann's mortal remains lay somewhere on the north side of All Saints, an oddly empty part of Hordle churchyard. Although the bland turf retained no vestige of the faithful, their memory, and that of their failed forest Eden, persisted. In the 1960s, Arthur Lloyd, a local historian whose interest in Mary Ann's story had been aroused by the broadcast of Housman's 'The Watchers', began a new investigation into the Girlingites, a last chance to record first-hand accounts. In 1961, Mr Thorne, Alice's husband, then aged ninety-seven, showed Lloyd a silver belt buckle, one of the items bartered for the sect's bills, and other tantalising relics: a black horsehair-stuffed sofa (perhaps the same under which she had sought shelter on that infamous winter's night in 1874), and a portrait of Mary Ann – an enlargement of her studio photograph, retouched and glazed in an oval frame, an icon to hang in the home of a believer, imbued with a reliquary quality and tinted to enliven the receding sepia.

But she was already lost even before she began, this woman disowned by the past, so little of her memory remained. It is ironic that a woman so articulate in her time has been left dumb by history, remembered in a few press cuttings and fleeting glimpses recorded in popular publications; secondhand impressions of a figure who seems barely a person at all, more a two-dimensional lithographic print. Mary Ann emerges from her historical interment only fitfully; a sly, liminal figure, a shape-shifting trickster. When did she begin and when did she die? While the saint's bones were picked clean by the worms of Hordle churchyard, her rustic gospel still echoed through the forest, merging into oral tradition as if, like Herne the Hunter – a shaman in a deerskin – or Robin Hood – a legendary outlaw giving to the poor – she had lived in folklore rather than in fact. Beyond record and beyond memory, Mary Ann remains a mystery. Sometimes I wonder if she ever existed at all; or if she might still be alive, an impossibly aged Mother Shipton still awaiting the millennium as the cars drive by.

Much extended since her troubled tenancy, New Forest Lodge was renamed Hordle Grange, and in the 1960s became a nursing

home. In 1987, the Great Storm stripped the house of its sheltering trees, felling more than a hundred macrocarpa, pines and oaks, and electrocuting two hundred pigs in the farm across the lane as one mighty tree pulled down an electric cable. The destruction opened up the house to public view, just as the Family's lives were exposed on their eviction. Their erstwhile commune is now a desirable country residence; although in the pastures still overlooked by Peterson's tower, bits of their mud huts are occasionally unearthed, as if the land were giving up their secrets. Unlike the industrious Shakers, the Girlingites left no clapboard villages or neatly-turned furniture to exhibit their simplicity; only cottages and barns whose daub and thatch have long since rotted back into the earth. And in the Tiptoe fields where Mary Ann's dream finally died, the hedgerows and muddied plots of turf betray no trace of her last stand.

But her stable-chapel has survived. In the twentieth century, this place of worship was turned into an engine room with concrete floors and, as sales particulars from 1929 proudly advertise, 'an Armstrong-Whitworth 4-h.p. petrol-paraffin engine, with Edmundson 50 volt dynamo and pump', producing quite a different sort of energy to that of the Girlingite rites. The building is

now a family home, but inside, the stable beams are still evident, as are the attic rooms from which the Children of God were so rudely ejected. Below, the hall-like space still seems to reverberate with speaking tongues and stamping feet, and the image of Mary Ann standing on a stool, arms *oraens*, preaching to the faithful.

In these quiet country lanes, memories of the sect are rare, although one Tiptoe resident recalls her grandmother, Tommy Ackland's daughter, talking of 'Mother Girling' and her 'queer folk'. Perhaps a faint air of shame hangs over those who joined the cult, or opposed it. Even in November 1976 the sensational *Reveille* could publish a somewhat tardy tabloid exposé – GAVE UP SEX TO LIVE FOR EVER – a contrast to other headlines that autumn devoted to 'Anarchy in the UK'. Meanwhile, a local historian, Jude James, responding to a letter in the *Lymington Times* about 'the passing away of the Shaker religious sect in the US', noted that accounts of the Girlingites did not 'make clear that Mrs Mary Ann Girling was a neurotic and probably also a schizophrenic whose influence for good was more than outweighed by the personal tragedy she brought to certain local families'. James concluded that 'Mrs Girling should be seen for what she was, and for this reason sympathy for the woman, no matter how misguided

GAVE UP SEX TO LIVE FOR EVER

Man and vife lived as brother and sister. All wordly goods were given up. It was a hard life. It was worth it, though. After all, the reward was eternal life. MARC ALEXANDER tells the strange, tragic story of the Walworth Jumpers

ON a September dawn 20 kneeling people gazed at a newly-dug grave and waited for a miracle. They expected to see Mary Ann Girling—who had claimed to be a female Christ—rise from the dead.

If they did not, it would mean that years of bitter hardship, the giving up of their worldly goods and the abandonment of physical love would have been in vain.

Suddenly three cried out that they saw her float out of the ground and began leaping up and down with joy. The others saw nothing.

Blaming [illegible] lack of faith, they sorrowfully trudged away from the parish churchyard in the village of Hordle, Hampshire.

So ended the last meeting of the Walworth Jumpers, the sect who had been convinced that they would live for ever if they gave up sex.

In Hordle today people remember their parents' tales of how the roads to the village would be jammed with crowds eager to see the delirious jumping marathons of these self-styled Children of God.

MARY ANN was born on April 27, 1827, at Little Glemham in Suffolk, to a farmer named Clouting.

In her early thirties she believed she had a vision in which Christ told her she was to be the messenger of his Second Coming which she must proclaim in the streets.

Hundreds flocked to hear her message, which was that Christ was about to return to earth, and those who wanted to avoid death could do so by giving up sex.

Even husbands and wives should live as brothers and sisters, she said.

This caused a lot of unhappiness in homes where only one person was converted. Mary Ann's meetings were often broken up by husbands angry because their wives preferred the idea of eternal life to them.

To spread the word further, Mary Ann began holding meetings in London in a converted railway arch at Walworth Road.

HUNDREDS queued to watch the Children of God leap up and down, calling out prophecies and putting themselves into trances. Here they earned the nickname of the Walworth Jumpers.

Sometimes they were barracked and even pelted with eggs, and Mary Ann felt that London was not the right place for her to carry out her mission.

In 1871 she had another vision in which it was revealed that she should take her followers and live in a house called New Forest Lodge at Hordle.

Although she declared she had no knowledge of the place, one of her wealthy disciples, a Julia Wood, located the village and by an amazing coincidence—or so the Children of God thought—found that there was a large house called New Forest Lodge standing empty.

Today the house is a nursing home, but in the heyday of the Jumpers over 160 people lived there.

Although sex was taboo in Mary Ann's kingdom, enemies of the movement spread ugly rumours of Jumping sessions turning into orgies and babies secretly born and buried in the Lodge grounds.

It was true, however, that in moments of leaping ecstasy the Jumpers did sometimes tear off their clothes, but probably what caused the most raised eyebrows was the women's clothing, designed by Mary Ann.

This consisted of a white smock and *trousers* (like a modern trouser suit), which was no doubt better for jumping in than long dresses.

LOCAL farmers offered the male members work, but Mary Ann refused to allow any of her followers to earn money.

All went well as long as the money donated by the converts lasted, but on December 15, 1874, the Jumpers were evicted for not paying mortgage interest.

Their belongings were dumped in Vaggs Lane, which runs past New Forest Lodge.

The Jumpers prayed through the freezing night in Vaggs Lane.

Later a farmer let them stay for a while in a barn where they slept on straw, but finally they ended up in a makeshift camp in a field at Tiptoe in Hordle parish.

Meanwhile, their benefactor, Julia Wood, was committed to an insane asylum by her family.

The Jumpers were now so short of money that they lived on only bread and cold potatoes, yet the magnetism of Mary Ann kept most of them faithful to their cause.

Then a girl of 23 died from the effects of malnutrition and cold.

The Jumpers, who had believed they were immortal, were shocked.

Mary Ann had to reassure them by declaring that the girl had died because of her lack of faith. From now on her flock must lead even purer lives.

This stilled their doubts for a while, but the next winter several Jumpers died of consumption.

Four years after their eviction from New Forest Lodge, Mary Ann announced that she was not just a messenger of Christ, but she was the Second Coming.

Some sceptics asked why she did not use her divine power to make life better for her disciples, but she replied it was impossible until the world accepted her as Jesus come a second time in woman's form.

Meanwhile three more Jumpers died because of the terrible conditions in which they lived.

Mary Ann explained their deaths were due to the fact they did not believe she was the Saviour.

IN 1886 Mary Ann was taken ill but she said that as she was not going to die there was no need for a doctor.

When one was finally brought in it was found she was suffering from cancer.

On September 18, 1886, she died — aged 59—after telling her 20 remaining disciples she would rise from the tomb.

New Forest Lodge, home of the Walworth Jumpers, as it is today. Now a nursing home, at one time 160 Jumpers lived here

Mary Ann Girling, who said she was Christ in the form of a woman

her motives, is justified, but surely not sympathy for what she did?'

In the 1980s, Arthur Lloyd compared the Girlingites to the new-age travellers being pursued by the authorities of southern England around the pagan sites of Stonehenge and Wiltshire. Regretting the fact that Mary Ann lacked a memorial, in 1987 Lloyd had a plaque fitted to a church buttress overlooking the approximate location of her grave. But like the Rufus Stone, it remains a disputatious site. In 2002, in response to plans to build a parish hall there, Jude James testified at a consistory court, called in the church itself, to the historical importance of the 'Shaker graves'. The Church authorities were not convinced, and despite a battle between the villagers as passionate as any of their predecessors' confrontations a century before, Mary Ann's last resting place will soon resound to the bustle of bring-and-buy sales. Its rough grass has now disappeared under concrete foundations, firmly sealing the thirteen unmarked graves which lie below; although, during the excavations, one villager spotted what was later confirmed as part of a human thigh bone in the spoil heap.

Epilogue

Live your beliefs and you can turn the world around
Henry David Thoreau

Running inland from Maine's jigsaw coast, the traffic on State Route 26 isn't enough to wake the faithful who lie at its verges, gathered in communal graves like mortal pastures marked with stones engraved with one word, 'Shakers'. Nor does the road disturb the last of the United Society of Believers, the five women and five men who still live here in the spirit of Ann Lee. In August 1784, as she lay dying, a deputation sailed from Sabbathday

Lake to see their leader for the last time. On their way back, the pilgrims were caught in a storm, only for Ann to appear and pacify the sea, just as she had done on that first voyage to the New World. But Ann the Word had already been dead for six hours, having told her friends that she saw a golden chariot coming to take her home.

In the tailwind of a passing pick-up truck, the modern world falls away as we cross the road. Brilliant white clapboards surround an oak tree under which a blacksmith is clanking hot iron on cold steel; beneath a flimsy marquee, a sewing-bee of quilt-makers goes about its business. Waiting for the next tour, we wander round the shop, with its homeopathic tinctures of rosewater, black and white postcards, and turned wooden pegs. Lying subversively among these homespun offerings is a pale yellow leaflet, a catechism which still retains its power after two centuries:

Purity of Life, Peace, Justice, Love

Equality of the Sexes in all departments of life,
Equality of Labour – all working for each, and each for all.
Equality of Property – no rich, no poor; Industrial Freedom.
Consecrated Labour; Dedicated Wealth; A United Inheritance.
Each using according to need.
Each enjoying according to capacity.

Such notions seem even further away now that they are most needed, reproving the world with its lost aspirations and future hopes, 'the interior realization that the same Divine Spirit which was in Jesus might dwell within the consciousness of any man, woman or child'. 'Sanitation, Health, Longeavity', 'Purity in thought, speech and personal habits', 'Freedom from debt, worry and competition', 'No Government without a God; No Body without a Head': these are utopian slogans for another dispensation, unfolding and demonstrating, embracing and confessing, abstaining and withholding.

As opposed to the common life of human generation and selfish gratification, this is held to be the

Resurrection Life!

We walk through interiors smelling of herbs and wood and mustiness and cleanliness, a scent which itself is a statement against change. Inside the meeting house, with its built-in pews and blueberry-, sage- and indigo-painted walls, the daylight is mediated by ancient wavy glass, and as the tour party files out, the footsteps fade away and the wooden floor reclaims its silence.

Twice a day the community assembles privately in this room, entering separately by sex through two doors. Upstairs, in another attic-like museum space, are the chairs Dickens so despised; simple knives and forks lie crossed on ironstone plates; poke bonnets hang on pegs. Presented with all this useful beauty, it is hard not to think of the contemporary value of these vintage pieces. Yet the building soaks up the present we trail behind us, subsumed in residual energy rising through the gently creaking heat, and out of the corner of my eye I see a figure hurrying down the stairs.

I was brought up in the Catholic faith. Religion meant stillness and obeisance; to move at all during Mass, other than to stand, kneel or sit would be almost sacrilegious. There was no shaking but silence as the vestmented priest intoned the Latin rites with his back to the congregation. At school assembly, in the green-painted hall which was once a tin church, I would look up at the mesmerising light forcing its way through the trefoil window, associating it with the drug-incensed liturgy of Benediction, during which I imagined that, like a miraculous saint, I too could levitate gently above the congregation, to the amazement of my friends and the confoundment of my teachers.

At the end of the Northern Line, in the recesses of Colindale's Newspaper Library, the scratchy microfilm scrolls through the *Daily News* for 9 January 1875. Next to a review of Charles Nordhoff's study of utopian societies is a letter headed 'Levitation'. 'When I was six years old . . . I firmly believed myself able, by an act of volition, to rise from the ground and float in the air . . .' claims the correspondent. 'The act always seemed to occur under peculiar mental conditions, hard to describe otherwise than as a state of singular vigour, confidence and exaltation of spirits. I would then say to myself, "Now I will rise in the air, and float to such and such a spot" . . . Drawing in my breath, and bracing all my muscles, so that the body was quite rigid, I would then find myself rising slowly and steadily off the ground, and moving through the air . . . the victory over gravity was delightful, and yet never struck me as having anything supernatural in it.' The anonymous writer concluded that such experiences, which still occurred, happened only in his unconscious, but 'even now, I find it hard to persuade myself that it is a dream . . .'

My father was born in Bradford in 1915, a year into the Great War, and two years before the Russian Revolution. His grandfather, my namesake, had been a fisherman in Whitby; his Irish Catholic antecedents had fled to England in the Hunger. My mother, however, chose Catholicism, as a teenager in the 1930s. Her grandfather had been a Methodist minister at Parkstone, a stern figure with an improbable beard cascading over his Victorian waistcoat, flanked by his mannish wife with her dark hair caught up in a voluminous pile on her head like some unstable hat. In photographs, this pair seemed to me to encapsulate austere flat-fronted suburban chapels and their dour services – as I imagined them – compared to our sacramental rituals, when the priest would hold aloft the Host in its monstrance, his hands swathed in an elaborately embroidered damask cope, the sun-ray burst of gilt surrounding the simple white wafer of adoration as though exposing Christ's Sacred Heart to children who moments later would be running home from school. And yet the Church taught me that we are all children of God; and as I hear Mass on the Feast of All Saints, reading from the Book of the Apocalypse – *Then I heard the count of those who were sealed, a hundred and forty-four thousand of them* – I wonder how different was the worship in that chapel converted from a Hampshire stable.

One afternoon in 1969, I came home from school to find my parents sitting around a circular table with their fingers on an upturned glass surrounded by cards with the letters of the alphabet on them. I remember my father's guilty look as I pushed open the door of the front room. Some months beforehand, my brother had died as the result of a car crash. He was twenty-three. Afterwards, 'messages' claimed that an asphalt lump, left by workmen on the side of the road, had caused the accident – a detail confirmed by my eldest brother, the only family member to have visited the scene. And just as the spirits said that Andrew's missing house keys were behind the fireplace in his house, so my brother arrived, having found them there. Other things happened in our house in Southampton around that time: passing figures in the bedroom, voices in the empty hallway, black crosses on landing doors; stories that now seem like dreams. And I thought of the place in which I was born, a Victorian semi-detached house with a slate turret, a wide mahogany staircase which doubled back on itself, and service bells still connected by wires to plaques in a kitchen where I was scrubbed in an old tin bath by the open fire, so my mother told me. This place, too, had its residue, as subsequent occupants, who had recourse to an exorcism, would attest.

'No one gets off at Sway,' says the guard as I buy my ticket on the train. I'm not sure if this is a complaint or a curse. I ride down Barrows Lane, past Peterson's piggeries, overgrown with nettles and buddleia like some abandoned prisoner-of-war camp. Their vaulted roofs and individual stalls set with dark arched openings resemble bunkers or catacombs, their uniform greyness made somehow bleaker by their architectural details. I peer through one of the unglazed windows into a chamber with an unmantelled fireplace, an unfinished space, the approximate cast of what a room should look like. It is vaguely disturbing, this animal-less factory, strewn with broken children's bikes and rusting cars, lacking only a butcher's block and hooks as a reminder of its true function.

Passing the turkey farm housed in what were once Peterson's Palladian stables, I pull over onto the verge. Perhaps, at this last moment, it might have disappeared in the previous night's gales. Nervously, I enter the access code into the electronic box; the metal gate swings open to admit me, and I am conducted through a narrow door into a dim stairwell. As I begin my ascent, I run my finger along the walls, much rougher than I'd imagined, a lumpy amalgam of shingle and cement as though, like Purbeck stone, they were filled with fossils. The solidness is deceptive: I'm told that the wind drives rain through these porous slabs, as if they were honeycombed. I pass panelled doors, but as I climb, the domestic cosiness is replaced by yellow 'Danger' signs and rooms filled only with feathers and droppings. Some are braced with shiny metal bars as if to bolt the tower together, holding it in a permanent tension. The spaces seem to change shape: some with round port-holes like some concrete ship; others with gothic arches making them look like monastery cells, only with their frames picked out in pink – a quirky kitschness which seems to reflect the seaside shell gardens of Southbourne, just along the coast.

The quiet is unnerving. As I ascend the last few steps, a gradual roar begins, resisting my advance. Out in the open, it rises to a crescendo. The air is forcing itself through the dome as if to suck me upwards and out of its arches. I stand in the well of Peterson's observatory, the rushing sound overcoming my senses, my body battered by the current which threatens to catch me up like a plastic bag and hurl me out where there would be no Ruskinian angel to save me, no spirit of the North Wind to catch me in her tresses and prevent me from falling into nothingness and the soft forest earth below.

And as I turn around, almost spun by the wind, the arches present a panorama of all Hampshire. To the east, the spires of Fawley's refinery and Southampton Water; to the west, Bournemouth, with its suburbs and distinctive red terracotta and brick water tower familiar from family days out. Northwards lies the forest and beyond it, Broadlands; southwards, the Isle of Wight hovers like a mauve ghost in the silver-gilt sea, barely there at all. The entire gothic-framed sequence is theatrically lit as the clouds shutter over the sun, creating angular shafts of intense light, their slanting rays making the view seem more unreal. My camera seems

to be malfunctioning. Perhaps the microwaves are to blame – I was warned not to go among the ominous, battleship-grey phone masts which stud the parapet below; maybe their electromagnetic radiation is what makes my head feel so light and my body so wired. The wind in which the tower sways tears at my clothes, as though this enclosed space were the focus of all the air in England, whirling around me. Unable to stand it any longer, I gather up my bag and, clinging to the metal ladder, descend into the winding gut of the stairwell, grateful for each window which brings me closer to the ground.

Below, at the foot of the tower around which peregrine falcons fly, the double porches have been converted into three elegant rooms with high ceilings and chapel-like windows. Beneath the coffee table in the central room is the trap-door to its now-empty vault. On a nearby shelf stands the brass plaque found there, having been discarded by wartime troops searching for treasure.

As the electronic gate closes behind me, I wonder, 'with the usual touch of melancholy that a past-marked prospect lends', what brought Mary Ann Girling and Andrew Peterson and Auberon Herbert here. This land seems marked with the stain of memory; and as I cycle down to the sea and the wind-blown site of Hordle's Saxon church, with its sad-leaning gravestones, I can think only of the drowned bodies of shipwrecked travellers, interred under the rabbit-cropped turf, victims of the grey and treacherous waters.

On the front at Milford, where the Solent breaks over boulders imported to conserve the coast, the police have stopped a carload of lads and are hitching at the hips of their shiny black trousers as they amble purposefully towards the suspected young offenders.

Here the possibility of the forest ends abruptly, the gravelly heath crumbling like fruit cake as it falls away in slabs to the sea. Here the land rises to a final peak before tailing off into Hurst's spit, another in the succession of promontories that spike this coast, curlicues of shifting sand and shingle whipped by the wind and the waves, from Portland Bill and its quarries, to Hengistbury's ancient headland, where Gordon Selfridge planned to build his modern Xanadu, and where, as children, we would roll down bracken-lined neolithic ditches.

Then these places seemed both strange and familiar. They seem the same today: reassuringly recognisable yet growing ever smaller as I age. Each year, as southern England sinks, the elements conspire to carve out grand vistas even as they threaten to tip retirement homes onto the beach below, there to join the remains of ancient forests and sea monsters, relics of a time before the flood engulfed England's animal spirits.

And even as other rivers flood and forests burn, Peterson's tower still casts its shadow, as though the land revolved around it, still telling out the years, mute and grey and useless and profound. But one day it too will topple into these deceptively decorative waters, and the island will sunder into a watery archipelago of chalk icebergs like the eroded Needles, glaciers crumbling into the sea. West Wight will devolve geologically, making a modern Avalon of Freshwater, on whose downs Tennyson wraps himself in his cloak to pronounce the air worth sixpence a pint, while Mrs Cameron's nitrate-stained hands conjure tableaux of angels, and over at Osborne, the Queen-Empress carefully replaces a princess's sculpted white marble hand under a glass dome, there to rest on its midnight-blue velvet pillow for eternity.

When the Camerons left England in 1879 with their possessions packed in their coffins, they were seen off from Southampton Docks by friends who watched as railway porters returned from the ship with photographs given to them in lieu of a tip. Perhaps they valued Mrs Cameron's art more than the dismissive Mr Ruskin, whose face she had been unable to capture and whose back she had thumped, saying he was 'not worthy of photographs!' Then she sailed down the Solent bound for Ceylon, where she would die on a tropical verandah, looking up at the stars, uttering her last word, 'beautiful'.

So too would my grandmother bid us goodbye from her New

Forest bungalow, with its Indian brass and ebony elephants, her candy-floss hair spread on the pillow as we were ushered in one by one to say farewell, while out in her secret garden, an arched gateway in the high privet hedge opened onto the heath, with its glassy-eyed ponies and flies hovering over their haunches, the purple heather and the spiky gorse, and in the distance, the dark woods in which we too might be lost forever.

At Keyhaven, the wind blows me like a cloud along the horizon; I sail rather than ride along an embankment bound on one side by waffle-like concrete slabs languorously lapped by bladderwrack, and on the other by reflecting pools of quiet water which lie like bits of the sky fallen into the sedge, while gulls and terns eddy overhead. A slit-eyed pillbox guards the approach to this fragile, tentative land, the terrain of bird-watchers and dog-walkers. 'Good light,' says one, as I focus my lens. There is a transcendence to the day, as though the sun has taken everyone by surprise, releasing them from their routines to rediscover the earth beneath their feet and the sea beyond the shore. Out in the Solent, the island ferries briefly synchronise before resuming the journey which inspired Tennyson's 'Crossing the Bar', its lines copied out in a shaky biro hand in my grandfather's pocket diary, its cover stamped with a map of the Isle of Wight.

Sunset and evening star and one clear call for me
And may there be no moaning of the bar when I put out to sea
I hope to meet my pilot face to face when I have crossed the bar.

Perhaps here, in this half-drowned place, it might be possible to escape. But Mary Ann would never leave, not in this life anyway, just as Peterson would never rise above the earth, for all his efforts to reach the sky. And down by the water at Lymington, I wait for the train back to Brockenhurst, where the sun is already beginning to set, casting long shadows on the forest heath.

LIST OF ILLUSTRATIONS

ACKNOWLEDGEMENTS

NOTES ON SOURCES

INDEX

ILLUSTRATIONS

TITLE PAGE: Stagprince: print by Linder, after Thomas Bewick; Frontispiece, p.3, map & 'Rufus's death', courtesy Christopher Tower Library, Lyndhurst; p.9 – Rufus Stone from *The Journey Book of England: Hampshire including the Isle of Wight*, Charles Knight & Co., London 1841; p.34; idealized etching of Mary Ann Girling from *The Graphic*, September 1886, 'from a portrait in oils, taken by Mr Edmond W.Wade in 1881'; p.48 – Lunardi's balloon from Vincent Lunardi, *An Account of the First Aërial Voyage*, 1748;

p.55 – Ann Lee phrenological likeness from William Oxley, *Modern Messiahs and Wonder Workers*, 1889; p.66 – Joanna Southcott's seal from John Timbs, *English Eccentrics & Eccentricities*, 1877; p.70 – 'Whirling Gift' from David R.Lamson, *Two Years' Experience among the Shakers*, 1848; p.76 – Fourier Phalanx from Mark Holloway, *Utopian Communities in America*, 1950; p.82 – James Burns from Harry Price Library, University of London; p.86 – spirit photographs from *Human Nature* September 1874; p.89 – Elder Frederick Evans, courtesy of the Shaker Society, Sabbathday Lake;

p.91 – 'Shaker Lady' from Hepworth Dixon, *New America*, 1867; p.99 & pp.122–3 – *Illustrated Police News*, 14 January 1872; p.133 – *'A Shakers' 'Service'*, courtesy Geoffrey Gale; p.142 – Ordnance Survey map, 1876, with railways added from 1888; pp.146, 148, 277 & 292 from *The Graphic*, 9 January 1875; pp.176–7 – 'The Ejectment from New Forest Lodge' from *Pictorial World*, 9 January 1875; pp.195 & 250 – Arthur Hughes, from George MacDonald, *At the Back of the North Wind*, 1871; p.199 – Broadlands from Edward Clifford, *Broadlands As It Was*,1890; pp.201, 205 – William & Georgiana Cowper, courtesy Trustees of the Broadlands Archives; p.207 – *Beata Beatrix*, courtesy Tate Britain; p.211 – spirit ship, courtesy Trustees of the Broadlands Archives;

p.215 – Frederic Myers from Eveleen Myers' album, courtesy

National Portrait Gallery, London; portrait of Edmund Gurney from Myers, *Fragments of Prose and Poetry*,1904;

p.223 – John Ruskin, carte de visite, 1863, courtesy National Portrait Gallery, London;

p.238 – Brantwood, courtesy Sheila Goddard; pp.239, 260, 266, 269, 275, 426, from Ruskin *Works*; p.246 – Rose La Touche, from Van Akin Burd, *John Ruskin and Rose La Touche*, 1979, courtesy the author; p.265 – Rose La Touche on her death bed, Tate Britain; p.295 – Mary Ann Girling, carte de visite, courtesy St Barbe Museum, Lymington; p.300 – *Medium and Daybreak*, 3 December 1875; p.306 – *The Graphic* illustration, 10 April 1875; p.310 – *Penny Illustrated Paper* sketch of Mary Ann Girling, 31 August 1878; p.326 – 'Mesmerism vs Shakerism' cutting, *Isle of Wight Times*, February 1876; p.340–1 – *Illustrated London News* supplement, 31 August 1878;

p.347 – Peterson's portrait from the *Occasional Magazine of the Milford-on-Sea Record Society*, June 1927 courtesy the late Diana Gould; p.348 – Paine by George Romney, courtesy Clare Goddard; spirit portrait from Andrew Peterson's *Essays from the Unseen*;

p.361 – Sketch of tower from ATTP's Order books; p.370 – Plan of Peterson's Tower, Crown copyright, National Monuments Record; p.372 – Aerial photograph of tower, courtesy Barry Nixon; pp.401, 406–9 – Illustrations from *Jump-to-Glory Jane*, 1892;

p.410 – Mary Ann Girling portrait from *Modern Messiahs and Wonder Workers*; pp.416, 417 – Portrait of Herbert & postcard of Old House, courtesy Hampshire Record Office; p.422 – Zeppelin over Lyndhurst, courtesy Christopher Tower Library, Lyndhurst; p.427 – Ruskin by Fred Hollyer, c.1894, courtesy The Ruskin Foundation (Ruskin Library, University of Lancaster); pp.429 & 434 – Lord Mount Temple with Mrs Leycester, & Miss Emily Ford, & Lady Mount Temple portraits, courtesy Trustees of the Broadlands Archives; p.440 – New Forest Shakers photograph from *Hampshire Advertiser & Southampton Times*, 23 October 1937; p.4 – Housman's portraits from *The Sheepfold* & *The Unexpected Years*; p.4 – *Reveille* cutting, courtesy Gordon Pomeroy.

All other photographs by the author.

ACKNOWLEDGEMENTS

My thanks to Mark Ashurst for giving me *The Sense of an Ending*; Michael Bracewell, for his constancy; Linder Sterling, for the original Shaker gift; Hui-yong Yu for her companionship in Maine; and for their friendship and encouragement, Adam Low, Hugo Vickers, Neil Tennant and John Waters.

At Fourth Estate, I'd like to thank Christopher Potter; Nick Pearson; Andy Miller for his early encouragement; Nick Davies for skilful editorial suggestions; Rachel Connolly for her copy edit; and the ultimate, elegant aid of Mitzi Angel for seeing it all through to completion. For her excellent work on the text design, Vera Brice; and Megan Wilson for her beautiful jacket design. Thanks, too, to my indefatigable agent, Gillon Aitken, for his faith.

Jude James supplied essential material and an eagle-eyed scrutiny of the manuscript, a task in which he was joined by his wife, Peggy James. On our explorations into the forest, Geoffrey Gale, whose work on the Shakers and the Girlingites long predates mine, shared his insights. I had a particularly helpful early conversation on utopianism and spiritualism with James Gregory, whose own chapter on the Cowpers appears in *Palmerston Studies*, edited by Miles Taylor. Both Geoffrey and James made generous last-minute contributions to the book for which I thank them.

Lawrence Popplewell's booklet, *Moving the Shakers*, was a useful and compendious primer on the Girlingites. In East Anglia, Mary Ann's descendent, Peter Oliver, and his wife, provided fascinating details on their family tree; at Hordle, Mr and Mrs Gordon Pomeroy allowed me to enter their former Girlingite chapel; Arthur Lloyd of New Milton shared his pioneering investigations into the New Forest Shakers; and Sarah Newman of Tiptoe helped with detective work. Peggy Phillips, Dorothy Johnson and Stanley Lane, also of Tiptoe, provided intriguing memories of the area, and of their forebears. And I would like to extend special thanks to Paul Atlas.

Thanks, too, to Ron and Pamela Ashurst; Vickki Broadbent; Andrew

Brown, John Carr; James Chatfield-Moore; Michael Collins; Mary Covert; Mark Curthoys, Emma Dolman, Nadine Fry; Sheila, Terry, and Clare Goddard; Sam Goonetillake) the late Daphne Gould, and her New Forest Shakers collection; R.Hatton-Gore, Bunhill Fields; Dr Brian Hinton and Dimbola Lodge; Ian Irvine, Peter Jerrome, Nigel Jones, Dr Jackie Latham; Peter Leslie and the Royal Victoria Country Park, Netley; Joyce Lewis, Sean Mackenzie, Jonathan Meades, Greg Neale, Barry Nixon, Janet Street-Porter, Jayantha Wijesinghe, Father Bill Wilson.

I have consulted many institutions, collections, and their archivists, among them the staff of the Christopher Tower New Forest Reference Library, Lyndhurst; Richard Smout, of the Isle of Wight, Newport; Steve Marshall and the St Barbe Museum & Art Gallery, Lymington; Jim Hunter and Red House Museum, Christchurch; Dr C.M.Woolgar and Karen Robson, the Hartley Library Special Collections, University of Southampton; the staff of the Hampshire Record Office; the National Monuments Record, Swindon; the staff of the British Library, and its Newspaper Library; Terence Pepper, Clare Freestone and the National Portrait Gallery; Southwark Local Studies Library; Stephen Wildman, Ruskin Foundation, University of Lancaster; Howard Hull and Brantwood House, Coniston; John R.Hodgson and the John Rylands University Library of Manchester; Joanna Banham, Gemma Nightingale and Richard Humphreys at Tate Britain; Stuart Comer at Tate Modern; New York Public Library. Their expertise and facilities have been inestimable. I'm particularly grateful to the Trustees of the Broadlands Archives for permission to quote from unpublished papers in their care.

In America, I'd like to thank Brother Arnold Hodd of the Sabbathday Lake Shaker family for his kindess; Alex Carleton and the Rogues Gallery crew of Portland, Maine, for creative inspiration and sartorial splendour; Frank Schaefer and Mary Martin, for their Provincetown refuge and companionship.

And here at home, I want to thank my brothers Laurence and Stephen, and my sisters Christina and Katherine, for their support; but most of all, my mother, Theresa, who has to put up with me. And lastly, my young friends Harriet, Jacob, Lydia, Max, Oliver and Cyrus, with whom forest expeditions are always fun, even when we get lost.

PHILIP HOARE,
Southampton, December 2004

SOURCE AND BIBLIOGRAPHICAL NOTES

Abbreviations of publications:

DN: *Daily News*
DT : *Daily Telegraph*
FC: *Fors Clavigera*, 1871–84
HA: *Hampshire Advertiser*
HC: *Hampshire Chronicle*
HI: *Hampshire Independent*
HN: *Human Nature*, 1867–77
IOWT: *Isle of Wight Times*
M&D: *Medium and Daybreak*, 1870–95
PMG: *Pall Mall Gazette*
SLP: *South London Press*
ST: *Southampton Times*
S&W: *Salisbury & Wilshire Journal*
Works: E.T.Cook & Alexander Wedderburn, ed., *The Works of John Ruskin*, The Library Edition, 39 vols, London, 1903–12

Abbreviations of sources

HL: Cowper-Temple papers, Hartley Library, University of Southampton
HRO: Hampshire Record Office, Winchester
NYPL: New York Public Library, Manuscripts & Archives Division
RHM: Red House Museum, Christchurch
SCL: Southampton Central Library (Local Studies)

All publications London, unless otherwise stated

Prologue

Page
1 'in the woods . . .' Wendy Boase, *The Folklore of Hampshire and the Isle of Wight*, Batsford, 1976, p.27
2 'like a beast . . .' *ibid*., p.28
2 'I bear to judgement . . .' John Chapman, 'The strange death of William Rufus', Donn Small, ed., *Explore the New Forest*, HMSO, 1975, p.28
2 'at this instant . . .' Boase, *op.cit*., p.29
3 'the Divine Victim . . .' *ibid*., p.31, expounding on Margaret Murray's 'discredited' theory in *The God of Witches* (1933).
3 'the persistence of . . .' Hugh Ross Williamson, *The Arrow and the Sword*, Faber & Faber, 1957, introduction. Williamson speculates that ritual sacrifice linked the deaths of William Rufus and Thomas à Becket. A follower of

Margaret Murray's theories, he also discusses Rufus's death in conjunction with witchcraft, Cathar heresy, and 'Uranianism' – 'the persistence of "unnatural love" as a mark of the heresy'. [introduction]

3 'a stupid and an accidental . . .' Mike Dash 'Accidental Death of an Anti-Christ', *Fortean Times*, No.48, Spring 1987, p.47

6 'witches gathered . . .' The self-appointed witch, Gerald Brosseau Gardner, claimed to have used a 'cone of power' to deflect the Nazis. Francis King went further, saying that the rite involved human sacrifice, as the coven performed naked, but greased like Channel swimmers: 'On this occasion, however, the oldest and weakest member of the coven volunteered to forgo the protective grease so that he might die from cold . . .and his life force might aid the spell.' [J.H.Brennan, *Occult Reich*, Futura, 1974, pp.150, 152]

7 'spreading like mantling . . .' Anthony D.Hippisley Coxe, *Haunted Britain*, Pan, 1975, p.86. Margaret Murray saw 'the earliest representation of a deity' as 'the figure of a man clothed in the skin of a stag, and wearing on his head the antlers'. [*ibid.*]

7 For verdant crosses, see Simon Schama, *Memory and Landscape*, HarperCollins, 1995, p.214 *et passim.*

PART I

Chapter One *A Voice in the Wilderness*

16 'wild amphibious race . . .' G.Crabbe *The Borough*, Letter XXII, J.Hatchard, 1810, p.4

16 'poet of the poor' D.C.Browning, ed., *Everyman's Dictionary of Literary Biography*, Pan, 1972, p.161

16 'an old fisherman . . .' Crabbe, *op.cit.*, footnote

17 'Marshes intersected . . .' M.R.James, *Collected Ghost Stories*, Wordsworth, 1992, p.561

18 'a figure in pale . . .' *ibid.*, p.135

18 'seven or eight . . .' caption, The Moot Hall Museum, Aldeburgh

19 'It was only yesterday . . .' Colin Ford, *Julia Margaret Cameron*, National Portrait Gallery, 2003, p.15

20 'helots of luxury' Chartist villages included 'O'Connorville' in Hertfordshire and 'Charterville' in Oxfordshire.

20 '17,927,609' figures from G.Kitson Clark, *The Making of Victorian England*, 1962, p.149, quoted Alan Gauld, *The Founders of Psychical Research*, Routledge & Kegan Paul, 1968, p.32.

20 'It is said . . .' Gauld, pp.63–4.

20 'means for spiritual . . .' *The Woodbridge Reporter & Aldeburgh Times*, 22 June 1871

21 'Mary Ann's own . . .' Mark Clouting's son Arthur was Ipswich's first Labour mayor, and a temperance preacher. Another of Mark's sons, Henry, was a trade union organiser, while a third of Mary Ann's nephews, John, was parish clerk at Little Glemham.

21 'impetuous, strong-willing . . .' William Oxley, *Modern Messiahs and Wonder Workers: A History of the Various Messianic Claimants to Special Divine Prerogatives, and of the Sects that have arisen thereon in recent times*, Trübner & Co.,1889, p.78

21 'Mary Ann married' Their marriage certificate records that George Girling of full age, bachelor, mariner, resident at Lowestoft, son of Samuel Girling, labourer, married Mary Ann Clouting [Clowting] of full age, spinster, [no occupation recorded] of Lowestoft, daughter of William Clouting [Clowting], farmer, at St John's Church on 2 May 1843. The ceremony was performed to the rites of the established church by Richard Watts Barker, curate, and the witnesses were Mary Ann Day and John Newson. [*DNB/GRO*]

21 'half and halfer' Peter and Doris Oliver, *Mary Ann Girling*, privately published, 2001

21 'went forth . . .' obituary, *East Anglian Daily Times* 20 September 1886. A later report described Mary Ann as 'a Suffolk servant girl', and in 1871, testifying to a congregation in Chelsea, she claimed the references of ' "Squire" somebody', perhaps one of her 'well-to-do' employers. [unsourced cutting 1874, RHM; *A Shakers' 'Service'*, p.7; *East Anglian Daily Times*, *ibid.*]

22 'female missionary' *ibid.* Mary Ann claimed she was raised as a Wesleyan and had been a class-leader for nine years, but left because 'they wanted to put her on "the plan" of the Circuit . . . and to make her preach for money'. [*A Shakers' 'Service'*, p.7]

22 'as many as eight'. In 1889, Oxley recorded that Mary Ann 'had ten children, eight of whom died in infancy, and two, a son and daughter, still survive'. His source was her own declaration to an audience in May 1879: 'She said that she was born in East Suffolk, of poor but honest parents, and she followed the business of a milliner and dressmaker for several years. At the age of 23, she married and became the mother of TEN! children all of whom, except 2, died in their infancy . . . She then described a dream which she had 21 years ago . . .' [Oxley, p.78; 'The Shakers at the Assembly Room, Poole', Popplewell] Given that ten years separate Mary Ann's marriage and the birth of her first surviving child, these claims do not seem so unreasonable.

22 'It was after . . .' Oxley, *op.cit.*, p.79. Oxley dates the beginning of Mary Ann's mission to 1868; Mary Ann appears to date it to Christmas, 1858, or 1864.

23 'a flash of light . . .' 'The Shakers at the Assembly Room, Poole', *Moving the Shakers*, Lawrence Popplewell, ed., Melledgen Press, Bournemouth, 1993, unpaginated

23 'Daughter! Thy sins . . .' Oxley, p.79

23 'his body became . . .' *HN* August 1877, p.372

23 'a thrill throughout . . .' Oxley, p.79.

24 'in the literal sense . . .' Peter Ackroyd, *Blake*, Sinclair-Stevenson, 1995, p.35

24 'When I was 30 . . .' Julian of Norwich, 8 May 1373, quoted *Independent*, 8 May 2003

25 'I have called thee . . .' Oxley, p.79

25 'the Holy Spirit . . .' Luke 3: 22

25 'odium and opposition . . .' Oxley, p.79

25 'into a realm . . .' *HN*, August 1877, p.373

25 'a literal interpretation'. One nineteenth-century commentor counselled: 'Beware of the Apocalypse which, when studied, almost always either finds a man mad, or makes him so'. [Ian Boxall, 'The use and abuse of apocalyptic', *Priests & People*, Vol.18, No.11, November 2004, p.405] Boxall notes that the Greek *apocalypsis* translates as 'unveiling'.

25 'to declare an end . . .' Oxley, pp.79–80.

27 'The only emaciated . . .' 'Another Account', 1875, Popplewell

27 'perfect presence . . .' *HN*, August 1877, p.372. The *Secular Review* of

11 April 1885 claimed that Mary Ann ran away from her husband in 1860. [Mary Heimann, 'Mary Ann Girling', *Dictionary of National Biography*, Oxford University Press, 2004, p.347]

28 'thrilling, and often . . .' *HA*, 23 October 1937

29 'island of errors . . .' Christopher Hill, *The World Turned Upside Down: Radical Ideas During the English Revolution*, Penguin, 1991, p.28

30 'utopia . . .' *ibid.*, p.34

30 'And all who . . .' Acts 2:44–5. James Gregory notes that the Girlingites had another direct exemplar in the White Quaker sect in 1840s Dublin, much publicised in British radical and mainstream press at the time.

31 'Bernadette knelt' The Feast of the Assumption, which established the Virgin Mary's physical ascension into Heaven, was instituted in 1850 and is celebrated with readings which include Revelations' description of the Woman Clothed with the Sun. The Dogma of the Immaculate Conception was proclaimed in 1854 and asserts that Mary was untainted by original sin. Bernadette's visions, four years later, were seen as confirmation of this rule of faith; she died of consumption in 1879, aged thirty-five, but when her coffin was opened in 1908, her body was found to be incorrupt.

31 'how she had been . . .' *HI*, 18 December 1875

31 'rough, uncouth . . .' Oxley, p.81

32 'She stands forth . . .' *HN*, August 1877, p.374

32 'a curious growth . . .' 'The Battle of the Town Hall', May 1876, Popplewell, *op.cit.*,

33 'Why not procreate?' 'Another Account', 1875, *ibid.* Rev Thomas R.Malthus (1766–1834) published his *Essay on Population* in 1798.

33 'Many of the males . . .' Oxley, p.82

33 'loose character' Census for 1871, RG10/1760

35 '. . .to all those . . .' John 1:10–13

35 'springing, elastic . . .' John Montgomery, *Abodes of Love*, Putnam, 1962, p.115

35 'MOBBING A FEMALE PREACHER' *Woodbridge Reporter*, 20 April 1871

40 'the Rights of Women', *ibid.*, 18 May 1871

40 'Literary, Scientific, and Artistic . . .' *ibid.*, 15 June 1871

40 'A Dreaded Visitor' *ibid.*, 17 August 1871

40 'an opportunity . . .' Paul Roach, 'Wandering Between Two Worlds:Victorian England's Search for Meaning', website.

40 'some printed handbills . . .' *Woodbridge Reporter*, 2 May 1871

42 'Such a disgraceful riot . . .' *ibid.*, 4 May 1871

42 'A Lover of Fair Play' *ibid.*, 11 May 1871

43 'would have been . . .' *Suffolk Chronicle*, ? June 1871

43 'deplored that such opinions . . .' *Woodbridge Reporter*, 8 June 1871. Frank Kermode writes of 'The tradition of those passionate artisan prophets, who assumed the role of the Emperor of the Last Days and led their free-spirited followers in search of the new Jerusalem, was still alive in the nineteenth century, as a sort of proletarian parallel to the more sophisticated imperialism of the ruling classes in Germany and England.' [*The Sense of an Ending: Studies in the Theory of Fiction*, Oxford University Press, 2000, p.14]

43 'MRS GIRLING AGAIN!' *ibid.*, 29 June 1871

45 'a good excuse' Another possible reason for Mary Ann's move was the fact that her brother Charles, born in 1840, had married Elizabeth Pester in Battersea in 1866. Leonard Benham's wife, Martha, also came from London.

Chapter Two *Turning the World Upside-Down*

47 'so reduced . . .' 'The First Aërial Voyage, September 15, 1784', Humphrey Jennings, *Pandaemonium: The Coming of the Machine*, André Deutsch, 1985, p.82

48 'The balloon . . .' Richard Holmes, *Shelley: The Pursuit*, HarperCollins, 1994, p.41

49 'these new mechanical meteors . . .' Davenport-Hines, *op.cit.*, p.124

49 'Twinkling . . .' Holmes, *op.cit.*, p.149. In the early twenty-first century, attempts to enlighten the dystopia of North Korea were made using radios floated on balloons.

49 'a framed point . . .' caption, 'Philip Brannon', Southampton City Art Gallery, May 2002. Brannon (1815–1890) produced guides to Southampton, Netley Abbey and his native Isle of Wight. Twice bankrupted, he later retreated to the island with his second wife and fifteen children, becoming Inspector of Nuisances in Shanklin. Nonetheless, he maintained his airier ambitions and in 1870, designed a navigable balloon.

50 'The Whale . . .' Philip Brannon, *Picture of Southampton*, 1850, republished Laurence Oxley, Alresford, 1973, p.16

50 'that the world might be . . .' Hill, *op.cit.*, p.17.

50 'The Camisards'. Another explanation for their name came from their habit of wearing their shirts outside their breeches. European heresies had ever reacted to persecution by spreading like ground elder: from the Antinominians, who believed in predestination and that they could therefore act as they wished on earth, to the Anabaptists, who believed in adult baptism on the grounds that no infant could be sentient of its faith.

50 'aerial psalmody' Charles Tylor, *The Camisards*, Simpkin, Marshall, Hamilton, Kent & Co./ Edward Hicks, 1893, p.213

51 'sobs and mental agitation' *ibid.*, p.68

51 '*L'Avertissement* . . .' J.F.Sollier, *The Catholic Encyclopdia*, New Advent web site

51 'they ranted profusely . . .' *Blackwoods Edinburgh Magazine*, March 1874, p.317

51 'mystical phalanx' W.H.G.Armytage, *Heavens Below: Utopian Experiments in England 1560–1960*, Routledge & Kegan Paul, 1961, p.42

52 'her Eyes glaring . . .' Anon., *An Account of a Dream at Harwich, In a Letter to a Member of Parliament about the Camisars*, Ben Bragg, 1708, p.12

52 'the whole Face . . .' Anon., *Clavis Prophetica; or, a Key to the Prophecies of Mons. Marion, and the other Camisars. . .*', J.Morphew,1707, p.2

52 'wou'd attest . . .' *A Relation of the Dealings of God to his Unworthy Servant, JOHN LACEY*. . . Ben Bragg, 1708, p.29

52 'the fact of some . . .' *Blackwoods*, *op.cit.*, p.317

53 'further degree . . .' Edward Deming Andrews, *The People Called Shakers*, Dover, New York, 1963, p.5. Geoffrey Gale notes there is no evidence that the French Prophets ever reached Manchester or that the Wardleys even existed; like Mary Ann, Ann Lee's orgins are surrounded by myth. [GG to PH, 5 December 2004]

53 'a strange power . . .' *ibid.*, p.302

54 '. . .Amend your lives . . .' *ibid.*, p.6

54 'It is not I . . .' Richard Francis, *Ann the Word*, Fourth Estate, 2000, p.28

54 'Permanent Spring', *ibid.*, p.31–2
54 'especially concerning . . .' Rufus Bishop & Seth Youngs Wells, ed., *Testimonies of the Life, Character, Revelations, and Doctrines of Mother Ann Lee. . .* Albany, New York, Weed, Parsons,1888, p.2–3
55 'When I felt my eyes . . .' Francis, *op.cit.*, 42
56 'her earthly tabernacle' *Testimonies*, *op.cit.*, p.5
56 'My flesh . . .' F.W.Evans, *Shaker Compendium*, D.Appleton, New York, 1859, p.125
56 'a kind of down . . .' Francis, p.44
56 'astonishing vision . . .' Mark Holloway, *Utopian Communities in America, 1680–1880*, Dover, New York, 1966, p.57
56 'clothed with the sun . . .' Revelations 12:1–2
56 'felt unspeakable joy . . .' Francis, p.44
57 'He then beat me . . .' Andrews, *op.cit.*, p.10
57 'surrounded by . . .' Holloway, *op.cit.*, p.56
57 'wilfully and contemptuously . . .' Andrews, p.11
58 'She had nothing to eat . . .' *Shaker Compendium*, *op.cit.*, p.133
58 'little ease', conversation with Linder Sterling, September 2002
58 'It is not I . . .' Andrews, p.1
58 'the *Christ* . . .' *Testimonies*, p.2, footnote
58 'utterly repugnant . . .' Holloway, p.65
59 'Earth's only Paradise' Ben Johnson, *The Alchemist*, quoted *The Deliverance and The Patience*, Richard Grayson, Book Works 2003, introduction. More's *Utopia* was 'the first. . . reflection of the New World in the literature of the old'; in 1583, Sir Humfrey Gilbert had carried a copy on the first British colonial expedition to America. [Krishan Kumar, *Utopia & Anti-Utopia in Modern Times*, Basil Blackwell, 1987, p.441]
59 'millenial convictions' Andrews, p.34
59 'new forest-homes . . .' Holloway, p.31
59 'a white, obscure . . .' *ibid.*, pp.40–1. Impersonations of the Woman Clothed with the Sun continue into the present century. The website of the Orthodox Church of Mother of God Derjavnaya in Russia declares 'The era of the Mother of God is coming', and exhorts, 'Angels, smite UFOs with the lightning of the Kingdom!'; while there were other echoes of mysterious aerial objects around Mary Ann's own birthplace: on Christmas Day, 1980, the US military base at Rendlesham was the site of a close encounter when, like the Shakers' burning tree, a UFO appeared to set the forest on fire.
59 'a large tree . . .' Francis, p.75
59 'fled to the . . .' F.W.Evans, *Shaker Communism*, James Burns, 1871, introduction
60 'I am commissioned . . .' *ibid.*, p.v
60 'the immense pines . . .' 'A Visit to the Shakers', *Blackwood's*, April 1823, pp.463–4
60 'all sunk . . .' Francis, p.78. The 1646 ballad, 'The World is Turned Upside Down', was the origin of the eighteenth-century song 'dolefully played' as Cornwallis surrendered at Yorktown in 1781. [Hill, p.380, Andrews, p.18]
60 'they were angels . . .' *ibid.*, p.140
60 'naked for a sign', Ackroyd, *Blake*, *op.cit.*, p.154. When the Shaker apostate, Thomas Brown, asked Mary Hocknell if it was true that 'in Mothers day, by her gift', the family danced naked, she replied, '. . . [Y]ou know how apt the ignorant and vulgar part of mankind, are to misrepresent what they see. If one

told they danced part naked, or with but few clothes on, another in telling the story, would leave out the part, or few, and so it was reported that we danced naked'. [Andrews, p.306]

61 'sometimes while . . .' Francis, p.141

61 'a certain efflux . . .' *et seq.*, *ibid.*, pp.181–2

61 'shaking their heads . . .' Andrews, pp.27–8

61 'as if there . . .' *ibid.*, p.29–30

62 'Their motions . . .' Chadwic Hansen, *Witchcraft at Salem*, George Braziller, New York, 1969, p.1

63 'federated communal order', Andrews, p.40

63 'being *unfriendly*', *Shaker Compendium*, p.141

63 'a British emissary . . .' Andrews, p.43.

63 'over Come . . .' Carol F.Karlsen, *The Devil in the Shape of a Woman: Witchcraft in Colonial New England*, W.W.Norton & Co., New York, 1998, p.9

63 'that He had . . .' Francis, p.246

64 'to bear . . .' Andrews, p.51. In 1643 there were 'divers sects of familists' in Barbados, and in the 1660s, exiled Ranter supporters of Nayler reconvened on the island. Later the Caribbean was a conduit of spiritualism via African shamanism and voodoo. There is a distinct black lineage in spiritualism's working-class roots and ministry to the dispossessed, from the Shakers' openness to black members (and Amerindian culture, with its own shamanistic and spiritualistic beliefs), to the Black Camisards of the civil war. Spiritualists such as Evans, Burns, and Owen were vocal opponents of slavery; while allegations of American influence on the Girlingites evoke modern notions of racism (as well as echoing 'black-faced' attacks on 'Indian-loving' Shakers). It is interesting, in this context, to note that the Girlingites played host to a pair of black Siamese twins who were born into slavery (see note to p.327). [Hill, p.254–5 *n*]

64 'the opium . . .' E.P.Thompson, *The Making of the English Working Class*, Pelican, 1980, p.418.

65 'imagination with magnetism . . .' Brennan, *op.cit.*, p.150

65 '*the Downfall* . . .' Thompson, p.128. Brothers was a naval officer until he received a new, heavenly commission, 'to lead back the Jews to Palestine'. In 1794 he issued a specific date for London's destruction, and claimed to have saved the city 'by his intercession with the Deity'. [John Timbs, *English Eccentrics & Eccentricites*, Chatto & Windus, 1877, p.194–6]

65 'walk leisurely into London' Timbs, p.196

66 'wrought such. . . .' Montgomery, *op.cit.*, p.83

66 'the bondage of the law' *ibid.*, p.84. Buchan also announced she was the Woman Clothed with the Sun. On her death, Buchan's partner, Reverend Hugh White, pointed to a hole in the roof (which he had made) as proof that an angel had taken her to heaven.

66 'O England! . . .' Thompson, p.422

66 'It is in vain . . .' *ibid.*, p.426

66 'was permitted by the Lord . . .' Oxley, p.26

67 'Then I heard . . .' Revelations 7:4

67 'Southcott left . . .' In the 1820s John Wroe, a Bradford woolcomber, succeeded Southcott and dedicating his Christian Israelite mission to the Jews, having himself publicly circumcised, and requiring his followers to do likewise. His New Jerusalem at Ashton, Lancashire cost of £9,200, but after charges of

immorality, he emigrated to Australia. His Lancashire temple later became the Star Cinema.

68 'orders' Andrews, p.57

68 'Put your hands . . .' Shaker leaflet, Sabbathday Lake

68 'the children of one . . .' Andrews, p.99

69 'Can Mr Owen reverse . . .' *Blackwood's*, March 1823, p.338. Robert Owen (1771–1858) used his father-in-law's cotton-mills at New Lanark on the Clyde as a model in his campaign against the abuses of industrialism. His *New View of Society* (1813) argued for a kind of proto-communism founded on co-operatives, and in 1817 he published 'A Brief Sketch of the Religious Society of People Called Shakers', extolling their 'habits of industry, temperance, order, and neatness'. [Andrews, p.131]

69 'I am come . . .' Holloway, p.104

69 'new empire . . .' *ibid.*, p.105. *Blackwood's* decried Owen's folly, 'when . . . all the honest money he had earned in Scotland . . . got dissipated in the dreary vanity of his great communistic whim in America . . .'; while the *Communist Manifesto* declared that the Owenites 'deaden the class struggle . . . to realise all these castles in the air they are compelled to appeal to the . . . purses of the bourgeois.' [August 1874, p.176; Laski, p.165]

70 'Nashoba' Frances Wright (1795–1852) was a ward of Jeremy Bentham, friend of Lafayette and of other European reformers. Robert Dale Owen (1801–77), spiritualist and abolitionist, came to New Harmony in 1825. As a Member of Congress, he was later instrumental in the foundation of the Smithsonian Institution.

70 'began to shake . . .' Andrews, p.154

70 'I see . . .' David Slosson, *Testimonies of the Life. . .of Mother Ann Lee. . .*, Hancock, Massachusetts, J.Tallcott & J.Deming, 1816, p.240

71 'where they lay . . .' Andrews, p.154

71 'heavenly thoughts' *ibid.*, p.155. The 'Era of Manifestations' also produced remarkable gift drawings of birds, animals, trees and abstract images of 'showers of blood' and 'the Sun clothed in Sackcloth and the Moon in Scarlet!!!' [*Heavenly Visions: Shaker Gift Drawings and Gift Songs*, curated by France Morin, The Drawing Center/UCLA Hammer Museum/University of Minnesota Press, 2001, p.13]

71 'diamonds of charity' Andrews, p.157

72 'such as would . . .' *ibid.*, p.170

72 'similar manifestations . . .' *ibid.*, p.175

72 'a brisk tattoo' Horace Wyndham, *Mr Sludge, the Medium*, Geoffrey Bles, 1937, p.5

72 'with her eyes . . .' *ibid.*, p.10

72 'at once recognised . . .' F.W.Evans, 'Shakerism and Spiritualism in their Moral Aspects', *The Shaker*, reprinted *HN*, 1871, Vol 5, pp.401–2

73 'that this form . . .' Andrews, p.175

73 'We are all . . .' Samuel Hopkins Adams, *Alexander Woollcott*, Hamish Hamilton, 1946, p.13. Woollcott, the theatre critic, was raised on the site of the North American Phalanx, New Jersey on Fourierist principles; his grandfather, John S. Bucklin, was President of the Phalanx.

73 'Rat-revelation' M.Russell & Clare R.Goldfarb, *Spiritualism & Nineteenth-Century Letters*, Fairleigh Dickinson University Press, New Jersey, 1978, p.51

73 'utter and systematic . . .' Nathaniel Hawthorne, *Twenty Days with Julian &*

Little Bunny by Papa, New York Review Books, 2003, p.44. Melville wrote, '... I feel that this Hawthorne has dropped germinous seeds into my soul. He expands and deepens down, the more I contemplate him; and further and further, shoots his strong New England roots in the hot soil of my Southern soul' ('an astonishingly sexual image', noted Newton Arvin in his *Herman Melville*,William Sloane Associates, NY, 1950). [p.138]

73 'Concordium' The Concordium was founded by James Pierrepoint Greaves and run by Charles Lane and Henry Gardner Wright. In 1843 it published *The New Age: A Journal of Human Physiology, Education, and Association*, concerned with 'hydropathy, mesmerism, phrenology, celibacy, pacifism, astrology, and a vegetarian diet shorn of all stimulants'. Greaves died after a hydropathic cure (in which subjects were wrapped in cold wet sheets) at Alcott House in 1842. Six years later the community also expired, from 'internal conflict'. [see J.E.Latham, *Search for a New Eden: James Pierrepoint Greaves, the Sacred Socialist*, Fairleigh Dickinson University Press, 2000]

74 'Since cotton, silk, and wool ...' Louisa May Alcott, *Transcendental Wild Oats*, Virginia Commonwealth University/American Transcendentalism website.

74 'to do away ...' *ibid.* After leaving Fruitlands, Charles Lane joined the Shakers at Harvard for the winter, only to return to England, where he married the following year.

75 'sentient beings ...' Holloway, p.138. Fourierism, as expounded by Frederick Law Olmstead, had a specific influence on American town planning and 'landscape architecture': Manhattan's Central Park, the 'People's Garden', was seen as a product of the Fourierist fever of the 1840s. Greg Neale sees a modern equivalent to a utopian movement in the TV show, *Friends* (whose coffee shop nexus, 'Central Perk', has its own relationship to Ruskin's St George tea rooms, run by Rose La Touche).

75 'Brook Farm' In the wake of these colonies came Modern Times, founded on Long Island in 1851 by America's first anarchist and founder of Ohio's Utopia, Josiah Warren. The community included a polygamist and a nudist. The local press declared 'the women of Modern Times dress in men's clothes and look hideous', and when another woman who ate only beans died of her diet, it was said that 'the people of Modern Times are killing themselves with fanatical ideas about food'. [Holloway, p.158]

75 'Daguerreotypist' *The House of the Seven Gables*, Penguin,1986, p.84. In 1856 Hawthorne visited Netley Abbey, and brought away a memory of its 'once polished marble pillars', now 'so rude in aspect'. ['English Notebooks' website]

75 'archangel Gabriel' Herman Melville, *Moby-Dick, or, The Whale*, Arion Press/ University of California Press, Los Angeles, 1983, p.323. In one of *Moby-Dick's* strangest chapters, Ishmael tells of the wild-eyed young man who, at the Shakers' 'cracked, secret meeting ... several times descended from heaven by the way of a trap-door, announcing the speedy opening of the seventh vial, which he carried in his vest-pocket; but, which, instead of containing gunpowder, was supposed to be charged with laudanum'. On joining the whaleship *Jeroboam*, he gains a 'wonderful ascendency' over its crew, declaring himself to be the archangel Gabriel and 'vicar general of all Oceanica'. When they encounter the *Pequod*, he warns Captain Ahab against attacking the White Whale as the 'Shaker God incarnated'. [pp.321–4]

76 'Bible Communists' Holloway, p.181

76 'In a holy community . . .' *ibid.*, p.183
76 'random procreation' *ibid.*, p.185. English spiritualists worried about such experiments in 'free love'. In his January 1868 'Letter from America' to *Human Nature*, J.H.Powell reassured them, 'Doubtless there are some in the mire, but the vast majority are rightly and morally opposed to it . . .'
76 'shares of Second-Coming Stock' *ibid.*, p.190

Chapter Three *Human Nature*

78 'faith is problematic' After the 2003 war in Iraq, the philosopher John Gray described Osama bin Laden's 'utopian vision of the future – a harmonious world in which the traditional institutions of government are no longer necessary', as 'an echo of 19th century European anarchists'. 'The history of the twentieth century is testimony to the undiminished power of the apocalyptic imagination', Gray added. 'Most people continue to believe that society is becoming progressively more secular, but . . . Communism had more in common with medieval millenarian movements than it did with anything in modern science – and at the start of the twenty-first century, the hold of apocalyptic thinking on politics is as strong as ever'. The fear of an imagined future distopia replaces the hope of a utopian one: in November 2004, Prince Charles was quoted as criticising 'social utopianism' as setting standards of unreal expectations. [*Independent*, 18 May 2003 & 11 September 2004; *The Tablet*, 17 January 2004]
78 'vast reaches of America' In *White Jacket* (1850), Melville writes, 'We Americans are the peculiar, chosen people – the Israel of our time . . . the pioneers of the world; the advance-guard, sent on through the wilderness of untried things, to break a new path in the New World . . .' In his introduction to Hawthorne's *The House of the Seven Gables*, Milton R.Stern notes, 'The history of America re-enacts the essential condition of the human race in its constant motion from Edenic expectation to the Fall of man and the consequent agonized struggle to rise again . . . the American claimant's Edenic expectations expressed by the pervasive American Dream – which, if it is anything, is a dream of triumph over time in a world that is endlessly New'. It is a literary trope most achingly expressed in Scott Fitzgerald's *The Great Gatsby*, with its last, mystical lines, 'somewhere back in that vast obscurity beyond the city, where the dark fields of the republic rolled under the night . . . So we beat on, boats against the current, borne back ceaselessly into the past.' [Kumar, p.80; Penguin, 1986, introduction; Penguin,1974, p.188]
78 'Utopia was priced out' At the beginning of the nineteenth century, the distribution of wealth in America had been relatively fair; by its end, more than half its wealth would lay in the hands of less than one per cent of the population.
78 'inventors of . . .' The Shakers' honesty and industry proved a specific paradigm for the new republic. With their inventions, they were 'unwittingly in the vanguard of the movement leading from a household economy to mass production'; yet when Evans denounced the idea of beauty for its own sake as 'absurd and abnormal', it was an ironic augury of a future in which Shaker furniture would sell for thousands of dollars, and when manufacturers would market 'Shaker kitchens'. [Andrews, pp.121,126]
78 'To the mind . . .' Holloway, pp.78–9
79 'intellectual celibates' Andrews, p.233

79 'Spiritualism originated . . .' F.W.Evans, 'Shakerism *vs.* Owenism', *Spiritual Telegraph*, 2 February 1856, p.157, spirithistory website. Owen's spiritualism promised a utopian 'Summerland', offering 'the living a community with the dead'. [Logie Barrow, *Independent Spirits: Spiritualism & English Plebians, 1850–1910*, Routledge & Kegan Paul, 1986, p.25–6]

79 'ancient costume' 'A Brief Account of Ten Seances Held at North Family, Mt Lebanon' May 1878, NYPL

79 'That noble . . .' F.W.Evans, quoted Barrow, p.260. Hammond's *Light from the Spirit World: The Pilgrimage of Thomas Paine, and others, to the Seventh Circle in the Spirit World* (Partridge & Brittan, New York, 1852), with its messages from Paine, communicated in Rochester in 1850–2, presaged Peterson's *Essays from the Unseen* a generation later. Rochester, the centre of the Burnt Over Region, was a 'free-thinking' town which in the 1830s openly celebrated Paine's birthday.

80 'John Brown' – see Barrow, pp.32–40

81 'the England and Irish . . .' *ibid.*, p.21

81 'one of the greatest . . .' *ibid.*, p.24

81 'spirits of devils' *HN*, 1871, Vol 5, p. 403

81 'would have . . .' *ibid.*, p.464. In 1871, Peebles held a joint convention in Cleveland with Elder Lomas of the Watervliet community; he was addressed as 'Brother' by the Society of Believers. Geoffrey Gale notes that it was Peebles who suggested the visit to Evans, and 'pleaded' with the Mount Lebanon Elders to let them go. [Evans MS, NYPL; GG to PH, 5 December 2004]

82 'Cosmology . . .' Barrow, p.194

82 'The Connexion' Roberta Elzey, *Founding an Anti-University*, courtesy Joseph Berke. At her installation at ICA East, Shoreditch, February 2004, Yoko Ono showed a poster of a building resembling the World Trade Center being blown up by 'Utopian Dynamite'.

82 'a kind of Universal Provider . . .' Anon., [C.Maurice Davies] *Maud Blount, Medium: A Story of Modern Spiritualism*, Tinsley Brothers, 1877, p.154–5. Burns was born in Ayrshire in 1835, the son of a smallholder; he came to London as a gardener at Hampton Court and discovered spiritualism via imported American texts.

83 'Psychological Department' *HN*, 1 April 1867

83 'with the upper portion . . .' *ST*, 9 January 1875

83 'exclaiming repeatedly . . .' *ibid.*, 30 January 1875

83 'Life in the Factories' *HN*, May 1867, p.116

84 'The Vaccination Humbug' *ibid.*, June 1867, p.174–5 p.72.

84 'alcoholic liquors . . .' *ibid.*, 'The Use of Fruit', July 1867, p.233

84 '*The Cases of the Welsh* . . .' W.M.Wilkinson & J.J.Garth Wilkinson, *The Cases of the Welsh Fasting Girl and Her Father. On the Possibility of Long Continued Abstinence from Food*, J.Burns 1870, p.11. William Martin Wilkinson was the lawyer brother of the homeopathist, mesmerist, and Swedenborgian anti-vaccinator, James John Garth Wilkinson.

84 'Her death was triumph . . .' undated cutting, tipped into above.

85 'organic particles' Thoreau noted that Sir Kenelm Digby believed 'exhausted lay fields' could attract 'vital spirits' from the air. [*Walden*, Princeton University Press, 1989, p.162]

85 'Walt Whitman . . .' *HN*, February 1876, p.49

85 'Music from the . . .' *ibid.*, Vol 5, 1871, p.480

85 'WHY WE SHOULD . . .' *ibid.*, March 1875, p.479. Peebles also wrote for

Human Nature, on 'Darwinism *vs* Spiritualism', and it was noted that the Shakers joined the Oneidans in accepting Darwin's theories. However, in another edition, J.W.Jackson stated that 'The fact that no Negroid people are thoroughly civilised. . .must be regarded as adequate proof of a radical unfitness', and claimed 'Of the organic inferiority of uncultured uncolonised America, indeed, no one doubts. . . Archeology abundantly demonstrates that America is now only passing through the epicycle of her colonial destiny.' [*HN*, May/June 1878; September & March 1875]

85 'a modern miracle . . .' 'A Letter from America', *ibid.*, January 1868, p.602–3

85 'alive and stuffed' J. J.Morse, *Leaves from My Life*, J.Burns, 1877, p.50–1. Lily Dale, a spiritualist camp set up in the Burned Over Region in 1879, still operates as a spiritualist community of two hundred homesteads.

86 'the baby sister . . .' 'Spirit Photography', MA (Oxon), *HN*, September 1874, p.395

87 '. . .The evidence for . . .' *HN*, December 1884, p.514

87 'by way of . . .' Roland Barthes, *Camera Lucida*, Vintage, 2000, p.31

88 'The whole ship . . .' F.W.Evans, manuscript diary, 7 July 1871, NYPL

88 'angelic children' Albums assembled by Frederic Myers' wife Eveleen contain images of their naked children as angels, and photographs of mediums with whom the Myers experimented. Under one portrait, of Eusapia Paladino, Eveleen wrote, 'led me a Hell of a Time. . .Very interesting but oh! so trying . . .' [album, National Portrait Gallery]

89 'dark little shop' Janet Oppenheim *The Other World: Spiritualism and Psychical Research in England 1850–1914*, Cambridge University Press, Cambridge,1985, p.43

89 'crowded with . . .' 'Elder Frederick & the Shakers', *HN*, September 1871, p.462

89 'we have seen . . .' *ibid.*, 'Phrenological Characteristics of a Shaker', p.464

90 'most interesting and profitable' J.M.Peebles to Antoinette Doolittle, 18 July 1871, Evans MS, p.24–5, NYPL

90 'splendid rooms' Evans to the Elders, Mount Lebanon, 2 August 1871, NYPL

90 '*An Opportunity* . . .' *Times* 3 March 1871.

91 'singular beauty . . .' W.Hepworth Dixon, *New America*, Hurst & Blackett, 1867, Vol II, p.92. He also wrote, 'The Shaker is a monk, the Shakeress a nun. They have nothing to say to this world; yet their church, so often described as a moral craze . . . at best a church of St Vitus, not of St Paul, will be seen . . . to have some singular attractions'. [p.89]

91 'The order of Shakers . . .' *Times* 3 August 1871. 'They certainly did manufacture alcohol for medical purposes, but there are plenty of records of Shaker brothers being the worst for wear or "having problems".' [GG to PH, 5 December 2004]

91 'that both England . . .' *ibid.*, 7 August 1871

91 'desperate, drugged . . .' Evans diary, p.155, NYPL

91 'great Babel . . .' Evans to Br Timothy, 15 July 1871, NYPL

91 'The poor breed . . .' Evans to the Elders, 2 August 1871, p.33, NYPL

92 'I am quite . . .' *ibid.* Evans told Dolittle, 'If I were Elder Otis & Co., I would sell out, and come to England. . .With Elder John as preacher, they would gather'. [26 July 1871]

92 'from one end . . .' *HN*, 1871, Vol 5, p.462

92 'Spiritualists' Vegetarian Banquet' *M&D* 22 February 1883, p.113

92 'I should do better . . .' Evans diary, p.45, NYPL

92 'They are . . .' To Br Timothy, 15 July 1871, NYPL. Evans thought Hardinge, whom he had met in New York, a 'wonderful medium', and would have liked to claim her for a Shaker ('it is a pity that Emma is married'). [To the Elders, 15 July 1871, p.20, NYPL]

93 'What have Spiritualists . . .' *HN*, 1871, Vol 5, p.463. When J.W.Fletcher visited 15 Southampton Row, asking, 'Is there any work for me to do?', Burns said, 'No. American mediums have ruined the cause here, and I wish none of them would ever set foot in England again'. [Barrow, p.131]

93 'women's rights . . .' *Shaker & Shakeress*, Vol III, No.8, August 1873, Mount Lebanon, New York, p.10. The journal began as *The Shaker* before becoming *Shaker & Shakeress* and, latterly, *The Manifesto*.

93 'Will Shakerism . . .' *ibid.*, Vol V, No.1, June 1875, p.4

93 'would have taken . . .' *ibid.*, Vol V, No.9, September 1875, p.67

93 'to inaugurate . . .' *HN*, 1871, Vol 5, p.464

93 'Single persons . . .' *Shaker Communism*, *op.cit.* Evans hoped Burns would publish *Shaker & Shakeress*, which he edited with Dolittle for a short period ('their views clashed with the other members . . . and by the end of 1875 they were replaced'). [GG to PH, 5 December 2004]

93 'party of proselytes' *HN*, 1871, Vol 5, p.462

94 'a young man . . .' Evans diary, p.60, NYPL. Haase had written to Evans before he came to England, and 'certainly intended to become a Shaker'. [GG to PH, 5 December 2004]

94 'if things suit . . .' Evans to Antoinette Doolittle, 26 July 1871, p.25, NYPL

94 'for political reasons' Geoffrey Gale, 'Elder Evans, Mrs Girling and the Children of God', Mick Gidley with Kate Bowles, ed., *Locating the Shakers: Cultural Origins and Legacies of an American Religious Movement*, University of Exeter Press, 1990, p.119.

94 'a great scientific . . .' Evans diary, p.28, NYPL, p.28

95 'if I wd pay . . .' To the Elders, 2 August 1871, p.31, NYPL

95 'thinks of going' Evans diary, p.264, NYPL

95 'A Welcome . . .' Gale, *op.cit.*, p.118

95 'Hills, mountains . . .' Montgomery, *op.cit.*, pp.72–3

95 'The dream of Utopia . . .' *Shaker & Shakeress*, Vol III, No, 1, January 1873, pp.6–7

95 'He stated . . .' 'Shakerism by David Brown', *HN*, 29 May 1876, Vol 10, pp.442–3.

96 'Shakerism . . .' *ibid.*, p.445. Oxley colourfully argued 'the rottenness' of Shakerism as 'Roman Catholicism pure and simple' with Mount Lebanon was its Vatican. 'Under the guise of liberty, it is, at bottom, a bondage as servile and intolerable as the ecclesiaticism born of Rome. . .which demands obedience to its behest as the passport to Heaven. . . damning all others to perdition'; its celibacy was 'a purely Romish device'. [p.21–22]

96 'trials have been . . .' Haase to Evans, 8 July 1871, Evans MS, pp.34–7, NYPL

PART II *O Clouds Unfold!*

'The great majority . . .' Kermode, *op.cit.*, p.8

Chapter Four *The Walworth Jumpers*

101 'other trades' Quakers also made their presence known in the morally integral production of food, from porridge oats to chocolate. Both John Cadbury and Joseph Rowntree were Quakers and founded model villages at Bourneville and New Earswick; in the USA, the Hershey company grew out of a Pennsylvanian Mennonite community.

102 '"First Month" . . .' Montgomery, *op.cit.*, p.36

102 'the time tables . . .' Rev C.Maurice Davies, *Unorthodox London:or, Phases of Religious Life in the Metropolis*, Tinsley Brothers, 1873, p.198

102 'standing on . . .' Peter Jerrome, *John Sirgood's Way: The Story of the Loxwood Dependents*, Window Press, Petworth, 1998, p.52.

102 'dimly visible . . .' Thomas Shaw, *Bible Christians*, Epworth Press 1965, p.78. The sect, founded by a Methodist named O'Bryan, rejected all human authority in religion.

102 'for refusing . . .' Davies, *op.cit.*, p.296. The Peculiar People persisted as conscientious objectors in the First World War and into the modern era, dressed anachronistically like their Sussex cousins, the Society of Dependents or 'Cokelers', whose own black bonnets and dresses recalled the Amish and Mennonites of Pennsylvania.

103 'derided, reproached, insulted . . .' Jerrome, *op.cit.*, p.83

103 'withdraw from . . .' Oxley, pp.82–3. The Bible Christians publically dissociated from the Girlingites: at their 'handsome Jubilee Chapel in East Road' near Bunhill Fields, Davies heard repudiations of 'the woman whose ministrations at Walworth have lately become notorious'. [Davies, p.110; *DT*, 28 December 1871]

104 'triumphant' W.Young Fullerton, *C.H.Spurgeon*, Williams & Norgate, 1920, p.354. Ruskin was particularly attached to the evangelist: '. . . I had a great lark with Spurgeon yesterday. I'm very fond of him, and he of me . . .' [7 January 1864, *Works* XXXVI, p.464]

105 'strictly descriptive . . .' Davies, introduction

105 'the leading criminal . . .' C.Booth, ed., *Life and labour of people in London*, MacMillan, 1890, quoted Andrew Harris, 'The Artistic Installation of Hoxton: Urban Space and Deindustrialisation', University College of London thesis, 2001

106 'On the plane . . .' Davies, p.1–2

106 'close to the Moorgate Street . . .' *ibid.*, p.3

106 'Colonel Wentworth Higginson . . .' *ibid.*, p.22. Thomas Wentworth Higginson served in the 1st South Carolina Volunteers; his book, *Army Life in A Black Regiment* (Fields & Osgood, Boston, 1870), is a classic account of the Civil War, and of black history.

106 'loud and long . . .' *ibid.*, p.78

106 'a splendid specimen', *Maud Blount*, p.2

106 'The very latest . . .' *ibid.*, p.16

107 'Spiritualism is . . .' Davies, p.169

107 'hope at a time . . .' Oppenheim, p.75

107 'black tippets . . .' Davies, p.150–1
107 'a sort of middle . . .' *ibid.*, p.165
107 'future life' *Things Heard and Seen: The Newsletter of the Swedenborg Society*, No.12, Autumn 2003, p.48
107 'decoded' Robert Upstone & Andrew Wilson, ed., *The Age of Rossetti, Burne Jones & Watts: Symbolism in Britain, 1860–1910*, Tate Gallery, 1997, p.192. Swedenborg (1688–1772), the son of a Swedish bishop, studied at Greenwich. As a scientist, philosopher and mystic, he was seen as a progenitor of spiritualism, which John Humphrey Noyes called 'Swedenborgianism Americanized'. Swedenborg believed that humanity came closest to God in sexual ecstasy, and each ideal 'conjugal partner' created 'an eternal, sanctified love'. His beliefs attracted many Victorians, from the Brownings to Rossetti, Baudelaire and Whitman. [Goldfarb, p.29; Upstone & Wilson, p.192]
107 'shilling seances' Davies, p.306
108 'Had I been . . .' *ibid.*, p.318
108 'I never break . . .' *ibid.*, pp.320–1
108 'It does certainly . . .' *ibid.*,p.339
108 'Little Miss Blank . . .' *ibid.*, p.340–1.
109 'Parsee doctor' *ibid.*, pp.342–3
110 'vivacious and apparently . . .' Oppenheim, p.18
110 'Sect-hunting . . .' *DT* 27 December 1871, p.5. The term 'Jumpers' was applied to early Welsh Methodists for their 'practise of leaping and dancing and jumping', taking Christ's instruction literally, 'Rejoice ye in that day, and leap for joy'; while the Primitive Methodists of Oldham had leapt in 1839, as a witness recorded: 'We had not long been in the chapel when the jumping began. Soon it became general all over the chapel. The minister said, "If you don't like that sort of work, you take your hats and leave us."' [Montgomery, p.20; Luke 6:23; Jerrome, p.120]
111 'others' *SLP*, 10 February 1872. Walworth Road's tramway was another conduit for potential Jumper audiences.
111 'Young Walworth . . .' Davies, pp.90–1
112 'peculiar bright gleam' *SLP*, 30 December 1871
112 'She had a large . . .' Davies, p.91
113 'betokening . . .' *SLP*, 30 December 1871
113 'a young good-looking . . .' Davies, pp.91–3
113 'that could have . . .' *SLP*, 30 December 1871
113 'ill-convenience' Davies, p.93–4
114 'were often . . .' Hill, p.143
114 'never given . . .' Davies, pp.94–7
115 'probationary believers' Oxley, p.83
115 'Once dead . . .' Davies, p.97
115 'with but little . . .' Andrews, p.8
115 'in the Resurrection . . .' Holloway, p.65
116 'endowed with . . .' Morse, *op.cit.*, pp.9–10
116 'whatever be . . .' Davies, pp.97–8. The magician Robert Houdin used ether when levitating his young son on stage.
117 'a performance between . . .' Jerrome, p.122
117 'Some of the men . . .' Davies, pp.98–9
118 'gift of the Spirit' Oxley, p.83. 'Violet' was probably the same woman

interviewed by T.A.Wylie ('The New Forest "Shakers",' *Occasional Magazine of the Milford-on-Sea Record Society*, Vol 4, No.1 June 1927).

119 'Mr Spurgeon's Return . . .' *SLP*, 30 December 1871

120 'Parents have . . .' *ibid.* The 'Eyewitness' of *A Shakers' 'Service'* thought it 'not pleasant to observe a great number of children, mostly girls, from babyhood to puberty. The Shakers might be forgiven much, but it is a serious offense to imbue young and impressible minds with such questionable "religious" principles'. [Montague, 1872, p.6] Peter and Doris Oliver speculate that in Hordle, the Girlingites may have been given unwanted or orphaned children – of whom the period produced many – to look after.

120 'matron of some . . .' *SLP*, 6 January 1872

121 'indecent behaviour . . .' *ibid.*, 10 February 1872

125 'Why Mr Ruskin . . .' *ibid.*, 23 March 1872

125 'infested, from . . .' *ibid.*, 17 February 1872

125 'a crowd of women . . .' *ibid.*, 27 April 1872

126 'Haase brought . . .' Haase may be the 'young gentleman of decidedly superior aspirations' with a 'decent black coat, white waistcoat and a watch chain . . . a geranium in his button hole, and his hair parted down the centre', seen collecting entrance fees at the Chelsea chapel. [*A Shakers' 'Service'*, *op.cit.*, p.5]

126 'had for some . . .' *Times*, 11 April 1872

126 'to have his . . .' Jerrome, p.128

126 'What she had . . .' *Times*, 11 April 1872

127 'did not altogether . . .' Jeremy Brown, 'The New Forest Shakers', thesis, p.8, HRO; Gale, *op.cit.*, p.119

128 'Artemus Ward' Andress claims the Girlingites were called Shakers 'after the appearance of Artemus Ward's comic sketch of his visit to the Shakers. . .in America . . .' [p.14] Illustrations of the Mount Lebanon family had appeared in *The Graphic* in 1870.

128 'We have received. . . .' *Times*, 29 March 1872

129 'Had she been . . .' Oxley, p.96

130 'The American Shakers . . .' *Times*, 26 December 1874. Some questioned the nature of Mary Ann's relationship to Julia, whom 'Eyewitness' heard Mary Ann introduce as a 'lady of fortune, both socially and with regard to her cause': 'She said, "This lady lives in the same house with me. Or rather," as if from a sudden prick of conscience, "she has kindly rented a house, and I live with her." A burst of derision incited Mrs Girling to another piece of indiscretion. "She does not get anything of of me," she said. A roar of laughter followed, when by a singular fatality she added: – "She frequently sees me in her visions at night." [p.8] The Taylors of Southsea seemed to be similarly affected (see p.335).

130 'She believed . . .' *ibid.*, 26 November 1875, reprinted 26 November 1885. Mary Ann insisted 'she had never "set her foot upon the American shore." The press of this country had totally misrepresented her and her followers . . .' [*A Shakers' 'Service'*, p.6]

130 'partook so strongly . . .' Charles Dickens, *American Notes*, Chapman & Hall, 1842, p.127

130 'The spirit searcheth . . .' F.W.Evans, *Autobiography of a Shaker, and Revelation of the Apocalypse, with an Appendix*, Albany, NY, June 1869, title page

130 'I so abhor . . .' Dickens, *op.cit.*, p.128

131 'I do not think . . .' Jerrome, p.126–8.
131 'They had even . . .' *ibid.*, pp.126–7
131 'a volley of stones . . .' *SLP*, 12 October 1872. Milton Hall seems to have been a generic, even sardonic name for a railway arch. After leaving Waterloo, the Girlingites had a brief sojourn in Finsbury (see Gale, p.122).
131 'a back slum in Chelsea . . .' Davies, p.104. 'Eyewitness' found the sect in 'one of the dirtiest and dingiest little bye-ways in London' at the end of a 'zigzag passage, as if leading to a mews. . .The sanctuary was a whitewashed barn, with a skylight above . . . and with the addition . . . of a half gallery. At the immediate right of the door was erected a sloping platform, on which were assembled the priestess . . . and her satellites'. [pp.4–5]
132 'gravitating towards . . .' Oxley, p.84
132 'Davies left' In the early 1880s, Davies organised a Guild of the Holy Spirit at 38 Great Russell Street (with one room as an oratory and the other for seances), holding twice-weekly services. Although still an Anglican minister, he proclaimed himself 'an ordained clergyman of the English branch of Christ's Catholic Church', and later moved his Guild to a suburban house, where his audiences dwindled. He died in 1910, having given up spiritualism to edit a translation of sources in Gibbon's *The Decline and Fall of the Roman Empire* for Cecil Rhodes. [Oppenheim, p.76]
132 'Shaker's Tea Meeting' *SLP*, 24 August 1872. Tea also had a strong association with temperance, although the Girlingites did not renounce alcohol.
134 'the gallery . . .' *et seq.*, *SLP*, 18 November 1871, quoting *John Bull*. 'Eyewitness' discerned a certain social divide in the sect, distinguishing 'that new breed found in London suburbs, between the lower and the middle classes' who were seated behind Mary Ann, and 'the humbler devotees' on the benches below. [pp.9, 10, 11, 6]
135 'transatlantic influence' The cotton famine was also a result of Lancashire workers refusing to work with cotton picked by slave labour.
135 'a decidedly American' *ibid.* Peter Oliver, Mary Ann's great-great-nephew, says his own Suffolk accent has often been mistaken for an American one.
136 'God had given . . .' Oxley, p.85. Mary Ann may have been inspired by the success of the Bible Christians on the Isle of Wight and in Southampton (especially Mary Toms' missionary work); it is also possible that Julia Wood had a connexion with the area.
136 'would be reflected . . .' R.Owen, *New Moral World*, 1840, p.206, quoted Dennis Hardy, *Alternative Communities in Nineteenth Century England*, Longman,1979, p.54–5. In 1849, James S.Buckingham proposed 'Victoria', a model town to be built on the banks of the Beaulieu River at a cost of £3 million, with five churches, two thousand houses, a university and a population of 10,000. ['National Evils and Practical Remedies', James O'Donald Mays, ed., *The New Forest Book*, New Forest Leaves, Burley, 1989, p.336]
136 '*Harmony Hall* . . .' Hardy, p.57. For six years Harmony Hall was the official Owenite community in Britain, comprising a series of farms of 1000 acres. Its collapse in 1845 announced the end of the Owenite movement in England, although William Galpin carried on a small, ascetic vegetarian community on a nearby farm. Harmony Hall later became an experimental school, but burnt down in 1920.
137 'those who . . .' Montgomery, p.179–82. Prince's Agapemone took its name

from early church 'love feasts', imitations of the Last Supper when the rich gave food to the poor.

137 'at no great . . .' *PMG*, 18 December 1874, p.7
137 'A London house . . .' *Times*, 26 December 1874
137 'He that works . . .' Hill, p.129–30
138 'howling and jumping . . .' 'The Ejectment of the "Shakers". . . ', 1874, Popplewell

Chapter Five *The New Forest Shakers*

139 'gate of heaven' Oxley, p.86
139 'Her assertions . . .' *Times*, 19 December 1874
140 'Woman, unknown . . .' Jude James, *The Story of Hordle Parish and its Churches*, Hordle Parochial Church Council, Millenium Edition, 1998, pp.2–3
141 'wonderful new town . . .' 'A Visit to the Shakers in Hampshire', *Irish Monthly: A Magazine of General Literature*, Dublin & London, October 1878, p.556
142 'an out-of-the-world . . .' *DN*, 18 December 1874
144 'communication by submarine . . .' *Kelly's Directory*, 1880, p.120
144 'An indulgence . . .' Robert Coole, 'The Judge's Tale', unpublished MS, 1992, p.68
145 'Nomansland' was so named because no-one was sure if it lay within the forest boundaries or not, or if its inhabitants could claim forest, or squatters', rights.
145 'Anabaptist' – statistics from James, *op.cit.*, p.5
145 'Forest Lodge' Despite local belief that the house was a hunting lodge on the Arnewood estate, no building is recorded on the site until 1867. The 1871 census shows its first inhabitants to be London-born George Smith, aged fifty-five and a farmer of thirty acres, living with his wife Emma, also fifty-five, and their son George, aged fifteen.
147 'All hail . . .' *Times*, 26 December 1874
148 'who considered . . .' *ibid.*, undated, but January 1875
149 '. . .Any one . . .' Oxley, p.86
149 'All persons . . .' 'The Hampshire Shakers', unsourced cutting, 1878, SCL
150 'At the expense . . .' Oxley, p.88
151 'a few mechanics . . .' *Times*, 26 December 1874
152 'The "Mother". . . ' *Pictoral World*, 9 January 1875, p.374
153 'such goods . . .' Wylie, *op.cit.*, p.27
153 'mannish bloomers' The Bloomer costume was invented in 1849 by Mrs Amelia Bloomer of New York, 'partly resembling men's dress. . .consisting of a jacket with close sleeves, a skirt falling a little below the knee, and a pair of Turkish trousers'. [*Chambers Twentieth Century Dictionary*, Edinburgh, 1900, p.101]
153 'Several of the . . .' *Pictorial World*, *ibid.*, p.374
153 'the pleasing strains' *HI*, 21 April 1875
153 'a Shaker band . . .' *West Sussex Gazette*, 31 May 1877, quoted Jerrome, p.25
153 'Upon the land . . .' *Times*, 26 December 1874
154 'on the lines . . .' Wylie, p.28
154 'and threw it . . .' *Irish Monthly*, *op.cit.*, p.563

154 'two of the most . . .' Wylie, p.28
154 'that the smaller . . .' undated cutting circa 1886, courtesy Jude James
155 'however rigidly . . .' *HI*, 21 April 1875
156 'a woman living . . .' *DT*, 7 November 1871
156 'extraordinary influence . . .' Andrews, pp.7–8
157 'Fearing the English . . .' A.T.T.P., Recorder, *Essays from the Unseen*, Printed for the Author & Sold by J.Burns, London, & King Bros., Lymington, 1885, p.5
158 'But what is concrete? . . .' *M&D*, 15 June 1883, p.369–71
160 'At the time . . .' Peterson, *op.cit.*, p.5–6
161 'There has been . . .' *Times*, 9 January 1875
161 'You cannot wonder . . .' *ibid.*, 29 December 1874
162 'caught the contagion . . .' Rev W.T.Andress transcripts, HRO, p.9. Lord Henry Scott, MP (1832–95) was created Lord Montagu of Beaulieu in 1885, and was a major contributor to the implementation of the 1877 New Forest Act.
162 'surrounded by . . .' Francis, p.293
162 'a new disease' Thompson, p.418
162 'the aftershock of electricity' Barrow, p.69
162 'every movement . . .' *ibid.*, p.71
163 'an occult spiritual essence . . .' *ibid.*, p.93
163 'I had seen . . .' Peterson, p.6. The *Zoist* was another precursor of *Human Nature*. Both propagated zoism, the doctrine that life originates from a specific principle.
163 'some fifty or sixty . . .' Barrow, p.80
163 'If my own life . . .' Russell & Goldfarb, *op.cit.*, p.69–70
163 'Scarcely . . .' *ibid.*, p.71
163 'magnetism' Elizabeth Longford, *Victoria RI*, Weidenfeld & Nicolson,1964, p.339
163 'Mr Lewis . . .' Barrow, p.81
163 'Esdaile had . . .' F.W.H.Myers, *Fragments of Prose and Poetry*, Eveleen Myers, ed., Longmans, 1904, pp.67–8
164 'wonderful things' Peterson, pp.6–7
164 'and felt certain . . .' *ibid.*, p.6
164 'a Shaker man . . .' *IOWT*, 9 March 1876
164 'how to do it . . .' *ibid.*, 23 March 1876
165 'that the simple . . .' *Times*, 29 December 1874
165 'mesmeric entertainments' Peterson, p.7
165 'I could silently . . .' *ibid.*, p.7
166 'With all due . . .' *Our Social Circle*, Vol I, No.2, p.107, June 1873, HRO 57M83/66
166 'very home of fancy . . .' Champion DeCrespigny, 1895, quoted Janet Rose, 'The New Forest Shakers: Religious Radicals in Nineteenth-Century Hampshire', Harris Manchester College dissertation, University of Oxford, 2001, p.39
168 'as Mother would . . .' Andress, p.4
168 'praising God . . .' *DN*, 19 December 1874
168 'wherein nameless infants . . .' *The Mayor of Casterbridge*, Penguin, 1978, p.212. The Shakers had also been rumoured to kill their babies: 'The fruits of their unlawful embraces, they conceal by the horrid crime of murder'. The Buchanites too would be accused of murdering their illicit children, and their

premises were searched by order of local magistrates for infant bones. [Andrews, p.91, 316; Montgomery, p.91]
168 'sin and shame . . .' Andress, p.116
169 'only one lapse . . .' Wylie, p.28
169 'aided by . . .' *Times*, 19 December 1874
170 'Converts . . .' *ibid.*
170 'and shed . . .' *HI*, 18 December 1875
171 'outside brethren' *ST*, 16 December 1874
171 'Behold! . . .' Barrow, p.39
171 'that they should . . .' Oxley, p.88
171 'Here liberty . . .' *Times*, 26 December 1874
171 'Her old imperious . . .' Oxley, p.86
172 'Those who . . .' *Times*, 19 December 1874
172 'the execution . . .' *ibid.*, 26 December 1874
172 'which. . .left them . . .' Oxley, p.89
172 'they thought it . . .' *Times*, 26 December 1874
173 'All who bought . . .' Oxley, p.88
173 'one of the most . . .' *Times*, 28 December 1874
173 'the Lord would . . .' *ibid.*, 18 December 1874
173 'a posse . . .' *ibid.*, 26 December 1874

Chapter Six *The Dark and Trying Hour*

174 'We bought . . .' Wylie, p.29.
174 'a scene probably . . .' *HC*, 19 December 1874, HRO 84M94/50/2
175 'no Irish eviction . . .' *DT*, undated, Popplewell – a comment from a visiting solicitor from London (Muskerry Tilson?), 'acting for the friends of Miss Wood'.
175 'conducted like . . .' Appendix I, Popplewell
175 'The men who . . .' *ST*, 26 December 1874
175 'having been . . .' *DN*, 17 December 1874
175 'their eyes . . .' *ibid.*, 19 December 1874
175 'the Lord might . . .' *ibid.*, 17 December 1874
175 'Praise Him' *ibid.*, 19 December 1874
175 'but however . . .' *ST*, 26 December 1874
176 'furniture, equipments . . .' *Times*, 18 December 1874
178 'It is the Lord's! . . .' *ibid.*, 26 December 1874
178 'This, however . . .' *HC*, 19 December 1874, HRO 84M94/50/2
179 'Would I accept . . .' *DN*, 21 December 1874
179 'singing and praying . . .' *ST*, 26 December 1874
179 'In this state. . . *Times*, 18 December 1874
179 'Ye friends of Jesus . . .' A.T.Lloyd *Ashleon: Magazine of Ashley School*, 1966
180 'and sturdily refusing . . .' Wylie, p.33
180 'of respectable appearance' *ST*, 26 December 1874
180 'One little fellow . . .' *Times*, 18 December 1874
180 'everything he had . . .' *ST*, 26 December 1874
181 'The only time . . .' *ibid.*, 21 December 1874
181 'in spite of . . .' *ibid.*, 26 December 1874
181 'We had "prayer". . . ' *DN*, 21 December 1874
181 'washed down . . .' *Times*, 26 December 1874
182 'If we are . . .' *DN*, 21 December 1874

182 'half-a-dozen . . .' *ibid.*, 18 December 1874
183 'Isaac told me . . .' *HC*,19 December 1874, HRO 84M94/50/2
184 'they all will . . .' *DN*, 17 December 1874
184 'not *compos mentis*' *ST*, 26 December 1874
185 'She speaks . . .' *Times*, 26 December 1876
186 'that the Shakers . . .' *Pictorial World*, 9 January 1875, p.374
186 'The barn has . . .' *DN*, 21 December 1874
187 'inconvenient women'. Collins' novel was published in 1860.
187 'the Community of Shakers' *PMG*, 18 December 1874, p.7
187 'An American' *ibid.*, 24 December 1874
188 'Two hundred and fifty . . .' *Times*, 26 December 1874
188 'oppressed peoples' S.H.Harris, *Auberon Herbert: Crusader for Liberty*, Williams & Norgate, 1943, p.45
188 'Individual Liberty' *International Voluntaryism*, (Series II), No.1, HRO 67M99/P26
188 'His life is unhealthy . . .' Harris, *op.cit.*, p.44
189 'as if I had . . .' *ibid.*, p.126–7
190 '. . .I see with . . .' *FC* Vol I, Letter 13, January 1872, *Works* XXVII, p.233
190 'We are both . . .' undated letter, Dimbola Lodge, Freshwater
191 'personal observation . . .' *Times*, 22 December 1874
191 'Mr Auberon Herbert . . .' *Vanity Fair*, 26 December 1874, p.346. The magazine was sensitive to notions of censorship having just been sued for libel.
191 'seemed to give . . .' *ST*, 26 December 1874
192 'a larger and more . . .' unsourced cutting, 24 December 1874
192 'It is quite . . .' *DN*, undated, 'The Ejectment of the "Shakers",' Popplewell
192 'It was vouchsafed . . .' *Times*, 26 December 1874
193 'to abate . . .' *ibid.*, 1 January 1875

PART III *Arrows of Desire*

Chapter Seven *The Sphere of Love*

198 'Low windows . . .' Edward Clifford, *Broadlands As It Was*, Lindsey & Co., 1890, p.5. Clifford (1844–1907) a minor Pre-Raphaelite who copied works by Burne-Jones and others, is also known for his book, *Father Damien and Others* (1905).
198 'their wise habit . . .' Clifford, 'Addenda', Georgiana Cowper, *Memorials of William Francis Cowper-Temple, Baron Mount-Temple*, privately published, 1890, p.140. Although William Cowper tried a vegetarian diet in his youth, he was later advised by Mrs Wagstaffe to eat meat.
198 'could not endure . . .' Clifford, *op.cit.*, p.6
198 'all those movements . . .' Barrow, p.89
198 'Conservative or Bourgeois . . .' Harold J.Laski, ed., *Communist Manifesto: Socialist Landmark*, George Allen and Unwin, 1948, p.161
200 'I still love . . .' WC, Journal, 9 November 1828, BR 51/5, HL
200 'and it is . . .' *The Christian*, 1 April 1885, BR 47/11, HL
200 'The townsman . . .' *PMG*, 28 December 1874
201 'the stamp . . .' W.G.Collingwood, *Ruskin Relics*, Isbister & Co., NY, 1903, p.219

201 'he runs . . .' Van Akin Burd, *Ruskin, Lady Mount-Temple & the Spiritualists*, Guild of St George Ruskin Lecture, Brentham Press, 1982, p.6
201 'serious-minded' *Memorials*, *op.cit.*, pp.37–8
201 'very beautiful . . .' Clifford, pp.6–7
201 'to bring . . .' Burd, *op.cit.*, p.9
202 'a holy and lovely . . .' *Memorials*, p.35
202 'self-supporting villages' Armytage, *op.cit.*, p.209
202 'Men of England . . .' *ibid.*, p.214–5
202 'people digging . . .' *ibid.*, p.216
202 'dooming men . . .' *ibid.*, p.221
202 'from a cottage . . .' *Memorials*, p.109
202 'There is . . .' *Vanity Fair*, 9 January 1875, p.19. Georgiana claimed her husband 'never aspired to the Cabinet'. [*Memorials*, p.63] Lord Radstock, who lived at Mayfield Park in Southampton, was a campaigning Christian and a delegate at the Broadlands conferences.
203 'He is a very . . .' Burd attributes this to Emily Cowper, but James Gregory notes that the observation is from the Dowager Countess Cowper, Anne de Grey, in her memoirs of her husband (WC's brother). [Burd, p.6; JG to PH, 4 December 2004]
203 'on which Ruskin . . .' Clifford, p.6
204 'could never . . .' Logan Pearsall Smith, *Unforgotten Years*, Constable, 1938, p.40
204 'and, without . . .' Clifford, pp.7–8
204 'Blessed Jenny' WC to GC, BR 43/20/7, HL
204 'My Precious Darling' *ibid.*, BR 43/25/10
204 'extremely stately . . .' Clifford, p.10–1
204 'black and white . . .' JR to Joan Severn, quoted Burd, p.24
205 'rejecting nothing . . .' J.Ruskin, *Modern Painters*, I, *Works*, III, p.624
205 'Burne-Jones' Clifford, p.7–8
205 'with that rare . . .' *Memorials*, p.65
206 'I am glad . . .' DGR to Mrs Gabriele Rossetti, 24 August 1866, *Letters of Dante Gabriel Rossetti*, Oswald Doughty & John Robert Wahl, ed., Clarendon Press,1965, p.603.
206 'consumption' In 1854 Siddal was treated for tuberculosis by J.J.Garth Wilkinson, the investigator of the Welsh Fasting Girl; Wilkinson believed vaccination was 'communism of the blood', and corresponded with Ruskin on the subject. [Barrow, p.188; Clement J.Wilkinson, *J.J.Wilkinson:A Memoir*, 1911, p.270]
206 'It must . . .' Virginia Surtees, *The Paintings and Drawings of Dante Gabriel Rossetti*, Oxford, 1971, pp.93–4. In 1855 Ruskin had suggested that Rossetti should illustrate Dante; his friendship with Rossetti and Siddal was another reason for the Cowpers to acquire *Beata Beatrix*. Ruskin thought Siddal 'as charming as the reflection of a golden mountain in a crystal lake', and a genius; he would kiss her in her coffin. Although relations between Ruskin and Rossetti deteriorated after Siddal's death, in 1866 Ruskin made a reconciliatory visit to the painter's studio in Cheyne Walk, 'expressing great admiration of the Beatrice in a Death-trance . . .' [Robert Hewison, *Ruskin, Turner and the Pre-Raphaelites*, Tate Gallery, 2000, pp.232, 132, 233]
207 'some union of strange . . .' F.W.H.Myers, *Essays: Classical & Modern*, Macmillan, 1921, p.552. In 'Rossetti and the Religion of Beauty' (*Cornhill*

Magazine, February 1883), Myers wrote, 'We can track his revelation to no source more explicit than the look in a woman's eyes'. George Frederic Watts (1817–1904) also drew Georgiana in pastels, and compared the Queen of Roumania to the 'beauty of the type of Lady Mount-Temple'. [Mary Seton Watts, *George Frederic Watts*, Macmillan, 1912, Vol II, p.189–190]

208 'Vision with . . .' *Journal of the Society for Psychical Research*, 1884, Vol 2, p.vii
208 'dressed in . . .' Brian Hinton, *Immortal Faces: Julia Margaret Cameron on the Isle of Wight*, Isle of Wight County Press, 1992, p.35
208 'Why does not . . .' *ibid.*, p.31
208 'this death . . .' Barthes, *op.cit.*, p.15
208 'the face of one . . .' Surtees, *op.cit.*, p.93
209 'these most . . .' Doughty & Wahl, *op.cit.*, Letter 1717, 24 August 1876
209 'Of course . . .' *ibid.*, Letter 1712, 2 August 1876
209 'She comes up . . .' Letter, 18 June 1876, Augustus Hare, *The Story of My Life*, George Allen, 1900, p.392
209 'my most womanly . . .' Doughty & Wahl, Letter 1716
209 'to one of . . .' Burd, p.8
210 'first woman medium' One historian claims that a British medium demonstrated for the benefit of Victoria in 1846, six years before the 'official' arrival of spiritualism from America. [G.K.Nelson, *Spiritualism and Society*, 1969, quoted Barrow, p.10]
210 'a spasm seized him . . .' BR 51/113/12/61, HL
210 'How I wished . . .' *ibid.*, 'Accounts of Seances, '61–77'
211 'The Lady expounder . . .' 2 September 1876, BR 44/5/6, HL
211 'with Planchette . . .' *ibid.*, /4
211 'seen in vision . . .' *ibid.*, /12
211 'No one I think . . .' *Memorials*, p.108
211 'I think there is . . .' BR 44/13, HL
212 '*time is ended* . . .' TLH to WC, 13 February 1879, Herbert W. Schneider & George Lawton, *A Prophet and a Pilgrim: Being the Incredible History of Thomas Lake Harris and Laurence Oliphant*. . . Columbia University Press, NY 1942, pp.313–4
212 'Evolution' '69–71 BR 45/8/1–2, HL
212 'the more frequently . . .' Montgomery, p.59
212 'literally perishing . . .' Schneider & Lawton, *op.cit.*, pp.124–5
212 'by His permission . . .' TLH to WC, 12 March 1875, BR 50, HL
213 'Go bathe . . .' *San Francisco Chronicle*, 21 June 1891, Schneider & Lawton, p.273
213 'electro-vital form' Armytage, p.280.
213 'Any one who . . .' *PMG*, 19 September 1886
213 'saw nothing . . .' *Memorials*, p.108
213 'Spirits form . . .' 2 November 1869, BR45/9, HL
214 'I saw you . . .' *ibid.*, March 1871
214 'I see you . . .' ibid., 1 April 1871
214 'Guardians are . . .' BR45/9, HL
214 'pre-Adamite' *ibid.*, February 1874
215 'so struck . . .' Gauld, p.175
215 'lest their . . .' *ibid.*, p.78
215 'manifest sanity . . .' *ibid.*, p.104

215 'all transmissions . . .' Gurney, Myers &.Podmore, *Phantasms of the Living*, SPR, 1886, preface
216 'They were sailing . . .' EG. to GC, 11 January 1875, BR 55, HL
216 'almost obsessively sombre' Gauld, p.156
216 'subliminal self' Upstone & Wilson, *op.cit.*, p.74
216 'He lay . . .' Gauld, p.177
216 'William James' William (1842–1910) and Henry James (1843–1916) were both interested in Swedenborg; Henry James was Vice President at the International Swedenborg Congress held in London in 1910.
216 'blameless and acute . . .' *ibid.*, p.181
217 'Mr Podmore's . . .' Trevor Hall, *The Strange Case of Edmund Gurney*, Duckworth, 1964, p.173
217 'catastrophe' *ibid.*, p.22
217 'homogenic love' Phyllis Grosskurth, *John Addington Symonds: A Biography*, Longmans,1964, p.272
217 'handsome, feminine . . .' *ibid.*, p.119
217 'For fifteen years . . .' Gauld, p.182
218 'complex nature . . .' *Fragments of Prose and Poetry*, Eveleen Myers, ed., Longmans, Green,1904, p.79
218 'end all things' Hall, p.175
218 'He beat against . . .' *ibid.*, p.80
218 'What hours . . .' *Fragments of Inner Life*, privately printed, 1893, p.16–17
218 'amid primeval forests . . .' Pearsall Smith, *op.cit.*, pp.42–3
219 'with intervals . . .' Clifford, p.18
218 'atmosphere . . .' Elizabeth Rundle Charles, *Our Seven Homes*, John Murray 1896, p.207
219 'We are informed . . .' George W.E.Russell, *The Household of Faith*, Hodder & Stoughton,1902, p.210
219 'He was at . . .' Clifford, p.19
219 'the negress . . .' *ibid.*, p.20
219 'told her thrilling . . .' BR 49, HL
220 'A humble . . .' Clifford, pp.14–15
220 'strange gatherings. . . .' Russell, *op.cit.*, pp.206–7

Chapter Eight *The Storm-Cloud of the Nineteenth Century*

221 'Is there . . .' James Dearden, ed., *John Ruskin*, Quince Tree Press, p.6. *Sesame and Lilies* was dedicated to Georgiana Cowper.
221 'going into . . .' Collingwood, *op.cit.*, p.214
221 'many people . . .' *Modern Painters*, p.224
221 'Spanish-born . . .' Tim Hilton, *John Ruskin*, Yale University Press, New Haven & London, 2002, p.36. Domecq was the daughter of Ruskin's father's business partner.
221 'a fair English girl . . .' *Works*, XXXV, p.277
222 'to see the show' Collingwood, p.214
222 'in getting nearer . . .' *ibid.*, p.216
222 'bright waving hair' *Memoir*, pp.7–8
222 'After a pause . . .' *Praeterita*, Vol III, George Allen, 1900, pp.58–9
223 'gleaming eyes . . .' Hilton, *op.cit.*, p.72
223 'You may be doomed . . .' *ibid.*, p.16
224 'I do not mean . . .' *The Stones of Venice*, Vol II, 1853, p.185, quoted Burd, 11

224 'every man . . .' Burd, p.11
224 'melancholy . . .' exhibition caption, *Pre-Raphaelite Vision*, Tate Britain, 2004
224 'third call from God . . .' Hilton, p.200
224 'a woman dressed all . . .' *ibid.*, p.140
224 'heard much of . . .' Ruskin, *Diaries*, p.245.
224 'seen a good deal . . .' *ibid.*, p.253; Simpson's shrieking woman, *ibid.*, p.483
225 'a remarkable . . .' Barclay Fox, 26 February 1844, *Independent*, 26 February 2004
225 'did not laugh . . .' Burd, p.11
225 'So far from . . .' *ibid.*, p.12
225 'St Chrysostom . . .' Clifford, p.9
225 'pretty' Burd, p.10
225 'Don't tremble' Letter 253, 4 December 1863, Van Akin Burd, ed., *The Winnington Letters, John Ruskin's Correspondence with Margaret Alexis Bell & the Children at Winnington Hall*, Harvard University Press, 1969, p.451
226 'with much pain' John Lewis Bradley, ed., *The Letters of John Ruskin to Lord & Lady Mount-Temple*, Ohio State University Press, 1964, p.26
226 'shd be all-powerful . . .' Burd, p.13
227 'often came . . .' BR 51/1, HL
227 '*You will become* . . .' 17 February 1864, BR 51/1, HL
228 'moving her fingers . . .' Burd, p.13
228 'a message . . .' *ibid.*, p.14
228 'I am very grateful . . .' Letter 9, 1864, Bradley, *op.cit.*, p.30
229 'noises at the . . .' BR 51/1, HL
229 'flushed cheeks . . .' Amice Lee, *Laurels & Rosemary: The Life of William & Mary Howitt*, Oxford University Press, 1955, p.222
229 'white as . . .' Mme Dunglas Home, *D.D. Home: His Life & Mission*,1888, p.29.
230 'more inclined . . .' *ibid.*, pp.56–7
230 'not produced . . .' *ibid.*, p.39
230 '. . .a lady who was . . .' *ibid.*, p.154
230 'that when the force . . .' *ibid.*, p.337
230 'quiver and tremble . . .' *ibid.*, p.43
230 'rich presents' *Maud Blount*, p.16
230 'Mr Home presently . . .' Home, *op.cit.*, p.370
231 'Now don't, sir! . . .' *ibid.*, p.53
231 'Vatican police' Home's story provides a particular insight into these oddly interlinked worlds. Having applied unsuccessfully to the English Consul, Joseph Severn, for help, Home retreated to Naples with a letter of introduction from Robert Owen to his son, Robert Dale Owen, then American Minister to the Neapolitan Court. Ruskin had met Severn, Keats's friend, when he first saw Georgiana in Rome in 1840; Severn's son Arthur would marry Ruskin's cousin, Joan. And after Severn was unable to help him, Home appealed to the Prime Minster, Lord Palmerston – William Cowper's father.
231 'listless & exhausted . . .' November 1874 BR 51/1, HL
231 'melodious voice' Burd, p.16
232 'I've found . . .' *ibid.*, p.16. Anna Maria Hall, herself an author, was the wife of Samuel Carter Hall, editor of the *Art Journal*; the couple championed

Home as 'the greatest of the mediums God has given to humanity'. [Oppenheim, p.34]

232 'idols being . . .' 10 July 1861, 'Accounts of Seances '61–77', BR 51/1, HL
232 'absolutely nothing . . .' Letter 17, 26 September 1864, Bradley, pp.41–2
232 'the result of spirits . . .' Burd, p.16
232 'Oh, that is George . . .' Jean Burton, *Heyday of a Wizard*, George G.Harrap & Co., 1948, p.167–8. Marryat's daughter Florence was herself a fervid spiritualist and author of *There is no Death* (1917). She declared that Florence Cook, Katie King's medium, was 'a beautifully made woman'. [*Fortean Times*, January 2004]
232 'Dialogue' E.T.Cook, *Life of Ruskin*, Macmillan, 1911, p.72
232 'manner and triviality' Letter 10, mid-April 1864, Bradley, pp.31–2
232 'It is so nice . . .' Home, pp.213–4
233 'Only fancy Ruskin . . .' *ibid.*, p.213
233 'When we last . . .' *ibid.*, p.168
233 'a rallying-point . . .' Wyndham, p.159
233 'spooky stories . . .' Longford, *op.cit.*, p.339. His surname was pronounced 'Hume'.
233 'lordly pleasure-marquee' *Rossetti Letters*, Vol 3, 1023 *n*
234 'The natural effect . . .' Wyndham, p.164
234 'Mrs Lyon . . .' *HN*, April 1867, p.64
234 'All the town . . .' Home, p.215
234 'Did you ever kiss . . .' Wyndham, p.177
234 'I was a mere toy . . .' *ibid.*, p.180
234 'mischevious nonsense . . .' *ibid.*, p.187
234 'bore. . .the aspect . . .' Burd, p.19
235 'earthly master' Hilton, p.650
235 'real witchcraft . . .' Letter 82, 4 January 1864, Bradley, p.29
235 'deceptive signs . . .' Burd, pp.19–20
235 'the nearest human . . .' Hilton, p.219
235 'I will endure . . .' *Works*,XXVII, p.13
235 'the life that *is*' Burd, 20
235 'For the sky . . .' 8 August 1871, *Letters of Ruskin*, Vol I, *Works*, XXXVII, pp.132–3
236 'I see the corruption. . . .' Letter 107, 22 May 1869, Bradley, p.201
236 'best state . . .' Sir Thomas More, *Utopia*, Everyman's Library, 1937, p.13
236 'infinitely foolish . . .' Sir Thomas More, *Utopia And Other Writings*, James J. Greene & John P. Dolan, ed., Meridian Classic, New York & Scarborough, Ontario, 1984, p.27
236 'Mr Harris . . .' Letter 112, 13 June 1869, Bradley, p.212–3
236 'I should like to meet . . .' Letter 59, 4 June 1867, *ibid.*, p.117
237 'told me wonderful . . .' Letter 121, 7 October 1869, *ibid.*, p.229
237 'I want to see . . .' 25 May 1871, *Letters of Ruskin*, Vol II, *Works*, XXXVII, pp.31–2
237 'take an acre . . .' 1874, *ibid.*, p.110
237 'comrades bound . . .' Matthew Teller, 'The Historical Framework', *Rough Guide to Switzerland*, Penguin, 2003, p.583.
239 'the strange *afflatus* . . .' Hilton, p.599
239 'the Empire of England . . .' Bruce Hanson, *Brantwood: John Ruskin's home 1872–1900*, Brantwood Trust, Coniston, p.20
239 ''Twill be more . . .' *Mayor of Casterbridge*, p.260

240 'MR RUSKIN'S GIFT . . .' *HN*, Vol 5, 1871
240 'go to nature . . .' *Modern Painters*, Part II, Section VI, *Works*, III, p.624.
240 'We will first . . .' *HN*, Vol 5, 1871.
241 'afraid of the Russians . . .' *FC*, Letter 1, January 1871, Vol 1, *Works*, XXVII, p.12
241 'the Kakotopia . . .' *ibid.*, Letter 8, August 1871, p.144
241 'That there be . . .' Hanson, p.16
241 'where it supercedes . . .' BR 57/59/1, HL
242 'cutting icebergs . . .' Armytage, p.292
242 'Gunpowder and steam hammers . . .' *General Statement explaining the Nature and Purposes of St George's Guild*, George Allen, 1882, p.7 *n*, BR 57/59/1, HL
242 'It is *not*. . . .' Letter 175, 4 August 1871, Bradley, p.314
242 'I know nothing . . .' M.S.Watts, *op.cit.*, p.263. Ruskin and Watts had much in common, not least in their unconsummated marriages to younger women: Ruskin to Effie Grey (whose portrait Watts also painted), Watts to Ellen Terry. Watts became a member of the Society for Psychical Research in 1884, Ruskin in 1887.
242 'wonderful folly . . .' 11 March 1878, H.Allingham & D.Radford, ed., *William Allingham's Diary*, Centaur Press, Fontwell, Sussex 1967, p.263
242 'A. First Article . . .' Joan Evans & John Howard Lighthouse, ed., *The Diaries of John Ruskin*, Vol I, Oxford at Clarendon Press, 1959, 22 October 1867
242 'where nothing . . .' *National Encyclopdia*, Mackenzie, undated, p.46
243 'the approach . . .' *Works* XXVIII, p.451. The museum, in a suburb of Sheffield, was furnished with specially-made gothic style cabinets, a cross between a chapel, a village hall and an art gallery; Ruskin appointed Henry Swan, a Quaker, vegetarian, shorthand expert and sandal-wearer, to curate his collection of minerals, shells, feathers and art.
243 'a little piece . . .' *Works* XXIX, p.98
243 'in a very short . . .' Dennis Hardy, p.107
243 'to leave this . . .' *Works* XVII, p.105
243 'To think . . .' *Proserpina*, caption, Brantwood

Chapter Nine *The Names of Butterflies*

245 '. . .a wreath of wild rose . . .' Greville M.MacDonald, *Reminiscences of a Specialist*, George Allen & Unwin, 1932, p.119
245 'quietly taking . . .' J.Ruskin, *Praeterita*, George Allen, 1900, p.104
246 'neither camera . . .' Greville MacDonald, *op.cit.*, p.102
246 'Archegosaurus' *Praeterita*, *op.cit.*, p.111
246 'Oh St Crumpet . . .' *ibid.*, pp.121–2
247 'Tower and steeple . . .' Hilton, p.309
247 'I think he wants . . .' *Works* XXXVI, p.399
247 'She is out . . .' Greville MacDonald, p.103
247 'and with her . . .' *ibid.*, pp.103–4
248 *Everything* . . .' Hilton, p.343. For her father's possible abuse of Rose, see *ibid.*, p.xiii
248 'the most extraordinary . . .' Greville MacDonald, p.108
248 'spiritual & earthly . . .' 13 November 1863, Van Akin Burd, ed., *John Ruskin & Rose La Touche: Her unpublished diaries of 1861 & 1867*, Clarendon Press, Oxford, 1979, p.90

249 '. . .And now she's . . .' Hilton, p.338
249 'tall and brightly fair . . .' *Works* XXXV, p.lxxv
249 'advancing towards . . .' George MacDonald, *Phantastes*,1858, Everyman, 1915, p.9–10. MacDonald (1824–1905) was originally a minister at Arundel; his later years were spent at Bordighera, Italy.
240 'a youth gorgeously attired . . .' *ibid.*, p.225
250 'I should have . . .' George MacDonald, *At the Back of the North Wind*, Strahan, 1871, p.375
250 'A lovely figure . . .' *ibid.*, p.378
250 'Come and see us . . .' BR 50, HL
251 'he had better . . .' William Raeper, *George MacDonald*, Lion, Tring, 1987, p.170
251 'first, I'm . . .' Hilton, p.351
251 'one of his mistresses . . .' Greville MacDonald, p.99
251 'was disgusted . . .' Hilton, p.118
252 'Such notions . . .' Greville MacDonald, p.101
252 'malicious disparagments' *ibid.*, p.107
253 'she will not . . .' Bradley, p.52
253 '. . .They may say . . .' *ibid.*, Letter 43, 29 September 1866, p.91
253 'lying would . . .' *ibid.*, Letter 49, c.20 October 1866, p.99
253 'I cannot write . . .' *ibid.*, Letter 52, 4 November 1866, p.104
254 'Last night . . .' RLT to GC, 29 October 1866, BR 55/7, HL
254 'Mama said . . .' *ibid.*, 9 November 1866
255 'not born . . .' Hilton, p.394
255 'I wish we *were* . . .' Letter 36, July/August 1866, Bradley, p.75
255 'only one can't press . . .' *ibid.*, Letter 82, 15 May 1868, p.161
256 'He is quite unnatural . . .' *ibid.*, p.188
256 '. . .I should like to tell . . .' undated letter, BR 55/7, HL
257 'She tried . . .' Letter 133, 8 January 1870, Bradley, p.247
257 'as storms . . .' *Memorial*, pp.65–6
257 'She has come . . .' Letter 147, 23 February 1870, Bradley, p.268
258 '. . .Would you come . . .' 10 January 1871, *Letters* Vol II, *Works*, XXXVII, p.27
258 'This semblance . . .' 20 September 1871, *ibid.*, p.36
258 'My dear William' Letter 172, 27 July 1877, Bradley, p.309
258 'plague-cloud' Hilton, p.491–2.
258 'most prevalent . . .' Burd, *John Ruskin & Rose La Touche*, *op.cit.*, p.63
259 'To-day we . . .' Greville MacDonald, p.117. For Rose's anorexia, see Hilton, p.308.
259 'both were for . . .' Greville MacDonald, p.20
259 '. . .I do not believe . . .' Letter 186, 13 August 1872, Bradley, p.328
260 'said I was . . .' Greville MacDonald, p.109
260 'I who believe . . .' Hilton, p.520
261 'I assure you . . .' *FC* Vol IV, Letter 48, December 1874, *Works*, XXVIII, p.220
261 'the first cottage . . .' Hilton, p.571
262 'notorious as . . .' *FC*, Letter 30, June 1872, *Works* XXVII, p.560
262 'desultory . . .' Hilton, p.473
262 'To read *Fors* . . .' *ibid.*, p.471
262 'flinging a pot . . .' *ibid.*, p.639. Ruskin lost the subsequent libel case, but Whistler won damages of just one penny.

262 "'rising" middle classes' *FC*, Vol III, Letter 29, May 1873, *Works* XXVII, p.530
262 'illusionists and antispiritualists'. The Egyptian Hall, 'England's Home of Mystery', decorated in 'Valley of the Kings' style, was the venue where John Nevil Maskelyne, a clock-maker from Cheltenham, turned mediums' effects into entertainment.
262 'Nor are we . . .' *ibid.*, p.488. Ruskin's quote is from *Hamlet*, Act I, Scene One.
263 'She struck him . . .' *FC*, Vol III, Letter 35, November 1873, *Works*, XXVII, p.667
263 'and if ever . . .' *ibid.*, Vol II, Letter 8, August 1871, *ibid.*, p.133
264 'an inquest . . .' *ibid.*, Vol II, Letter 24, December 1872, *ibid.*, p.432
264 'maintenance and eduction' *ibid.*, p.436
264 'the woman . . .' *ibid.*, Vol V, Letter 49, January 1875, *Works*, XXVIII, p.246
264 'chiefly . . .' Hilton, p.582
264 'quite sure . . .' *ibid.*, p.581
264 '*Of course* . . .' Lucia Gray Swett, *John Ruskin's Letters to Francesca and Memoirs of the Alexanders*, Lothrop, Lee & Shephard, Boston, 1931, p.118
265 'The last solemn promise . . .' Brantwood caption, 1876
265 'He saved others . . .' Greville MacDonald, pp.123–4
266 'The Plague . . .' *FC*, Vol IV, *Works* XXVIII, p.229
266 'Dined with the Prince . . .' 18 November 1874, *Diaries*, Vol II, p.824. Prince Leopold, Duke of Albany, (1853–84) died from a haemorrhage after a fall in 1884, shortly after the birth of his first son. His courtier and secretary, Sir Robert Collins, was also a keen spiritualist, and an influence on Ruskin's return to the seance table.
267 'it is so precious . . .' 10 August 1875, *Letters*, II, *Works*, XXXVII, pp.173–4
267 'darling Grannie' JR to GC, 18 February 1876, tipped into diary, BR 58/5, HL. Georgiana's diary for 1875, covering the peak of the seances with Ruskin, is missing; likewise, pages in her 1874 diary, covering Rossetti's visit to Broadlands, are torn out.
267 'October 9th . . .' 17 October 1875, *Diaries*, Vol II, p.866
267 '. . .Utter blackness . . .' 20 October 1875, *ibid.*, p.866
267 'where I had . . .' 21 October 1875, *ibid.*, p.866
267 'curious violent attack . . .' *ibid.*, pp.867–8
268 'with some difficulty' Edward Wakeling, ed., *Lewis Carroll's Diaries*, Vol 6, 3 June 1875, Lewis Carroll Society, 2001, p.396
269 'Bright at last' *Diaries*, Vol II, pp.875–6
269 'peculiarly exercisable . . .' Barrow, p.81
270 'like the sea' Ann Thwaite, *Emily Tennyson*, Faber, 1996, p.46
270 'distinct but very small . . .' 4 August 1873, BR 51/1, HL
270 'often left her body . . .' Burd, p.23
270 'a long life . . .' Burd, p.24
270 'gifted with second sight' *Diaries*, Vol III, p.876
271 'Broadlands, 14th December.' *Letters of John Ruskin to Charles Eliot Norton*, Houghton, Mifflin, Boston, 1904, p.124–5
271 'quite crushed' *Diaries*, 15 December 1875
272 'December 21st . . .' *ibid.*, p.867
272 'seen and described . . .' Burd, p.26
273 'that she had . . .' BR 58/5, HL
273 'looking quite happy' Hilton, p.611

273 '...At Broadlands...' 13 January 1876, *Letters ... to Charles Eliot Norton*, *op.cit.*, p.126–7
273 'being brought...' 1 February 1876, *ibid.*, pp.128–9
273 'as of a longed-for...' Myers, *Fragments of Inner Life*, pp.90–1
274 'She came...' *FC*, Letter 71, November 1876, *Works*, XXVIII, pp.740–1. The figure of Ursula's martyred virgins has since been revised (it was suggested that the Roman numerals had been misread), but her feast, abandoned by the Second Vatican Council, has been restored. She is now regarded as the patron saint of youth.
274 'So dreams...' *ibid.*, Letter 20, August 1872, *Works*, XXVII, p.344
274 'period of...' Cook, *Life of Ruskin*, pp.276–7
275 '*There she lies*...' Hilton, p.628
275 'Meaning was...' *ibid.*, p.632
276 'and leaving...' ' Myers, *Fragments of Inner Life*, pp.90–1
276 'the only *definite* thing...' Cook, *Life of Ruskin*, pp.430–1

PART IV *The Countenance Divine*

'As a living soul...' Barthes, p.65

Chapter Ten *This Muddy Eden*

279 '*Monday*...' *Irish Monthly*, October 1878, p.556
280 'The pitiable...' *Times*, 4 January 1875
280 '...The Shakers...' BR 51/1, HL
280 'of any house...' *DN*, 31 December 1874
280 'Meant to visit...' GC diary, BR 58/5, HL
281 'Their furniture...' *Times*, 4 January 1875
282 'Mr Henry Doman' Doman (1823–1900) was the author of *Songs of Lymington* and *Songs of the Shade*, morbid, Pre-Raphaelite-influenced verses with titles such as 'The Dead Darling'. He published his poems on the advice of William Allingham, then a customs officer in Lymington; he was also a friend of Coventry Patmore, the poet who had introduced Ruskin to the PRB, and who also lived in the town. Doman was probably the 'well-informed resident of Lymington' with 'the confidence of Mr Cowper-Temple of Broadlands' who wrote to Herbert in December 1874, 'giving him the details of the position of the community so far as he could ascertain them.' [Harris, p.159]
282 'Since the publication...'*ibid.*, 6 January 1875
282 'for the poor creatures' *Pictorial World*, 9 January 1875
283 'On the facts...' H.C.Lopes, 15 January 1875, BR 49, HL
283 'Hon Sir...' Isaac Batho, 15 January 1875, *et seq.*, BR 49
286 'Whether by fanaticism...' *Times*, 9 January 1875
287 'at Ashley Arnewood...' Harris, p.159
287 'obscene stories...' undated, Popplewell
287 'Sir, -...' *Times*,10 January 1875
288 'trustworthy correspondent' *DN*, 19 December 1874
288 'that the men...' September 1878, Popplewell
288 'Off started another...' *HI*, 19 June 1875
288 'Did not David...' *South London Chronicle*, 18 November 1871, quoting *John Bull*

289 'much pity' *Times*, 10 January 1875
289 '. . .This nondescript tribe . . .' *HA*, 30 January 1875
290 'I hereby promise' *PMG*, 12 January 1875, pp.4–5
290 'a very clever woman' Harris, p.159–60. A local expressed it in more vernacular terms: 'Wal, I doan't known wat she believes, and what she doant, but I do know as Mother Girling is a darned clever woman'. ['The Southampton Bus', Popplewell]
291 'When a man . . .' Montgomery, p.139. The Doukbours emigrated from Russia in 1899, funded by Tolstoy who empathised with their vegetarian and pacifist beliefs. Their protests of stripping naked and burning their houses continued into the 1950s, when they undressed in a Canadian court to demonstrate against the possibility of a third world war.
291 'grand actress' Andrews, p.33
291 'The Shaker Settlement . . .' *The Graphic*, 9 January 1875. In 1870, *The Graphic* had published illustrations of Shaker meetings by J.Boyd Houghton, depicting Evans and the dancing Families of Mount Lebanon (see Andrews, pp.145, 146, & 339)
293 'THE "SHAKERS". . . ' *The Graphic*, 9 January 1875, p.27.
294 'But since . . .' Barthes, p.113
294 'gone mad . . .' *ibid.*, p.117
296 '. . .One of the Shakers . . .' *HA*, 20 January 1875
297 'An eye witness . . .' *ibid.*, 13 January 1875. As late as the 1950s, a 'Peculiar' couple in Halifax were charged with manslaughter for allowing their two children to die without medical attention.
297 'something the matter' *IOWT*, 23 March 1876
298 'Ellen Benham . . .' *HA*, 13 January 1875
298 'The professed . . .' *DN*, circa 13 January 1875
298 'the hand of the infant . . .' *M&D*, 8 May 1874, p.289
299 'She had . . .' *ibid.*, 3 January 1873, p.8
299 'I say friend . . .' *ibid.*, 28 February 1873, p.101
299 'HELP FOR . . .' *ibid.*, 8 January 1875, p.25 – a reprint of Glendinning's letter to the Glasgow *Daily Express* 1 January 1875, p.9. Glendinning (1835–1910) was also a vegetarian and opened vegetarian restaurants in London. He declared that 'Either the discoveries made by Mumler, Stainton Moses, Beattie and others, have now been confirmed, or a very eminent man. . .has been the victim of a marvellous and inexplicable delusion'. A close friend of James Burns, he attended the latter's funeral in 1895. [*The Veil Unlifted*, Whittaker & Co., 1894, p.111]
301 'THE NEW FOREST SHAKERS . . .' *ibid.*, 13 March 1875, p.172. Frederick Nutt Broderick (1854–1913) was, like his father, a well known Island photographer.
301 'the sympathy and kindness. . . .' *HA*?, 23 January 1875
301 'that you will obtain . . .' Andress, p.19. 'Saradin' of the *Secular Review* claimed to have 13 misspelt letters from Mary Ann.
303 'very respectable . . .' *S&W*, 20 February 1875. One report (*ST*, 20 February 1875) claimed that Harry Burdon's father had already succeeded in taking his son 'by force', only for the boy to escape back to Hordle. It seems Girlingism had a particular effect on impressionable and perhaps weak young minds.
303 'cutting out . . .' *Weymouth & Portland Telegram*, 1875, Popplewell
304 'If your son . . .' *ST*, 20 February 1875
305 'Shaker teachers . . .' *ST*, 27 February 1875. Herbert's last deadline fell on

24 February; he even sent his wife to make a final, feminine appeal to Mary Ann to stay.

306 '*These singular people . . .*' *The Graphic*, 10 April 1875, p.351

306 'our blessed benefactor . . .' *DN*, 21 December 1874

306 'that attempts will . . .' *Pictorial World*, 9 January 1875, p.374

307 'Dr Maskew . . .' *Manchester Guardian*, undated cutting, February 1875

308 'Those poor suffering . . .' *Times*, 6 March 1875

308 'being bound . . .' *Penny Illustrated Paper*, 6 March 1875

309 'the crowning act . . .' *ST*, 6 March 1875

309 '*Whether his attention . . .*' *et seq.*, *Hansard*, 8 March 1875 [222] p.1394 & 18 March 1875 [223] pp.30–1

312 'two young doctors' *HI*, 17 March 1875

312 'Oh, Lord . . .' *ST*, 13 March 1875

312 'one inmate' 'I told him he was dying', said Surgeon-Major Buckley, who found the man with his excised gut lying beside him, 'and asked him if he wished to see his clergyman? He said no, he was not going to die, and he should be alright in the morning.' [*ST*, 16 January 1875]

312 'the Shakers are mad' *DT*, undated, Popplewell

312 'We are not . . .' quoted *HI*, 7 August 1875. Colney Hatch, later known as Friern hospital, was built by George Myers, the same contractor responsible for Netley's military hospital.

313 'There is no . . .' *The Views of Vanoc*, Kegan Paul, Trench, Trübner, 1911, p.281. White had his own ideas on utopian settlements ('Mr Lever's experiments at Port Sunlight prove that decent housing accomodation is the most effective prescription for sterlising the unfit known to science') and would advise the Russian government on the establishment of a forced Jewish colony in Argentina. In *A Modern Utopia*, H.G.Wells writes, 'Do you realise just where the propositions necessary to a modern Utopia are taking us? Everyone on earth with have to be here . . . Mr Chamberlain, and the King. . .(no doubt *incognito*) . . . and Mr Arnold White.' [*ibid.*, p.280; Nelson & Sons, 1904, p.37]

313 'As to the . . .' Andress, pp.20–2

313 'on the simple . . .' *Times*, 15 March 1875

313 'the most marvellous . . .' exhibition caption, *Pre-Raphaelite Vision*, *op.cit.*

313 'There were three . . .' *Times*, 15 March 1875

314 'the noise of rain . . .' *ST*, 13 March 1875

314 'might soon . . .' *Times*, 26 December 1874

315 'Much of the land . . .' *ST*, 13 March 1875. In February 1875 three gentlemen from London visited the sect, offering to buy back New Forest Lodge, but on condition that the Girlingites reduced their numbers, 'the estate being much too small for supporting so many people'. Another neighbour who 'expressed much interest in their fate' was the eighty-six-year-old Admiral Sir George Sartorius, a local celebrity who had recently sent the Admiralty his plans for 'the war ship of the future', complete with steam battering ram. Then there was the arrival of a box from Holmsley station, addressed to Mary Ann: 'Dear madame I hope these few things will be found useful to you in your afflictions. Please write and tell me your views of the second coming of Christ, and why you withdrew yourself from the world and dwell in the wilderness, yours truly, J. W. Fudge' – Inside was 'some butter, scented soap, tea, safety pins, one bottle of ginger wine,

envelopes, notepaper, and pins'. The source of this bizarre, Beuysian compendium, somewhere between a food parcel and Joanna Southcott's box, was never identified. [*S&W*, 20 February 1875; *ST*, 13 March 1875; *HI*, 27 November & 17 March 1875]

315 'ankle-deep . . .' *HI*, 24 July 1875. In May 1875, W.E.Ecke, an auctioneer and surveyor, of Hyde Park Gardens, led a campaign to raise £3,000 to buy 108 acres near Ringwood for the sect, but on their inspection, the land was declared unsuitable.

316 'we, the Shakers . . .' *Shaker & Shakeress*, Vol V, No.3, March 1875, pp.18–9. 'So far as fanaticism goes, the "Bible Christians" have not been much worse than were the Shakers, when the Shakers were as young . . .' Evans acknowledged that both held celibacy 'as a necessary condition of Resurrected Souls. But while Shakers respect the injunctions – "Not to touch a woman" – Girleyites [sic] seem to consider, that being now resurrected, they can throw off restraint. They do not hesitate to practise great sexual familiarity in public meetings.' [*ibid.*]

317 'the Girling woman', Gale, p.120. When Evans returned to England in 1887, one elder suggested that the now leaderless sect might be 'gathered' to Shakerism, but Evans dismissed the notion. [GG to PH, 16 January 2004]

317 'this very clever lady . . .' *Irish Monthly*, October 1878, p.563.

317 'emigration agents . . .' *ST*, 23 January 1875

317 'that they should . . .' unsourced cutting, 1874, RHM

317 'resident of Southampton' *HI*, 7 August 1875. American awareness of the Girlingites extended beyond Shaker circles. In 1875, the Boston journal, *Living Age*, reprinted a *Spectator* piece on the sect (written in response to Herbert's first letter to *The Times*); and in 1879, *The Globe Encyclopedia*, also published in Boston, mentioned the Girlingites in its entry on Shakerism: 'They indulge much in dancing, and live huddled together in a hovel' – evidence of Mary Ann's impact having carried across the Atlantic. [*Littell's Living Age*, 12 Februay 1875, Littell & Gay, Vol IX, pp.440–2; *The Globe Encyclopedia of Universal Information*, Estes & Lauriat, Vol V, p.588, *Making of America* website]

317 'four or five . . .' *ST*, 13 March 1875

318 'fast, loudly-attired . . .' *ibid.*, 20 March 1875

318 'gladly accepted . . .' *Irish Monthly*, October 1878, p.564

318 'crowded to excess' *HI*, 6 June 1875

318 'regenerating' *Vanity Fair*, 24 April 1874, p.229; *DN*, 21 December 1874. 'We should be all Sankeys and Moodys, all Pauls, all Christs, all good', Mary Ann told her Exeter audience. [*HI*,18 December 1875] Dwight Moody (1837–99) and Ira Sankey (1840–1908) arrived in Liverpool in 1873 for a two-year tour of England; their exhortative evangelism drew on popular songs, and offended High Anglicans in the process.

318 'revivalist . . .' Rose, p.19, citing J.Ritson, *The Romance of Primitive Methodism*, London, 1909, p.78; Alresford reference from *HI*, 12 June 1875

318 'could bring together . . .' *HI*, 10 November 1875

318 'The roadway . . .' *S&W*, 3 April 1875

318 'On Thursday last . . .' 'The New Forest Shakers', July 1875, Popplewell

319 'Such char-a-bancs . . .' Harris, p.178

319 'most improperly . . .' 'Lymington: The Shakers', September 1875, Popplewell

319 'roughs' unsourced cutting,1 March 1875, RHM

319 'the treatment of fugitive . . .' *ST*, 23 October 1875

319 'THE SHAKERS', *ibid.*, 9 October 1875
319 'with a hymn book . . .' *S&W*, 23 September 1875.
319 'a spare woman . . .' *ST*, 23 October 1875
320 'she had never been there . . .' *Times*, 26 November 1875
320 'the reason . . .' *ST*, 23 October 1875
320 'mesmeric entertainments' 'Shakerism *v* Mesmerism', November 1875, Popplewell.
320 'but because . . .' *HI*, 27 November 1875.
320 'charged with . . .' *T*, 26 November 1875
321 'The life . . .' *HI*, 18 December 1875
322 'a very curious composition' *S&W*, 11 December 1875. The Girlingites' hymnal was presumably published locally, perhaps by Henry Doman. Their singing was said to be 'a sort of chant . . . a peculiar, irregular melody, but pleasing – the female voices being particularly good, and displaying some culture in psalmody'. [*A Shakers' 'Service'*, p.6]
322 'during which . . .' *Times*, 17 December 1875
323 'a gaunt woman . . .' W.H.Gardner, ed., *Gerard Manley Hopkins, Poems & Prose*, Penguin, 1985, p.244
323 'prophetess towered . . .' *ibid.*, p.18
324 'loathed for . . .' *ibid.*, p.19
324 'a great increase . . .' 'The Shakers', late May 1876, Popplewell
324 'the Isle of Wight . . .' *FC*, Vol 6, Letter 64, April 1876, *Works* XXVIII, p.585
324 'dealer in Marble Ornaments' Raymond V.Turley, *Isle of Wight Photographers, 1840–1940*, University of Southampton, 2001, p.110
324 'a young man . . .' *Lymington Chronicle*, 12 May 1881, quoted Turley, p.114
324 'Shaker Camp' *Hampshire Telegraph*, 28 January 1876
325 'Mrs Girling . . .' *IOWT*, 17 February 1876
325 'Mrs Girling and the whole . . .' *Hampshire Telegraph*, 16 February 1876
325 'to the eternal . . .' *IOWT*, 17 February 1876
325 'We fear bad . . .' *Hampshire Telegraph*, 19 February 1876
327 'afterwards he went . . .' *IOWT*, 17 February 1876
327 'Sgt-Major Millin . . .' *ibid.*, *et seq.*, 23 March 1876. Millin's rank fluctuates from Sergeant to Sergeant-Major, as does the spelling of his name, and his place of residence. The Knights were probably responsible for the visit of another sideshow entertainment to the Girlingites – albeit one more amicable, and more extraordinary. On 27 September, their Hordle service was attended by 'the Two Headed Nightingale', Millie-Christine, a pair of black pyopagus Siamese twins joined at the base of the spine. They were born into slavery in North Carolina in 1851, and later brought to Europe to perform, touring with P.T.Barnum. Able to duet with 'herself' in five different languages, Millie-Christine performed at the Town Hall in Ryde in September 1877, and the 'wonderful dicepbalous lady' subsequently visited the Girlingites – a sensational 'freak' visiting a sect themselves regarded as a sideshow. [*Poole & Bournemouth Herald*, 27 September 1877]
333 'forced himself . . .' *Isle of Wight Observer*, 7 May 1881, *Lymington Chronicle*, 12 May 1881, quoted Turley, pp.111–4. The Taylors' house, Glenmore, still stands in The Circle, Southsea. In January 1880, Mrs Young, one of the Ryde Girlingites, was 'rescued' from Tiptoe by her husband, while the now apostate Charles Knight diverted Mary Ann's attention (a year later, Mrs Young returned to the colony). Knight, who would be twice declared bankrupt, went on to take one of the few photographs of Queen Victoria

amused, during her Jubilee visit to Newport in 1887 – an image which he retouched and advertised as 'THE QUEEN LAUGHING'. On being shown to Her Majesty by her indignant daughters who wanted it stopped, Victoria is said to have replied, 'Well, really, I think it is *very like*. I have *no* illusions about my personal appearance'. [Turley, p.117]

336 'of lath-like . . .' 'Battle of the Town Hall', May 1876, Popplewell
336 'the Shaker community . . .' *HN*, August 1877, pp.370–4
337 'two or three . . .' *Irish Monthly*, October 1878, p.561
337 'admit that . . .' May 1876, Popplewell
337 'that the girl's . . .' Montgomery, p.116
337 'of leaving . . .' *Times*, 13 February 1877
338 'After a four . . .' unsourced cutting, 1878 SCL
338 'a strong and useful . . .' *Lymington Chronicle*, 30 July 1878, RHM
338 'He was always . . .' *Irish Monthly*, October 1878, p.564
339 'making . . .' 'Ejectment of the Community . . .', late August 1878, Popplewell
340 'The scene . . .' *Illustrated London News*, 31 August 1878
342 'a visit of . . .' 'The Evicted Shakers', September 1878, Popplewell. In Chelsea, 'Eyewitness' had seen a dancer 'suddenly leave the arena . . . displaying as well she could in her face, a simulated sleep' in a 'burlesque of Blind Man's Bluff'. 'Be not afraid of her!' said Mary Ann. 'It is only the spirit of the Lord directing her to find the lost one!' [p.12]
343 'If Mrs Girling . . .' Coole, p.68
343 'moonlight flight' September 1878, Popplewell
344 'like-minded . . .' *Times*, 23 September 1878
344 'where all . . .' 'Mrs Girling "Interviewed". . . ' 'Rambler', October 1878, Popplewell
344 'a young woman . . .' *ibid.*, 'Death of a Shaker', May 1876.

Chapter Eleven *Mr Peterson's Tower*

346 'There must be . . .' *The Stones of Venice*, Pallas Editions, 2001, p.77
346 'Eternal Peace' Coole, p.87
346 'the most important . . .' Nandor Fodor, *Between Two Worlds*, Parker, New York, 1964, p.6, Roach website. Gladstone also proposed sending a fleet in search of Atlantis, in the wake of Ignatius Donnelly's 1880 study on the submerged utopia.
348 'giving the Public . . .' Peterson, p.1
348 'strange doctrines' *ibid.*, pp.7–8
349 'of a peculiar . . .' Morse, *op.cit.*, pp.9–10
349 'spiritualist hotel' Barrow, p.127
349 'might prove to be . . .' Home, p.337
349 'materialisation . . .' *TWENTY-TWO DIFFERENT PHOTOS OF THE 'KATIE KING' SERIES* . . . J.Hawkins Simpson Sands, 1903, pp.3–4. Crookes is supposed to have had an affair with Florence Cook, who was joined at his Mornington Crescent house by her sister Kate and Mary Rosina (Rosalie) Showers, both suspected of doubling as Katie King. Showers was later caught standing on a chair, pretending to be the spirit 'Florence Maple'. [Oppenheim, p.20]
350 'half a medium . . .' Peterson, pp.10–11
350 'the cocoa-nuts . . .' *M&D* 8 November 1878, p.714
350 'Mrs Olive . . .' *ibid.*, 3 January 1873, p.12

350 'gutteral . . .' Peterson, p.11
351 'a lady-like . . .' *ibid.*, pp.11–12
351 'heart derangement' *ibid.*, p.14–15
351 'electro-positive' Count von Reichenbach was a 'naturphilosophical' spiritualist who believed in 'odic force', a Norse term for 'a personification of the elements of nature'. [Barrow, p.74, 298]
351 'The Sensitive . . .' *ibid.*, p.17–18
352 'intellectual looking' *ibid.*, p.23
352 'well known Eddy family' *ibid.*, p.27. This was the same family with whom Evans had conducted spiritualist experiments at Mount Lebanon.
352 'pale-faced . . .' Peterson, p.32–3
353 'The medium . . .' *M&D*, 21 December 1883, p.802
353 'his very face . . .' Peterson, p.42
353 'tied by one leg . . .' *ibid.*, p.35
353 'Men like Paine . . .' *ibid.*, p.37
353 'highly favoured . . .' *ibid.*, p.38
354 'unlawfully . . .' *Times*, 16 January 1877
355 'It almost surpasses . . .' *ibid.*, 17 January 1877
356 'the same spirit . . .' Peterson, p.39
356 'spiritual vagrants' C.R.Woodring, *Victorian Samplers: William & Mary Howitt*, Laurence, Kansas, 1952, p.199. The Davenports were professional mediums and showmen, 'awfully good at wriggling out of the knots that bound them hand and foot in a large cabinet'; their act inspired Maskelyne and Harry Houdini. [Oppenheim, p.26] The sense of spiritualists as 'vagabonds' or 'vagrants' echoed the notion of Mary Ann as a show-woman/ gypsy.
356 'as a rogue . . .' Oppenheim, p.69. Two weeks after the Lawrence trial, the British National Association of Spiritualists recorded 'its disgust and indignation' at the 'fresh proceedings against Dr Slade for a matter already disposed of by course of law'. In 1878, Rev Andrew Jukes wrote to William Cowper about reports in *Medium and Daybreak* and *Human Nature*, 'the most wonderful thing I have yet heard of in modern spiritualism . . . They are written by "M.A.Oxon", and by the Rev Thos.Colley, M.A. late of the Royal Navy . . . one of the materialised spirits, which came out of Dr Monck's side, was offered and accepted and swallowed a glass of water, which water Dr Monck almost immediately afterwards vomited forth out of his own mouth. What does it mean?' Colley, formerly a curate in Portsmouth, offered £1,000 to anyone who could prove Monck was a fraud, but when Maskelyne claimed to have done so, Colley refused to pay, and was taken to court in 1907. Alfred Russel Wallace testified on his and Monck's behalf. Maskelyne never received his reward. [*Times*, 2 February 1877; 2 February 1878, BR 53/ 13, HL]
356 'modern Babylon . . .' Susan M.Gay, *John William Fletcher, Clairvoyant, a Biographical Sketch*. . . E.W.Allen, London 1883, p.291
356 'tears rolled down . . .' Peterson, p.493
356 'scarcely been sitting . . .' *ibid.*, p.49
357 'who on earth . . .' *ibid.*, p.47
357 'the infinite . . .' Roger R.Easson, *William Blake*, 1972, p.60
357 'Spiritualism will teach . . .' Peterson, p.64
357 'unknown to themselves . . .' *ibid.*, p.39

357 'ill-developed Sensitives . . .' *ibid.*, p.51
358 'spiritual paintings' See *Spike Island*, p.327–8. Arnold White's essay on multiple personalities, 'The Unseen', cited another Mary Barnes who manifested 'no fewer than ten distinct and separate personalities', including a 'blind imbecile' ('her absolute blindness was proved by placing a book between her eyes and the paper') who could 'draw admirably' – even though the 'normal' Mary Barnes could not draw at all. [*Vanoc*, p.146]
358 'freedom . . .' *ibid.*, p.68–9; a reference 'to the Cholera raging in Egypt', noted Peterson.
358 'the sacred liberty . . .' *ibid.*, p.71
358 '. . .I, your guide . . .' *ibid.*, p.495–501
359 'You are thinking . . .' *M&D*, 15 June 1883, p.370
359 'outdoor paupers' *HA*, 23 January 1875
359 'the shadow . . .' Harris, p.213. One-third of able-bodied men were unemployed in the 1880s.
359 '[T]he poor-rate . . .' *M&D*, 15 June 1883, p.371
360 'Note – This Book . . .' Peterson's Order Books, 2 vols, HRO. The 1881 census of 'The Towers' lists Charlotte M.Peterson, 64; Anna Johnston, 38; Charles Johnston, 52; Charlotte L.Johnston,14; Elisa Wehrfritz, 46, (born in Germany, presumably Charlotte's governess); and four servants. Peterson was at 4 Verulam Buildings, along with Edward Brown, an unmarried thirty-six-year old from Brixton, presumably his manservant.
362 'practically indestructible' *M&D*, 15 June 1883, p.370. Rollo Massey was later MP for Christchurch.
362 'thinking of . . .' Order Book, *op.cit.*
363 'is it to be . . .' Coole, p.165
364 'A VISIT . . .' *M&D*, 15 June 1883, p.370
364 'So from . . .' Peterson, p.132
364 'The most conspicuous . . .' *M&D*, 15 June 1883, p.369
365 'into a realm . . .' *HN*, August 1877, p.373
365 'Looking southward . . .' *et seq.*, *M&D*, 15 June 1883, p.370–1
368 'hopes of making . . .' Coole, p.80
369 'The Tower is not . . .' *M&D*, 17 August 1883
369 'Keep the *top room* . . .' Order Book, HRO. The completion of the tower may have been further delayed by family grief: Peterson's grandson Andrew died in India in 1884, aged 32; his mother, Peterson's daughter, Anna, died at Arnewood Towers in 1885.
371 'by reason of . . .' *Pearson's Magazine*, June 1898, p.637–8

Chapter Twelve *The Close of the Dispensation*

373 'farming was . . .' Harris, p.215. In May 1878 Herbert announced his intentions to convert Ashley Arnewood for use as a sectarian school.
374 'gossip' *ibid.*, p.225
374 'the greatest storm . . .' Aileen Kelly, programme notes for Tom Stoppard, *The Coast of Utopia*, National Theatre, May 2002
374 'Very little . . .' 'A Row at the Shaker Encampment', March 1881, Popplewell. In spring 1879, rumours that Mary Ann had died were disconfirmed by her appearances in Salisbury, and Poole, where, wearing a dark blue dress and jewellery and flanked by five female Girlingites in white and three brethren, she was challenged on the recent deaths in her Family. 'It

was a wonder all the community were not dead, considering the hardships they had undergone', she said. 'Where, then did the ungodly go at death?' she was asked. 'Hell is the grave', she replied. And if there is no hell, then where do they go? 'Down to the Fish Shambles', shouted a wit. ['Shakers at the Assembly Room, Poole', Popplewell]

374 *'The Shakers' House . . .'* 1881 census, RG 11/1191/75–6. It is a nice irony, perhaps, that the 1881 census has been digitalised by the Mormons to retrospectively claim the entire human race for their Church of the Latter-Day Saints.

377 'George Frampton' Frampton had already served a month with hard labour for his failure to pay. 'I cannot help myself', he told the court, 'God has forbidden me.' [Coole, p.74] Frampton was embraced and kissed by his brethren as he was taken to the 1.50 train for Winchester, where was held for a month, although, perhaps in deference to his status – in effect, a political-religious detainee – he was not forced to wear prison uniform.

379 'several others . . .' Oxley, p.94

380 'lady of wealth' *ibid.*, p.33

380 'Except for . . .' *ibid.*, p.109. James Jersham Jezreel raised £100,000 for his temple, its square feet intended to shelter the 144,000 sealed people. His monument survived into the late twentieth century as a ruin, emblazoned with a giant symbol of the Last Trumpet.

380 'thus adding . . .' *ibid.*, p.34

380 'they appear . . .' *ibid.*, p.132

380 'habited in . . .' Anon., *The Mother: The Woman Clothed with the Sun*, Field & Tuer, 1885, p.13

381 'threatened destruction . . .' Oxley, p.133

381 'the *inner* body . . .' *The Mother*, p.154

381 'The Second Coming . . .' *ibid.*, p.169

381 'It is noteworthy . . .' Oxley, p.134. Andrew Jukes wrote to Georgiana Cowper (who believed in the duality of God) of a woman 'who called herself "Mother Theresa"' and who 'claimed with the absolute conviction that belongs generally to madness to be the identical women prophesised of in Revelation, whose son was the wonderful Man-Child, who in 3 years (this was in Oct. 1878) was to rule all nations with a rod of iron . . .' [3 January 1884, BR53/9, HL]

382 'sickness and death' *et seq.*, Andress, p.14–17.

383 'But some will ask . . .' Corinthians 5:35–44

383 'greater than . . .' Oxley, p.91. Mary Ann told another Baptist minister, Rev.T.W. Scammell of Lyndhurst, that 'Christ manifested the male attributes, I am manifesting the female attributes'. When Scammell protested 'that there have been no authenticated miracles or somebody raised from the dead wrought by you', she replied, 'This is an evil age, and my powers are curtailed by this unbelief'. [HRO 26M79/PZ3, Brown, p.6]

383 'spirit manifestations' *ibid.*, p.92

384 'There were . . .' *ibid.*, p.94

384 'a relic . . .' *ibid.*, p.92

384 'the evidence . . .' *ibid.*, p.92–3

385 'In some extraordinary . . .' Andress, p.9

385 'The Mysterious Woman . . .' *ibid.*, from *Dundee Evening Telegraph*, 27 March 1882

386 'Photography has something . . .' Barthes, p.82
386 'What these marks mean . . .' Andress, p.12–13
388 'This extraordinary document . . .' Oxley, p.94
388 'One can understand' 'Dagonet', (G.R.Sims) *The Referee*, undated cutting, RHM
389 'their deaths were due . . .' Oxley, p.93
390 'Sometimes my daughter . . .' Coole, p.77
390 'feloniously killed . . .' 'Death at the Shaker Encampment', 1883, Popplewell
391 'no one . . .' *HC*, 14 July 1883
391 'and many . . .' Oxley, p.94
391 'dazed and doubtful' *ibid.*, p.95
392 'excursionists' *S&W*, 3 July 1886
392 'Summer Season . . .' 1886, Popplewell
393 'There is perfect decency . . .' 'Death of Mrs Girling', September 1886, *ibid.*
393 'ill from cancer . . .' *Times*, 29 September 1886
393 'If I did not feel . . .' cutting, circa 1886, courtesy Jude James
393 'A sight of Him . . .' *Times*, 26 November 1985 (reprint)
394 'The agony . . .' Oxley, p.95–6
394 'would not . . .' *S&W*, 2 January 1886
394 'You have . . .' A.T.Lloyd, 'The Shakers of Hordle', *Hampshire Magazine*, Vol 2, No.1, November 1961, p.17
394 'Why do you . . .' Oxley, p.96
394 'Mrs Girling had . . .' *Times*, 29 September 1886
395 'persecution . . .' *Lymington Chronicle*, 23 September 1886, RHM
395 'Who is the . . .' *Times*, 29 September 1886
396 'I have not . . .' *ibid.*, 27 September 1886. 'A compound of inspired evangelist . . . fraud and maniac', Stead embarked on a sensational campaign in 1885, when he pretended to solicit a thirteen-year-old girl for sex. He sought to expose Victorian hypocrisy, but was imprisoned in Holloway for three months. He was released in January 1886, and later joined the Society for Psychical Research, investigating spirit photography and producing automatic writing. In 1894, he edited *Borderland*, a magazine to examine 'all mysterious phenomena occurring in the borderland between science and superstition' (a metaphysical *fin-de-siècle* interzone coined by Stainton Moses). His son's death in 1908 convinced him of the truth of spiritualism; and having perished on *Titanic* in 1912, Stead subsequently appeared in spirit photographs of his own. [J.Canning, ed., *100 Great Nineteenth-Century Lives*, Methuen, p.447; advertisement, *The Veil Unlifted*]
396 'Henry Doman' Doman's poetic eulogy set Mary Ann in company with Joan of Arc, Mohammed, and 'Swedenborg's wild fancies', paying tribute to her 'sad heritage of want and pain,/A great heart, and uncultivated brain'. [Andress, p.25]
396 'Since her death . . .' Andress, p.6
397 'on account . . .' *Standard*, quoted *HA*, 4 December 1937
397 'then brothers Chase . . .' Andress, p.6–7
399 'the leader . . .' All Saint's Burial Register, 1886, No.614, Christopher Tower New Forest Reference Library
399 'a primitive kind . . .' Andress, p.7

PART V *A New Jerusalem*

401 'I will arise . . .' 'The Hampshire Shakers', unsourced cutting, 1878, SCL

Chapter Thirteen *In Borderland*

403 'For strange . . .' A.Herbert, *Windfall and Waterdrift*, Williams & Norgate,1894

403 'carried off . . .' *The Unexpected Years*, Jonathan Cape, 1937, p.125–6

404 'introspective . . .' *Times* obituary, quoted Roger Fulford, *DNB 1951–60*, p.518. A.E.Housman (1859–1936), the eldest of seven children, declined to add his name to a 1910 petition for 'Woman Suffrage', telling his brother: 'Even if I were actually in favour of woman suffrage in the abstract, I think I should like to see some other and less precious country try it first: America, for instance . . .' [L.Housman *A.E.H.*, Jonathan Cape, 1937, p.174]

404 'free rendering' *Echo de Paris: A Study from Life*, Jonathan Cape, 1923, introduction. Housman's play, *Victoria Regina* (1934) was produced in America by Gilbert Millar, with designs by Rex Whistler. It was performed in London in 1937, and was a major success, earning him £15,000.

404 'something quite small . . .' *The Unexpected Years*, *op.cit.*, p.50

405 'a prose Browning' *Everyman's Dictionary of Literary Biography*, *op.cit.*, p.466. George Meredith (1828–1909), was born in Portsmouth, and wrote 'intellectual' novels such as *The Egotist* (1879) and *Diana of the Crossways* (1885).

405 'Yes, there are . . .' (Harry Quilter, ed.), *Jump-to-Glory Jane*, 1892, introduction, p.26

405 'Its motive . . .' *ibid.*, p.23–4. Quilter claimed the poem was also a satire on Christian Socialists, 'a sly *reductio ad absurdum* to the doctrine which Kingsley set such store by; the connection between physical health and religious feeling . . . Jane . . . mistakes her increase of happiness for increase of virtue, "to enjoy is to obey" is her spiritual creed'. [*ibid.*]

405 'A revelation . . .' *ibid.*, verse 1

405 '. . .As I drew . . .' *Unexpected Years*, p.117

406 'A good knee's height . . .' *Jump-to-Glory Jane*, verse 6

407 'It really seemed . . .' *ibid.*, verse 19

408 'Her end was beautiful . . .' *ibid.*, verse 36

409 'Some have died . . .' Andress, p.7–8

409 'all the children . . .' *ibid.*, p.15–16. The Girlingites' burials echo those of the Shakers, who eschewed gravestones for 'a mound of earth, or perhaps a shrub or tree, not as a memorial but rather a contribution to the earth's fertility and beauty'. [Andrews, p.198–9]

409 'This unconscious imitator . . .' Oxley, p.140–1

410 'information . . .' *DNB*, p.1275–6. Boase wrote on religious figures for the *Dictionary of National Biography*.

410 'the only wealthy . . .' *National Encyclopedia*, *op.cit.*, p.271

411 'providing . . .' *S&W*, 9 October 1886

411 'new church' The tin church, known as St Augustine's, had stood on Abbey Hill in Netley for six years. It was advertised at £250: 'The nave is 40' by 26', chancel 17' deep, an organ chamber and vestry. Building of corrugated

iron, substantial and very pretty'. [K.A.Ford, *Netley Abbey Village*, Kingfisher, Southampton, 1990, p.14] On arrival at Tiptoe in November 1886 it was renamed St Andrew's, but was later struck by lightning and subsequently demolished.

412 'a Port of Entry . . .' Ruth Silvera, 'Memories', Oliver, *op.cit.* The Silveras, Mary Ann's surviving descendents in the Caribbean, believe that William worked at a shop run by Mr Isaac T.C.Brooke, which he subsequently took over. Brooke was the witness to William and Martha's marriage, performed by Rev Wilde at Newport on 17 March 1891. According to David Silvera, Martha 'was known as a staid person, with no sense of humour'. [Ruth Silvera, Oliver, *op.cit.*; David Silvera, website] George Girling died on 14 July 1900, aged seventy-five, and was buried in Ipswich town cemetary.

413 'coal gas . . .' Victoria Mary Bailey, death certificate, 6 November 1931, *ibid.* p.343

413 'respecting the unjust . . .' Harris, p.161

414 'never recovered . . .' *Memorials*, p.83

414 'falling over . . .' *ibid.*, p.87

414 'My dear Aunt . . .' 17 January 1893, BR 55/70, HL

415 'I know . . .' *Liberty*, Vol 3, No.100, 23 May 1885, *Against Politics* website. Herbert's plan was to buy land and resell it as smallholdings 'the main object being the multiplication of landowners and those interested in and living on the land.' Acreage was acquired in Berkshire, Cambridgeshire, Wiltshire and Essex. Like Ruskin's St George experiment at Totley, the Company failed; yet it augured William Morris's *News from Nowhere* (1890), which envisioned 'the England of some remote future under realised communism'. [L.Jebb, *The Small Holdings of England*, John Murray, 1907, p.144; John William Mackail, *DNB*, Vol XXII, Oxford University Press, 1922, p.1073]

415 'I have had a lot . . .' *et seq.*, Harris, p.296. Theosophy was founded in 1875 by the Russian-born Madame Helena Petrovna Blavatsky and the American, Colonel Henry Steel Olcott. Employing 'animal magnetism' and mediumship, it aspired to be a science rather than a religion, and garnered such followers as Alfred Russel Wallace, William Crookes, W.B.Yeats and Oscar and Constance Wilde, partly attracted by its liberal sexual attitudes (as evinced by Blavatsky's attachment to Annie Besant).

415 'a bed-sitting . . .' *DT*, 22 August 1907. Scraps of Clair Herbert's diary, dated November 1889 to April 1890, indicate that Old House was tenanted for many years and only latterly by a man called Skew – probably the source of the *Telegraph's* story. [110 M89/296 HRO] The diary also includes a faded photograph of George Veal, the farmer who gave the Girlingites final sanctuary: a benevolent-looking, silver-haired gentleman with a polka-dot cravat. As a widower in his sixties, Veal came to live at Old House; his connexion with the Herberts may explain why he offered the sect his field in Tiptoe.

416 'for the most . . .' *DT*, 22 August 1907. Ernest Westlake, born in 1855, also wrote *Bacchic Eros*, an outspoken account of his marriage. In 1916, he and Ernest Thompson Seton, the American pioneer of scouting, founded the Order of Woodcraft Chivalry, an alternative scout movement. Three years later Westlake set up his own forest Eden at Sandy Balls, near Fordingbridge. Here he preserved ancient oaks and beeches, and planned to stock his park with the surviving fauna of the Stone Age. On his death in 1922, Westlake

was buried on his estate in a replica Bronze Age barrow. The site is still run by his grandchildren as a caravan park.

416 'perfect good manners' Harris, p.297. Sir Edward Grey, who later married Pamela Tennant, was Liberal Foreign Secretary when the First World War began. On the eve of the war, he told Lord Glenconner, Pamela's first husband, 'The lights are going out all over Europe. We shall not see them lit again in our lifetime'.

417 'The Ethics of Dynamite' Harris, p.321; for spiritualist miners, see Barrow, p.114

417 'the small group . . .' 'What is Anarchy?', *Westminster Gazette*, 7 August 1894, p.320–1

417 'How the British Army . . .' Harris, p.325–6. The 1895 manoeuvres in the New Forest, lead by the Queen's third son, Arthur, Duke of Connaught, and conducted on 31 August with 13,000 troops, caused severe disruption and resulted in many claims for compensation.

418 'one of the most . . .' R.M.Ebeling, *Freedom Party*, website

418 'In the heart of the New Forest . . .' *DT*, 22 August 1907

419 'the most independent . . .' *Sketch*, 28 August 1907. Herbert and his daughter hosted an annual 'Old House Tea', with its open invitation, 'As Long as the Tea-Pot Lasts'. 'His guests found a most unconventional host, clad in baggy, homespun trousers, loose woollen shirt, and shapeless coat . . .' Eight thousand attended the last event, 'and there was not a cab or brake of any kind for miles around to be hired for getting there'. [James O'Donald Mays, ed., *The New Forest Book*, New Forest Leaves, Burley, 1989, p.338; *DT*, 22 August 1907]

419 'The grounds . . .' *DT*, 22 August 1907.

419 'a chapter from . . .' *Daily Mail*, 22 August 1907. Other Californian utopias included the short-lived Altruria, Halcyon's Temple of the People, and Thomas Lake Harris's own Fountain Grove in Santa Rosa.

420 'Dr Baraduc . . .' *Illustrated London News*, 17 August 1907, p.245

420 'The Coming Trafalgar . . .' *ibid.*, 31 August 1907, p.311

420 'mighty angel' John Coats, Theosophical Society leaflet, c.1940

421 'You contemplate . . .' E.A.Greenwal, *The Point Loma Community in California, 1897–1942*, University of California Publications in History, Vol 48, 1955, p.154

421 'summer vacation . . .' Armytage, p.286

421 'Nan's brother' Herbert's heir, Lord Lucas, was an equally vociferous and able Liberal politician. He lost part of his leg in the South African War, yet insisted on serving in the next war, first in the Army, then training as a pilot. On succeeding him as Baroness Lucas, Nan married another pilot, Lieut-Colonel Howard Lister Cooper, RFC, in 1917. They had two daughters, and lived at Woodyates Manor, Salisbury.

422 'Minstead' Conan Doyle died in Crowborough, East Sussex, where he was buried in a vertical position in his own garden, but in 1955, when the house was sold, his remains were reinterred, horizontally, in Minstead churchyard.

422 'book tests' – see Pamela Glenconner, *The Earthen Vessel*, John Lane, 1921

423 'Zeppelin' On 17 June 1917, Zeppelin L.48 flew over Orford Ness and sailed past Woodbridge, bound for Harwich where it intended to bomb the port, only to be shot down over Theberton – the village in which George Girling was born. The airship took five minutes to fall, an interval which spared the lives of its three survivors. The rest of the crew – sixteen airmen – died, and

were buried in the local churchyard. A portion of the airship – its charred metal skeleton almost silvery with ash – is preserved in the church porch. By coincidence the propaganda postcard of Lyndhurst under bombardment by a Zeppelin (p.422), was sent, in 1916, to Vernon Ellis, 39 Dormitory, R.A.Barracks, Harwich.

423 'Dead, dead . . .' 'C.N.', *M&D*, 20 February 1874, p.121. Nonetheless, the new age persisted even during Armageddon. In a magazine produced at Netley's vast hutted hospital during the First World War, the editor, Caesar Caine, noted, 'Often I have been surprised and sometimes carried off my feet as it were, by finding Tommies who . . . have studied Spiritualism and are familiar with the works of F.W.H.Myers and Sir Oliver Lodge. Others again, have been attracted to Christian Science, and practise its tenets in connection with their healing'. [*Spike Island*, p.249]

423 'so far as the existing . . .' Jennings, *op.cit.*, p.350

423 'made of dead men's souls' *FC* August 1871, Letter 8, quoted Hilton, p.492

424 'blanched sun . . .' Jennings, p.350

424 'I have been . . .' *Letters of Ruskin*, Vol II, *Works*, XXXVII, p.110–1

424 'the sword . . .' WC to JR, April 1879, BR 44, HL

425 'in a state of great . . .' Hilton, p.667

425 'with perfect knowledge . . .' *ibid.*, p.690

425 'Rosie-Posie' *ibid.*, p.671

426 'Some wise . . .' *Praeterita*, *op.cit.*, p.112–3

427 'the fireflies . . .' MS facsimile, 18 June 1889, *Works*, Vol XXXV, p.562

428 'During this last . . .' Letter 234, 30 May 1888, Bradley, p.386

428 'sunk to rest' *Fragments of Inner Life*, p.89. Ruskin's Guild would 'influence the founders of the National Trust and the modern Welfare State.' [Hewison, p.271] For many years, Ruskin's papers resided at the Bembridge School in the Isle of Wight.

429 'smiles flickered . . .' Clifford, p.24

430 'an obscure sect . . .' J.Betjeman, 'Lord Mount Prospect', *London Mercury*, 1929/ Tragara Press, Edinburgh, 1981, p.10–11

430 'curious Gothic pinnacles' *ibid.*, p.26

430 'Ruskin's designs' W.E. Nesfield is the accepted architect for Babbacombe.

430 'strange, charming . . .' Edmund Gosse to Robert Ross, 22 December 1892, Margery Ross, *Robbie Ross: Friend of Friends*, Jonathan Cape, 1952, p.24–5

430 'full of surprises . . .' Campbell Dodgson to Lionel Johnson, 8 February 1893, R.Hart-Davis, ed., *The Letters of Oscar Wilde*, Ruper Hart-Davis, 1962, p.868

431 'my darling Mother' CW to GC, 27 February 1890,BR 55/11, HL

431 'the Sibyl . . .' Barbara Belford, *Oscar Wilde: A Certain Genius*, Bloomsbury, 2001, p.231

431 'I wonder . . .' CW to GC, 27 May 1891, BR 57/11/8, HL

431 'I don't . . .' CW to Juliet Deschamps, 8 June 1890, BR 55/11/2, HL

431 'The only thing . . .' CW to GC, BR 57/15/16, HL

431 'Oscar is . . .' *ibid.*, BR 57/50/2, HL

431 '. . . I very much . . .' *ibid.*, 9 September 1893, BR 57/50/7, HL

432 'a place . . .' M.Holland & R.Hart-Davis, ed., *The Complete Letters of Oscar Wilde*, Fourth Estate, 2000, p.538

432 'Are there . . .' *ibid.*, p.541–2

432 'My Own Boy' *ibid.*, p.544

432 'a gorgeous . . .' *ibid.*, p.868

433 'has become . . .' *ibid.*, p.547
433 'by which . . .' Pearsall Smith, p.41
433 '"arch-natural". . . ' Hannah Smith to GC, 1 August 1880, BR 57/5/1, HL
433 '. . .I do not accept . . .' *ibid.*, 25 August 1882, BR 57/5/5, HL
433 'a loathsome description' *ibid.*, 5 May 1877, BR 57/61/15, HL. In 1889, Harris claimed that Ann Lee had appeared to him in a vision. Having told him 'things too painful to narrate', she began whirling, 'which she could not stop'. As a result of this visit, and in a gesture which would have been anathema to Lee, Harris proclaimed himself 'The Lord, the Two-in-One . . . God manifest through the flesh'. But the flesh would be his undoing: in 1901 he was forced to marry his 'leading disciple' to forestall public outrage, and ended up as a 'drivelling, sensual old man in a private hospital, with an overwhelming desire to hug and kiss women'. [Oxley, p.70–1; Montgomery, p.60]
433 'exciting nature . . .' Rev Andrew Jules to GC, 27 December 1876, BR 53/15, HL
433 'He has been . . .' Logan Pearsall Smith, ed., *A Religious Rebel: The Letters of H.W.S (Mrs Pearsal Smith)*, Nisbet, 1949, p.85. After their split from Harris, the Oliphants had set up a new sect in Palestine, where Alice 'felt compelled into high-minded but unreticent intimacy' with Arabs, 'no matter how degraded and dirty they were. It was a great trial to her to do this, and she felt that she was performing a most holy mission.' [Hannah Smith, p.86 *n*] After her death in 1886, Oliphant married Rosamund Dale Owen, daughter of Robert Dale Owen and granddaughter of Robert Owen.
434 'a mysterious creature . . .' *ibid.*, p.102
434 'carelessly thrown . . .' *Memorials*, p.82
435 'perfectly clear . . .' *Romsey Advertiser*, 18 October 1901, BR 47, HL
435 'The Menace . . .' Philip Hoare, *Wilde's Last Stand*, Duckworth, 1997, p.160
435 'He very nearly . . .' *A Religious Rebel*, *op.cit.*, p.126
435 'I have not yet . . .' GC to Mrs Russell Gurney, undated, Burd, p.27
435 'against God . . .' Hannah Smith, 3 October 1893, *A Religious Rebel*, p.132
435 'false, all false . . .' *Laurels & Rosemary*, *op.cit.*, p.333
435 'the tidings . . .' Helen Gill Viljoen, ed., *Brantwood Diary of John Ruskin*, 1971, p.506

Chapter Fourteen *Resurgam*

437 'A map . . .' G.F.Maine, ed., *The Works of Oscar Wilde*, Collins, 1948, p.1028
437 'We can see . . .' Armytage, p.315. Edward Carpenter was born in 1844 to an upper-class family in Brighton and educated at Cambridge. He took holy orders, but lost his faith in orthodox Christianity in his twenties. As a young university lecturer in 1880, Carpenter made his own sandals and grew vegetables to sell at Sheffield market, and for some months lived at Totley, Ruskin's communitarian settlement. In the anarchist journal, *Freedom*, Carpenter exhorted readers to leave the cities 'for a more natural life on the land'; he regarded *Walden* as 'the most vital and pithy book ever written'. [Armytage, p.310] Thoreau's influence, and that of Ruskin and Whitman, was evident in *Towards Democracy*, published in 1883 as a plea for the reconciliation of man and nature, a mission also reflected in Carpenter's

campaign for the understanding of the 'intermediate sex'. He met his lover, George Merrill, a young man from the slums of Sheffield, in a railway carriage in 1891, and the pair lived together – to public outrage – at Carpenter's house, Millthrope in Derbyshire, until Merrill's death in 1927. Carpenter died two years later.

438 'a costume which . . .' Wylie, p.29

438 'THE INNER SECRET . . .' *HA*, 23 October 1937

438 'strange disconnected . . .' Andress, p.7–8

438 'literary and newspaper . . .' *ibid.*, p.10. This may be the same unnamed source whom Housman cited in his letter to Wylie; see note to p.447.

439 'the marks . . .' *HA*, 6 November 1937

439 'Padre Pio' Pio was said to emanate perfumed odours, to read 'the minds and consciences of people speaking to him', and to be present in two places at once, a talent also claimed for Mary Ann. The stigmatic visionary, Anna Katherine Emmerick, a German nun who died in 1824, was said to have lived for years on water and communion wafers. More recent stigmatics include Mary Ann Van Hoof, a Wisconsin farmer's wife who in 1950 claimed that the Virgin Mary had appeared to her with apocalyptic messages, and said she felt the wounds of Christ; her followers recorded that her body itself 'would convulse and assume the shape of a cross'. [*Catholic Life*, June 2002, p.26; Sandra Zimdars-Swartz, 'Suffering, Knowledge, and Exploitation: Apparations as Apocalyptic Experience', *Encountering Mary*, Princeton University Press, 1991, p.265]

439 'If the photograph . . .' Andress, p.9

441 'Let not . . .' Proverbs 3:3. 'Religion' itself derives from the Latin contraction, *religare*, to bind together.

441 'This photograph . . .' *HA*, 23 October 1937

441 'I remember when . . .'*ibid.*, 30 October 1937

441 '. . .I was one . . .' *ibid.*, 4 December 1937

442 'still lamenting . . .' Lloyd, *Hampshire Magazine*, 1961, *op.cit.*, p.18. In 1948, seven years after Lizzie Chase died, Annie Stephens, Elder Evans' only successful English convert from his 1871 mission, died at Mount Lebanon.

442 'little doubt . . .' *HA*, 30 October 1937

442 'Although nobody . . .' Augustus John, *Chiarscuro*, Jonathan Cape, 1954, p.24

443 'slums under trees' *Picture Post*, 29 January 1949, Vol 42, No.5

443 'in their green . . .' exhibition, 'Sven Berlin' St Barbe Museum, Lymington, 2003

443 'Blitz' In the Second World War, the folklorist and environmentalist, Rolf Gardiner, bemoaned war's arboreal abuse: 'Wood derivatives fuelled and greased the trucks. The tyres were made from wood alcohol, and the explosives came from waste products of pulp mills'; he even complained that 'propaganda films were made of wood cellulose acetate'. [Wright, p.236] While other English purists regarded the Forestry Commission firs as Teutonic invaders, Gardiner was suspected of German sympathies, to the extent that he was said to have planted a forest in the shape of a swastika. Conversely, in the days before D-Day and the invasion of Europe, Allied forces were hidden in the New Forest to avoid detection by the Germans. The poet Keith Douglas, who would be killed on 8 June 1944, two days after D-Day, wrote his last poem in St Luke's church in Sway.

443 'Who do you . . .' *The Unexpected Years*, p.117. The house Housman shared with his sister Clemence was 'Greycot', 11 King's Road, Ashley. [A.T.Lloyd, *New Milton in Old Picture Postcards*, Zaltbommel, 1985]

444 'The elder's voice . . .' 'The Watchers', *The Listener*, 22 September 1949, p.497
444 'The call had come . . .' *The Unexpected Years*, p.117
445 'cloistral internment' *The Sheepfold*, Duckworth, 1918, p.18. These folk remedies are echoed in Pamela Pope's romantic reworking of the Girlingites' story, *Neither Angels nor Demons* (1992), in which Mary Ann saves a boy's leg from amputation with a compress of comfrey.
445 'Tom as he lay . . .' *ibid.*, 68. The scene delayed publication of *The Sheepfold*, as Housman was told he might face prosecution if he did not modify it. But he found another publisher, 'the book had quite a fair success . . . and we had no trouble from the police'. [*Unexpected Years*, p.322]
445 'a very comely youth' *The Sheepfold.*, p.129
445 'to wash black sinners . . .' *ibid.*, 164
445 'disappears from history . . .' *ibid.*, p.191–3
446 'public mission' *ibid.*, p.194
446 'they laughed . . .' *ibid.*, p.210
446 'These were . . .' *ibid.*, p.223
446 'a tall tower-like . . .' *ibid.*, p.258
446 'He don't much like . . .' *ibid.*, p.261
446 'a pleasant-looking . . .' *ibid.*, p.264
446 'house in the trees' A.T.Lloyd, *Lymington Advertiser & Times*, 20 September 1986
446 'light and spacious . . .' *The Sheepfold*, p.264
447 'a controlled birth-rate' *ibid.*, p.272
447 'a hundred and twenty . . .' *ibid.*, p.267
447 'in an Eastern richnesss . . .' *ibid.*, p.333
447 'No headstone . . .' *ibid.*, p.344
447 'as wide across . . .' *ibid.*, p.3. During his research, Wylie wrote to Housman, who replied, 'My book . . . was almost entirely fiction, especially the first half. My only source of information – in so far as Mrs Girling suggested the circumstance of "Jane" – were – [Wylie discreetly omits the name] and talks with old inhabitants of Hordle who had memories of the "Shakers".' [p.22]
448 'a decent Christian burial' *New Milton Advertiser & Lymington Times*, 22 November 1958
448 'quite incapacitated' *M&D*, 22 March 1885. Peterson still pursued his experiments with William Lawrence, but complained, 'A more thriftless, happy-go-lucky man I never came across . . . on many accounts; he kept me waiting half an hour. For 35 minutes after coming, he sat almost like a log. Then he got up and and took up a pencil and paper and wrote: "The impatience of your desires is frustrating their fulfillment. Henry Tudor".' As Peterson had been expecting Henry Plantagenet, this was doubly annoying. Lawrence then assumed the persona of Harry Vernon, a costermonger from Whitecross Street, and signed off as Ned Kelly, the armoured outlaw. [*ibid.*, 11 February 1889]
450 'a mournful spectator . . .' R.D.Massey, 'Peterson's Tower', *The Lymington Guide*, Town Improvement Association, W.Mate & Sons, Lymington, 1915, p.56
450 'delightful freehold . . .' *Arnewood Towers, Particulars for Auction*, 24 February 1921, Hewitt & Co., Lymington & New Milton, Fox & Sons, Bournemouth & Southampton
451 'windows open' According to Syd Corbyn, the tower's windows were glazed,

but were smashed when lightning struck; only then was a conductor installed. Ironically, it is because the tower was not reinforced with steel or iron – which by would have corroded and caused decay – that it has survived. In 1990 renovation works installed galvanised steel armatures on each floor, and the cupola was reinforced with a stainless steel 'spider'.

451 'psychic charge' One medium in the spiritualist colony of Lily Dale, New York State, claims that the 'nineteenth-century style of physical mediumship', such as spirit drawings, is no longer seen because 'The world wide web is suffocating the world, blocking our connection with the spirit world'. ['Ghost town', *Independent on Sunday Review*, 21 November 2004]

452 'silver belt buckle' Charles Knight of the Ryde Girlingites claimed he had given the sect £25 to settle their baker's bill, but Isaac Osborne denied this. Gordon Pomeroy, who lived in Hordle Grange, has since been shown a brooch which the owner's family claimed to have received from Mary Ann in a similar barter.

453 'Tiptoe fields' The encampment was set in a field opposite the junction formed by Wootton Road and Mount Jireh Lane; here the Girlingites lived in six 'soldiers-hut like tents', partly wooden, with 'tar' roofs. [May 1879, Popplewell] After the Osbornes' death, a railway carriage was placed on the site; known as 'Granny Barnett's' and tenanted by an elderly lady assumed to have been a Girlingite (possibly 'Violet'). In the 1930s a detached house was built in a corner of the field, although the rest of the land remains open, bounded by hedgerows. Rose Cottage, the house in which Lizzie Chase lived, and which appears to have been shared with other Girlingites, also still stands, and was once known as 'Quakers' Cottage'. I am grateful to Peggy Phillips, Sarah Newman, and the memoirs of Mr Syd Corbyn for these facts.

453 'an Armstrong-Whitman . . .' *Illustrated Particulars . . . Hordle Grange*, Rumsey & Rumsey, 1929

454 'Mother Girling' Mrs Dorothy Johnson to PH, 31 November 2003. Other local memories include those of children being sent across the lane 'with something for the Shakers'. [Sarah Newman to PH, 22 September 2004]

454 'the passing away . . .' Jude James, *Lymington Advertiser & Times*, 8 July 1972

455 'GAVE UP SEX . . .' *Reveille*, 14 November 1976

455 'Shaker graves' A row of thirteen Girlingite graves ran at a ninety degree angle from the east end of the church, towards the northern boundary of the churchyard. Mary Ann's grave was identified as the most southerly – and therefore nearest to the building – in 1927, when the then vicar, Rev Boys-Smith, told Wylie that a succession of three trees planted on her grave had died 'for some unknown cause', and that another had been planted recently. In the last photographs of the site before construction began, the stump of this tree was still visible in the grass.

The burial record for All Saint's lists a number of Girlingites, although unlike the four consumptive young women who died up to 1878, their ages indicate that the community's viscissitudes had done them little physical harm. Leonard Benham, died on 14 September 1885, aged sixty-seven. Isaac Osborne died on 19 December 1908, aged eighty; like Mary Ann, his entry was marked by a note from the vicar: 'One of Mrs Girling's former followers known as "Shakers"'. Henry Osborne died on 29 May 1909, aged seventy-six; his was probably the thirteenth grave, after Mary Ann's: Eliza Osborne died on 23 February 1917, aged eighty-four. Cornelius Chase died on 10 October 1917, aged seventy-three. George Frampton of Bashley – one of the few long-term local converts, and once gaoled at Winchester – died on 4 February 1931, aged eighty-six. Lizzie Chase, the last known Girlingite, died on 15 October 1941, aged ninety-five years. All were interred in the churchyard at All Saint's, but their graves appear to be unmarked. See map, p.523.

Epilogue

458 'Purity of Life . . .' Eldress M.Catharine Allen, *The American Shakers:A Celibate, Religious Community*, The United Society, Sabbathday Lake, Maine, 1974. Among other visitors to Sabbathday Lake was Wilhelm Reich. He invented his orgone machines in Maine; zinc-lined containers to gather unspent sexual energy from the atmosphere – a modern version of Swedenborg's beliefs, perhaps.

460 'When I was six . . .' *DN*, 9 January 1875. Frederick Evans contributed information on the Shakers to Nordhoff's study, *The Communistic Societies of the United States* (1875), which declared 'Communism is a mutiny against society. Only whether the communist shall rebel with a blugeon and a petroleum torch, or with a plow and a church, depends upon whether he had not or has faith in God'. Utopia's history in twentieth-century America continued to be a troubled one, in a world whose aspirations shifted from garden cities to gated communities. After Mark Holloway asked, in the 1950s, 'what has become of the *Koreshans* (1902), founded by Cyrus ('Koresh') Teed, who believed that we live on the inside of a hollow sphere which also contains the sun, moon, planets and heavens complete?', he would have his answer in David Koresh's Branch Davidians, seventy-six of whom died in the 1993 siege of their Texan compound, a holocaust to echo the Doukhobors (who still exist in the Canadian wilds) and their naked arson and apocalyptic gospel. One writer saw the sectarians of Waco as 'having more in common with Shakers than Charles Manson'; while their leader's 'New Light' revelation, that he was husband to all one hundred women in the group, was redolent of Thomas Lake Harris or Brother Prince. [Andrews, p.204; Holloway, p.218; Aaron Hicklin, *Independent on Sunday*, 13 April 2003] Meanwhile, Girlingism has its own strange parallel in the Children of God, also known as The Family, a decidedly uncelibate sect with its origins in 1960s southern California, with by their 'End Time Prophet' and polygynist, David Berg, who in 1969, prophesying a disastrous earthquake, led his group into 'exile' in the south west, before starting a series of communities, propagating their belief that sexuality was an expression of faith, and that the Holy Spirit is feminine.

461 'Then I heard . . .' Revelations 7:4. Ian Boxall points out that 'the famous number 144,000 is symbolically a number of *inclusion*': the holy number of twelve, multiplied by itself, multiplied by a thousand. [Boxall, *op.cit.*, p.407]

464 'with the usual . . .' *Mayor of Casterbridge*, p.152

466 'not worthy of photographs!' Hilton, p.744

466 'modern Avalon' Brian Hinton ascribes a utopian intent to the Isle of Wight festivals of 1968–70, a combination of 'a religious coming together, of a grown up boy-scouts camp . . . a bohemian escape to a land of free love and illegal substances, of a waking dream, even of medieval pilgrimage'. He also records an eccentric exchange in the Commons, when Tom Driberg, the

maverick Labour member, defended the festival goers: 'These young people were behaving like the earliest Christians in the Acts of the Apostles, who had all things in common'; to which the Tory, Patrick Cormack replied, 'What nauseating claptrap'. [*Message to Love: The Isle of Wight Festival*, Sanctuary/Castle Communications, 1995, p.180] Modern utopian festivals include Glastonbury in Somerset, and the Burning Man in Black Rock Desert, Nevada, where a temporary town of 30,000 often naked people neither buy nor sell, and where a giant wooden effigy is burnt to symbolise their freedom from orthodoxy – for a week, at least.

466 'beautiful' Hinton, *Immortal Faces*, *op.cit.*, p.5

468 'Sunset and evening star . . .' Alfred, Lord Tennyson, 'Crossing the Bar', as inscribed in D.G.Moore, diary/address book, 1968

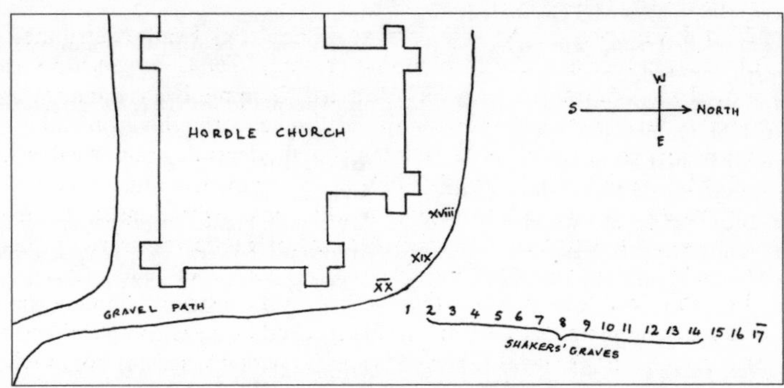

Girlingites' last resting place, All Saint's, Hordle.

INDEX

INDEX

INDEX

INDEX

INDEX

INDEX